The Bigger Picture

black dog publishing
london uk

Today, more than ever, the places where we live and work are undergoing profound change.

Climate change has emerged as the defining issue of our time, but equally we are all affected by the reshaping of world economies and rapid urbanisation, the pressures on natural resources and instability of energy markets. These significant factors underline our global interdependence and demand new approaches to design, conservation and stewardship.

The landscape design and planning firm EDAW was founded early last century. Our core ambition and achievement has always been the creation of a brave new world with places to live, work, learn and enjoy leisure time that were not just functional, but were beautiful and inspiring. That ethos continues today and is strengthened by our goals of integrating environmental, social and economic sustainability as we enter a new era as Design + Planning at AECOM.

As designers and planners we are in a unique position to address current global challenges. We operate at the point where science and culture meet; we understanding complex issues, work at all scales, resolve technical challenges and produce creative and dynamic solutions. Our emphasis is always on collaboration, not just within our in-house multidisciplinary teams, but also with clients, consultants and local communities. Time and again this method of working has demonstrated that we can produce the most effective and robust results—whether the project is managing an entire river system or designing a new city, creating an urban park or planning a wind farm.

Our work in the future will involve further embedding this philosophy of joined-up thinking and joined-up working. Solutions for coping with the changing world will require an increasingly collaborative and multidisciplinary response, where all skills sets are truly integrated in the pursuit of technical and design excellence. Our growing body of knowledge continues to be shared with our offices around the world making it possible to deliver global expertise to local communities.

We see the future as an opportunity for positive change, where we will continue to improve our ability to anticipate change and build in flexibility, extra capacity and adaptability. We can design new neighbourhoods, towns and cities with walkable neighbourhoods, with open spaces that increase biodiversity, with improved air quality, and reduced flood risk.

Making better places to live strengthens social structures, improves health and reduces crime. What's more, these principles apply at both the city and suburban scale. Along with creating a functional and social outcome, each of these responses provides the opportunity for realising places that reflect the culture of communities and places through design. The aesthetics of placemaking must be more rooted in local geography, people and materials. While most of the evidence suggests we are just at the start of this phase of change, there is no time to waste. The time for prototypes is over.

To demonstrate our collaborative and multidisciplinary approach, the many issues we address and the areas in which we work, this book collects together some of our most recent projects from around the world. Exploring an entire spectrum of schemes from land management to creating new communities, from creating a new city park to developing a business strategy for a million acres of land, they illustrate our working process from initial research and analysis, the creation of new planning and assessment tools, integrated economic, environmental and social sustainability and the goal always to produce beautiful and creative designs while always considering the bigger picture.

Jason Prior
President, Design + Planning at AECOM

Here and now

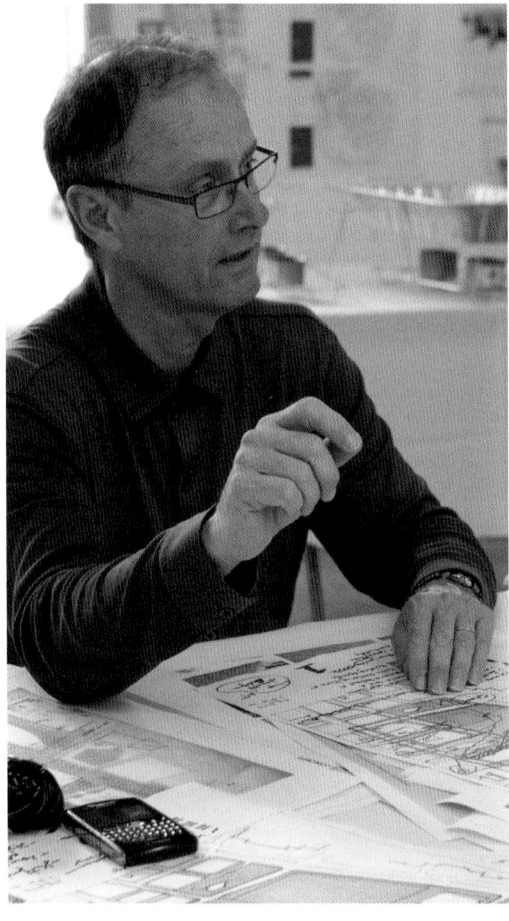

At work

Joe Brown, chief executive of AECOM's Planning Design and Development division who in 2009 received the American Society of Landscape Architects' highest award for lifetime achievement. A visionary landscape architect with a career of more than 35 years at EDAW AECOM, Brown's much-praised contributions to the profession include the promotion of design and planning as a fusion of art, science and nature.

The challenge of shaping the environment to meet changing human needs and mitigate human impact has always been complex. From large-scale projects such as planning cities or managing water systems to the smallest detail of a new city park, the ability to analyse problems and find solutions has been crucial to improving the quality of life and conserving environments and resources.

A critical moment in environmental awareness was on Christmas Day 1968 when one of the astronauts on the Apollo 8 mission photographed the Earth from space. The blue and white globe, suspended in a dark void, looked small, fragile even. It was finite. On that planet was all life and all life was dependent on the limited resources it could provide.

Despite the continuing expansion of the environmental movement and increasing knowledge and understanding of human impact on the planet, the challenges are greater than ever. While the full global effects of climate change are yet to be revealed, work is already in progress to find new ways of dealing with flood and drought, high winds, unstable and extreme weather patterns, rising seas, increasing temperatures and more. There are other major factors affecting life on the planet too. Worldwide economic change has seen old and established economies faltering and new ones emerging. People migrate to find work, be close to resources and move away from inhospitable climates. At the same time populations continue to grow, existing cities are under pressure as the majority of the human race now lives in urban environments and new cities and communities are being established to cope with this phenomenon. Against a background of diminishing resources, there is continued demand for faster and more accessible travel and communications, for more water and greater energy supplies.

Finding the balance between meeting human needs and caring for the environment has always been at the heart of Design + Planning's work. The founding of the firm can be traced to Garrett Eckbo, an American of Norwegian parentage who was born in New York in 1910 and was raised in California. His formative years coincided with the flourishing of the Modern Movement, in the years after the First World War, when architects and designers were among those who felt the urgency to create a new and better world.

Eckbo would have been aware of this influential new work as he studied landscape architecture at the University of California, Berkeley. And later, at Harvard, he attended lectures by Bauhaus founder Walter Gropius and the architect/designer Marcel Breuer, both of whom had fled Germany. He listened and sympathised with their Modernist manifesto—that architecture and design had a social role and could help improve the quality of life. The ideas became his beliefs and would stay with him for the rest of his life.

As the United States was emerging from the wretched years of the Great Depression and as Europe was going to war in 1939, Eckbo set up in business with Ed Williams, an environmental planner and landscape architect. They chose to form their partnership in liberal California and their vision was to practice design that was informed by knowledge, that expressed ideals as well as ideas and that enhanced people's lives while respecting nature. While Eckbo zealously believed that design could promote social equity, Williams was an open-space enthusiast who, long before the environmental movement, saw the importance of managing urban growth and conserving natural environments. They came from different backgrounds, but were united in the realisation that by integrating design and planning it was possible to take a progressive stance and create environments that furthered the collective good. Their work included private gardens and parks along with landscapes and recreation spaces for public housing projects.

The firm revolved around design and planning, but the work was considerably broader than just creating beautiful places. There was always a strong interest in the sciences, contemporary art, finding ways of addressing social and economic issues, integrating landscape with architecture... making, in other words, a 'total landscape'. As projects became larger and increasingly complex, the practice drew on the skills and knowledge of other professions to work collaboratively. By 1945 a new partnership, Eckbo, Royston, and Williams, was formed to include landscape architect Robert Royston. Francis Dean, another landscape architect, became a partner in 1953; Royston left in 1958, and the firm then changed its name to Eckbo, Dean, and Williams. Don Austin, landscape architect, became the fourth partner in 1964. In 1967, the firm incorporated as Eckbo, Dean, Austin, and Williams. Throughout this time the firm was working on college campuses and landscapes for corporate headquarters along with large civic projects such as public parks. Eckbo wrote his seminal book *Landscape For Living*. These were important years for the firm based in California—the time of the Civil Rights movement, rapid economic growth, the John F Kennedy presidency and assassination, space exploration and, with the Apollo missions, and the start of the environmental movement.

In 1973, the firm again changed its name, this time to EDAW. This was the year of the oil crisis when the Organization of Arab Petroleum Exporting Countries declared they would no longer ship oil to countries supporting Israel in the Yom Kippur War. For the first time the world felt the effects of the rising power and economic strength of the Middle East. For some, there also came the realisation that countries were part of a global economy, and that the world was an interdependent place.

As the firm was evolving, so its work escalated from small-scale and private projects to larger scale work for corporations and governments. Environmental planning work flourished in the 1970s as the United States began to embrace a greater consciousness of these issues. The firm's work had by then reached Britain and the Middle East, and was growing eastward across the United States. In 1989, EDAW merged with Australian landscape architects and engineers to plant a foot firmly outside the US. In 1992, the acquisition of a planning and economic development firm in the United Kingdom spread EDAW across three continents and heralded the beginning of a global practice where landscape design, planning and environmental practice were recognised as professions with a role in shaping communities, towns and cities on a par with architects.

Growing economies in the Middle East and Asia became sources of important work for EDAW with projects from private gardens to city planning and urban design. And as global travel became more accessible and popular, there was considerable work creating resorts in South-East Asia including Thailand, Malaysia and the Philippines.

As the firm matured, the projects it won continued to be larger and more complex and it became clear this scale of project required new approaches. Along with working more closely with clients and other professionals, came the commitment to working more closely with local communities. The firm took a new direction with the recognition that to be relevant it was important to be culturally aware and so it was crucial to have a local presence. The great strength was in having a global operation with worldwide experience that could be brought to bear at a local level by sharing knowledge. And this was increasingly being facilitated by digital technologies which enabled the speedy access and dissemination of research or information to wherever it was needed. For example, a team working in Qatar on an aspect of water management would be able, within seconds, to access data on similar projects in Australia or the United States. In addition to constructing a vast database of knowledge, the firm employed experts in areas such as satellite-based geographic information systems (GIS) and created a number of computer-based analytical and measuring tools. Among the most recent being the Sustainable Systems Integrated Model (SSIM) an integrated land-planning tool that measures environmental, economic and social sustainability.

Creative collaboration

The ideas-driven approach to work involves multidisciplinary collaboration. Regular design summits draw together staff from offices around the globe to share knowledge and experience.

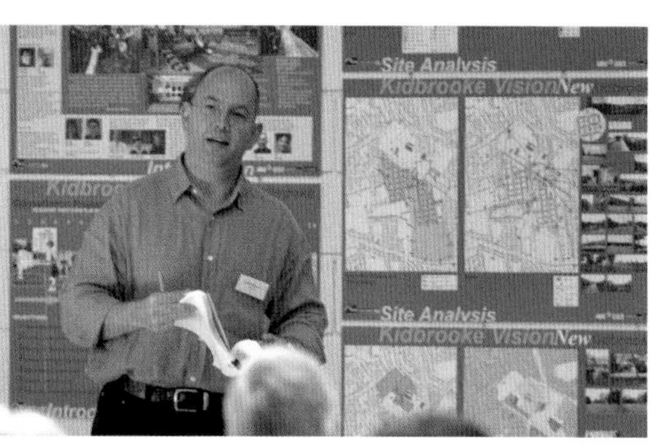

Creative process

For powerful and robust solutions, staff from different disciplines work together throughout the project from site visits, to preparing models and creating plans.

By 2000 EDAW had become a very large land consultancy involved in schemes from urban planning and urban regeneration to environmental management and resort design. During the early years of the new millennium, the firm expanded internationally with projects across the United States and throughout Europe and Asia that were growing in scale and dealing increasingly with profound environmental and social issues. In 2005, EDAW joined AECOM, an expanding family of companies offering integrated services in engineering, transportation, planning and environmental expertise.

As EDAW AECOM has grown and adapted to the demands of new projects, its belief in the strength of multidisciplinary and collaborative work has grown too. While landscape architects, spatial and environmental planners and urban designers have continued to make up a large proportion of the staff, they have been joined by architects, ecologists, botanists, hydrologists, economists, community consultation experts, graphic designers, writers. Every project draws together a cross-disciplinary team, where appropriate additional skills and expertise are brought in from other consultancies.

The strength of this way of working is that the power of the integrated team is greater than the sum of its parts. The approach is founded on the commitment to an analytical process that provides a collaborative framework and begins from the ground up by understanding the context and the inherent challenges—the physical, environmental, ecological, economic, the social and historic. From this stage a range of possible options is evolved and they are tested to find the most robust solution. This is not about imposing a style, but is a flexible and adaptable process. Whether the project is in Mexico City or Moscow, Mumbai or Manchester, it is possible to forge a team combining international knowledge with local expertise.

And it is this unique way of working which secured EDAW AECOM the American Society of Landscape Architects' Landscape Architecture Firm Award for 2009—the society's highest honour. Along with recounting the firm's 70 year history from its founding by partners Eckbo and Williams, the submission outlined the powerful fusion of art and science in all projects, the annual intern programme run since 1980 which fosters young talent and which won the ASLA's Landscape Architecture Award of Excellence in 2000, the commitment to social, environmental and economic sustainability and the global experience and expertise which is delivered to projects of all scales.

The annual awards also marked the lifetime achievements of former EDAW AECOM president Joe Brown with the 2009 ASLA Medal. Brown is currently chief executive of AECOM's Planning Design and Development as well as the global architecture, building engineering, project management and economics teams. Celebrating a career of more than 35 years with EDAW, Brown's contributions have included raising the profile of the landscape architecture profession, promoting the importance of the spaces between buildings as the connective tissue of towns and cities and stressing that design and planning is a fusion of art, science and nature.

Looking to the future, as the impacts of climate change are felt and proposals for mitigation and adaptation evolve further, the need for cross-disciplinary working will increase. The methodology has remained consistent to the ideals originated by Garrett Eckbo over 70 years ago—linking environmental and social progress to create an improved quality of life.

Debate and communication

Actively participating in current debates on issues including climate change, rapid urban growth and the careful use of natural resources, staff regularly contribute to conferences and professional seminars.

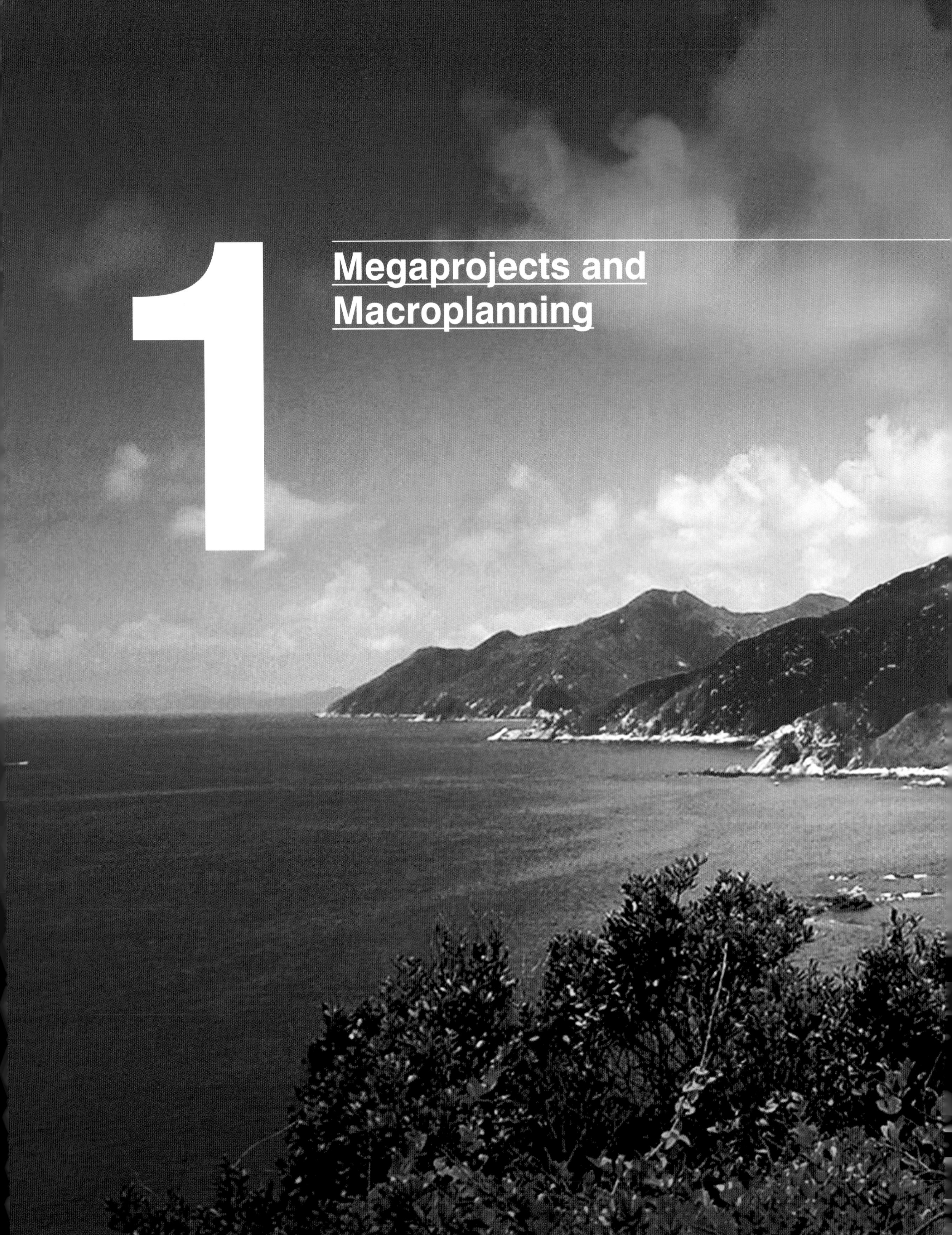

1 Megaprojects and Macroplanning

“The success of big-scale projects rests on setting out to

achieve the extraordinary,

avoiding token gestures and ensuring transparency and good communications with everyone involved from local residents and businesses to the media and, of course, the client.

David Higgins
Chief Executive, Olympic Delivery Authority

Concept

A twenty-first century model of sustainable urban regeneration

Context

Inner city/temperate

Lower Lea Valley Regeneration; 2012 Olympic and Paralympic Games Masterplan and Legacy Masterplan Framework, London, UK.

Threaded with canals, roads and rail lines, water pipes, sewers and electricity pylons, the Lower Lea Valley has long been the service entrance for London. At the start of the new century it was a run-down and melancholic place, but with the growth of the capital shifting eastwards it provided the opportunity for one of Europe's largest regeneration projects, a home for the 2012 Olympic Park and a new park for London.

Opposite
Shape of things to come

The legacy of staging the 2012 Olympic and Paralympic Games in London will include a beautiful new park in the east of the capital. While some of the main sporting venues, such as the Olympic Stadium, will be reduced in size and retained, the sites of temporary venues will become areas for development.

Lower Lea Valley Regeneration; 2012 Olympic and Paralympic Games Masterplan and Legacy Masterplan Framework, London, UK

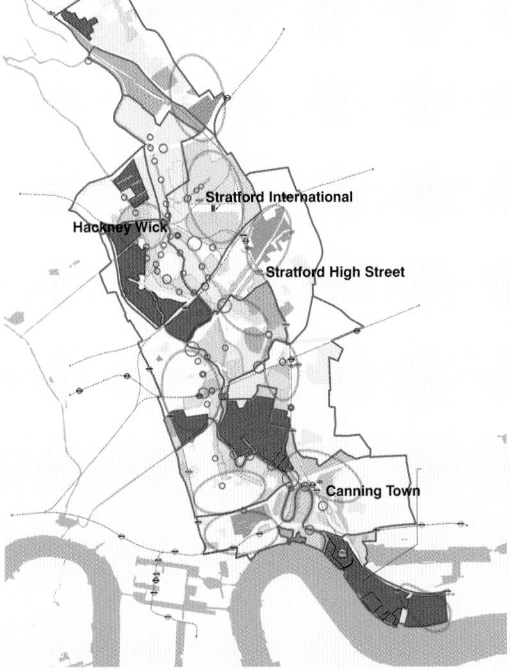

LLV composite proposals map

- Potential pedestrian/cycle crossing
- Upgraded pedestrian/cycle crossing
- Potential vehicular crossing
- Upgraded vehicular crossing
- Town centre uses including commercial, retail and leisure
- Town centre uses + mixed uses
- Strategic employment locations
- Locally significant industrial sites
- Areas with potential for industry-led mixed-use
- Safeguarded wharves
- Rail, underground, DLR
- Sub-area boundaries
- Potential new housing areas
- Social infrastructure—area of search

Above
First steps

The Lower Lea Valley Opportunity Area Planning Framework provided a blueprint for how the valley could change. It built on the strategic planning policies set out in the 2004 London Plan for an area of nearly 1,450 hectares, extending from the Thames in the south to Leyton in the north, straddling the borders of Newham, Tower Hamlets, Hackney and Waltham Forest. Central to the vision was to enhance the area's unique network of waterways and islands to attract new investment and opportunities, and to transform the valley into a new sustainable, mixed-use city district, fully integrated into London's existing urban fabric.

Opposite
Valley vision

The site of the Olympic Games seen in its regional context of East London with Stratford on the eastern edge of the Olympic site. Linking Hertfordshire with the River Thames, the River Lea can be seen flowing through the core of the area.

As an integrated part of London's fabric, it is possible to see how the regenerated parkland with greatly improved transport connections will act as a catalyst for improvement in the wider area and shift the capital's centre of gravity eastwards. Map from DFL/LDA.

Creating an exemplary setting for the 2012 Olympic and Paralympic Games, the 30th Olympiad, has been just one step on route to the transformation of a large swathe of run-down land in East London. The vision was to create a high-quality public space to act as the catalyst for regeneration. Following the tradition of London developments based around green spaces, the concept was to create a new park with the land at its periphery being a magnet for investment and development. Along with repairing the damaged urban fabric, the regeneration scheme included the long-term vision of leaving a lasting legacy of new communities, an improved quality of life for existing ones and a new well-served urban district with world-class sports facilities. The staging of the Games was seen as a landmark event taking place during the making of the new park; one of the largest European parks in more than a century.

Close to Stratford, the new park occupies a site at the southern end of the River Lea which flows from the Hertfordshire countryside southwards through London and into the River Thames tidal estuary. The northern part of the river flows through the Lee Valley Regional Park and part of the vision was to transform low-value land in the south to create a green corridor linking the Thames and the heart of London with the countryside at its edge.

Lower Lea Valley

Work on these interlinking projects began with an appraisal of a large area of the Lea Valley. Broad in its scope and encompassing almost 1,500 hectares, the research work evolved to set out a vision for the future and it started to identify opportunities for working towards regeneration.

The vision on how to effect positive, long-lasting and sustainable change was rooted in the landscape's history and the area's most prominent and potent feature—its water. The goal was to revitalise this neglected area by creating 35,000 new homes and as many as 50,000 jobs along with schools, healthcare facilities, community centres and sporting amenities. Expected to take a generation to complete, the sustainable scheme will also include improved public transport and transport infrastructure and better connections to the rest of the capital. The vision's seven themes included Water City celebrating the area's rivers and canals and completing the missing link connecting the Lee Valley Regional Park with the Thames as a continuous green corridor. The second theme in the vision was the identification of Thriving Centres, including Stratford and Canning Town, where new development could be concentrated. The third was Neighbourhoods and Communities where mixed-use schemes would ensure an improved quality of life for all. Other themes focused on creating active and dense areas of industry and employment opportunities, improved communications and social, economic and environmental sustainability. The final theme was the 2012 Olympic and Paralympic Games. The regeneration strategy was well under way before the Games were a consideration, but they were incorporated into the vision as an important catalyst for regeneration of the wider area.

The opportunities document provided clarification on the social, economic and regeneration challenges and the scale of effort that would be required to effect significant, lasting and positive change.

Leytonstone
High Road
Leyton
Homerton
Maryland
Stratford
Hackney Wick
Stratford
Pudding Mill Lane
Plaistow
West Ham
Bow Church
Bow Road
Bromley-by-Bow
Mile End
Devons Road
Stepney Green
Langdon Park
Canning Town
Limehouse
All Saints

Above
Breaking news

The jubilation seen in the West End when London was pronounced the 2012 host city in 2005. It was clear from the start that local community involvement was essential to the making of the Olympic Park and its subsequent successful transformation into a new London district.

Opposite
Transformation

The energy and excitement of staging the Games is evoked in powerful graphic visions, top, of how the public areas around the concourse could look and function. It requires an athletic leap of the imagination to create such an event from the run-down, near-derelict landscape, bottom.

Olympic Park

The land designated for the Olympic Park (more than 230 hectares) occupies around one fifth of the whole Lower Lea Valley regeneration zone and flanks a two kilometre stretch of the River Lea. In addition to having the river at its heart, the site incorporated a network of canals and a tangle of infrastructure including pylons, roads, sewers and rail. It was disfigured by run-down buildings and dereliction, and was surrounded by poor and badly served communities. Local neighbourhoods were identified as some of the poorest, youngest and most ethnically diverse in the entire city. They suffered from a lack of jobs, a lack of amenities and limited public transport connections with other local areas and the rest of London. Significant parts of the land were contaminated with pollutants from decades of low-value industry and landfill including thousands of tons of rubble dumped here following the widespread destruction caused by the Blitz in the 1940s.

The long industrial history of the place stretches back to the Middle Ages when the flat marshlands were studded with windmills grinding flour for the city's bakers, later the canals helped generate wealth as the means of transporting goods from London's docks to the rest of the country, in the past century industries sprang up making the first transistors and valves for early television sets, creating some of the earliest plastics, Lee Enfield rifles and toys. However, in recent decades manufacturing collapsed and the place languished. Its decline was halted as a result of London's rapid development in the early years of the new century when the place was identified as an area for potential growth. Despite its sense of dislocation and deprivation, the Stratford area is within eight kilometres of central London. The city's expansion eastwards provided the opportunity for regeneration of an entire urban district with development on a scale not seen since Victorian times.

Ideas evolved to create a new park around the upgraded river and network of canals. Work on the public realm would be accompanied by improving local transport infrastructure to link the district with the centre of London and neighbouring communities. With the 2012 Olympic and Paralympic Games as the catalyst for regeneration and a profound and lasting change, investment would be accompanied by the creation of a distinctive and positive image for the area.

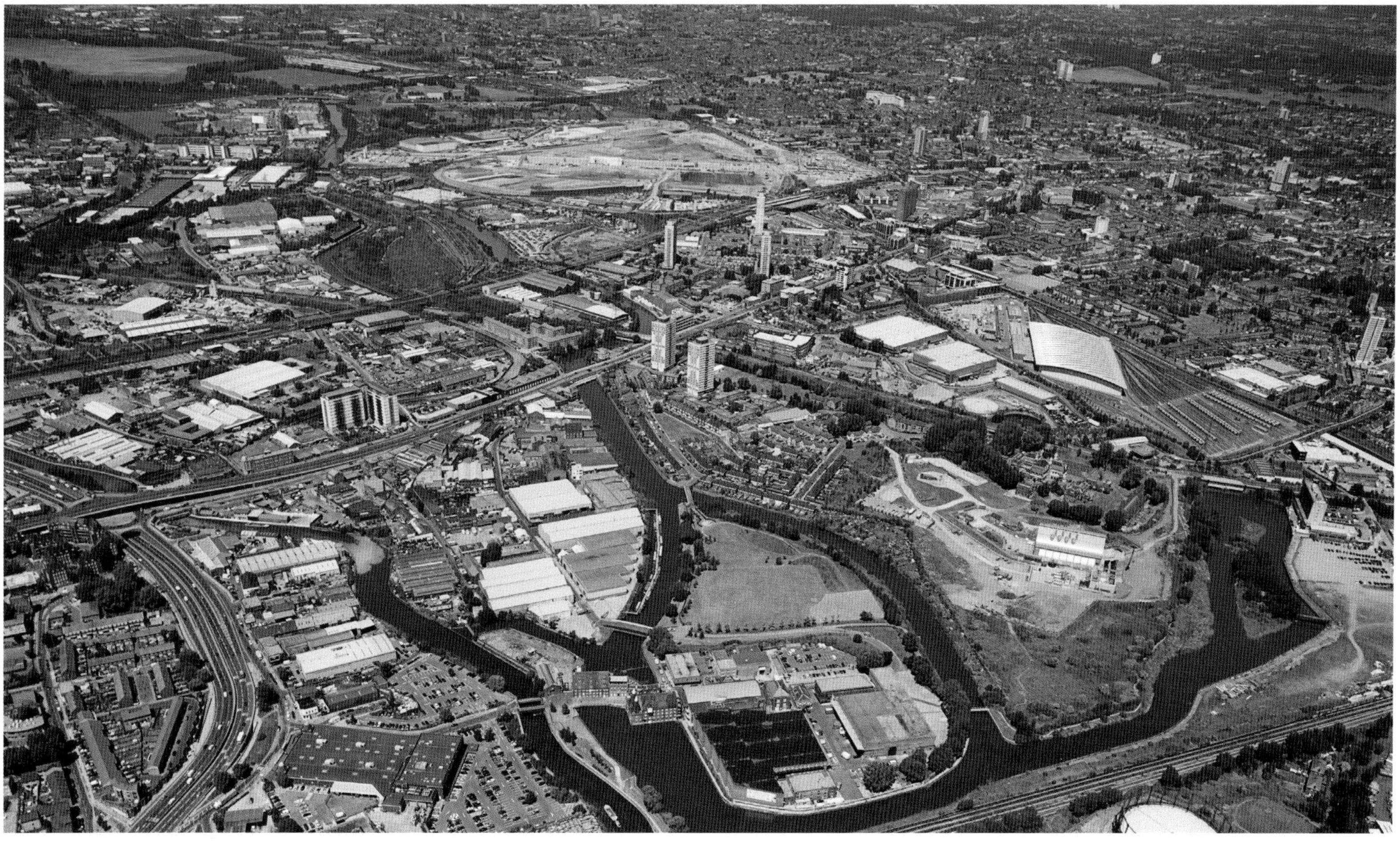

Right
Olympic Park Masterplan

A colour-coded diagram of the Olympic Park showing some of its layers of construction. The sporting venues appear in pale blue, with back-of-house facilities and service areas in patches of red, and waterways in dark blue. Floating above here is the concourse which provides internal pedestrian circulation through the site and spectator access to all venues. The uppermost layer of the diagram, in red, is the Loop Road. This encircles the park site and provides service access to the back-of-house areas and athlete access to the venues. From this diagram it is possible to understand the park as a vast stage set where the complexity of running the Olympic and Paralympic Games necessarily involves tremendous logistical planning, controlled access and security considerations.

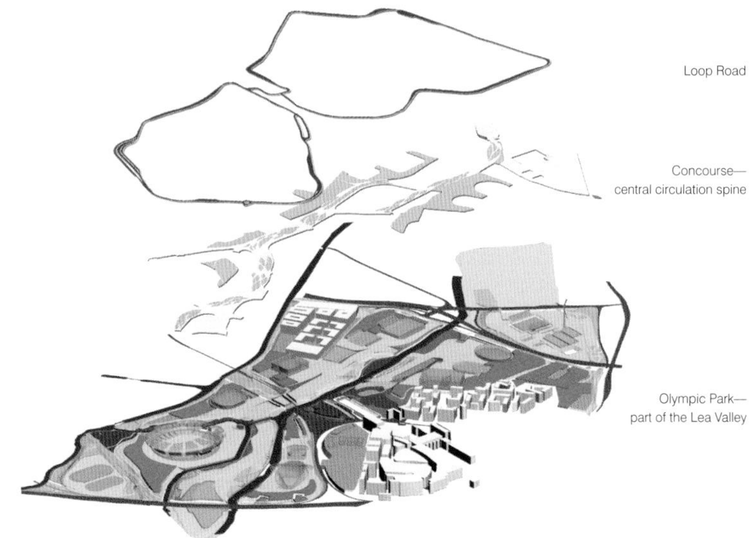

Masterplans for the Games and for the parkland that would be their legacy were prepared and gained planning permission. As a powerful expression of intent, these permissions formed the core of London's bid for the 2012 Games. Following the announcement that London was the chosen venue, the next phase was to develop the concept masterplan. Planning permission was secured in a landmark joint decision made by the four host boroughs of Tower Hamlets, Hackney, Newham and Waltham Forest with neighbouring authority Greenwich.

Created around water the 230 hectare site, of which 120 hectares will form new parklands, flanks a two kilometre stretch of the River Lea. It has an open and semi-rural character in the north and a dense, urban feel in the south, closer to the Thames. The southern portion also includes the canal network. The design is conceived as a two-tier landscape with the rivers and canals forming a lush, green lower level core and with an open platform above creating the setting for the 2012 Olympic and Paralympic Games. At the upper level, the grand concourse follows the north–south flow of the river leading spectators through the linear site on a grand processional route. The concourse links all of the main Olympic venues from the VeloPark cycling centre in the north by a team led by Hopkins Architects, to the grand stadium designed by a team led by HOK Sport, and the Aquatics Centre by Zaha Hadid, both anchoring the south of the site.

Above
During the Games

Looking south towards the River Thames and the former Millennium Dome, now The O2 arena, this early visualisation of the Olympic Park by EDAW AECOM, Foreign Office Architects, HOK and Allies and Morrison, shows the main sporting venues clustered around the central river valley. The concept of integrating permanent and temporary venues formed part of the design from the start. Linking these buildings, the broad concourse forms a strong central spine weaving its way from north to south and crossing the river at key points.

The creation of the park involved a complex sequence of compulsory purchase orders to acquire the site, followed by a systematic clearing and remediation of the land. This included excavating, treating and cleaning around 1.5 million cubic metres of soil, eradicating an infestation of Japanese knotweed and other invasive species, reusing around 90 per cent of materials generated from demolition within the site, removing more than 50 pylons and placing electricity cabling in two underground tunnels more than six kilometres in length, and cleaning up more than eight kilometres of waterways. In addition, work was carried out to improve wildlife habitat and biodiversity with extensive planting of native species including oak and ash, willow, birch, hazel, holly, blackthorn and hawthorn, and to ensure that construction work followed established sustainability principles using recycled materials and ensuring that 50 per cent of materials by weight were transported by sustainable means including by waterways and rail.

The creation of the park is underpinned by environmental, economic and social sustainability with the goal of minimising any adverse impacts during the design and construction of the park, its venues, infrastructure and surrounding housing to leave a lasting, high-quality place.

In terms of environmental sustainability, key gains include transformation of the near-derelict site and bringing the land into public use by creating significant new green space in East London.

All construction has been carried out to maximise the careful use of resources such as using recycled material and optimising opportunities for the efficient use of water. In addition the new utilities infrastructure was designed to meet the long-term needs of this part of the Lower Lea Valley ensuring that 20 per cent of the total energy demand from the permanent Games facilities will be met by new on-site renewable energy sources. At the heart of the park's infrastructure is the Energy Centre with biomass boiler and a combined cooling heating and power plant for the Aquatics Centre and 2012 Olympic Stadium. Other aspects of environmental sustainability included improving natural habitat, a network of cycle ways and footpaths and a range of improvements to the public transport system including the high-speed Javelin train's seven minute journey to central London, an extension to the Docklands Light Railway, increased capacity on the Jubilee Line and the upgraded Stratford International Station.

In economic sustainability, the goals included creating new high-value jobs, investing in infrastructure to attract businesses to the area, and adding value to the land and encouraging investment through the new park.

Social sustainability is embedded by creating high-quality public spaces and homes which are attractive and well served. Places where people can enjoy being part of a community, enjoy healthy lifestyles, and be proud of their neighbourhood.

Above and opposite
Games, transformation, legacy

Images above show the progression of works on a riverbank section of the site where areas of natural habitat are preserved and enhanced and the brownfield land is made ready for the Games. The middle image shows the land in Games mode with the broad concourse at the upper level and walkways close to the water. After the Games the site is transformed into the legacy state where temporary parts of the concourse are removed and trees and plants gain stature as the park matures. The stages of evolution are also shown in the visualisations opposite where the excitement of the Games is depicted in the top two images, and the future park is shown below.

Below
Biodiversity

Habitat protection enhancement and creation have been carefully considered throughout the design process, which included a biodiversity action plan.

Occassional tree and shrub planting provide structural diversity and cover that benefit species such as birds. Flower-rich grassland is an important aspect of the site's existing ecology. A high herbaceous component provides greater diversity of nectar, seed and food plants.

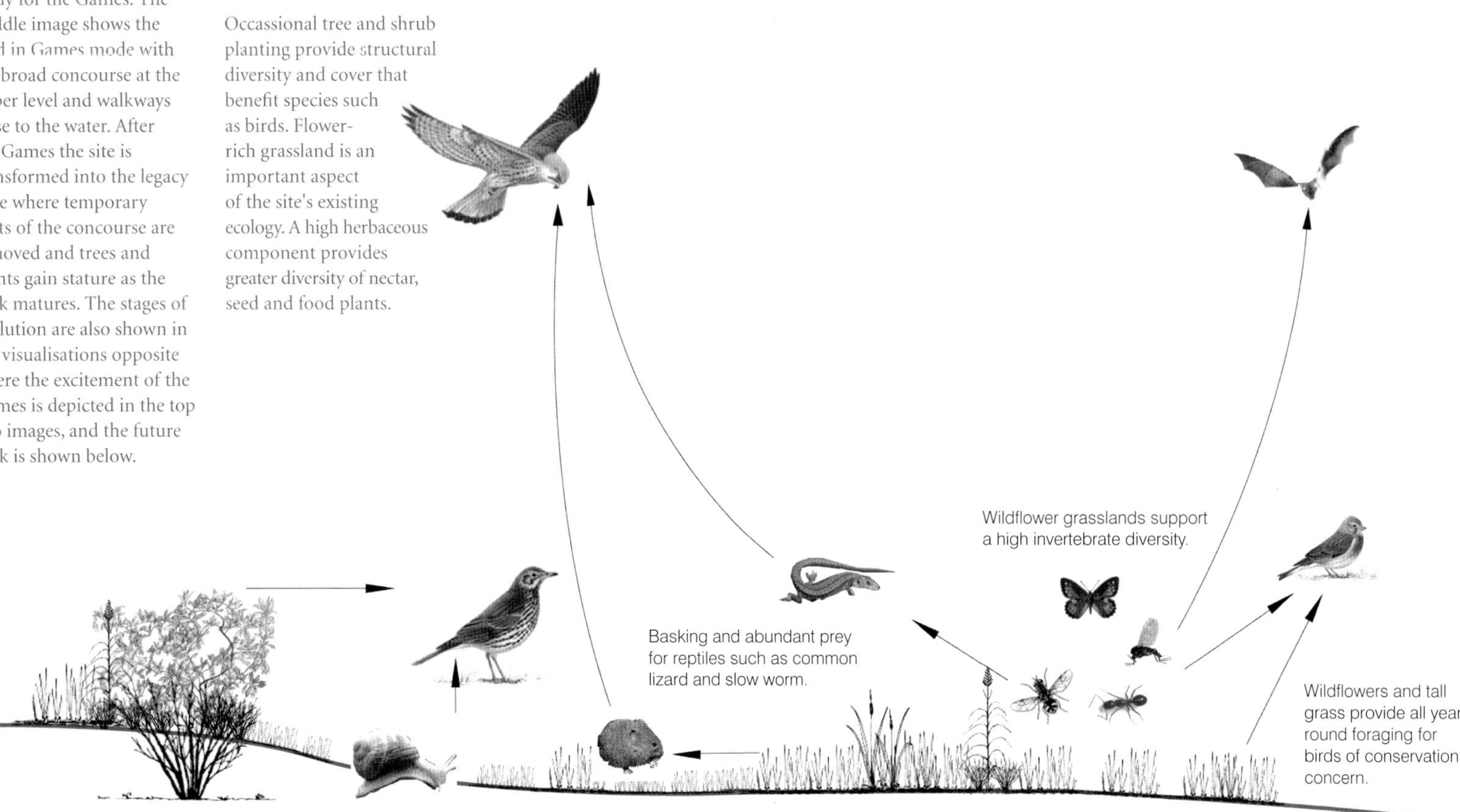

Wildflower grasslands support a high invertebrate diversity.
Basking and abundant prey for reptiles such as common lizard and slow worm.
Wildflowers and tall grass provide all year round foraging for birds of conservation concern.

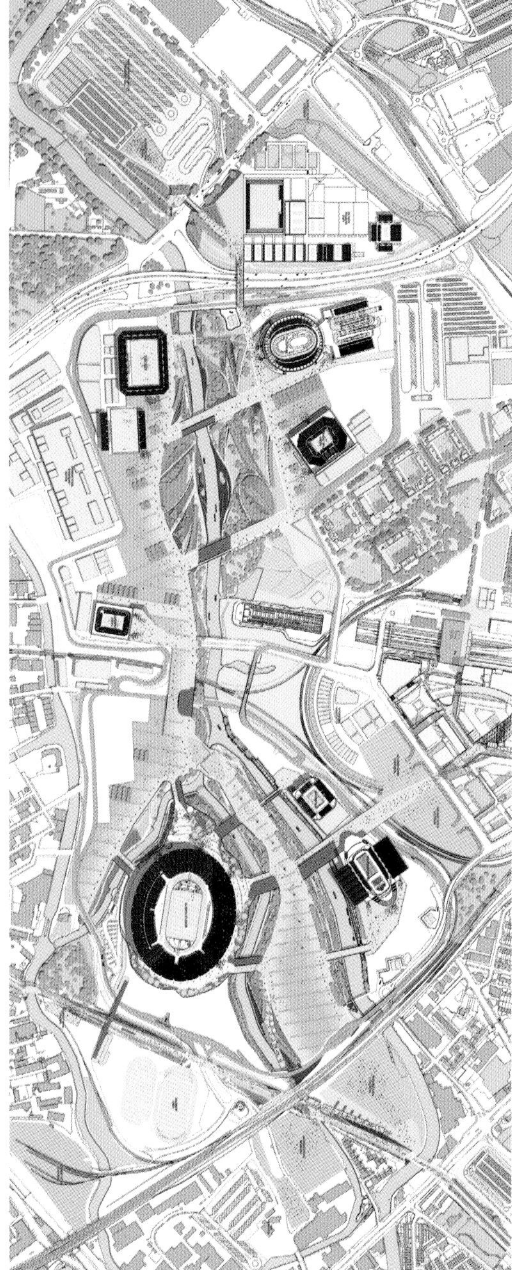

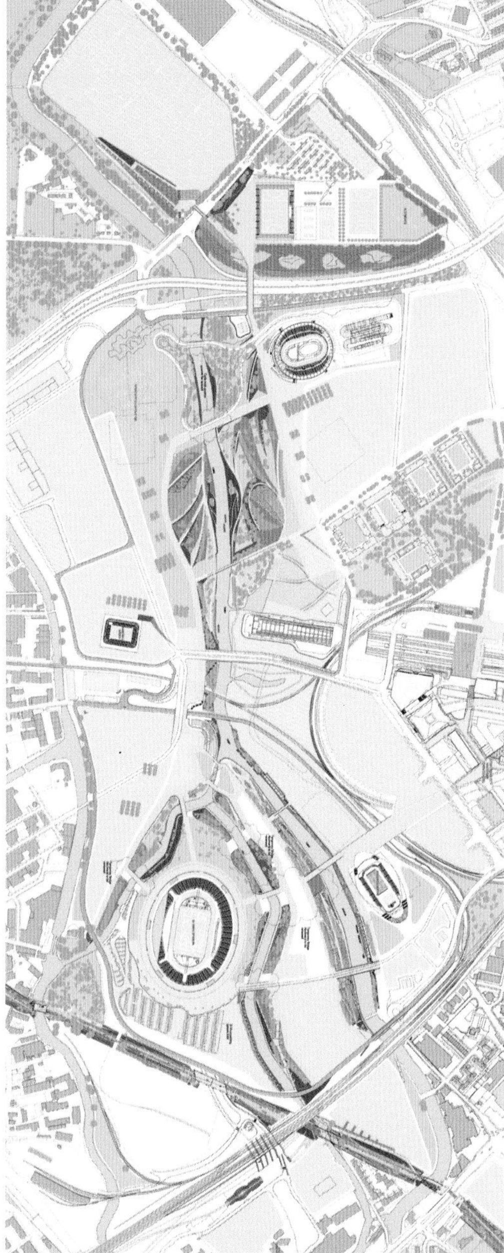

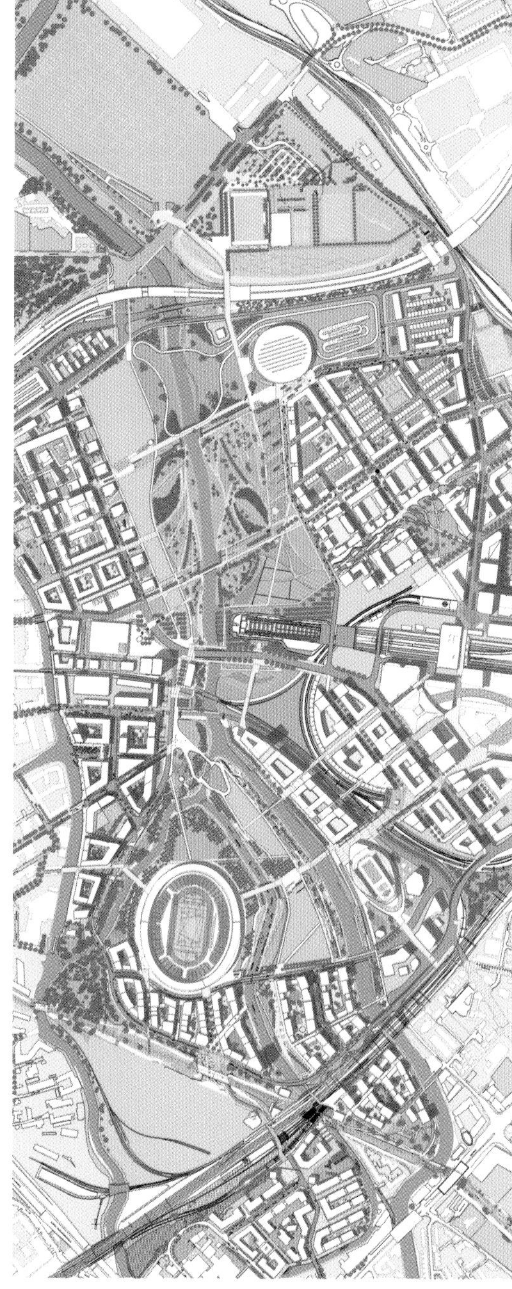

Left to right
Starting at the finish

Designed in reverse order, first as a completed park with the Olympics occurring as an event along the way. The evolution of the site moves from being a stage for the 2012 Olympic and Paralympic Games to the transition phase when permanent venues are downsized and temporary venues decommissioned and removed to create sites for new development. Green areas and restored waterways remain intact throughout. On the far right, the completed parklands are shown with the prominent Olympic Stadium and Aquatics Centre, in the south, and Velodrome, in the north, in place, and new development around the circumference of the legacy park. Also in the legacy site, the Loop Road and concourse are downsized and a number of temporary bridges are removed.

Legacy

From the outset, the London 2012 Olympic and Paralympic Games and their legacy were planned together. The Legacy Masterplan Framework for the park underpins the development and further regeneration of the area.

The legacy ambition is for a new piece of well-connected and well-served city in the east of London. Truly a mixed-use scheme, plans include 10,000–12,000 new homes in addition to those in the Olympic Village, and more than 11 hectares of commercial space along with three new primary schools, a secondary school, and a sports' focused national skills academy which will be located in the Olympic legacy stadium. In addition there will be an arts academy and primary school in the Olympic Village, a new business and higher-education hub around the legacy of the international media and broadcast centre in Hackney Wick, along with healthcare provision, training and jobs, social and cultural facilities.

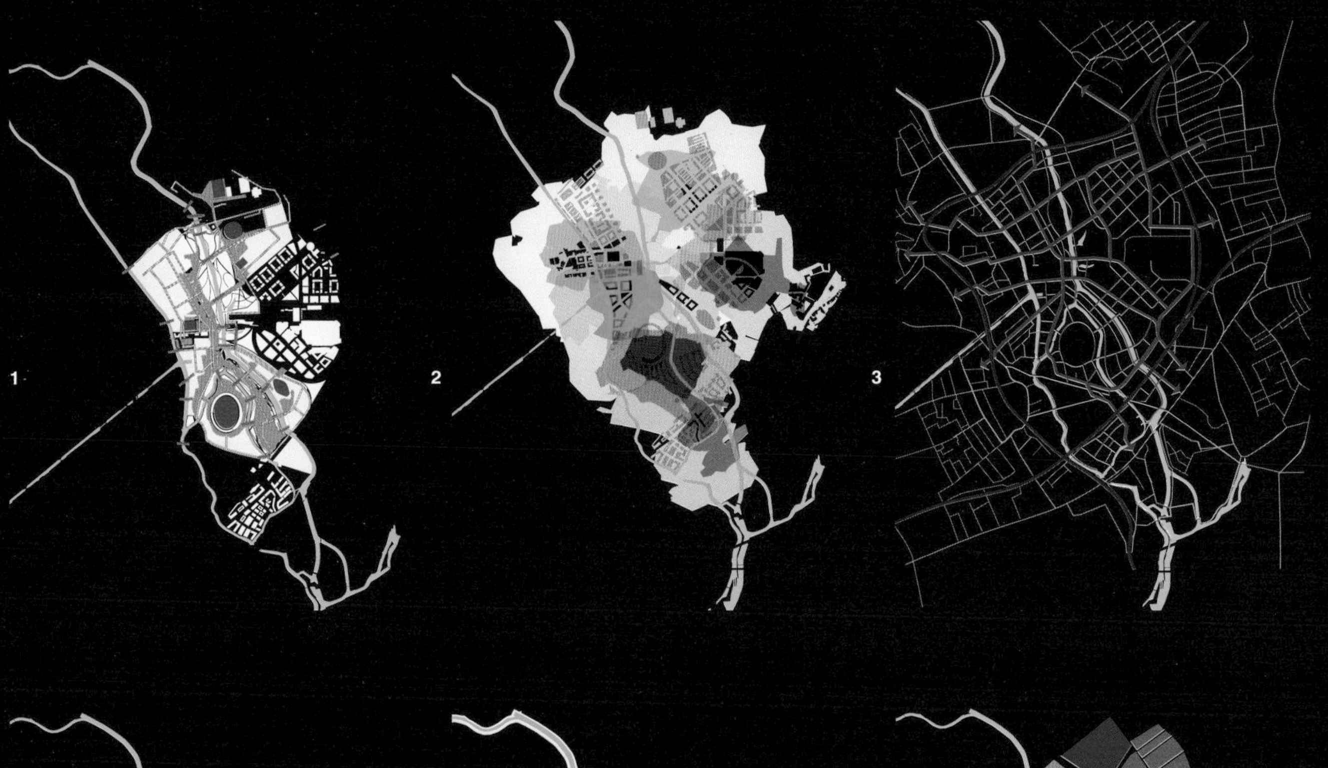

Six spatial concepts
1 2012 Olympic inheritance
2 Neighbourhoods and centres
3 Connections
4 Open space and parklands
5 Water city
6 Field evolution

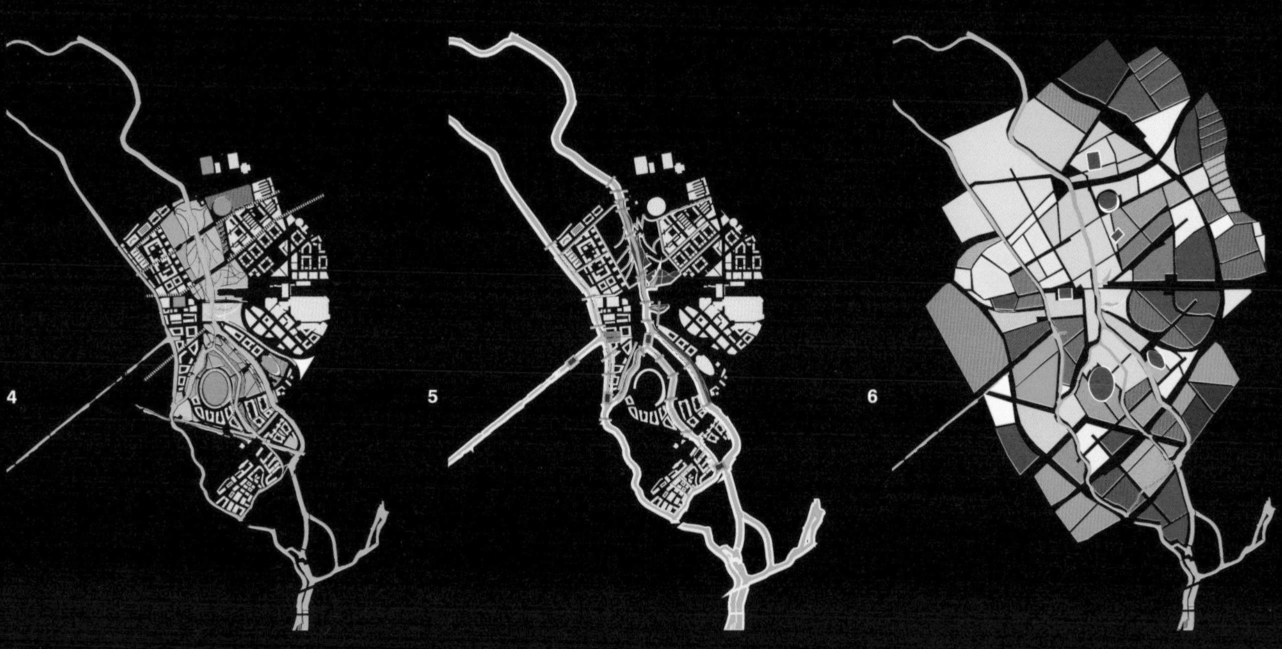

With the end of the 2012 Olympic and Paralympic Games, work will start on new development in and around the park. Six new legacy areas will be created:

Stratford Village—which includes plans for 1,500–1,800 homes, a primary school and a new local high street.

Hackney Wick East—which includes plans for the development of the broadcast and media centre, 2,000–2,400 homes, a 6,000 seat multi-use sports stadium and an ideas store and creation centre.

Stratford Waterfront—which includes plans for 1,800–2,000 homes, the Aquatics Centre, and a lively waterfront.

Olympic Quarter—which includes plans for the legacy stadium, 2,700–3,200 homes, Olympic gardens and a sports focused education facility within the stadium.

Pudding Mill—which includes plans for 800–960 homes, in excess of 600,000 square metres of commercial space and an active local plaza with cafes and restaurants.

Old Ford—which includes plans for 1,200–1,400 homes, a primary school, a new marina and the retention of the Old Ford Lock structure.

All the areas will include other leisure amenities, and as part of the plan the Aquatics Centre and Velodrome will be retained for future sporting use. To bring about this change, at the close of the Games the park enters its transformation phase with the removal of perimeter fences and opening up the site. The green core of parklands flanking the river and canals remains intact and open for the public to enjoy through a network of towpaths, footpaths and cycleways as the natural systems continue restoring themselves and grow stronger. Meanwhile, all new work is focussed on the upper level where the Games took place.

Economically, the area will be transformed. Thousands of new jobs will be created and training opportunities will be made for local people. Benefits will be felt in the wider area too as a result of the cross-city transport improvements in London, new investment in homes and jobs and the events to be staged in the sporting venues.

Right
A sense of place

A diagram of the character, uses and activities in the future parklands as an extension of London's city fabric.

Opposite

Looking south-east towards the River Thames, and with the prominent Olympic Stadium in its downsized legacy mode, this slice of the future parklands shows development around the edges of the site and green space in the centre close to the restored and revived waterways.

Victoria Park
The Greenway
Waterworks River
Legacy stadium, a sports-focused education facility
Greenway Park
Olympic South Park
Rail tracks
Aquatics Centre

Opposite

Close-up of the south-eastern corner of the legacy development with Olympic Stadium in the centre background and the Greenway cutting a swathe across the site.

Above
Timelapse

Evolution of the site as it may take place. Clockwise from top left, from 2012 to 2015, 2015 to 2020, 2020 to 2030 and 2030 to 2040.

Hackney Wick East

1 Legacy park frontage
2 Multi-use sports venue
3 Employment, research and creativity
4 Canal-side housing

Stratford Village

1 Legacy park frontage
2 Local high street
3 Central community school
4 Family housing
5 Velodrome and VeloPark

Stratford Waterfront

1 Waterfront promenade
2 Balconies on the water
3 East–west links
4 The Aquatics Centre

Old Ford

1 Public space: new marina
2 New primary school
3 Legacy park frontage
4 New built canal
5 Courtyard buildings

A quartet of images from the EDAW AECOM, KCAP and Allies and Morrison team, showing a vision of the future as development transforms the Olympic site into a new city district.

Hackney Wick East, former site of the media centre, temporary hockey, and handball arena, transformed into a multi-use sports venue. The temporary hockey arena is removed to free up new parklands.

Stratford Village, the athletes' village becomes new housing and a school. The Velodrome remains in place as an important national venue for cycling events.

Stratford waterfront is created where the temporary waterpolo venue is decommissioned and frees up development space for a new city district with views over the water. The Aquatics Centre is reduced in size but retained.

Old Ford, where back-of-house facilities are dispensed with to make way for development incorporating the canal with a new school and marina.

Concept

The creation of mainland China's first coastal park system

Context

Coastal/tropical

Shenzhen Coastal Park System Strategic Plan, Shenzhen, China.

In the past, urban growth in the fast-expanding city of Shenzhen has marched across landscapes free from restraint. More recently, protection of the environment has risen up the agenda to take precedence over unfettered development. This project involved assessing and analysing the ecological value and development potential of the natural resources along a 150 kilometre stretch of the city's eastern coastline, and then devising a series of strategic coastal parks to support sustainable management of the area's natural resources.

Opposite
Boom town

Until the 1980s Shenzhen was little more than a fishing village surrounded by rice paddies, however, after being designated as a Special Economic Zone, the rate of growth has been phenomenal. In the hinterland of Hong Kong, the megacity of more than ten million people continues to expand at a rapid pace.

Shenzhen Coastal Park System Strategic Plan, Shenzhen, China

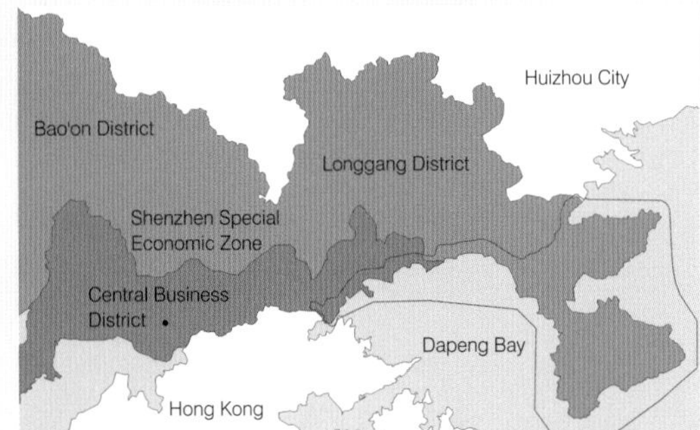

Above
Regional context

To the north of Hong Kong, Shenzhen's latest explosion of growth has been eastwards towards a beautiful area of mountains and coast. In previous years, land has been flattened for development, but more recently the urge has been to protect areas of particular environmental value. The desire to protect the landscape is also driven by the recognition that China's new urban populations need natural places to visit and enjoy as a break from city life. The strategic plan has created a viable framework for the first coastal park system in mainland China, and protects one of the last remaining pieces of unspoiled nature in the Pearl River Delta region, a megalopolis of 60 million people. The comprehensive plan preserves a unique coastline with reserves for parks, forests, mountains, water systems, beaches and terrestrial freshwater and marine ecosystems, achieving a balance between urban growth and resource protection.

Opposite
Majestic beauty

Using methodical and scientific research, analysis and site surveys, the project team was able to assess the various qualities of the area and delivered sustainable planning and sensitive resource management recommendations to the city's planning authorities.

In the Pearl River Delta, one of China's most dynamic industrial regions, Shenzhen has grown from being a fishing village to an economic powerhouse with a population of ten million in the space of just a few decades. Its potential was unleashed in the late 1970s when Shenzhen was designated the country's first Special Economic Zone. Today it is one of the world's fastest growing cities.

On the South China Sea and bordering Hong Kong, this manufacturing boom town has expanded at a frantic pace. And with the latest phases of urban development heading eastwards, the metropolis looked poised to spill out into the nearby coastal landscape. Ecologically rich, visually stunning and sparsely populated, the area is dominated by mountain ranges and valleys, woodlands and wetlands. It also has more than 150 kilometres of unspoiled coastline, one of the largest stretches of unblemished coast in the country.

The municipality knew that the effects of a new explosion of growth could be devastating since it had already experienced unfettered development when the young city grew westwards. Here, the rapacious urban expansion resulted in the wholesale levelling of mountains and the incessant march of construction. To avoid the same fate for Shenzhen's eastern area, the city's planning authority took the progressive option of managing future development by restricting building sprawl and by protecting as much as possible of the remaining natural environment.

The progression towards ecological stewardship has removed sensitive and fragile areas from the danger of eradication and ensures that the growing urban population will have easy access to a beautiful landscape, natural open spaces and the opportunity for healthy outdoor pursuits. Protection of this stunning landscape will also provide economic benefits by attracting tourists to the region and it is expected to have a positive impact on Shezhen's image, moving from its perception as a gritty industrial hub to a place with a beautiful and extensive natural environment.

In striking the balance between the potentially conflicting goals of expansion and ecological protection—the solution has been to evolve a strategic plan that creates development zones around a string of new coastal parks, the country's first regional coastal park system. The scheme has helped to redefine new ways to control development and integrate nature preservation in mainland China.

On route to completing the plan, the initial steps in accommodating this sustainable growth were to assess the area's attributes and its potential. At the beginning of the process the focus of attention was along the coastline, but it soon became clear that results would fall short of expectations by concentrating attention on just a narrow band of land. With so many interconnecting and overlapping ecosystems, habitats and land uses, a broader vision was required. Eventually the planning authority took the bold step of taking in an entire landscape of around 300 square kilometres.

To begin to understand the particular qualities and characteristics of the landscape, an audit was conducted of the natural, historic and cultural resources under threat. Elements explored included agricultural use, local geology and topography, water resources and woodlands along with features such as ancient villages, flora and fauna. The work also served to highlight the area's ecological richness. Environmental damage and endangered species were also recorded, and so too was scenic value.

To collect the information, field investigations were conducted during the course of six months involving landscape architects, environmental planners, developmental economists, urban designers and architects. They spent extensive time on site during different seasons to experience, observe and record the natural, cultural, social and economic resources from land and from sea. The teams collaborated with local experts including professional hikers, academics and environmental groups to further understand the existing resources in the study area and how they had been changed as a result of recent developments.

These field investigations were coupled with the extensive use of remote-sensing data including aerial photography and satellite imagery, plus historical and current land-use planning. To gain a holistic understanding of the area, the layers of information were compiled using a geographical information system (GIS) database.

With the resource information logged, it was evaluated and analysed. The GIS mapping made it possible to identify the different grades of environmentally sensitive areas and other less precious land that would be useful for future growth. This information is now used by the city as a reference for future development; by setting out principles and guidelines it acts as a strategic framework. Work on the strategic plan has also included advice on sustainable planning and resource management recommendations for the planning authorities.

Water quality sensitivity zones

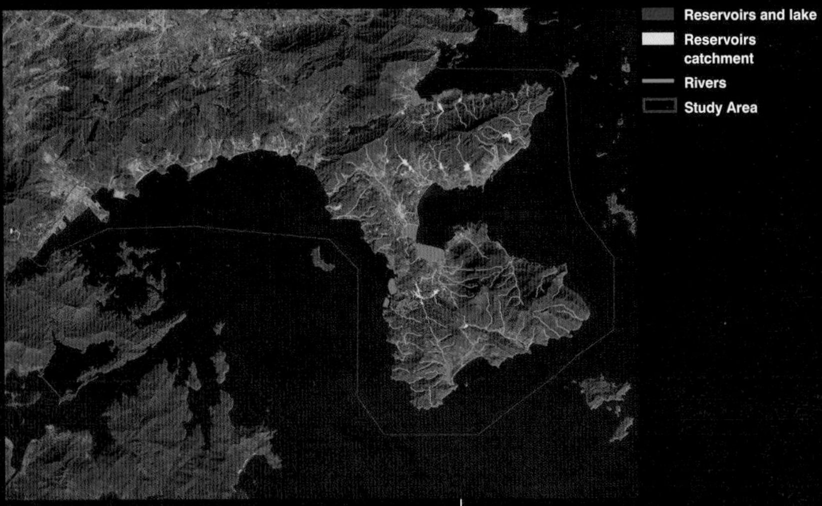

Reservoirs and lake
Reservoirs catchment
Rivers
Study Area

Slope analysis

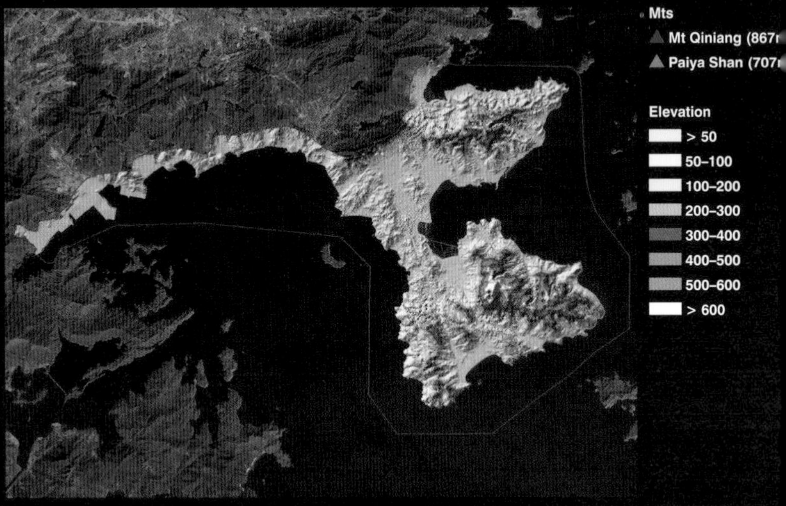

Mts
Mt Qiniang (867
Paiya Shan (707
Elevation
> 50
50–100
100–200
200–300
300–400
400–500
500–600
> 600

Sensitive biological areas

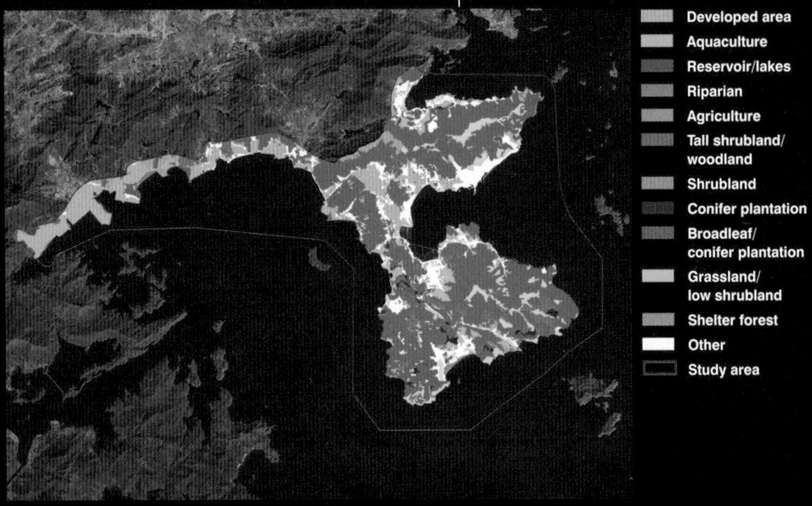

Developed area
Aquaculture
Reservoir/lakes
Riparian
Agriculture
Tall shrubland/ woodland
Shrubland
Conifer plantation
Broadleaf/ conifer plantation
Grassland/ low shrubland
Shelter forest
Other
Study area

Pollution and hazard analysis

Polluted/haz areas

Primary and protected farmlands

Primary farmland (medium-high sensitivity)
Protected farmland (medium-low sensitivity)
Study area

Marine environment

Coastal sediment
Reclaimed la
Silty clay
Sandy silty c
Silty sand
Sandy silt
Medium sanc
Fine and mec
Coarse and r
Fine sand
Clayey silt
Grit
Sand
Sand gravel
Gravel

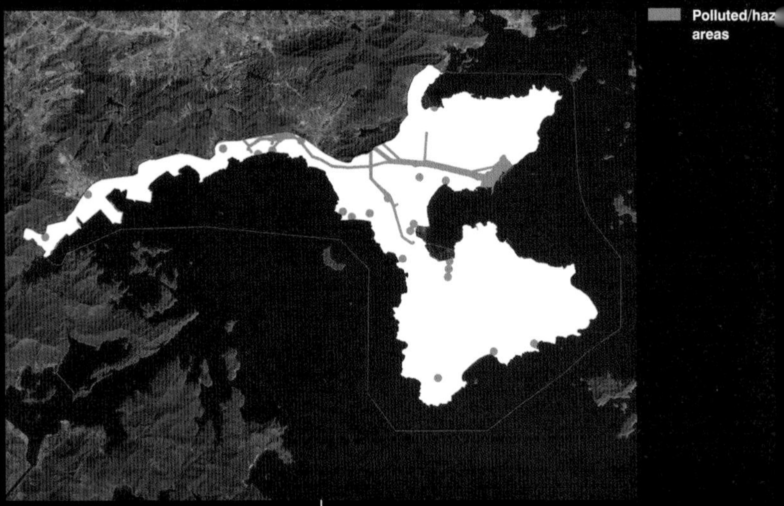

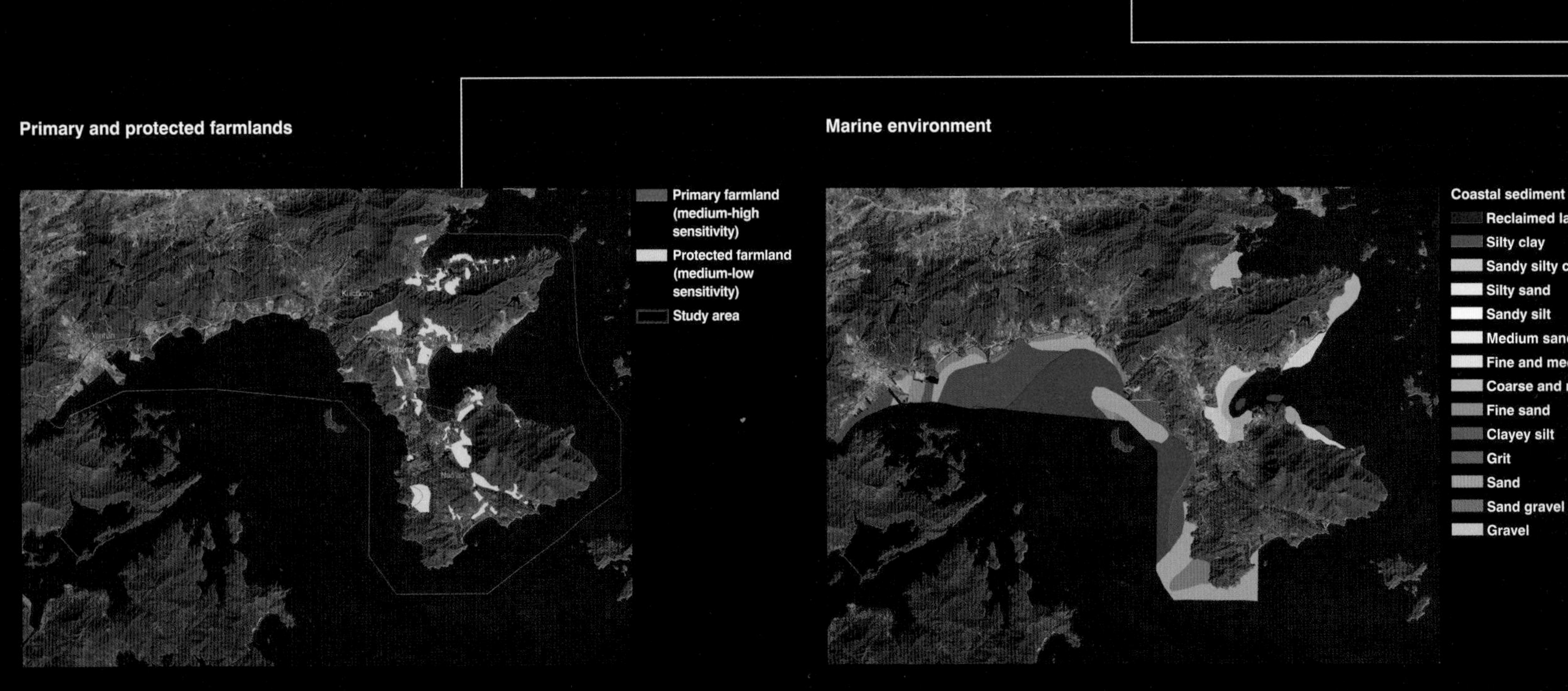

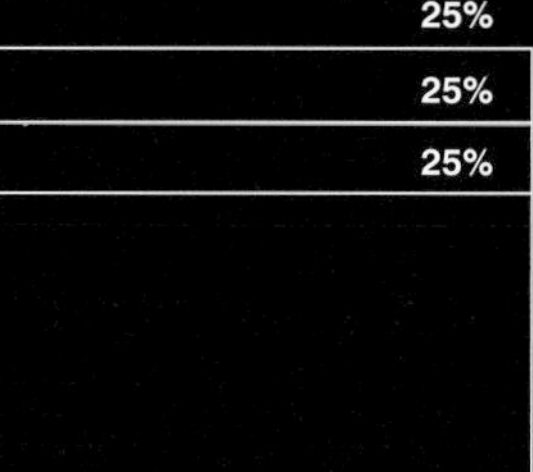

Composite resource sensitivity

10%
15%

Left
Analysis and assessment

The study area was analysed to identify its many components from water sensitivity zones and slope analysis to pollution and sensitive biological areas. These different qualities of the area were then combined into a composite image to indicate areas of greatest and least environmental sensitivity.

Overleaf
Strategic plan

By understanding the qualities of the site, it was possible to identify areas in need of most protection and those where public access could be encouraged. The result is China's first coastal parks system, which sits to the east of Shenzhen and within easy reach of the city. Following the development of the strategic plan, further work in the area included the design of the country's first scenic coastal road, by Yangchou Point and Egong Bay.

Maluanshan Country Park
Da/Xiao meisha Seashore Park
Beizai Point Coastal Park
Shayu Chong Coastal Park
S
1
2
To Hong Kong
To Hong Kong

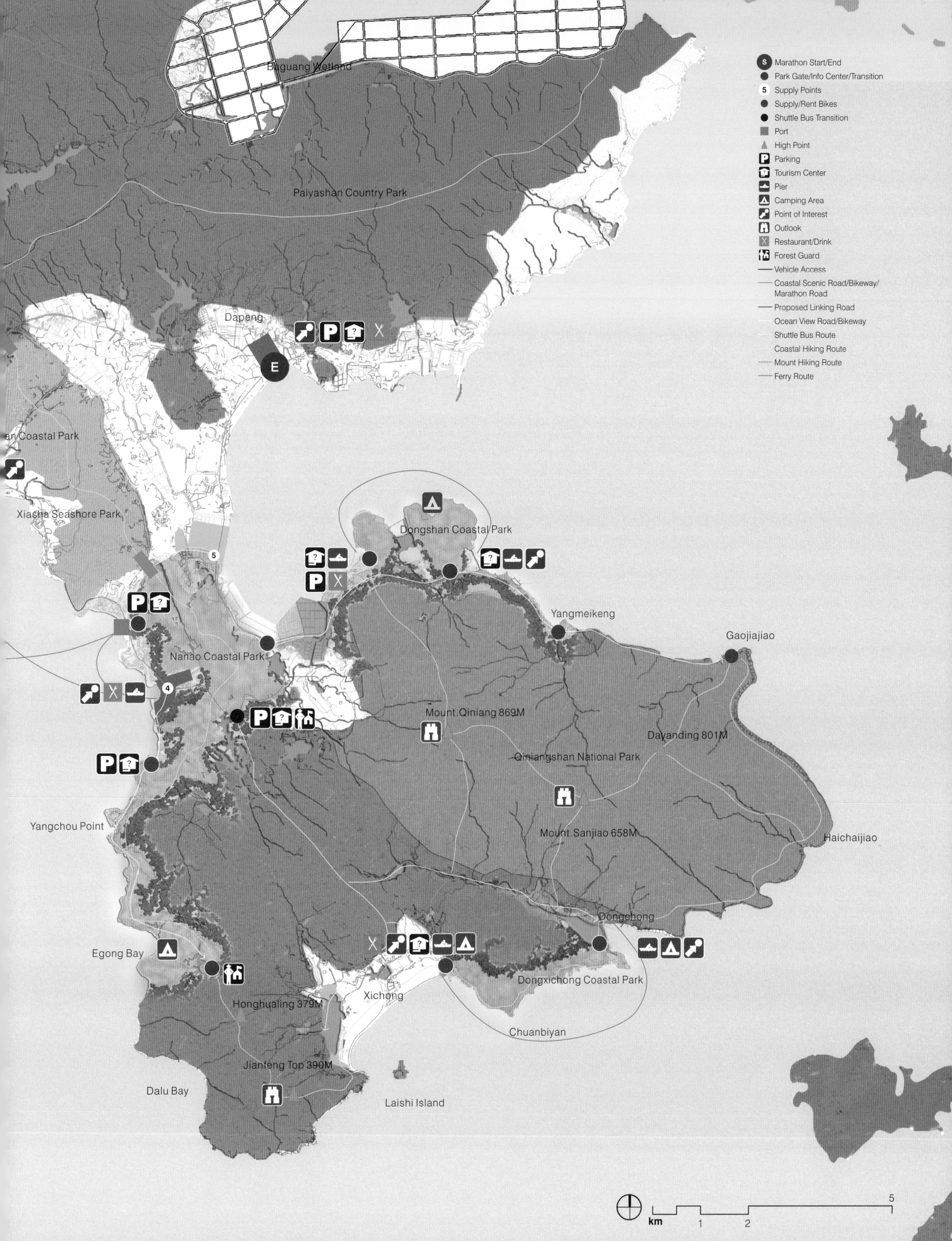

Marathon Start/End
Park Gate/Info Center/Transition
Supply Points
Supply/Rent Bikes
Shuttle Bus Transition
Port
High Point
Parking
Tourism Center
Pier
Camping Area
Point of Interest
Outlook
Restaurant/Drink
Forest Guard
Vehicle Access
Coastal Scenic Road/Bikeway/ Marathon Road
Proposed Linking Road
Ocean View Road/Bikeway
Shuttle Bus Route
Coastal Hiking Route
Mount Hiking Route
Ferry Route
Baguang Wetland
Paiyashan Country Park
Dapeng
Xiasha Seashore Park
Dongshan Coastal Park
Yangmeikeng
Gaojiajiao
Nanao Coastal Park
Mount.Qiniang 869M
Dayanding 801M
Qiniangshan National Park
Mount.Sanjiao 658M
Yangchou Point
Haichaijiao
Dongchong
Egong Bay
Dongxichong Coastal Park
Xichong
Honghualing 379M
Chuanbiyan
Jianfeng Top 390M
Dalu Bay
Laishi Island
km
1
2
5

With the multi-layered composite picture of the region complete, the next phase of work began on understanding where to create the protected areas and parks and how to manage public access. The creation of a new system of country parks was proposed with a hierarchy of land types, the most sensitive being heavily protected, the least sensitive providing public access. Protected areas encompassed those with special landscape value and sensitive habitat, preserved historical sites including some traditional villages, precious marine ecosystems and existing and restored wetland with public access to recreation. The coastal parks, also described as decoy areas, are less environmentally sensitive. Here outdoor activities are concentrated away from the more sensitive ecological reserves and people have access for intensive uses such as walking trails, museums and visitor centres.

Alongside the concept of a parks system, development opportunity areas were also identified to answer the city's need for expansion. This phase of work began with further analysis that explored existing transport infrastructure and connections, scenic and landscape values, and development capacity as well as a review of the city's existing planning strategy for the area. International case studies were referred to from California to the coast of Spain where comparisons on tourist capacity, activity, park management and programmatic organisation were conducted. There was also a review of Shenzhen's existing system of protected areas which were cross-checked with the project's earlier GIS findings. This comprehensive work identified a sequence of areas suitable for development to accommodate the city's inevitable growth.

Concentrated away from precious natural landscapes, many of these development areas are around the coast and will be linked with a new coastal road. Along with providing access to beaches which have the potential to become a regional attraction, this road also ensures good connections with the heart of Shenzhen where work is underway reviewing the city parks and open spaces to make connections with the new rural parks.

Opposite and left
A walk in the park

Part of the research work identified historic villages which are to be preserved for their traditional architecture. New walking trails, opposite, provide China's new urbanites with the opportunity to get close to nature.

Overleaf
Local distinctiveness

Preservation of architectural and natural heritage has moved up the agenda in recent years as awareness grows of the value of local distinctiveness and the sense of place. The creation of a new system of coastal parks and municipal-level ecological reserves is a progressive one for China.

Concept
Transforming a dessert island into a major cultural and resorts destination for an economy in transition

Context
Desert/arid

Saadiyat Island Masterplan, Abu Dhabi, UAE.

With rapidly growing populations and the need to plan for a post-oil, carbon-limited world, the Gulf States are poised for considerable change. Abu Dhabi is among those taking the lead in economic diversification and a central part of its vision is investment in tourism, especially cultural tourism.

Opposite
Island vision

Rising from the desert sands, the Saadiyat Island vision for a post-oil economy is rooted in culture and tourism. The 2,700 hectare project will include world-class museums and galleries by Frank Gehry, Jean Nouvel and Norman Foster.

Saadiyat Island Masterplan, Abu Dhabi, UAE

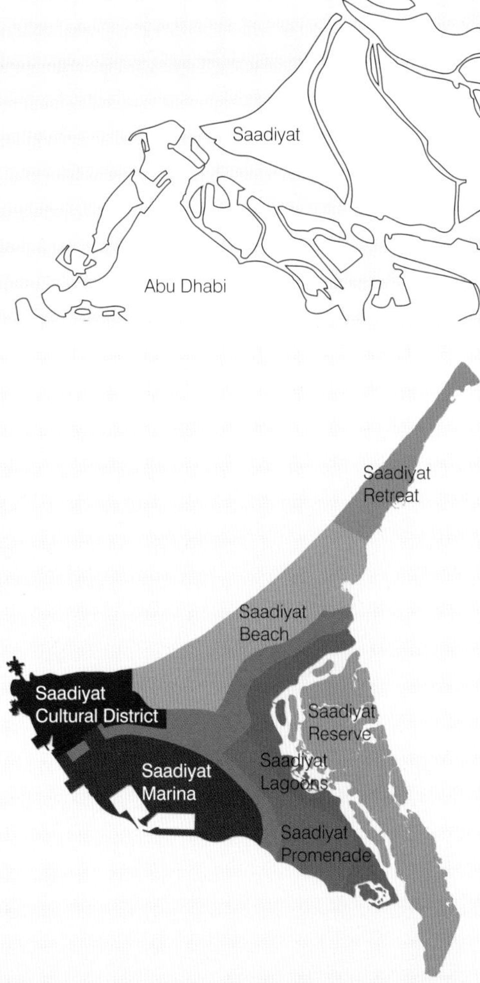

Above
Context

The triangular shaped island seen in relation to the city of Abu Dhabi. In its natural state the landscape is composed largely of dunes and mangrove lagoons fringed with white sand beaches. The masterplan envisages creating a sequence of areas each with a strong character.

Opposite
Masterplan

Composed of distinctive districts, the island's masterplan shows the high density areas of the Marina District in the south and the Cultural District to the west, with lower density development for the resorts along the north-facing coast and the restored mangrove and lagoons area to the east. The design creates a coherent, fluid and pedestrian-oriented movement. Neighbourhoods and character areas are linked to each other intuitively through lanes, streets, boulevards and open spaces. Integrated public transit catalyses the benefits of the urban density and integrated mix of land uses.

The ambition for Saadiyat Island is to use cultural tourism as a driver to create sustainable mixed-use development. Saadiyat's vision integrates a world-class cultural district with buildings by Frank Gehry, Norman Foster and Jean Nouvel, a public transport system, and homes for 160,000 people, along with schools, civic facilities and a range of tourist resorts. Saadiyat will also accommodate 220,000 daytime workers, many of them in knowledge-based industries related to the cultural institutions including museums and galleries. The island is well placed to boost its tourist trade being within relatively short flying times from most of Europe and from Asia. In fulfilling the vision for the 2,700 hectare island, it is anticipated that visitor numbers to Abu Dhabi will achieve a fourfold increase to reach eight million by 2030.

Saadiyat, which means "happiness" in Arabic, is a natural island about half the size of Bermuda, and is located just 500 metres off the coast north of the city of Abu Dhabi. Until now, this expanse of sand dunes and mangroves has been sparsely populated and undeveloped. However, because of its proximity to the city it has been identified as an ideal location for new and exemplary urban expansion in Abu Dhabi's long-term vision and framework for anticipated wider growth called "Plan Abu Dhabi 2030". The city's population increase has already been explosive, with a further projected rise from 930,000 in 2007 to more than three million in 2030. Saadiyat Island is one of the first projects in the Plan Abu Dhabi programme of expansion, and, unusually, development of infrastructure has been used to stimulate demand and investment.

Work on the masterplan began with assessing and understanding the local and regional economies and the likelihood of considerable change due as a result of the move away from extensive oil production. After analysing and exploring a number of possibilities, cultural development was identified as the trigger for investment, and at the heart of the scheme is a world-class arts development called the Cultural District. Here, a long stretch of coast at the western corner of the triangular island will be studded with landmark buildings sited prominently on the shoreline. These include the world's largest Guggenheim Museum by Frank Gehry, along with the first outpost of the Louvre, a vast and delicate domed structure by Jean Nouvel, and a memorial museum designed by Norman Foster dedicated to the founder of the UAE, Sheikh Zayed. The ambition is that Saadiyat will become a beacon for cultural experience and exchange in the Middle East.

To support the Cultural District and build on the island's tourism potential, the development plan also incorporates a range of high-quality resorts on the north-facing coast overlooking the Arabian Gulf, and more modest schemes around the mangrove lagoons in the east. In addition, there is a marina in the south with the capacity to berth the new generations of large-scale yachts. The residential development includes homes at all scales and costs making it possible for people with a wide range of incomes to live on the island. The plan is for well-served and thriving communities in high-density residential development with generous community, healthcare and educational services and amenities, easy access to shops and leisure facilities and an extensive public transport system, including light rail.

Along with economic and social sustainability, there is a strong environmental component to the work. This includes designing for a reduced reliance on private cars, generous public space, energy-efficient construction techniques, making careful use of natural resources, protecting dunes and the coastline and restoring mangrove wetlands.

The texture of development across the island will vary considerably, with the south of the island close to the mainland the most intensely developed, while northern areas provide a contrast with open, natural landscape and long white-sand beaches overlooking the open water.

Saadiyat Retreat
- Boutique eco hotels

Saadiyat Beach
- International tourist destination
- Nine kilometres of natural beaches
- Five-star hotels and resorts
- Private and public beach clubs
- Championship golf course with luxury residential

Saadiyat Cultural District
- Guggenheim Abu Dhabi
- Louvre Abu Dhabi
- Sheikh Zayed National Museum
- Performing arts centre
- Office campus
- Boutique hotels
- Retail and commercial environment
- Luxury townhouses and apartments

Saadiyat Lagoons
- Luxury low-rise waterfront residential
- Waterside living
- Tidal lagoon system

Saadiyat Reserve
- Eco centre
- Boutique eco hotel
- Championship golf course
- Luxury residential water-side living

Saadiyat Marina
- World-class marina
- Maritime Museum
- Luxury apartments
- Central business district
- Leisure and entertainment facilities
- Commercial and retail environment

Saadiyat Promenade
- Family resort
- Dynamic beach lifestyle
- Boardwalks with cafes and restaurants
- Leisure and entertainment facilities

Vision and planning strategies

The emerging island-wide masterplan focuses on seven distinct development areas, each intensifying the natural potential of the island's physical resources, its unique exposure to views, and the prevailing winds. The vision incorporates a series of dynamic strategic goals as follows:

Excite The intensification of proposed urban density, balanced and carefully punctuated by well-defined open areas and relationships to the natural hinterland, responds to the needs of human interaction. The scale of development is carefully considered across the island creating a setting for excellence in architecture and the public realm.

Enrich The mixed-use land programme in the urban areas leverages the focused areas of density and open space to encourage an attractive and complementary blend of lifestyles, emphasising cultural diversity, community cohesion, easy access to leisure and the pursuit of excellence in knowledge-based industries. Elsewhere, a combination of resort hotels, villas and landscaped apartments responds to the rich opportunities of the natural landscape, in particular in the intertidal zone where land meets sea, creating dunes, beaches, mangroves and lagoons.

Connect The emerging masterplan stresses coherent, fluid and pedestrian-oriented movement. Neighbourhoods and character areas are linked to each other through a lattice of lanes, streets, boulevards and open spaces. Integrated public transit catalyses the benefits of urban density and integrated mix of land uses, linking the lower density districts to these.

Sustain The environmental programme guides responsible development. Natural ecological systems are identified, conserved and extended, especially in the resort areas. Indigenous plantings are integrated throughout. Urban density and compact development in the urban areas protect and define open space.

Succeed The development plan emphasises a rational delivery process. It is designed to be highly flexible, allowing incremental phasing by related development partners who may proceed independently and effectively at different rates. The simple, clear urban patterns and well-defined precincts and neighbourhoods enable incremental build out to achieve coherence at every stage, while providing appropriate and flexible planning options to respond to changing market conditions.

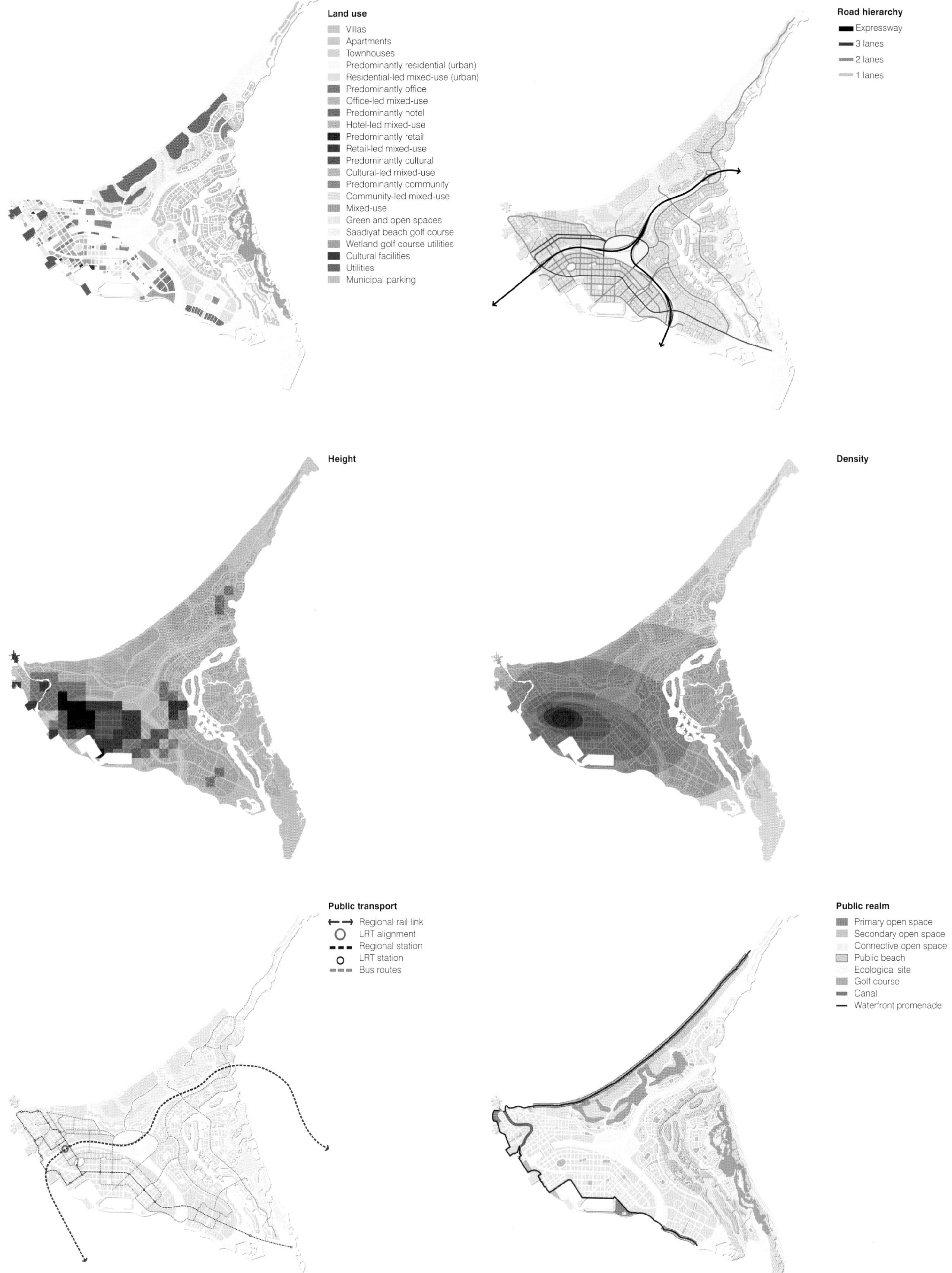

Land use
Villas
Apartments
Townhouses
Predominantly residential (urban)
Residential-led mixed-use (urban)
Predominantly office
Office-led mixed-use
Predominantly hotel
Hotel-led mixed-use
Predominantly retail
Retail-led mixed-use
Predominantly cultural
Cultural-led mixed-use
Predominantly community
Community-led mixed-use
Mixed-use
Green and open spaces
Saadiyat beach golf course
Wetland golf course utilities
Cultural facilities
Utilities
Municipal parking
Road hierarchy
Expressway
3 lanes
2 lanes
1 lanes
Height
Density
Public transport
Regional rail link
LRT alignment
Regional station
LRT station
Bus routes
Public realm
Primary open space
Secondary open space
Connective open space
Public beach
Ecological site
Golf course
Canal
Waterfront promenade

Sustainability goals

At the start of the masterplan evolution, guidelines were embedded into the process to ensure maximum environmental, social and economic sustainability. The goals were to:

- Protect natural water resources and conserve potable water.
- Reduce carbon emissions associated with fossil fuels.
- Maximise diversion of waste from landfill.
- Conserve, restore and enhance ecological habitat to reflect the local natural heritage and enhance biodiversity.
- Minimise dependence on private car use.

With the main principles in place, the more detailed level of design has seen the island divided into distinct areas each with its own strong character. For example the focus of the main resorts area is along the nine kilometres of sandy beaches on the north-west coast which will become home to a world-class golf course and around 30 international hotels, including a landmark project with a seven-star rating, providing a total of more than 7,000 rooms. Meanwhile, in the south of the island, the Marina District will be a cosmopolitan residential area designed around the new marina with a dynamic cluster of high-rise towers and a long ribbon of urban park. Meanwhile, the eastern wetlands with their characteristic lagoons and meandering waterways will see much of the natural landscape restored and protected. There will also be pockets of development including luxury residential schemes, a championship golf course, a marine research facility, small-scale eco hotels and a park with sporting and equestrian facilities. And there is the Cultural District where the international landmarks of the Guggenheim and the Louvre and the Sheikh Zayed memorial museum anchor the extensive public-space system of parks and canals. Here, too, will be a mix of high-density residential development, seafront promenades, high-quality shopping with restaurants and cafes and a beautiful canal to frame views of the major buildings.

The development density of the urban areas is high for the region—for example, the Cultural District is approximately the same density as central Paris, while the Marina District will achieve a density somewhere between central London and Manhattan. This concentration of residents served by neighbourhood shops and services and supported by mass transit, will create a walkable and engaging city. In addition, this level of urban density radically decreases energy and resource use compared with more widely dispersed urban and suburban communities. Expressed as tons-of-oil-equivalent (TOE), the UAE as a whole consumes around ten tons-of-oil-equivalent per capita, the highest rate of energy consumption in the world. In contrast, a resident of Saadiyat Island, is expected to use around five tons, with the corresponding decrease in carbon footprint.

Top
Future city

A visualisation of Saadiyat rising up from the sea with the landmark Frank Gehry-designed Guggenheim Museum on the left, and lattice dome of the Louvre designed by Jean Nouvel on the right and the city on the horizon beyond.

Bottom
Marina District

An early impression of the large-scale marina with the city as a dynamic backdrop. The completed marina will be capable of accommodating the latest generation of large-scale yachts and leisure boats.

Sustainability features

During the process of the masterplan development, sustainability goals became embedded in the design with the following features:

- Rehabilitated ecological habitats, including vastly expanded mangrove wetlands and lagoon systems.
- A dense urban core, to maximise resource and energy efficiency.
- Multi-modal links to an island-wide mass tram and water-taxi system.
- District cooling, to improve overall system efficiency.
- LEED green building rating system, to provide an enforceable strategy for improving the environment.
- Mixed-income housing, to reduce the amount of peak-hour traffic on the approach bridges.
- Reduction of expansive, undifferentiated open space, to minimise water consumption and increase urban density, thereby improving environmental performance.
- Minimised landfill, with the new island shorefront matching the exisiting one.

Opposite
Lagoons and reserves

Plans include restoring lagoons and areas of mangrove which will not only enhance the aesthetic appeal of the island but will also protect and extend wildlife habitat.

Left and below
Lifestyle and leisure

Visualisations of the resort areas with luxury hotels in beautiful landscape settings.

Among the key challenges of the Saadiyat Island project have been to weave together economic, social and environmental sustainability through culture-based tourism, the creation of new jobs and a healthy natural landscape with enhanced ecosystems. The approach is unusual for this region. The project is designed as an economic machine and will be a platform for creating sustainable wealth through knowledge-based industries as part of Abu Dhabi's strategy for a diversified and open economy no longer heavily dependent on oil revenues. By creating a cultural and civic infrastructure, Saadiyat provides the resources that a booming population and a growing middle class need to compete on a global level. Crucially, finding ways to retain human capital is important as the region's economy moves away from oil dependency, and it is intended that Saadiyat will become a catalyst for wider development in the region.

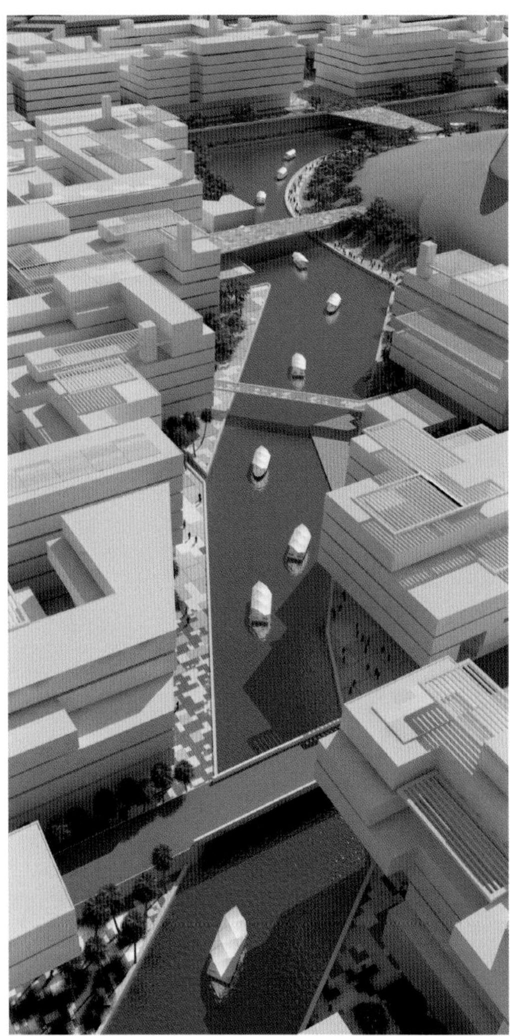

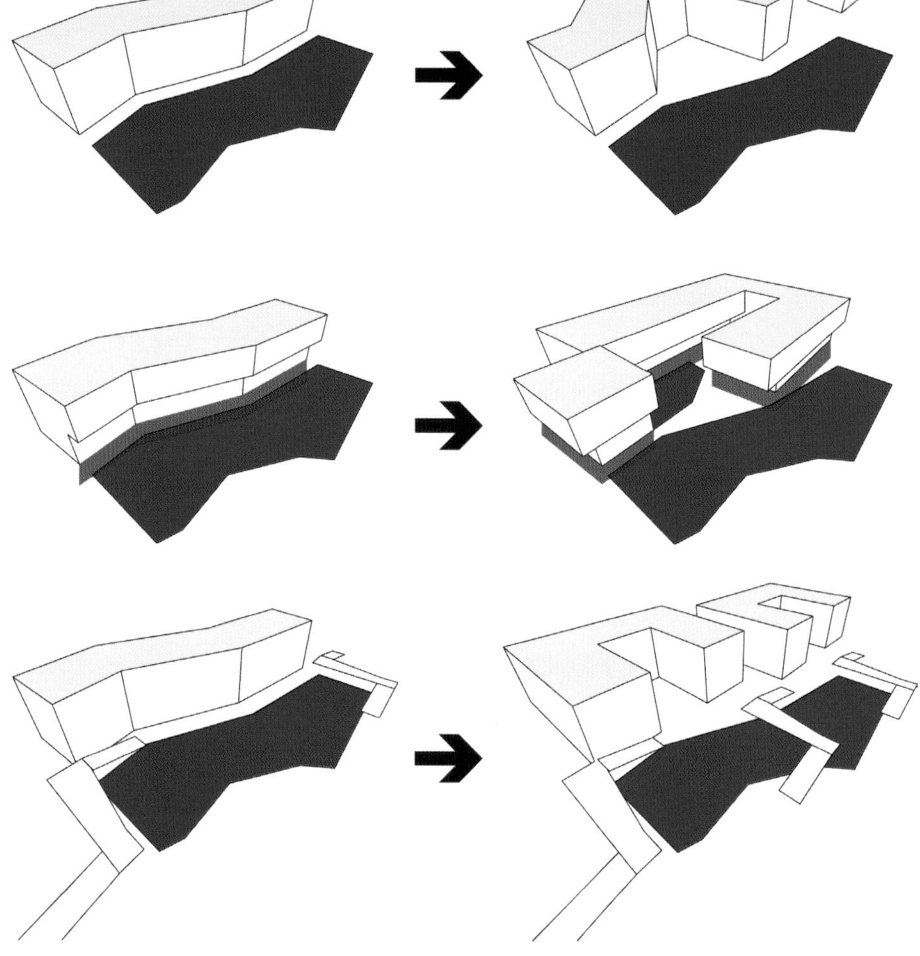

Above, right and opposite
Cultural District canal precinct

The canal is a significant feature in the west of the island creating the opportunity for beautiful public space, boat trips and a piece of urban fabric with water views. The illustration, centre, shows how waterside buildings can be articulated horizontally and vertically to create interesting spaces with shading and great views. Bridges across the canal connect different neighbourhoods. Opposite, innovative architecture has the potential to create attractive and welcoming public spaces.

The Cultural District will be characterised by its high-profile museums, galleries and performance spaces. These uses will be integrated into an urban environment that is human in scale and responsive to the needs and desires of those who live and work in, or visit the district. With a broad mix of uses in a multi-layered environment and with a diverse population, the district will be home to communities including artists, designers and others involved in the creative industries.
There will be two substantial, world-class art museums—extensions to the Louvre and Guggenheim museums—housing international collections of modern and Islamic arts, and an international performing arts centre. Saadiyat's Cultural District will also be home to a new national museum commemorating the life and times of the UAE's founder, His Excellency the late Sheikh Zayed bin Sultan Al Nahyan. A grand canal will thread through the heart of the district, creating a distinctive landscaped promenade and boat route. The waterway will be lined with cultural pavilions, international galleries, exclusive shops and restaurants, and boutique hotels on multiple levels, which will create an extraordinary setting for the 'cultural temples' that will establish this district's reputation. Some of the most fashionable residences in Abu Dhabi will have views across this exceptional space.

Waterfront parks and linear gardens connected by a promenade will complement the canal creating gathering spaces for cultural and entertainment events.

The Cultural District will incorporate space in which creative industries and research and development activities can flourish, alongside regional conference and event facilities, which will contribute to the generation of a well-rounded urban cultural environment. The district will also be home to a wide range of people, with a variety of housing types including luxury apartments, townhouses and live/work artists studios. Visitors will have a choice of luxury, resort and boutique hotels, and will be entertained in the district's theatres, cinemas, bars and restaurants. The Cultural District covers some 245 hectares and will be home to approximately 30,000 residents, provide workspace for around 37,000 workers and attract several thousand visitors each day. Its core components and supporting uses will combine to generate an active mixed-use district comparable to other international cultural quarters.

Concept
Working together to find a balance between conservation and development

Context
Rural, riverine/temperate

Big Darby Accord Watershed Masterplan, Ohio, USA.

Facing the apparently conflicting demands of environmental conservation and community growth, this vast Mid-western landscape of more than 22,500 hectares needed a long-term plan to establish future priorities.

Opposite
Big Darby context

Seen from the air, the Big Darby Accord study area is an intricate patchwork of settlement, agricultural fields and natural landscape. Concern about development encroaching on the green spaces created the need for a strategy for development control and environmental protection.

Plain City Georgesville Rd
Walker Rd
Main St
Scioto & Darby Rd
Leap Rd
Brown
Alton & Darby Creek Rd
Roberts Rd
Beach Rd
Walcutt Rd
Spindler Rd
Norwich
City of Columbus
Roberts Rd
Hilard-rome Rd
Renner Rd
Trabue Rd
270
70
Feder Rd
Fisher Rd
Hilard-rome Rd
142
Phillip Rd
iddle Pike
W Broad St
Prairie
Walnut St
40
Franklin
Hellbranch Run
Hall Rd
Clime Rd
Jack Nicklaus Fwy
Georgesville Rd
Demorset Rd
Roberts Rd
Galloway Rd
270
Big Darby Creek
Little Darby Creek
Darby Creek Dr
Bausch Rd
Big Run South Rd
Bolton Field Airport
Alkire Rd
Bukey Rd
Holt Rd
Georgesville
Grove City
Grove City Rd
Georgesville – Wrightsville Rd
Kropp Rd
Madison County
Franklin County
Lukkens Rd
Harrisburg Pike
Smith Ditch
Norton Rd
Lamb Rd
Big Darby Creek
Pleasant

Wild at heart

The Big Darby Watershed area has provided a playground for generations of Ohians. In addition to being a place for recreation and enjoying close connections with nature, the beautiful landscape gives the area a distinctive character, a robust natural water management system and ecological richness.

To work towards creating a successful plan, a set of goals was outlined. These were to:

- Meet the water quality goals established by the Ohio Environmental Protection Agency through land use changes and best management practices.
- Locate the highest density growth in areas that have access to infrastructure such as centralised sewer and transportation.
- Create recurring funding streams for plan implementation including a new community authority and tax increment financing.
- Develop new open space and water quality monitoring programmes.
- Establish an advisory board to oversee development in a consistent manner across multiple jurisdictions in the planning area.

Water is the unifying element in this large-scale project which has inspired communities to work together in a model of regional co-operation. At the centre of the state of Ohio, the Big Darby watershed is an expansive tract of land which runs across six counties. Much of it is in agricultural use and has a low density of development. It has also been enjoyed as a playground and place for recreation by generations of Ohians. However, because of the site's proximity to the state capital Columbus, it is vulnerable to sprawling suburban development and the attendant pollution threat to ecosystems and habitats. The area for consideration in the Big Darby Accord Watershed Masterplan, is approximately 15 per cent of the total watershed; the planning area runs along the western boundary of Franklin County, west of the City of Columbus.

Concern about encroaching development and increasingly stringent state regulations on water quality led to a historic meeting of representatives from ten local governments to discuss the need to protect the watershed for the common good and to develop a co-ordinated and long-term vision for the site. A balance had to be found between protecting and enhancing water quality in a network of local streams, and enabling development in a managed way that reduced its impact on the land. A unified approach and shared goals in conservation and development were the only positive way forward.

The process began with uniting the authorities under the umbrella of the Big Darby Accord which soon established a set of principles and then evolved a plan for future action over 20 to 30 years. The resulting plan is intended to serve as a multi-jurisdictional guide for development and conservation, combining long-term environmental stewardship with economic and community growth. Extensive public participation and consultation also played a key part in the process.

Historic environmental studies established baseline information to inform the analysis. The Big Darby Creek is the major water body running through the watershed; it is joined by tributaries including Little Darby Creek, Hellbranch Run, and Clover Groff and Hamilton Ditches. While the landscape flanking the Big and Little Darby Creeks is lush, wooded and beautiful, Hellbranch Run, and the Ditches have been severely affected and degraded over time. The exceptional qualities of the Big Darby Creek is reflected in its designation as a State and National Scenic River. Overall, the watershed is rich in plant and animal habitats and is recognised as one of the most biologically diverse aquatic systems in the Midwest, home to 38 state and federally listed aquatic species.

To help protect the watershed, development moratoriums had been in place for more than three years before the accord was established. Because multiple jurisdictions had authority for zoning, development regulations, and provision of services, it became clear that new pressures on the land were greater and needed to be addressed consistently and collectively by all accord jurisdictions. Adoption of the plan allowed the moratorium to be lifted.

An analysis of existing conditions including environmental and water resources, land uses and zoning, transport, water and sewer infrastructure and capacity, and community facilities was the first step in the planning process. Critical environmental attributes such as hydrology, soil, geology, vegetation, natural habitats and biodiversity were analysed using geographic information system (GIS) modelling, and ranked to ensure that the most sensitive areas such as stream corridors and wetlands are protected, while less sensitive areas could become the focus of potential development. This analysis provided a foundation for the plan's conservation strategy.

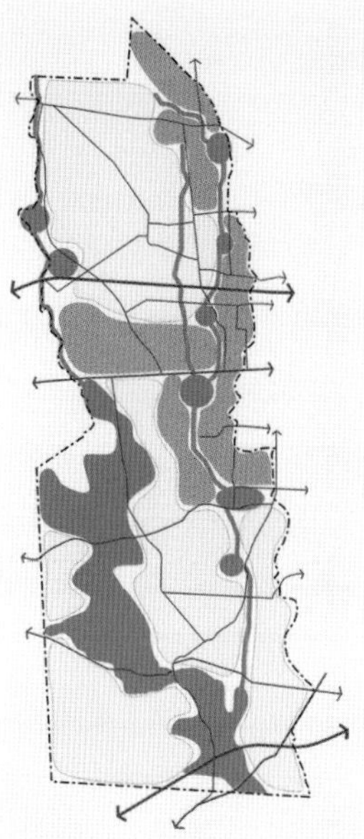

Scenario A

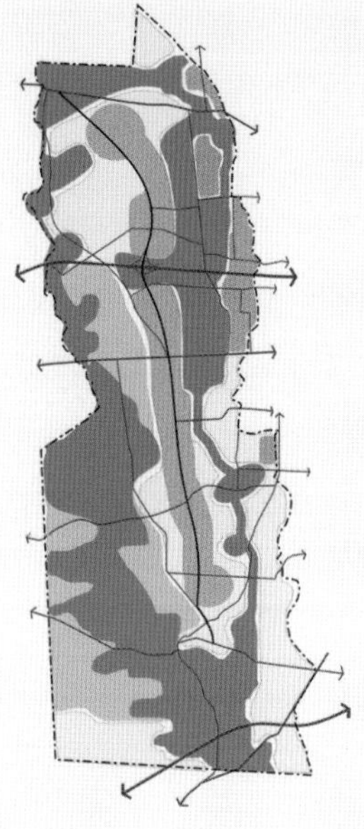

Scenario B

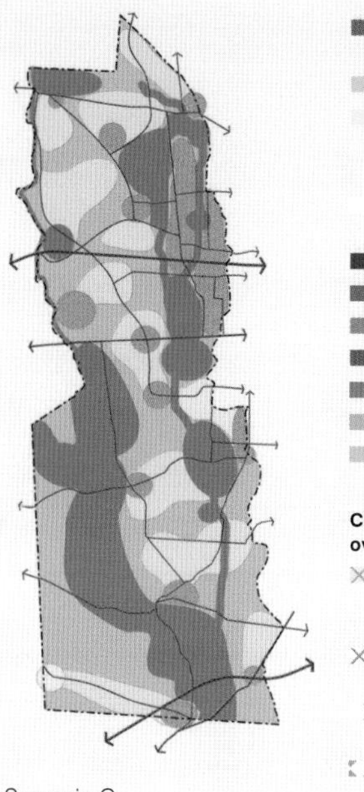

Scenario C

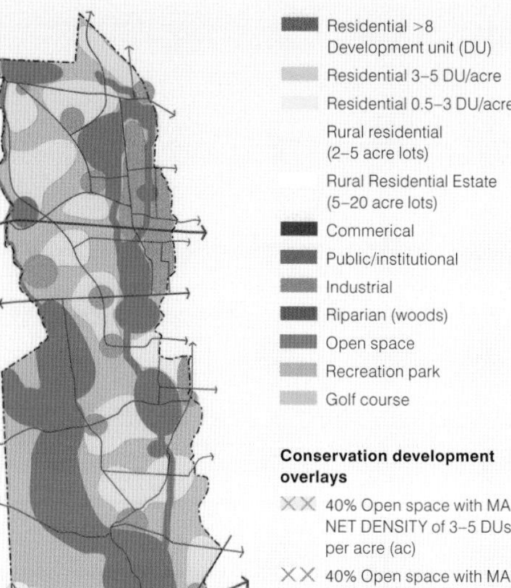

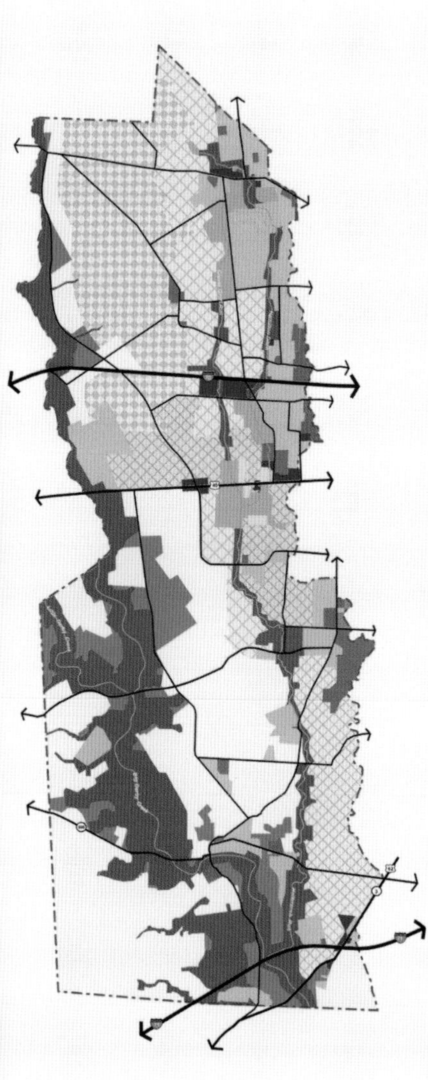

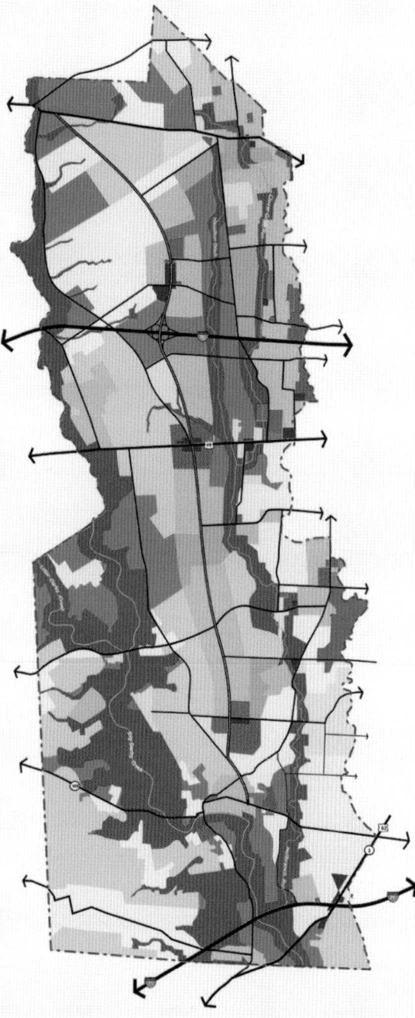

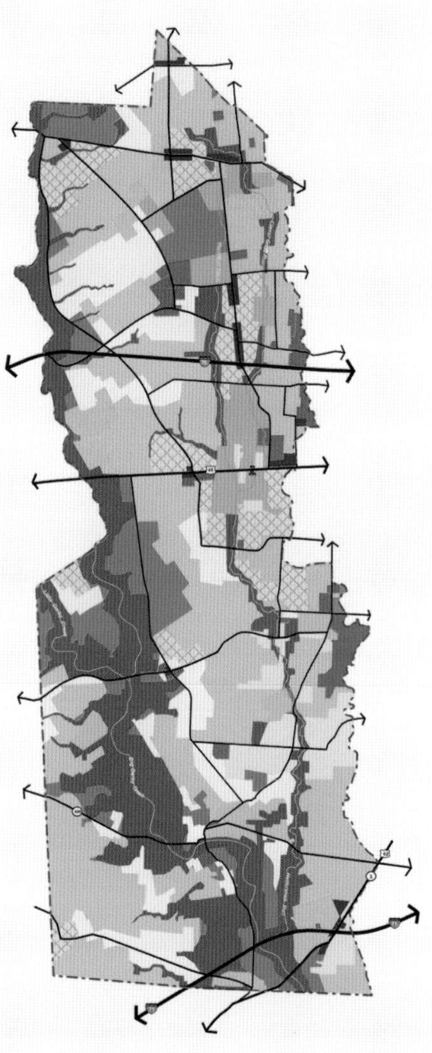

Scenario A: concentration of development

This scenario closely mirrors policies that existed at the time of the study. With an emphasis on residential development, it shows largely rural-scale development with a significant amount of conservation development. This approach promotes an open-space network that is accomplished through private developments and a required open space set aside. In this scenario, agricultural uses are replaced with development. More dense development is located in the eastern portion of the study area.

Scenario B: central corridor development

The main concept of this scenario is to create a corridor concentrating new development through the central portion of the study area. This development corridor corresponds with the lesser environmentally sensitive areas. Densities beyond the development corridor transition to open space and agriculture. This scenario provides an expanded interconnected network of parks and open spaces along the main stream corridors.

Scenario C: pockets and clusters

This scenario is based on developing village clusters, or nodes of denser development. The nodes of development include a mix of uses including residential, commercial and public/institutional. Along with development clusters, Scenario C provides for continued agriculture uses and includes expanded open space/buffer areas. While the scenario does include some conservation development areas, it relies primarily on pre-designated open spaces and farmlands to form an interconnected open-space framework.

Preferred land-use scenario

Conservation strategy

Following assessment, analysis and testing options, the project's outcome is a preferred scenario of land uses which identifies potential development areas, particularly focused on the new town centre in the north-west, shown in pink, along with areas for protection and enhancement.

The special pilot residential area denotes state-of-the-art LEED-certified sustainable development to be implemented subject to specific performance standards. The tier designations denote the following, Tier 1—important hydro-geologic considerations including 100 year floodplains, wetlands, in-stream sensitive habitat areas, critical groundwater recharge and pollution potential zones; Tier 2—important resource considerations, highly erodable soils, and woods; Tier 3—planned parks, open-space corridors and buffers based on habitat sensitivity, connectivity and other planning considerations.

A system of tiers in the conservation strategy identifies land areas of protection based on unique environmental resources identified during the environmental sensitivity analysis. A majority of the sensitive features are associated with areas of high potential for groundwater and surface waterflow exchange, areas of high groundwater pollution potential, floodplains, wetlands, and stream corridor zones. Combined, the tiers represent a connected green infrastructure network and goal of conserving around 10,000 hectares of land.

The development strategy acknowledged the need to provide around 20,000 new homes in the area. Development scenarios were formed that explored different ways to spatially accommodate future growth and retain property rights while still protecting sensitive resources. The plan explored options for a Transfer of Development Rights (TDR) programme as a mechanism to help create the conservation strategy and direct growth. The scenarios were run through a hydrological model to determine water quality impacts for nitrogen, phosphorus, total suspended solids, and flow levels. Discussions and debates were held regarding the scenarios, associated development patterns, and their ability to meet new water quality regulations.

The preferred plan recommends a high-density, mixed-use scenario combining homes, schools, shops and offices with new infrastructure including sewers and generous open space in a new town centre. The plan encourages the application of eco standards set out in Leadership in Energy and Environmental Design (LEED) building principles and management of stormwater through an integrated system of site, community and regional-level systems that emphasise filtration, green roofs, permeable paving, dry and wet swales, and rainwater harvesting. Transitioning away from this urban zone, pockets of clustered conservation development are encouraged in rural areas.

The plan includes the aspiration of meeting tough new water quality goals established by the Ohio Environmental Protection Agency, removing or reducing pollutants, and developing systems for long-term monitoring of water quality. Other conservation goals include conserving almost half of the accord plan land area, more than 10,000 hectares, and creating a connected green infrastructure network of wetlands, floodplains, wooded areas and special habitats. Building in flexibility, it is anticipated that the plan will adapt and evolve over time to accommodate changing circumstances and to incorporate the latest best practices.

To review development projects and ensure they match the shared aspirations of the masterplan, an advisory panel has been set up with representatives of each jurisdiction and other interested parties including The Nature Conservancy and The Affordable Housing Trust.

The cornerstone of the Big Darby Accord is collaboration among authorities and the local communities. Since its foundation, jurisdictions have been working to update their local planning codes and regulations to ensure consistency with the plan's recommendations. A first of its kind in Ohio, the scheme has demonstrated the power of collaboration and the potential of joined-up thinking in an exercise in green planning which incorporates science, engineering and land-use planning critical to creating and ensuring the longevity of sustainable communities. The Big Darby Accord Watershed Masterplan is described as a "living" document, its contents are intended to be updated and reviewed over time in response to changing conditions and pressures.

The Big Darby guide for development and conservation

As a multi-jurisdictional guide for development and conservation, key points of the Big Darby Accord Watershed Masterplan are that it:

- Identifies and prioritises environmentally sensitive areas.
- Directs development to a new high-density, mixed-use town centre to manage growth responsibly.
- Identifies mechanisms for co-operative revenue sharing and requires new development to pay for itself.
- Directs the accord partners to take specific steps to ensure the plan is fully implemented.

Concept
Bringing the country into the city

Context
River delta/subtropical

Jiangxin Island Vision and Concept Masterplan, Nanjing, China.

In a reversal of the trend for growing cities to build over agricultural land, at Jiangxin Island, a large farming area could be conserved and enhanced as part of the city.

Opposite
Jiangxin Island masterplan

A process of detailed analysis identified areas to preserve and enhance along with areas with the potential for development. The concept is to retain the sense of place through the powerful natural, historic and cultural references of Jiangxin and guide development so that existing elements and new activities can comfortably coexist.

Rural resonance

The avenues of distinctive towering metasequoia trees are characteristic of the island and line many roadways. They evoke a strong emotional response from local people and will remain a distinctive feature of the place in the future.

As Nanjing's rapid growth pursues its course of expansion across the Yangtze River, Jiangxin Island close to the east bank would appear to provide a prime location for the westward march of skyscrapers and highways. Because of its ideal location the island was identified for redevelopment and the city authorities commissioned a vision for the future. The brief for the vision was that the scheme should benefit the city, the island and its residents, as well as creating a sustainable framework to guide future development.

To fulfil the brief a multidisciplinary team was assembled comprising urban designers, landscape architects, environmental and economics experts to develop a sensitive plan and design that would respond to the island's physical attributes as well as its ecological, social and economic status.

A detailed survey was also conducted among island and city residents to gain a thorough understanding of the way of life on the island and, importantly, their vision of the future. Responses from residents showed that most families have lived on the island for more than two generations and they enjoy their way of life. Most residents work in agriculture or tourism and the young generation want to remain living locally if more job opportunities can be provided. Most of the residents believe that tourism development will increase their job opportunities and income.

Meanwhile, the majority of those questioned in Nanjing perceive the island as a special place because of its beautiful agricultural landscape and quietness. However, accessibility was considered to be poor and overnight accommodation is limited and could be enhanced.

Jiangxing Island is a slender but substantial land area of around 12 kilometres in length. It lies close to the east bank of the Yangtze and the main part of Nanjing city with its population of more than six million and rising. The land is largely agricultural in use and has evolved a unique character with an attractive landscape, roads lined with distinctive metasequoia trees and many examples of traditional Chinese rural agricultural buildings. There is a total population of just under 5,000 households and agricultural land area is approximately 660 hectares with 60 per cent of the population working on the land.

Work on the vision and masterplan considered the whole island, an area of around 15 square kilometres, and began with surveying and understanding its particular qualities and potential. Farming includes around 260 hectares of vineyards, 60 hectares of fruits, 200 hectares of leeks and 130 hectares of other vegetables. From June to September the island hosts a grape festival when farmers celebrate the harvest and people from all over the city come to help pick the grapes. In the knowledge that Nanjing will continue to grow and that there will be increasing importance and value in high-quality public space, the vision evolved to propose that the island could become a leisure destination within the city. It could become an authentic rural retreat for the urban population, providing a link between city dwellers and the natural landscape, places to walk or cycle, go fishing or stay on a farm. In addition, the place would also continue to operate as a series of farms providing fresh food to local residents.

Above
Coexistence

A photomontage of how new development along the fringes of farming land can sit harmoniously with the working landscape.

Left
Rural life

Most of the island's residents have lived there for more than two generations and around 60 per cent of them work on the land and live in villages.

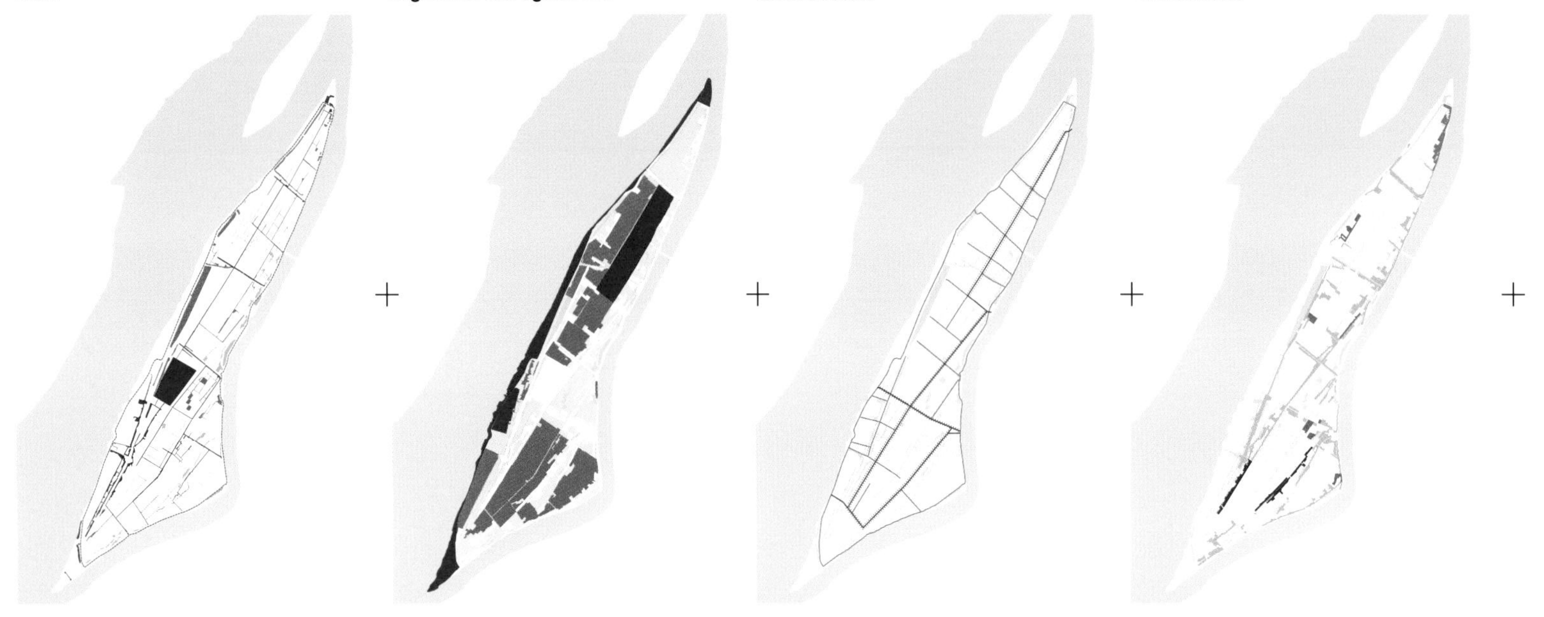

Public facilities

Industrial heritage

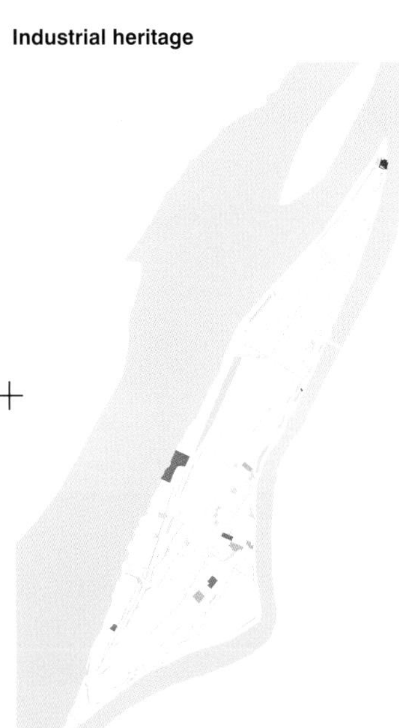

Tourism development

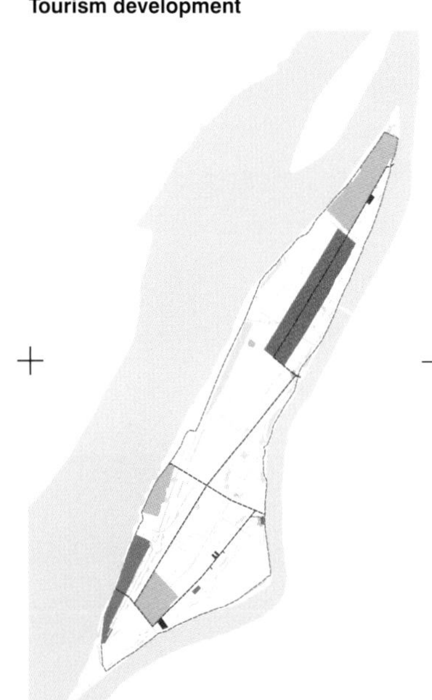

Above and opposite
Land uses

Instead of adopting the *tabula rasa* approach often used in Chinese development, the conservation and development framework is derived from careful analysis of the existing situation. Elements including settlements, infrastructure and agricultural use have been separated out from each other and then combined to produce a sensitivity overlay.

This multilayered composite denotes areas of high, medium and low sensitivity and directs development towards the least sensitive areas.

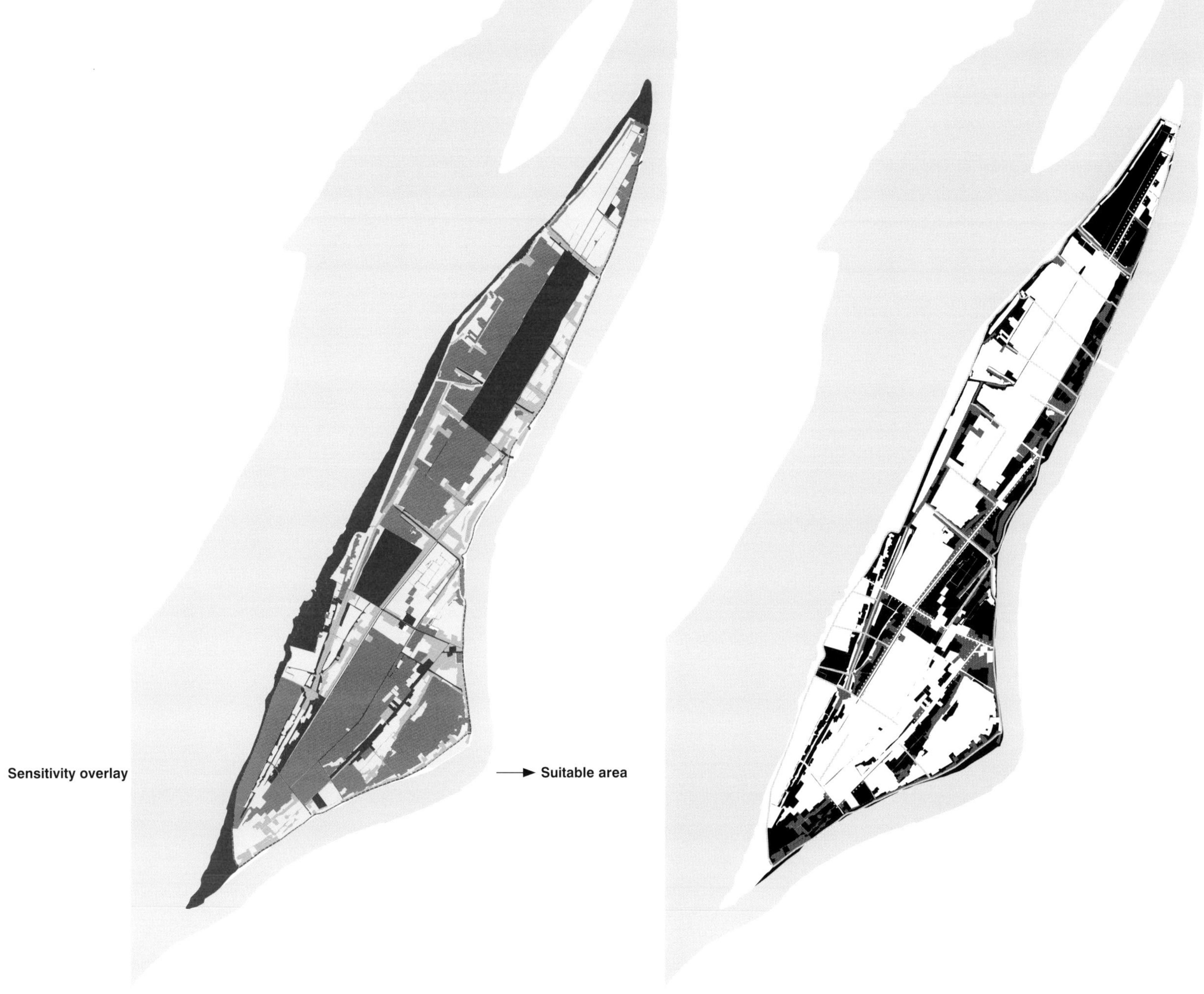

Evaluation grade

A High sensitivity—to be protected

B Medium sensitivity—to be conserved and adjusted

C Low sensitivity—to be developed

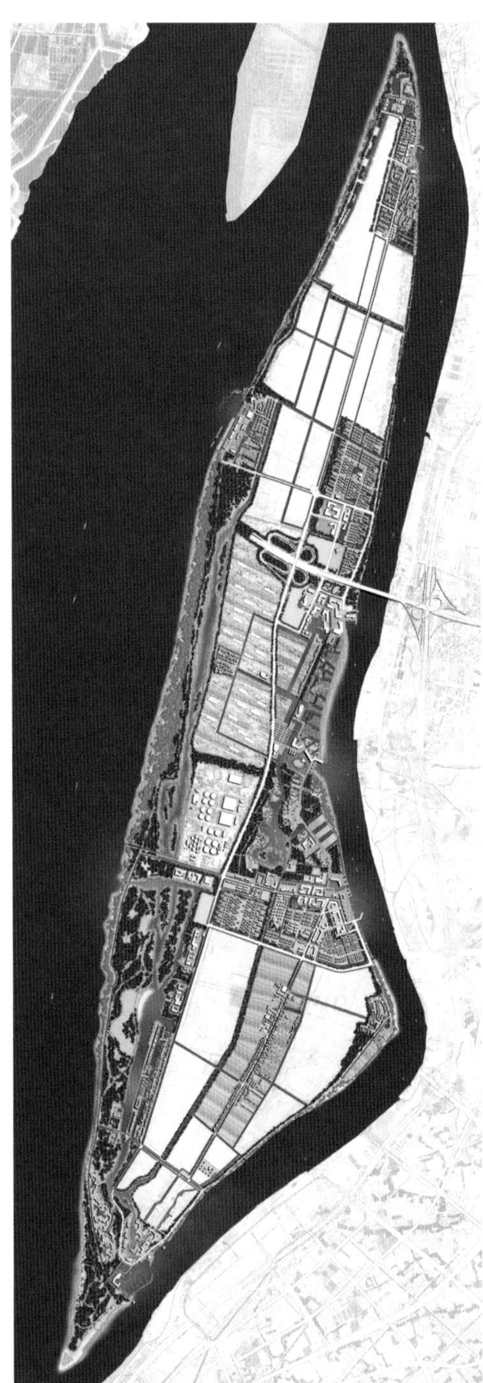

Shape of things to come

A visualisation of how existing land uses and new development could be integrated. Retaining much of the existing agricultural use and natural area, helps provide a distinctive character and context for future development.

This innovative idea meant that the fabric of the island could be woven more closely into that of the city by one vehicular bridge, three ferries and one cable car connection. In addition there would be a development of sustainable tourism, building on the distinct character of each of the existing seven villages and promoting additional amenities such as fishing. Large-scale development would be discouraged.

The plan also proposed that existing farms would be maintained and expanded to grow high-yield organic crops. Existing farmers and residents will be encouraged to remain on the island to fuel the evolution of local agricultural-tourism. Ultimately, the unique character of the island will be maintained and local residents will be allowed to continue their way of life, with expected future improvements. Existing roads lined with indigenous metasequoia trees will remain a key identifying feature of the island. The planning strategy included seven stages:

- Making new connections to the city.
- Setting up green transportation—electric buses and electric water taxis would be the main means of transportation on the island and the plan limits vehicular traffic and public parking to a small area, thereby freeing up the rest of the island for pedestrians and cyclists.
- Strengthening the island's character and identity.
- Creating an environmentally sound water system which includes restored wetlands that form ecological and habitat corridors, and recycling grey water.
- Setting up a green open-space system.
- Enhancing the local quality of life.
- Developing organic agriculture.

Local farm houses will be concentrated in two areas, supported by a basic infrastructure, and clustered around key amenities including schools, clinics and community centres. The design of the new buildings will reflect the spirit of the traditional Chinese rural architecture found on the island, while addressing the specific lifestyle needs of local residents and farmers. A park has been planned at the centre of the island as an extension of the urban park located across the river on the east bank, and will feature botanic gardens, an educational wetland park, a petting zoo and a performance centre.

Developing the character and distinctiveness of the seven villages includes ideas such as creating one place as a hub for artists, developing a floating food market, renovating old farm houses for bed and breakfast accommodation, creating a flower farming area, a village where folk customs are preserved, and an area for fishing and a fish market.

Unlike many large-scale projects in China that call for large-scale visions, the Jiangxin Island masterplan proposes a modest approach which retains and builds on the distinctive sense of place and local culture.

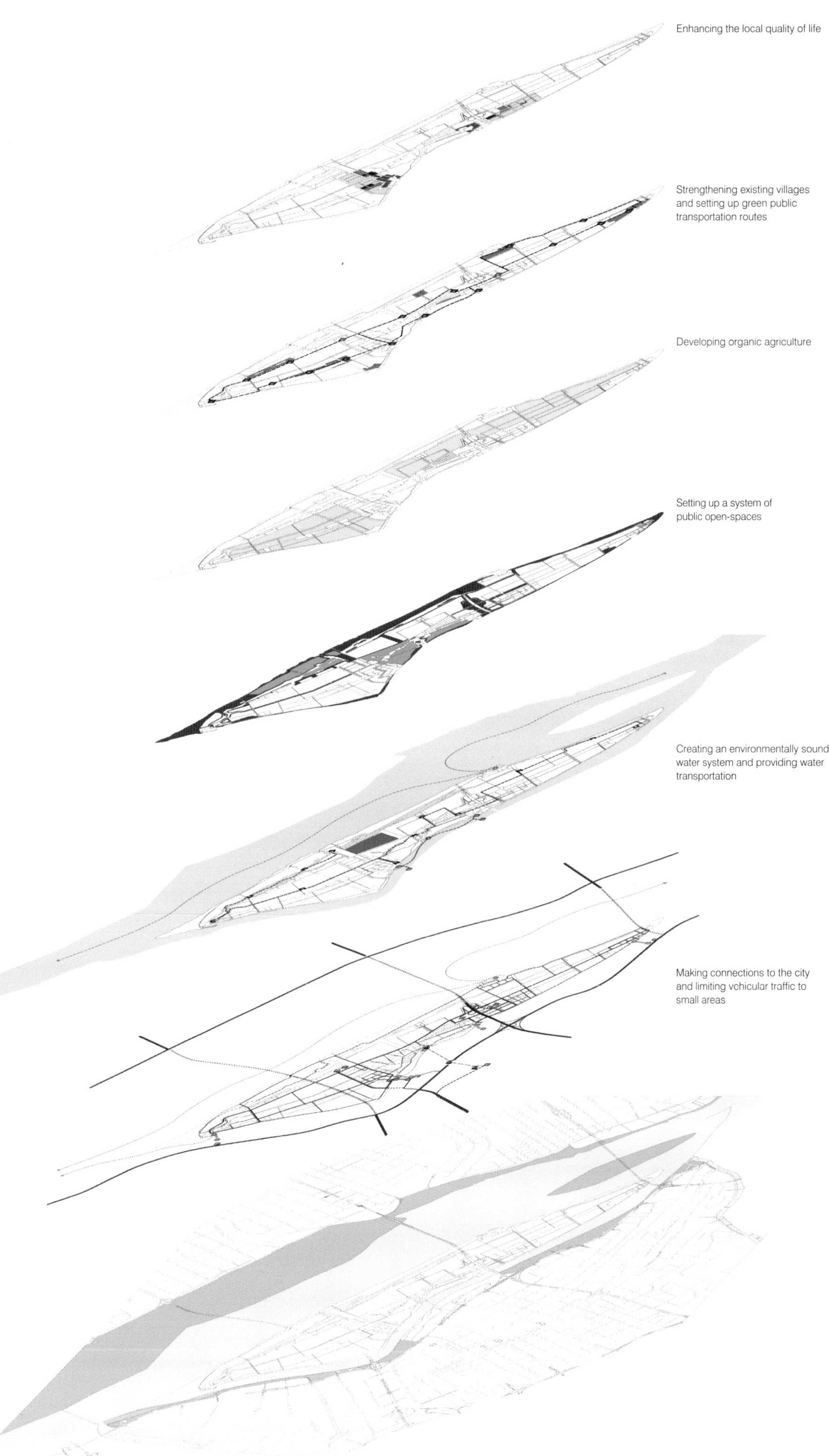

Exploded diagram

The diagram shows the layers of intervention which are not just concerned with conservation, but are also focused on enhancement. Proposals include developing more organic agriculture, an open-space system for public use and improved transportation connections between the island and city.

Concept

A sustainable million-acre plan combining high-quality development with a rigorous conservation programme

Context

Coastal/temperate

Opposite
Quality of life

The rich natural environment of forested land, waterways and beaches provides a picturesque setting for new development. High-quality interventions including architecture and infrastructure such as this footbridge are designed in sympathy with the landscape. The company's environmental programme has been key to maximising the appeal of the place. Large portions of the land totalling almost 69,000 hectares are to be protected forever.

St Joe Business Strategy, Florida, USA.

For most of the twentieth century, The St Joe Company grew forests for timber and turned trees into paper. However, at the end of the century, it changed direction from a paper manufacturer to a real estate developer. For guidance in how best to create new communities, resorts and infrastructure in the increasingly popular Florida Panhandle, the company sought a strategic plan for its holdings of almost one million acres of land.

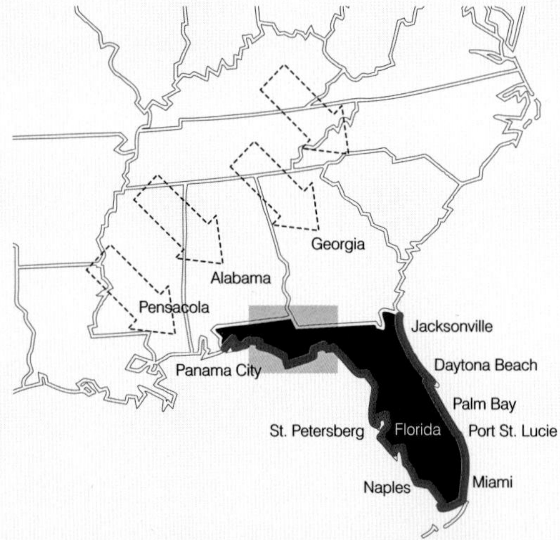

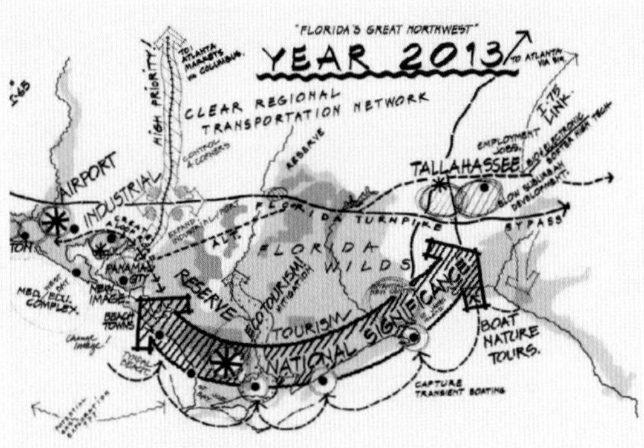

Above
Context and concept

A map of Florida's coast showing the location of St Joe's land within the panhandle. A conceptual sketch indicating the area's potential for development including connections to major transport routes and high-quality tourism.

Opposite
Regional placemaking

Land-use plan showing infrastructure, environmentally sensitive areas for protection, conservation projects and, in yellow, the extent of St Joe holdings.

Acknowledging that the beauty and ecological diversity of the landscape is its greatest asset, Florida's largest private landowner, The St Joe Company, has pursued a policy of high-quality development with a rigorous conservation programme.

Creating a vision and plan for an entire region combined opportunity with responsibility for making environmentally, socially and economically sustainable development. The vast scale of land ownership presented the rare opportunity for regional placemaking which combines high-quality mixed-use development and infrastructure with joined-up conservation programmes which include preservation of ecological resources by being able to direct infrastructure such as roads and trails away from environmentally sensitive sites, protecting watersheds and creating wildlife corridors. Concentrated primarily in north-west Florida, The St Joe Company's one million acres or 400,000 hectares, includes approximately 140,000 hectares, within 16 kilometres of the coast of the Gulf of Mexico.

The scope was to create a market-based, long-term vision for the types of development that would be realistic and appropriate for the land, and what portion of the total would be viable for development. Because of its history of use for forestry, this land in the north-west corner of Florida was largely undeveloped, and provided an outstanding setting for new homes and resorts along the Gulf of Mexico.

Working alongside St Joe's management team and asset-management specialists, a consultancy team was assembled including land planners, economic specialists, ecologists, engineers, facilitators, and information technology specialists who were rapidly able to assimilate data and structure. Work on the vision and strategy included interactive workshops and an assessment of the real estate market. From this initial stage of consultation it was possible to create an overall market responsive approach to masterplanning, identifying clear opportunity sites and potential markets that would increase development activity.

Research and market analysis highlighted the main market as the baby boomer generation, aged between 45 and 60, and particularly those seeking a high-quality of life. Places with the greatest appeal would be those offering attractive and authentic architecture, a sense of belonging, and a healthy lifestyle in a beautiful, natural and well-managed environment. With developable land in limited supply, high-quality development within a high-quality landscape would maximise the land value and ensure that investments remained strong.

Moving from the vision, a set of core principles evolved to ensure than development could meet, or even exceed, expectations. The principles included the pursuit of authenticity, respect for the past and for the environment, preserving what is special and unique, integrating local architecture, landscape and art and promoting civic infrastructure such as an improved airport and roads, new education and healthcare facilities and promoting economic development.

Working at such a large scale on land spanning more than 280 kilometres east to west, and incorporating 23 local governments, one of the most challenging decisions was where to start. A set of bold, ten year corporate objectives became the foundation of the company's business plan.

Creation of 'true places'
Protection of environmentally sensitive areas
Conservation projects
St Joe Holdings
Public Ownership
Other Lands

Creation of 'true places'

1 WaterColor
2 RiverCamps
3 WindMark Beach
4 SouthWood

Protection of environmentally sensitive areas

1 Devil's Swamp
2 West Bay Sector Plan
3 Hobbs Pasture
4 Aspalaga Bluffs
5 Torreya St Park
6 Sweetwater Ravines
7 Sumatra Tract
8 Tate's Hell
9 Bald Point St Park
10 Wacissa River
11 Snipe Island

Conservation projects

1 WaterColor Inn
2 WaterSound Beach
3 Devil's Swamp Mitigation Bank
4 Bay to Bay Greenway
5 RiverCamps on Crooked Creek
6 Breakfast Point Mitigation Bank
7 West Bay Sector Plan
8 Panama City Crayfish Conservation Area
9 Lathrop Bayou Conservation Area
10 Wetappo Creek Conservation Area
11 WindMark Beach
12 Tupelo Bend Waterfowl Area
13 SummerCamp Beach
14 Gopher Tortoise Relocation Area

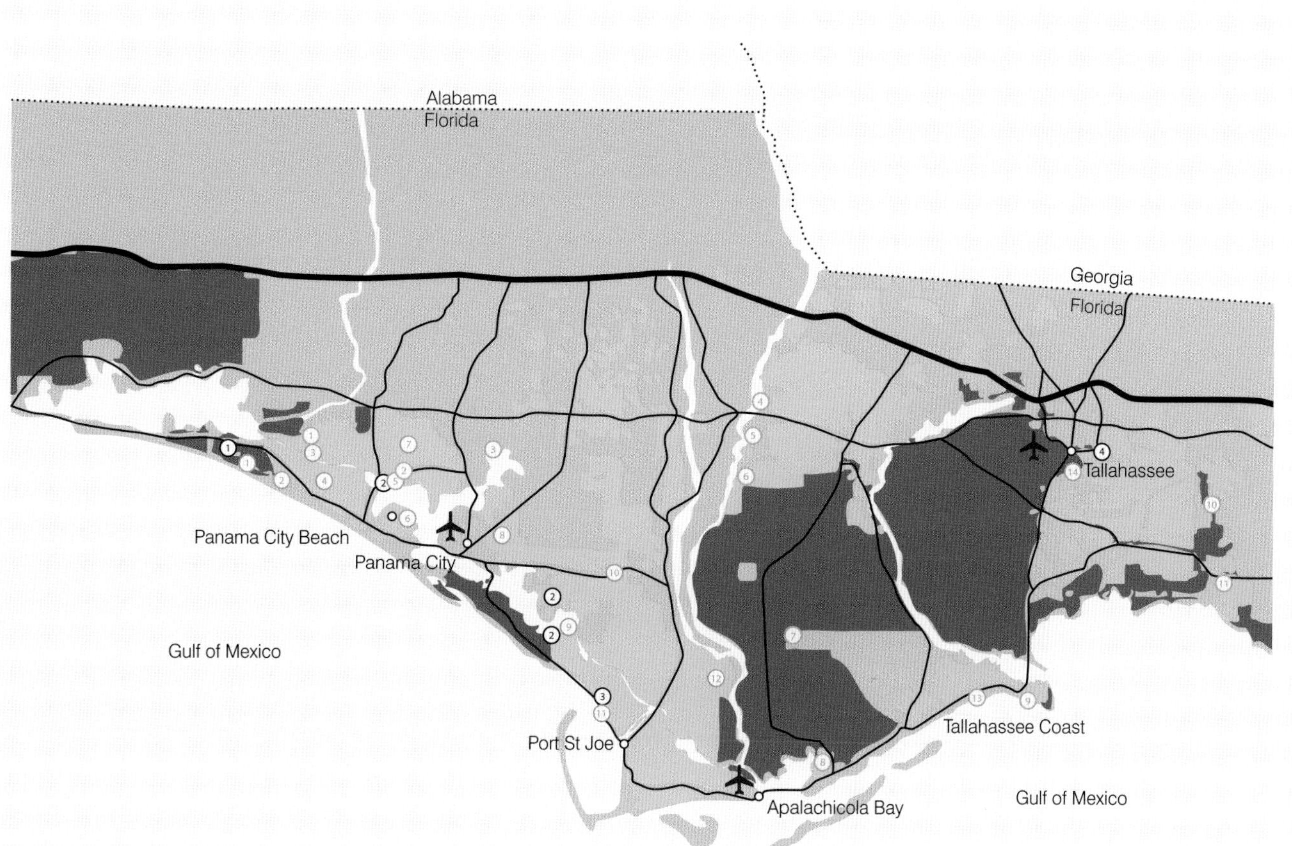

A decade later, these objectives led to:

- Land-use entitlements in development or in process totalling more than 50,000 residential units and more than 1,300,642 square metres of commercial uses over approximately 20,000 hectares.
- Development of more than 20 mixed-use masterplanned communities.
- The successful planning, permitting, financing and construction of a new international airport, the Panama City Bay County International Airport scheduled to open mid-2010.
- Approval of a 29,000 hectare sector plan and detailed specific area plans for the largest comprehensive masterplan and set of policies in the State of Florida's history.
- Improved regional transportation including the development of a historic agreement with the Florida Department of Transportation planning for more than 320 kilometres of improved road and four new state roadways.
- Entitlement and development of a new, beachfront, mixed-use retail and entertainment destination on 70 hectares and over 93,000 square metres.
- Relocation of a five kilometre coastal segment of a US highway inland opening up five kilometres of new Florida beachfront land for development of a new masterplanned resort community.
- Demolition of an abandoned paper mill resulting in the repurposing and entitlement of over 40 hectares of waterfront land for mixed-use development and city revitalisation.
- A partnership to improve regional healthcare resulting in the development of two new hospitals and two additional regional medical centres.
- Approval of a sustainable plan of development and entitlements for a 9,300 hectare island.
- A regional conservation strategy leading to land sales and permanent protection of almost 69,000 hectares.

Below
Landscape and lifestyle

Water's edge development set into the landscape below the treeline.

Opposite
A sense of place

Understanding that the special qualities of this Florida landscape were its greatest asset, the development has included extensive environmental and habitat protection and enhancement. Among the first stages of work on the St Joe project was a piece of research and market analysis which identified that buyers would be drawn largely from the baby boomer generation aged between 45 and 60. Knowing this type of buyer would be in search of a high quality of life, development had to be of the highest standard with attractive and authentic architecture in communities with a sense of belonging, offering a healthy lifestyle in a beautiful, natural and well-managed environment.

The company's environmental programme has been key to maximising the appeal of the place. Large portions of the land, a total of almost 69,000 hectares, have been set aside as sites to be protected forever. And in each new community around 40 per cent of all land is reserved for parks and open spaces. To carry out the conservation and to guide land and environmental management St Joe employs biologists, wildlife experts, foresters, architects, engineers and planners. The land management programme includes pioneering new approaches to wetland restoration, coastal dune protection, forest thinning, protecting water quality, eradicating invasive plant species and pursuing a policy of native planting. Meanwhile in wildlife conservation, work is under way protecting threatened and endangered species including the flatwoods salamander, gopher tortoise, sea turtle, Panama city crayfish and the red cockaded woodpecker.

To complement the work on the natural environment, an equal attention to detail is being paid to new development. Each community is designed with its own distinctive character, for example WaterMark Beach, near Port St Joe, has been designed to celebrate and preserve the architecture of old Florida, while Southwood near Tallahassee has the feel of a small college town. WaterColor's built environment is based on classic Southern homesteads. This 200 hectare community and resort includes high-quality homes, parks, a white-sand beach, and woodland trails, three golf courses, a tennis centre, the Ogden Museum of Southern Art, a retail centre and the award-winning WaterColor Inn.

Here the environmental policy has included protection for the choctawhatchee beach mouse. To offset small impacts to habitat at the WaterColor community, the developer partnered with the US Fish and Wildlife Services and the Florida Department of Environmental Protection to introduce six pairs of beach mice to more than 32 hectares of protected habitat at WaterSound Beach. Raised boardwalks across the dunes helped to keep people away from the habitat. In addition WaterColor was one of the first Walton County developments to install and maintain low-level sea-turtle friendly lighting. WindMark Beach has become the first community in Florida to be Wildlife Friends Lighting certified; this national programme promotes the protection of wildlife by minimising light pollution.

Environmental Systems

“The most important strategy to protect habitats from

fragmentation and loss is to reverse the approach of development planning:

landscape should lead the way for urban development. A multifunctional ecological infrastructure must be identified and planned in advance of any development plan. This proactive approach to preservation is even more important and urgent in developing countries, such as China, than elsewhere. Landscape architecture has nothing to do with gardening: landscape architecture is the art of survival, and it is an art of integration between 'smart preservation' and 'smart growth', and it is an art of the wise integration of various natural and cultural processes, of stormwater and flood, biodiversity, recreation, and aesthetics, on the site and across scales.

Dr Kongjian Yu
Dean and Professor, Graduate School of Landscape Architecture, Peking University
President, Turenscape

Concept

Regeneration of an industrial landscape the size of Manhattan with restored habitat, improved public access and greater flood management

Context

West coast bay/temperate

South Bay Salt Pond Restoration Project, San Francisco Bay, USA.

After more than a century as a centre for industrial salt production, a vast area of San Francisco Bay is being restored to its natural wetland state. Taking place over the coming 50 years, this is the largest transformation of its kind on the US west coast.

Opposite

A kaleidoscope of colour

Lining the South Bay, the patchwork pattern of salt ponds is clearly seen from above in a startling array of colours. While this industrial site has created a barrier to public access to the water, restoration plans include remedial environmental work, enhancing habitats and creating a public amenity. The initial three restoration areas are Eden Landing Ponds, Alviso Ponds and Ravenswood Ponds.

Eden Landing Ponds
Ravenswood Ponds
Alviso Ponds

South Bay Salt Pond Restoration Project, San Francisco Bay, USA

Above
Salt ponds and tidal marshes

Shallow man-made salt ponds are separated by levees and use the process of natural solar evaporation to extract salt from sea water. During the course of this process the ponds go through a spectrum of colour changes. Levels of salinity are indicated as microorganisms in the water change their hues. In low to mid-salinity ponds, green algae provide the dominant colour; in mid-salinity ponds a brine shrimp can create an orange cast and in high salinity the algae changes again and shifts the colour to pink and even a deep red. Other factors play a role, too, in creating this palette of colour as the presence of iron in the earth also adds to the redness. While the landscape can appear desolate and dessicated, salt ponds provide productive resting and feeding grounds for dozens of bird species including migratory shorebirds and waterfowl travelling on the Pacific Flyway migration route over this part of the coast.

Tidal marshes offer a range of varied habitats including heavily vegetated marsh plains, open mudflats and slough channels. Together they offer habitat for a variety of fish and wildlife including the salt marsh harvest mouse and the California clapper rail, both threatened with extinction. The rich mudflats of the tidal marsh create important feeding grounds for willets and other shorebirds. Meanwhile, the winding sloughs and channels that cut through the marsh are protective nursery areas for young fish including steelhead.

Above right

The landscape has a desolate beauty where remnants of the old industry can still be found and nature is regaining a hold in conquering the land.

While piecemeal work has taken place over recent years to remediate small areas of San Francisco's South Bay, this latest plan provides the opportunity to restore an entire ecosystem and landscape. On an epic scale at more than 6,000 hectares and with its patchwork of colourful red, orange, pink, green and white salt evaporation ponds, the South Bay Salt Pond Restoration Project's three central aims are to transform this unusual post-industrial landscape into restored wildlife habitat, to improve flood protection and to create wildlife-oriented public access and recreation.

Since the 1800s, as much as 90 per cent of the tidal marsh around the shores of the bay have been lost to agriculture, development and industrial salt production. Large swathes of the landscape were dyked and drained which resulted in dramatic change, not just in the way the landscape looked, but also in its ecology. The changes also severely affected the ways the wetlands functioned, so they could no longer perform as giant water filters preventing sediment flooding into and polluting the bay. They also helped with flood protection.

Salt production became a dominant industry in the South Bay and has occupied much of the coastline. In recent years the ponds have been operated by Cargill which, at its peak, was producing around one million tonnes of salt a year. At the turn of the twenty-first century, Cargill decided to consolidate its operations and offered for sale more than 6,000 hectares of shoreland south of San Mateo Bridge. It was acquired by and will be managed by a consortium including the California Department of Fish and Game and the US Fish and Wildlife Service.

Aimed at improving the physical, chemical and biological health of San Francisco Bay, a plan has evolved to help the environment revert to its natural state incorporating a variety of land types including tidal marsh, non-tidal marsh, mudflats, managed ponds and other wetland habitats.

The restoration has been informed by a planning process which included surveying and assessing the site, understanding its qualities and assets, and producing an Environmental Impact Statement (EIS) to analyse the long-term restoration alternatives. Detailed maps of the restoration areas were developed using geographic information system (GIS) for the impact assessment to illustrate how the restoration would be implemented in multiple phases over the 50 year planning period. The EIS included explorations of three alternative approaches to restoration. The first suggested no action, the second placed restoration emphasis on managed ponds and the third with an emphasis on restoring tidal habitat. The preferred option is to strive for a 90/10 balance between tidal and managed ponds through incremental phased implementation and careful adaptive management and monitoring.

1. No action

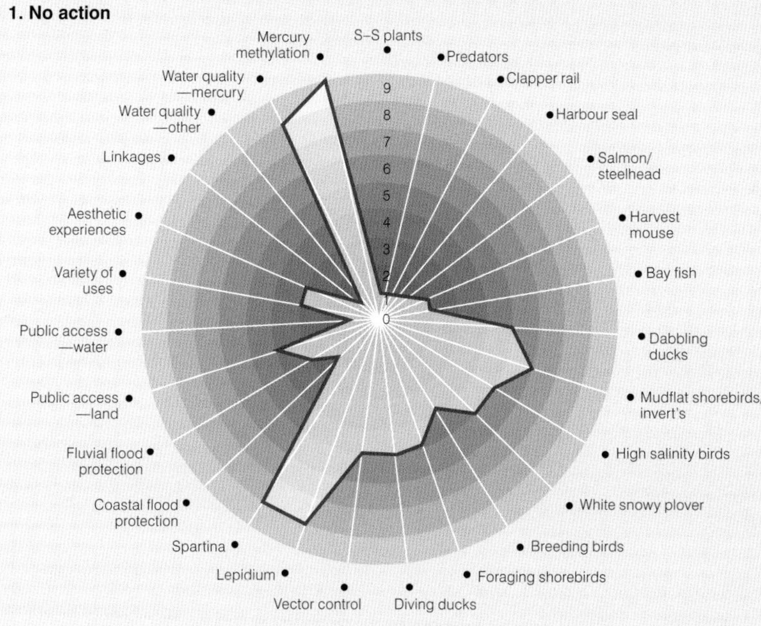

2. Managed pond emphasis

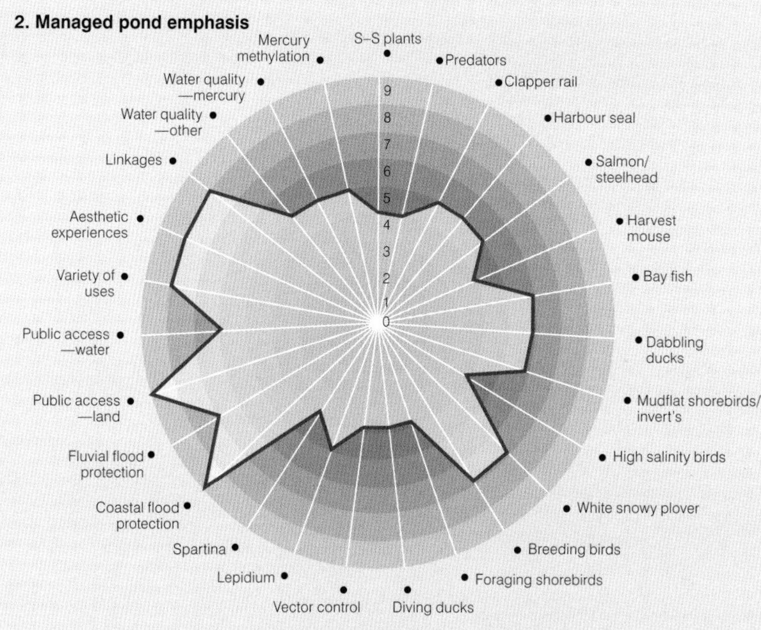

3. Tidal emphasis

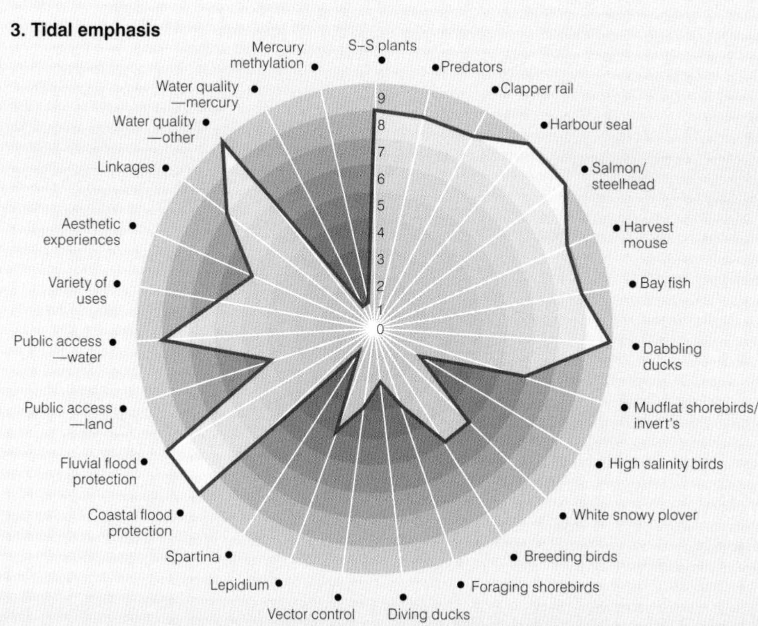

4. Mixed

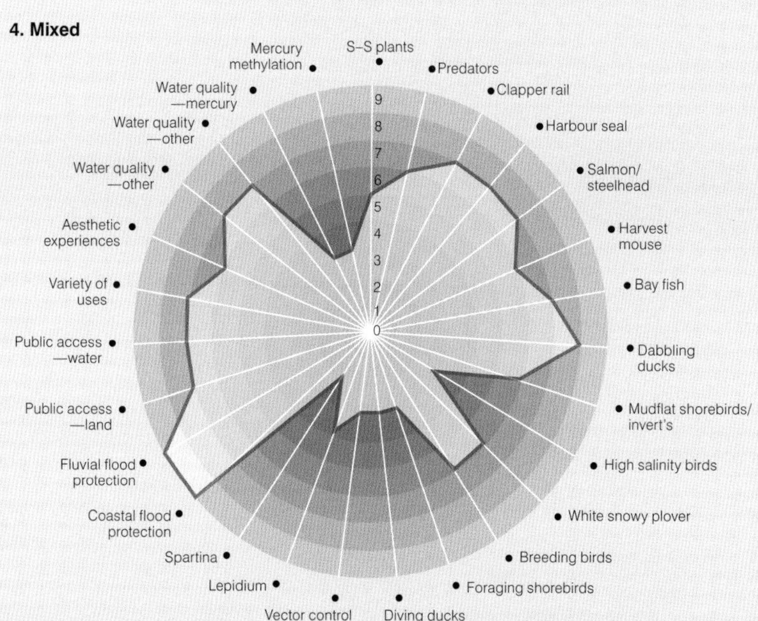

Long-term options as measured against success criteria

To plan for the future, it was important to understand the different options for management and use. Clockwise from bottom left, these charts denote the projected results for different levels of intervention including placing an emphasis on tidal areas, taking no action, placing an emphasis on managed ponds and taking a mixed approach.

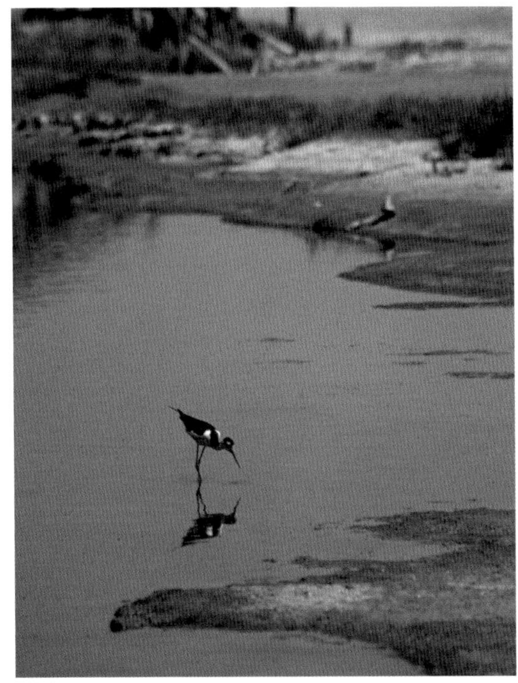

Above and opposite
Tide and flood

The highly distinctive landscape is threaded with meandering waterways. Restored tidal wetlands act as buffers against rising sea levels and increase the carrying capacity of local creeks, flood control channels and rivers by reconnecting these areas to their historic floodplains.

Right

Diagram showing sediment cycling in the South Bay.

While a restoration strategy and programme has been developed, it is expected to evolve further as work on pilot projects is implemented and results are monitored over time. Using an adaptive management process, changes will be closely monitored at every stage of the process. Along with progress towards goals, the monitoring will also detect unexpected negative effects from the remediation work. Once a problem is detected, the process also ensures that action will be taken to implement a solution.

Involving the combined skills and expertise of state and government agencies, conservation groups, scientists, engineers and landscape architects, the work includes breaching some levees and allowing the tidal water to ebb and flow into the salt ponds. However, some ponds will remain virtually untouched because of their capacity to provide resting, foraging and breeding places for migratory birds. As the water quality improves, fish and other marine life will be encouraged back into bay areas which in turn will attract a greater variety of birds. Recent projects have seen the return of birds including pelicans, American avocets and double-crested cormorants, but concern remains for endangered species including the California clapper rail and the salt marsh harvest mouse.

Integrated with habitat restoration, flood protection measures will be increased for coastal and inland communities to take account of the impact of remediation works and also rising sea levels resulting from climate change. In some places this will entail restoring and building up levees, while in others flood capacities will be increased in local creeks, flood control channels and rivers by widening their mouths and by re-establishing connections to historic flood plains. Wetlands perform important functions here. Restored tidal wetlands act as buffers against rising sea levels and increase the carrying capacity of local creeks, flood control channels and rivers by reconnecting these areas to their historic floodplains. Tidal marshes have their role too. As sediment washes into newly opened salt ponds, it accumulates and begins to establish new tidal plains for marsh vegetation. Once tidal marshes are established they become very efficient sediment traps. In effect, they tend to preserve themselves as they age. For this reason, new tidal marsh areas are likely to keep pace with changing sea level conditions if sediment is available in the system. A further bonus is that tidal marshes are highly biologically productive and capture significant amounts of carbon from the atmosphere.

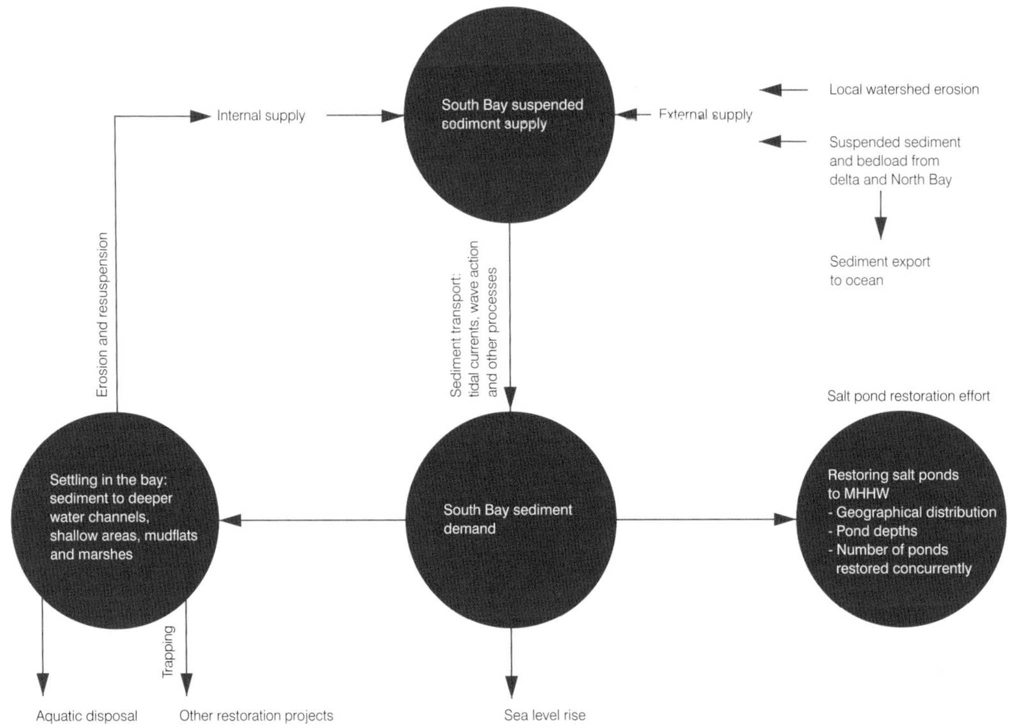

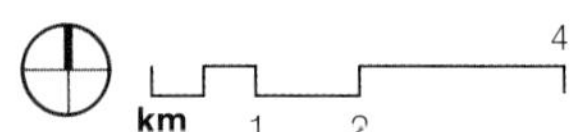

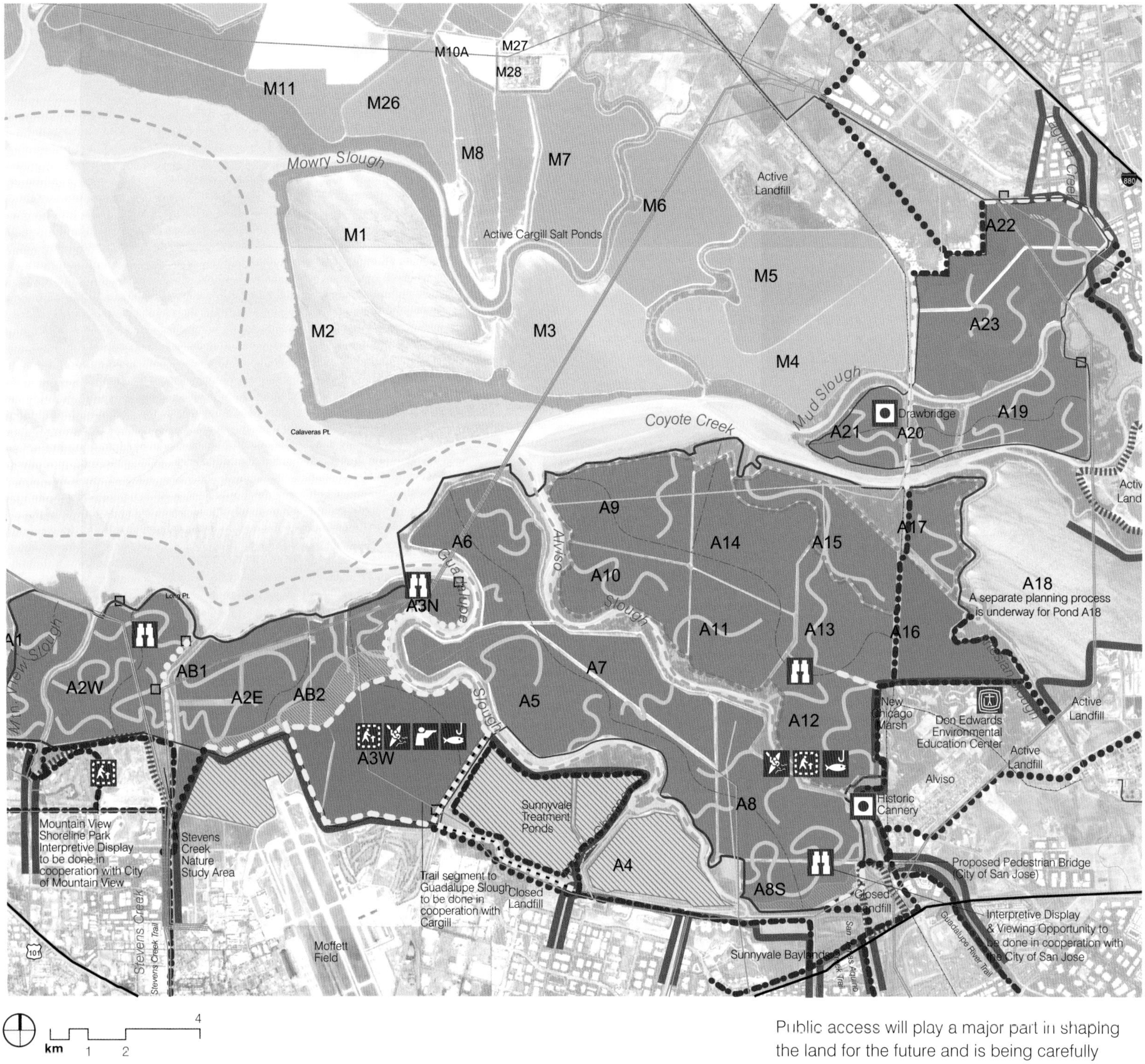

Alviso Ponds

- Project Area

Infrastructure Features
- Highway
- Railroad
- Wastewater Outfall
- PG & E Access Points
- Hetch Hetchy Aqueduct
- Overhead Power Transmission Line
- Sewer Force Main
- Distribution Line

Habitat Feature
- Tidal Habitat
- Upland Transition Area
- Managed Pond
- Managed Pond (outside project area)
- Initially Reversibly Tidal; Ultimately Tidal

Flood Management Features
- Proposed Flood Protection Levee
- Existing Flood Protection Levee (outside project area)
- High Ground*

* Level of flood protection not specified

Recreational Features
- Existing Trail (to remain)
- Proposed year-Round Trail
- Proposed Seasonal Trail
- Proposed Water Trail
- Proposed Vehicular Access
- Proposed Trail (outside project area)
- Interpretive Trail
- Historic Site
- Fishing
- Kayak Launch
- Hunting
- Viewing Opportunity
- Environmental Education Centre

Public access will play a major part in shaping the land for the future and is being carefully balanced with the habitat restoration to ensure that the requirements of wildlife and humans are not in conflict. New recreational facilities will include land trails for hiking and cycling along with water trails for kayaking. This trail system will close the gaps in the regional Bay Trail Project, and there will be opportunities to link the engineered pond tracts to existing nearby parks. To help visitors interpret and understand this distinctive environment, viewing platforms will be located at intervals along walkways offering great vantage points and information about the land, plants and wildlife. There will also be plenty of opportunity to learn about the recent past of this unusual working landscape and the entrepreneurial spirit that built it along with the restoration work that is currently in progress.

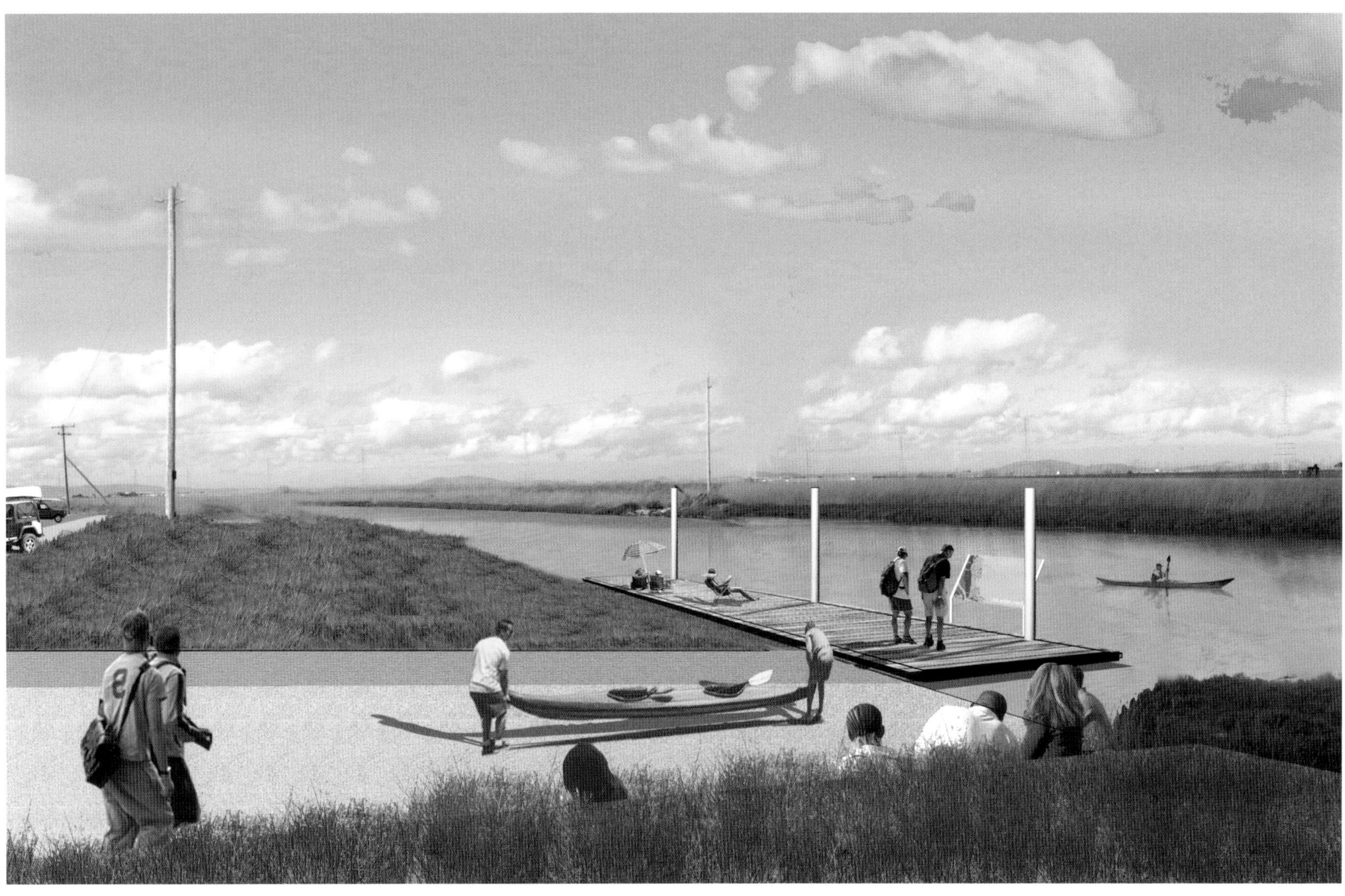

The first phases of implementation will be undertaken at salt pond complexes in Alviso, Ravenswood and Eden Landing.

In the southernmost portion of the bay, the sequence of ponds at Alviso will be subject to a series of improvements in phase one, to be completed by 2012. The work includes enhancing more than 100 hectares of shallow pond habitat with 50 nesting islands for migrating shorebirds such as avocets and stilts. At the same time the plan connects more than 360 hectares of ponds to the bay, creates tidal marsh for endangered species and shallow water habitat for pelicans, cormorants and ducks, and there is work on opening four kilometres of new bay trail.

At the Ravenswood Ponds on the western shore, the plan includes enhancing almost 100 hectares of pond habitat for nesting and resting shorebirds including the snowy plover. A one kilometre trail will be opened, along with installing interpretive displays, two new viewing platforms near pond habitat and existing tidal marsh, plus a viewing area and interpretive station at Bayfront Park. Key to the work at Eden Landing Ponds on the eastern shoreline, is restoring 255 hectares of tidal habitat for endangered species, and creating more than 90 hectares of pond habitat for a variety of birds including phalaropes and eared grebes. There will also be six kilometres of new trails, an interpretive site with raised walkways and viewing platforms overlooking the remnants of the historic salt works and a kayak launch at Mount Eden Creek.

Restoring tidal marsh at this scale is expected to take several decades to complete. As the wetlands evolve over time, understanding of the restoration project will also evolve and science will be playing a major role in deepening the understanding of these natural systems.

Opposite
Alviso Ponds

Plans for the Alviso Ponds area in the southernmost point of South Bay include enhancing shallow ponds with nesting islands for migrating shorebirds connecting a large area of ponds to the bay creating new tidal marsh for endangered species and shallow water habitat for pelicans, cormorants and ducks. There are also proposals for a new bay trail.

Above
Eden Landing

In the future, restored ponds and waterways will provide a beautiful landscape for a range of sporting activities. Shown here, at Eden Landing on the east side of the South Bay, proposals include a kayak launch and trailhead. There is also a plan for an interpretive site with raised walkways and viewing platforms overlooking the remnants of the historic salt works. The long-term vision for habitat restoration includes restoring tidal habitat for endangered species, and creating pond habitat for birds including phalaropes and eared grebes.

Visions of the future

Future educational uses of the ponds and marshes. Above, at Ravenswood Ponds on the west side of the bay, this image shows school children enjoying panoramic views of the waterscape from the new viewing platform and interpretative station. Opposite, understanding the historic salt works at the Eden Landing viewing platform and interpretive station.

Concept
A wetland park incorporating natural waste water treatment systems

Context
Temperate oceanic monsoon climate/ industrial plant

Shanghai Chemical Industrial Park Natural Waste Water Treatment System, Shanghai, China.

In a fusion project uniting landscape design, environmental expertise, water engineering and academic knowledge, a natural wetland treatment system has been created to improve industrial waste water, the first system of its kind in China. This highly functional installation also provides the ecological, landscape and recreational benefits of a beautiful wetland park.

Opposite
Through the wetlands

Accessed by boardwalks and pathways, a green ribbon of grasses and trees runs between the industrial plant and the local community.

Shanghai Chemical Industrial Park, Natural Waste Water Treatment System, Shanghai, China

Function and beauty

The water treatment system is designed to be highly functional and beautiful. It creates a buffer zone around the huge industrial facility. Boardwalks make it possible to gain access deep within the site to enjoy the water, and a variety of wetland plants and wildlife, particularly the wildfowl attracted to the site.

With its lush reedbeds, extensive sequence of lakes, ponds and weirs along with boardwalks and a new visitor centre, this wetland park is located within one of Shanghai's largest petrochemical industrial complexes, providing a welcome green oasis for staff and the local community. In addition to providing an attractive recreational space and wildlife habitat, this wetland also works hard as a natural waste water treatment system for the industrial park. This facility is home to more than 40 petrochemical and pharmaceutical production plants run by international blue-chip companies including global giants Bayer and BP.

Combining the skills of landscape architects, engineers, ecologists, and academics, the natural treatment system creates a model for the polishing and recycling of treated industrial waste water at a rate of more than 22,000 cubic metres per day. Innovative design components include shallow-water oxidising ponds for chemical oxygen demand (COD) removal, and two parallel free surface wetlands systems for COD, biochemical oxygen demand (BOD), nitrate and heavy metal removal. The system design evolved in response to growing environmental awareness in China, public concerns about issues of health and safety and water quality, and the willingness of forward-thinking industries to adopt a responsible attitude towards the impact of a booming economy on the environment.

Located south-east of Shanghai along the north coast of Hangzhou Bay, the Shanghai Chemical Industrial Park (SCIP) has been established as one of the country's first industrial zones specialising in the development of petrochemical and fine chemical businesses. The owners and managers of the gigantic 3,000 hectare complex generated a brief for a water treatment system that would purify industrial waste water effluent to a level suitable for recycling within the industrial park, thereby reducing overall water demand, or for discharge into the ecologically sensitive Hangzhou Bay. Achieving these goals would improve effluent to the Level IV National Standard for Surface Water Quality (NSSWQ). Any proposed treatment system must also ensure compliance with groundwater and soil standards.

During work on the treatment system design, it became clear there was an opportunity to broaden the scope of the project beyond its purely functional requirements. Using the latest ideas in ecological engineering, it was possible to take the innovative step of combining the new waste water facility with the provision of natural wetlands as wildlife habitat and a recreational space for the park's employees and visitors, and also to benefit local communities living adjacent to the park. The treatment system is also of interest to the scientific community, and a research centre has been established as part of the wetland area.

The design of the 30 hectare wetland system follows a long, linear, L-shaped route following the park's boundary, providing a green buffer for neighbouring residential areas. Waste water from the industrial park has already undergone the first phase of cleaning before it reaches the wetlands. While this treatment removes much of the ammonia, BOD and total phosphorus (TP) from the effluent, waste water entering the wetland treatment system is still highly saline, and contains significant concentrations of COD and nitrates. The treatment system provides waste water 'polishing' to remove these remaining pollutants. The wetlands are also designed with a degree of treatment flexibility: effluent water quality and volume is likely to change as new industrial facilities come on-stream, and the system can accommodate these variations maintaining discharge standards with minimal operational changes.

On entering the wetlands, waste water passes through a research area, before flowing slowly through two large, shallow ponds where pollutants are oxidised, then into a long sequence of wetland cells. Here, different blocks of planting including bulrushes, reeds and wetland grasses, act as natural filters. Plant species were selected for their saline tolerance and also their filtering function —with different species able to remove different pollutants from the water. In the final phases of the system, water enters a network of open ponds and broader swathes of flowering wetland vegetation. This botanical wetland can be explored by boardwalks and bridges that are connected to the wetland visitor centre with its conference, meeting and education rooms. Viewing platforms within the centre, and also on the central island of the botanical wetland, enable visitors to observe the abundant and diverse wildlife attracted to the wetlands. By the end of the process, most of the water is returned to the industrial park for reuse, with any excess being released into Hangzhou Bay.

A rigorous operation and monitoring programme is in place which offers a quick response to water quality changes. Researchers assess the effluent from each industrial facility before it enters the natural treatment system. The chemical, physical and biological condition of the wetlands is also checked to avoid the build up of pollutants in the water or soil. Continuous research is conducted to track removal rates of specific water effluent constituents such as heavy metals and organics, and to refine the system to target specific pollutants. Finally, water quality is closely monitored at points throughout the wetland system to minimise the risk of accidental pollution discharge.

Even in the early stages following construction, the innovative natural treatment system has attracted considerable interest from other industries in China, and has set a new benchmark in the country for ecological engineering and water treatment.

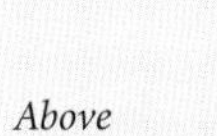

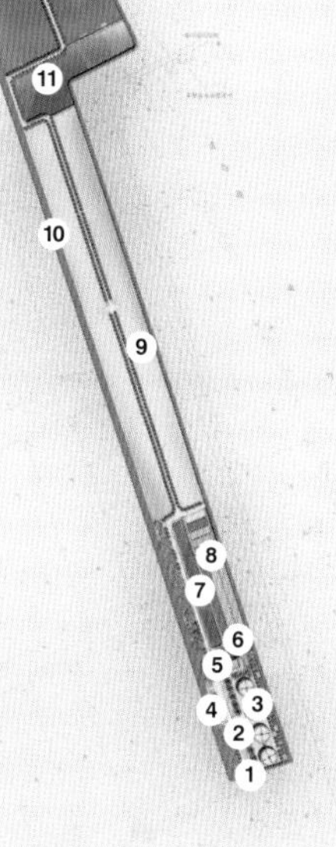

1 Research entrance
2 Pump house
3 Trickling filters
4 Research station parking
5 Laboratory facilities
6 Header pond
7 Bypass channel
8 Research wetlands
9 Shallow water for COD oxidation
10 Forested buffer
11 Combined flow mixing ponds
12 Submerged berms
13 Reed wetland
14 Flow control wiers
15 Cattail wetland
16 Bulrush wetland
17 Maintenance road and access ramps
18 Pump house
19 Bird observation tower
20 Reed wetland
21 Open water
22 Cattail wetland
23 Bulrush wetland
24 Maintenance road and access ramps
25 Marsh walk
26 Botanical wetland
27 Visitor centre building
28 Maintenance building
29 Visitor centre parking
30 Habitat Island and observation towers
31 Lakeside promenade
32 Stone wier sculpture
33 Outflow to canals

Above
Masterplan

Water from the industrial plant enters the treatment system at the lower end of this plan. The main components of the wetlands are:

Research wetland cells

The research wetlands are located at the southern end of the site near the effluent inflow, with a total of seven wetland cells making up the unit. Three cells are 85 x 7.5 metres, and four cells are 20 x 7 metres. These research cells make experiments possible that enquire into the characteristics and removal efficiencies for specific constituents of the effluent, cell configurations and various vegetation types as well as providing research opportunities for local universities.

The COD degradation ponds

Water enters two parallel, COD degradation ponds, each with an area of approximately 7,300 square metres. Water spends a minimum of 4.5 hours in these shallow, gravel-lined ponds, where it is exposed during the day to natural ultraviolet-light and aeration from algae. While much of the COD is difficult to degrade, this design exposes the COD to an intense, oxidising environment before it enters the free surface wetland.

Free surface wetland

The free surface wetland has a total area of just over 22 hectares, comprising almost 19 hectares of wetland and 3.5 hectares of open water. It is divided into two parallel treatment systems. The upstream wetland cells, where the majority of the treatment occurs, are designed with dense stands of emergent vegetation with no open water to maximise treatment efficiency.

Criteria for plant species selection in the free surface wetland included salinity tolerance, proven performance in treatment wetlands, and ability to grow at controlled water levels. Regional and local species were sought, with aesthetic considerations also playing a role in the selection. Using the above criteria, wetland plant species including *Phragmites communis*, *Typha spp*, *Scirpus tabernaemontani*, *Zizania cadiciflora* and *Ruppia maritima* were selected for core treatment areas.

Botanical wetland

The final section of the treatment system forms a botanical wetland, designed to have a greater diversity of wetland plants and habitats. An additional 25 plant species were selected for the botanical wetlands based on their aesthetic characteristics and hardiness.

Below

A cross-section showing the composition of part of the wetlands.

Wetlands system

This working landscape is an attractive and enjoyable place for the industrial plant's employees. As it flows from the industrial facilities through the system, waste water is channelled through a primary treatment plant before it enters the natural wetlands system. This initial cleaning process ensures that effluent is of a consistent quality before it enters the wetlands, with many key pollutants removed from the water.

Concept
A fusion of ecology and design

Context
Coastal prairie, coastal scrub/Mediterranean

The Presidio: Fort Scott Creek and Historic Gardens Project, San Francisco, USA.

Like many urban open spaces worldwide, the Presidio public park in San Francisco has been seeking to balance complex and conflicting public space demands including historic preservation and ecological conservation and recreation. To find solutions that unite ecology and design, park staff and main user groups took part in a process that included an on-site conceptual masterplanning workshop and the production of a book documenting the techniques and lessons learned for integrated ecology and design.

Opposite
Fort Scott Creek

The lush, densely vegetated creek with historic palms at the Presidio has evolved over centuries from an area of coastal scrub to being part of a frontier outpost for Spanish, Mexican and US armies. Today, it is used as a public park.

The Presidio: Fort Scott Creek and Historic Gardens Project, San Francisco, USA

With plans to improve public access, enhance the visitor experience and protect the landscape, the Presidio's management trust was interested in exploring how best to establish successful integrated uses. In a pilot project, a series of workshops was run to draw together the skills and different approaches of designers and ecologists to produce a range of options. The workshops focused on a three hectare area within the Presidio park site called Fort Scott Creek and Historic Gardens. Flanking a natural spring and small waterway, the land had been identified as the site for a future sustainability-themed education and visitor centre.

At the southern end of the Golden Gate Bridge, the Presidio is a parkland area of just over 600 hectares which forms part of the vast 30,550 hectare urban national park called the Golden Gate National Recreation Area. The Presidio served as a military post from 1776 to 1994. Established as a Spanish fort, it was also used by the Mexican Army before becoming an important US Army base. The land has a complex land use history including military occupation and large-scale reforestation, it includes areas of preserved native habitat, and an extensive collection of buildings from historic structures to homes for more than 3,000 people. Among its many uses, the site became a temporary encampment in 1906 for thousands of people made homeless in the San Francisco earthquake. Designated a National Historic Landmark District in 1962, it was incorporated into the wider recreation area in 1972 and the Presidio Trust was established in 1996 to preserve and enhance the Presidio as an "enduring resource for the American public".

In this piece of exploratory work, a team comprising landscape architects, a restoration ecologist, a wildlife biologist and the trust's technical experts set out to develop a conceptual design plan to enhance, interpret and integrate the unique features of the creek site. The method of interdisciplinary working was chosen to test the idea that the integrated collaboration of designers and ecologists could produce more informed design solutions than those resulting from independent working patterns.

The client's key goals were:

- To develop the restoration of Fort Scott Creek and determine what role it might play in relation to other riparian corridors, as well as the wider historic landscape.
- To knit the district together and tie the historic garden and community garden to the ideas of sustainability and stewardship.
- To create an educational landscape with evolving experiences.
- To develop a landscape design that would create opportunities for children and adults to come into meaningful, intimate contact with nature.

For those taking part, this was an opportunity to explore new ways for designers and ecologists to work together by understanding their different approaches and reconciling working methods. Set against a background of the increasing demand for sustainable urban design, primary differences and potential friction included the urge of ecologists to exclude human activity and for designers to encourage it. However in this collaboration all effort was concentrated on acknowledging differences but finding common ground.

The intensive week-long, on-site project began with understanding the area's history and assessing existing conditions. At the heart of the promontory with views towards the Golden Gate Bridge and the sea, the Fort Scott study area is partly wooded and partly open land with a sequence of buildings formerly used as officers' quarters, a native plant nursery, historic buildings and protected landscape. To the south-east of the main fort, the creek is a wooded valley.

The next phase of work involved hearing the varied views of stakeholders including representatives from local volunteer groups, historic preservationists, restoration ecologists, maintenance and operations staff and architects working on the new sustainability centre. The fruitful session included bringing together groups who had not previously met, understanding different and sometimes conflicting interests in the site and finding ways

art driven metrics = aesthetic appeal people use and enjoyment

"success is being provocative, profound, memorable"

design world

- site interpretation
- site design
- grading and drainage
- planting plan
- visualisation
- engineering
- plans and specs
- cost estimates
- construction management

?

innovation
identity
usability
adaptability
form
function

high design

fusion zone

high science

Key EDAW values

create enduring solutions
seek cultural and environmental fit
foster positive change
advocate collaborative exchange of ideas

science driven metrics = ecological health of natural ecosystem sustainability

"success is when the hand of man is not evident"

ecology world

- soils
- hydrology
- water quality
- geomorphology
- plant ecology
- wildlife ecology
- human ecology

?

restoration
regeneration
rehabilitation
enhancement
preservation
management

to move forward together towards a shared vision. The consultation produced a list of goals and objectives.

Following this an ecology and design charrette was run with stakeholders. Here people formed small groups to explore the four themes of historic preservation, recreation, education and environment. Debate centred on concerns which included rehabilitating the historic landscape, the role of ecology, whether to partition off areas for protection, the extent of public access and the style of future maintenance. From here concept diagrams and alternative scenarios developed into a conceptual plan incorporating ecology, history and public use which have provided a strong base for the Presidio Trust's next phase of development.

In addition to the plan, the pilot study offered the opportunity to document the experience of designers and ecologists working in close collaboration. At the conclusion of the workshop, the team recorded the process identifying points of successful integration and the missed opportunities for collaboration. This was published in a manual for ecologists and designers called *Design + Ecology in Practice*.

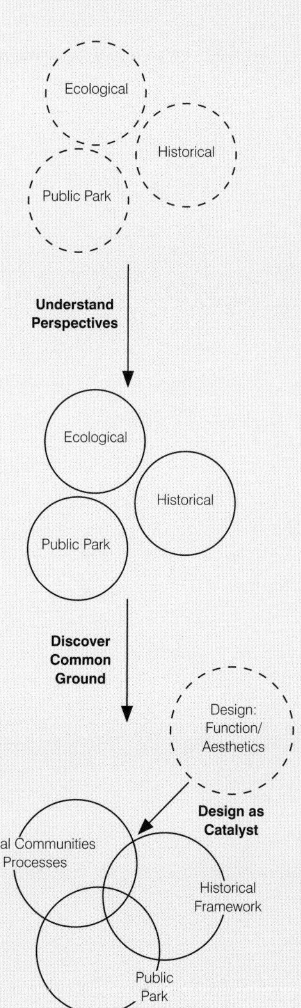

Left
Constructing a middle ground

The goal of the week-long session was to create an integrative design process where the design and ecology team worked in collaboration with the Presidio Trust and with the multiple stakeholders. Of greatest importance was the integration of ideas and the development of solutions that brought multiple perspectives towards a fruitful middle ground.

Above
Design and ecology fusion

Landscape architects have begun to take on a larger role in understanding and developing urban ecological systems. They are beginning to appreciate an ecological process-based understanding of landscapes and environmental concerns, and learning to access and incorporate ecological knowledge into their design processes.

Taking advantage of the multi-layered park to overlap programme and activities.

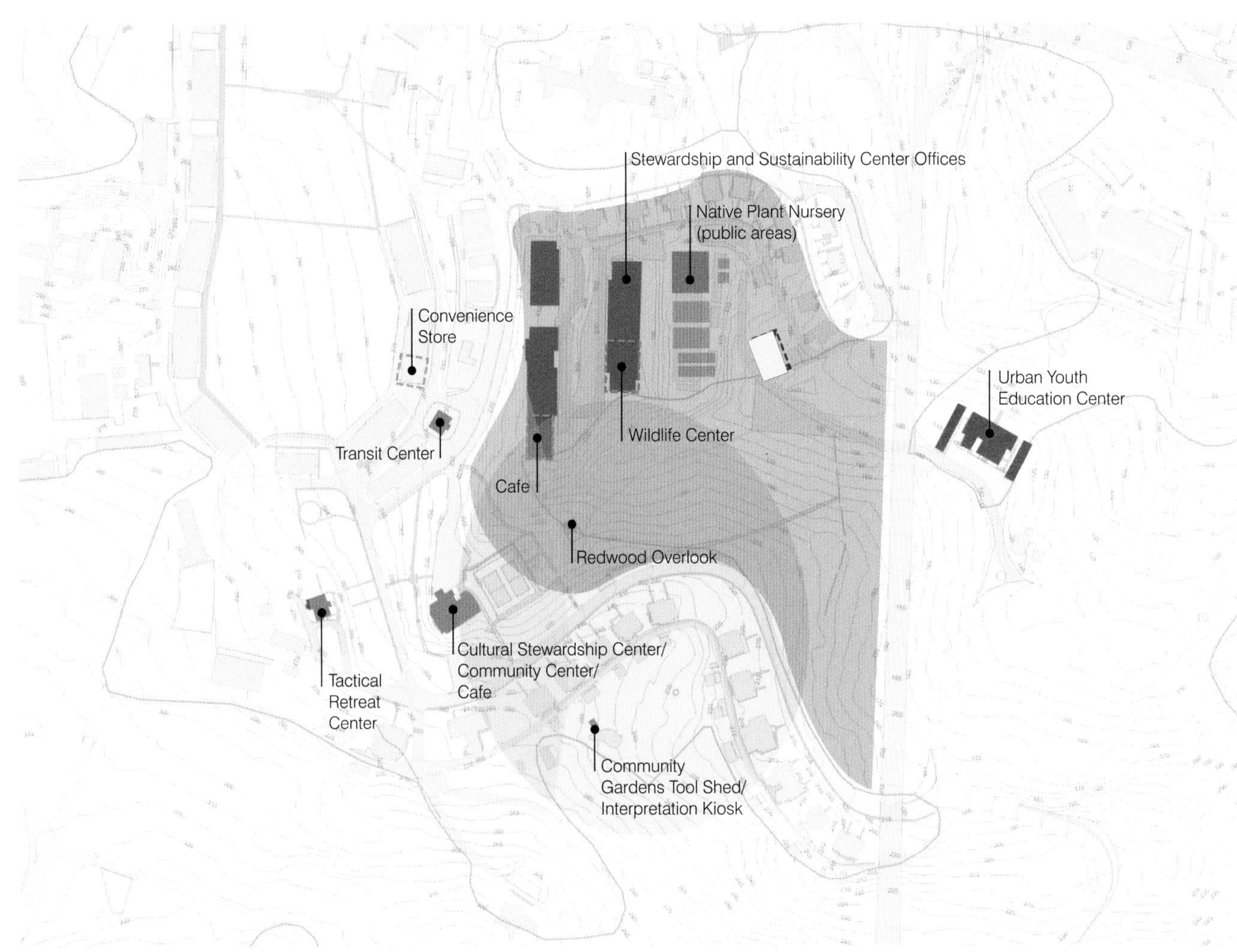

Fort Scott Tactical Retreat

- Existing buildings
- Stewardship and Sustainability Center (SSC)
- Fort Scott Creek Tactical Retreat Center
- Historic retreat

Overlapping program and activities

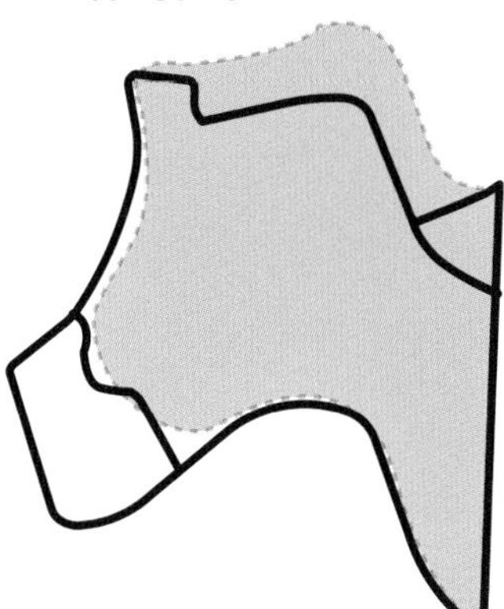

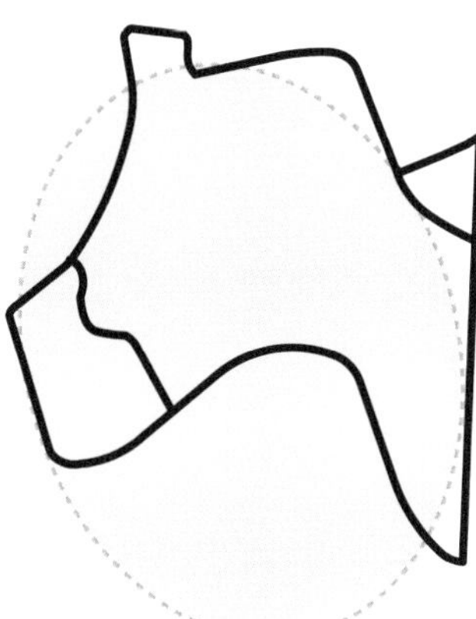

Stewardship and sustainability
The Stewardship and Sustainability Center is planned for the northern edge of the creek.

Tactical Retreat Center
This provides meeting spaces, outdoor classrooms, walking trails, views and a historic garden.

Botanical/community and historic gardens
Currently used for growing native plants and as community gardens, the creek area could combine working and historic gardens.

Alternative scenarios for public access

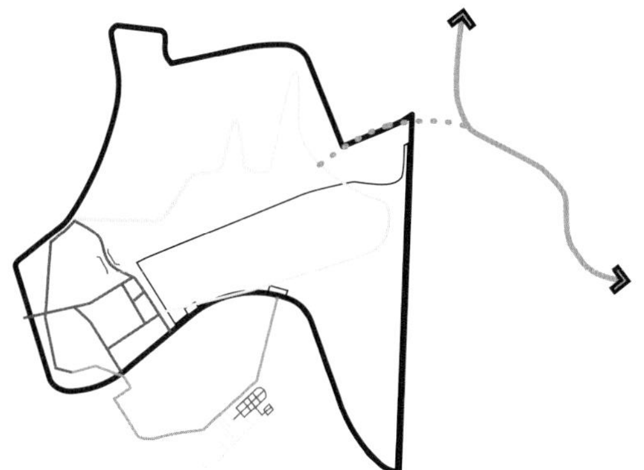

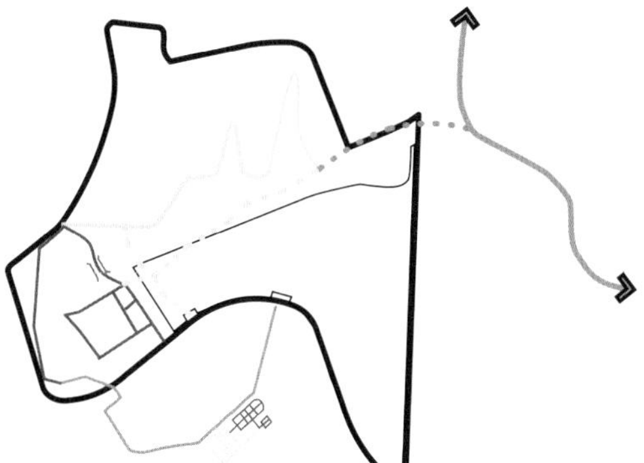

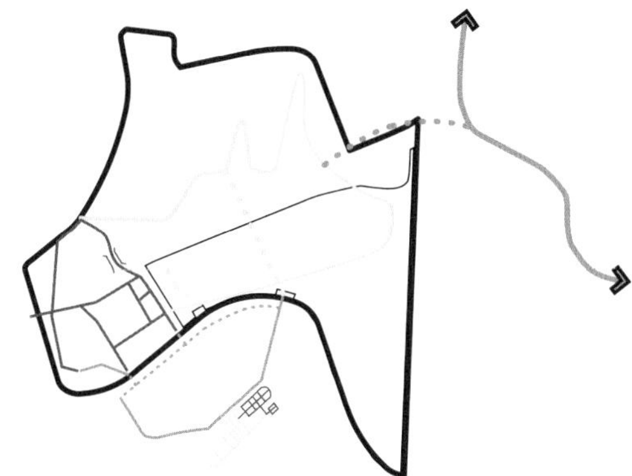

Perimeter nature trails
Relegating paths to the site's perimeter would limit human access and disturbance within the riparian zone.

Seasonal trails
Narrow seasonal trails would provide controlled access to the heart of the site.

Permanent accessible pathways
This approach prioritises public use and access over wildlife enhancement.

Alternative scenarios for the riparian corridor

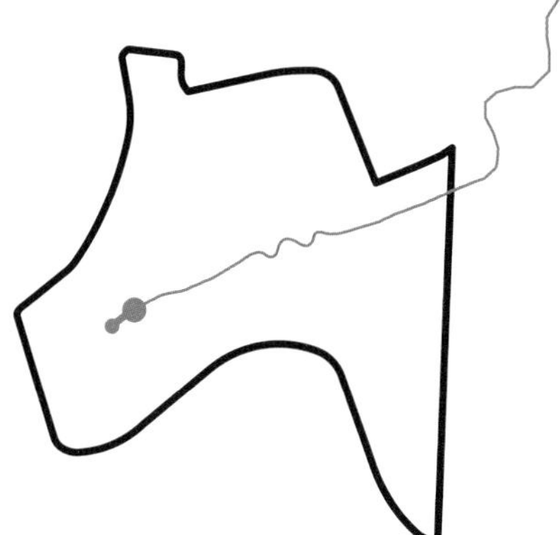

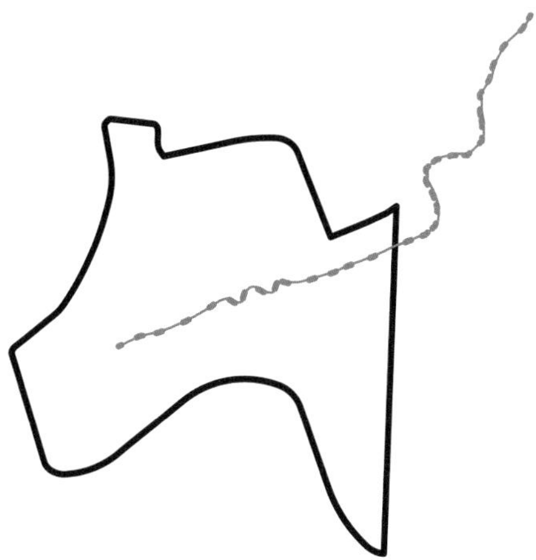

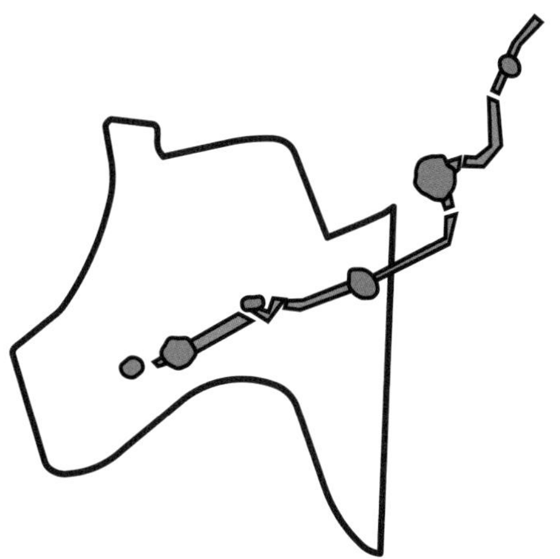

Ecological restoration
Enhancement actions might focus on eradicating certain non-native species and planting natives.

Water-quality enhancement
Features would include incorporating the capture of stormwater runoff into small treatment wetlands.

Water as design elements/ features
Along the entire creek corridor structures, trails and other facilities would provide gathering points.

Alternative scenarios for a happy medium

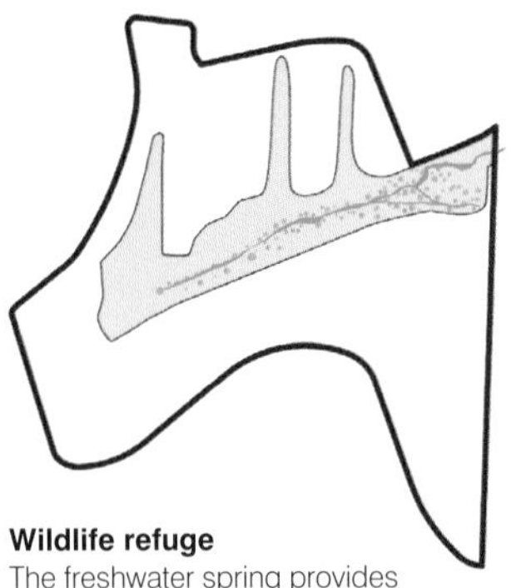

Wildlife refuge
The freshwater spring provides a significant attraction to wildlife including the violet green swallow and the varied thrush.

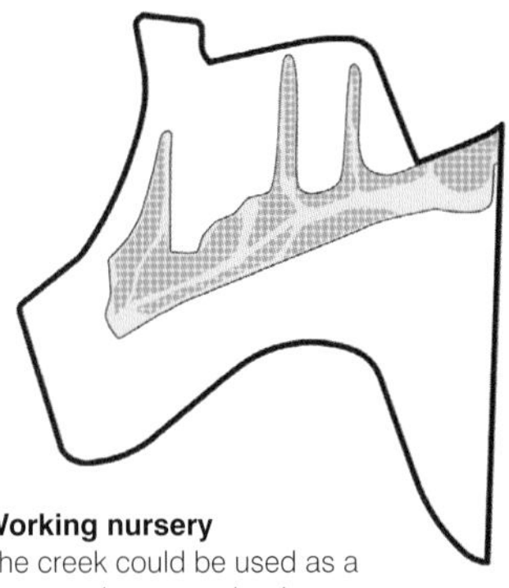

Working nursery
The creek could be used as a large-scale nursery landscape with paths and enlarged aquatic zones.

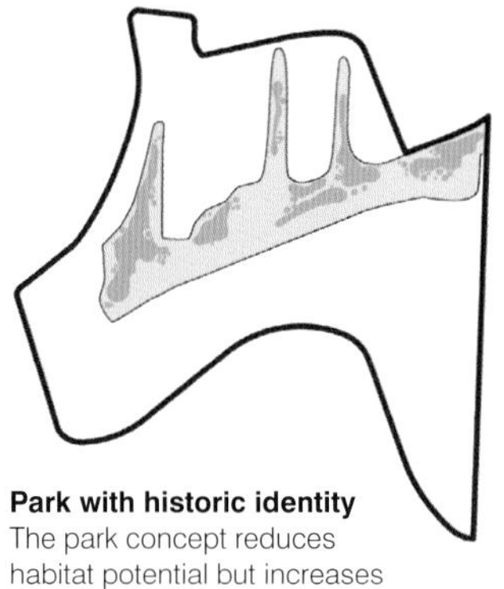

Park with historic identity
The park concept reduces habitat potential but increases public access.

Alternative scenarios for habitat fragmentation and wildlife viewing

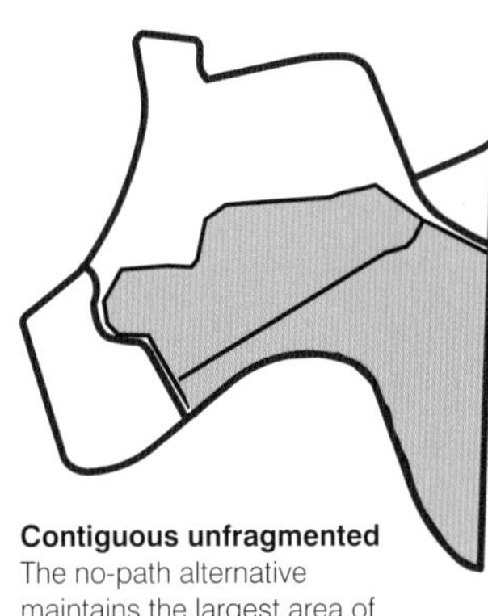

Contiguous unfragmented
The no-path alternative maintains the largest area of contiguous wildlife habitat.

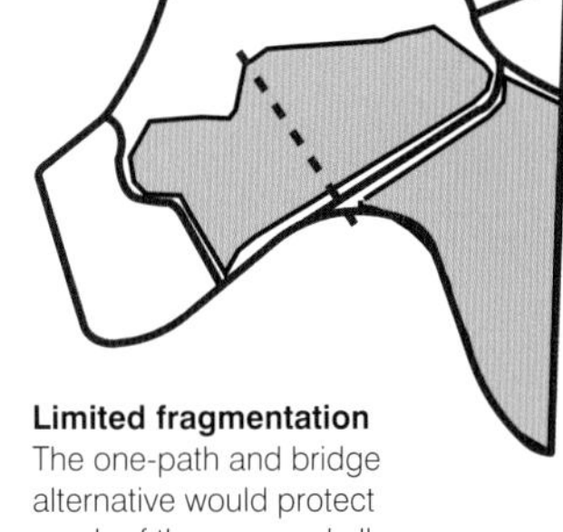

Limited fragmentation
The one-path and bridge alternative would protect much of the area and allow visitors to observe wildlife.

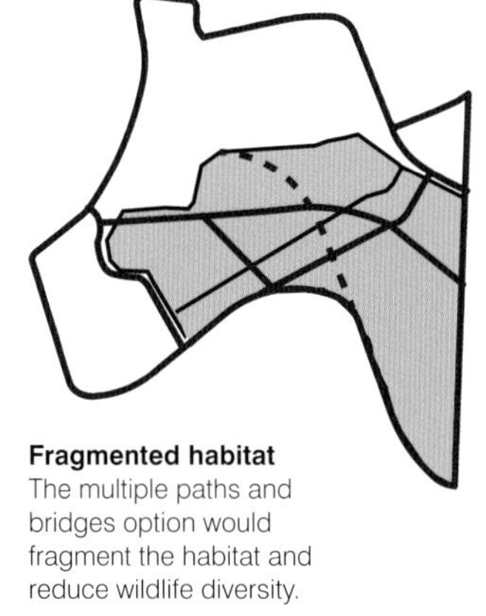

Fragmented habitat
The multiple paths and bridges option would fragment the habitat and reduce wildlife diversity.

Alternative scenarios for balancing wildlife habitat with public use access

Wildlife enhancement
Public use

Alternative 1
This preserves the creek, but the human experience and opportunities for contact with nature are minimised.

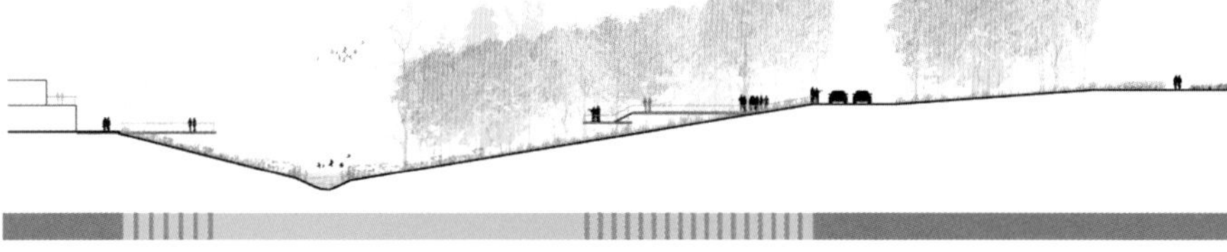

Alternative 2
This facilitates more public access and experience with urban natural areas, but imposes potential significant impacts to the natural area.

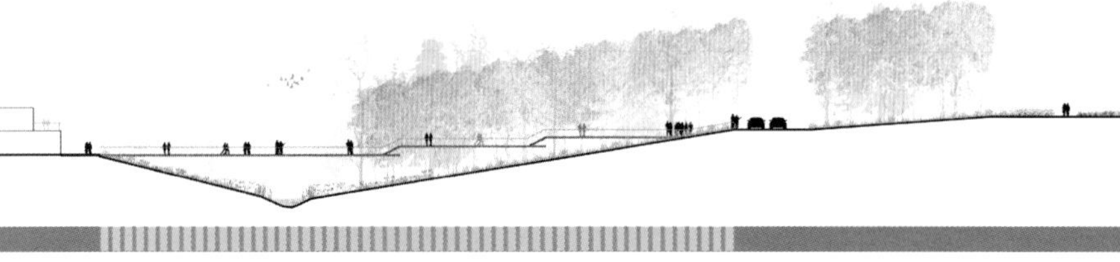

Alternative 3
This brings public experience into the natural area by maximising public contact with urban natural systems. However, this alternative imposes direct human impacts on the creek that are difficult to control.

Stewardship and Sustainability Center

Fort Scott Creek ecological restoration

Historic forest

Historic gardens and community garden

Alternative scenarios for historic forest area restoration

The historic forest is one of the more contentious ecological components of the site. There is no simple solution that satisfies all stakeholders, and so the solution must be a compromise.

The three restoration alternatives, shown below, are:

1 to leave as it is,

2 to transform the understorey,

3 selectively remove and replace canopy species.

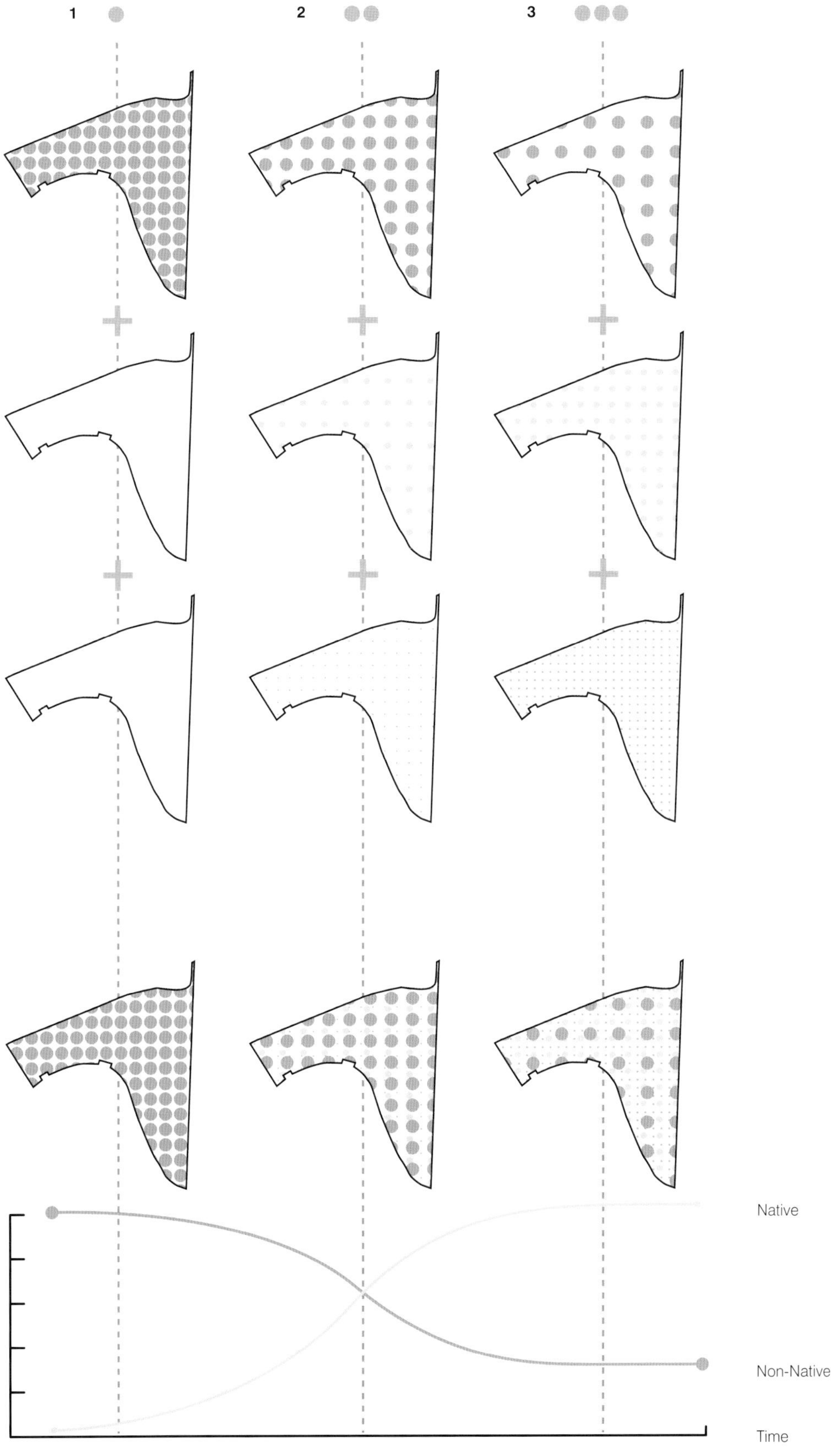

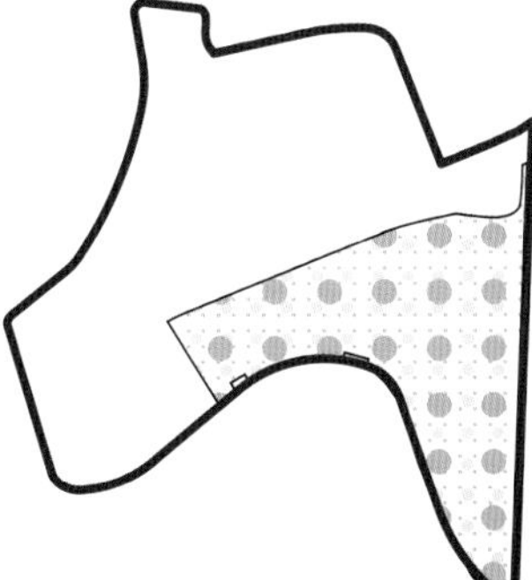

This alternative shows the transformation from eucalyptus to native forest.

Right
Conceptual plan

The conceptual design incorporates some overlapping programmatic elements desired by designers, ecologists, historians and recreation advocates. For example, to balance wildlife viewing opportunities with habitat preservation and enhancement, there is only limited access provided to the river corridor.

Below
Conceptual section

The section through the site indicates the topographic changes and variety of proposed garden types. Concept planning for Fort Scott forced the charrette team to find compromises between approaches that emphasised ecological value and those focused on public access. The proposed solution has a more active and culturally defined upper area with a restored habitat condition in the lower area and visual access from pedestrian bridges and viewing platforms.

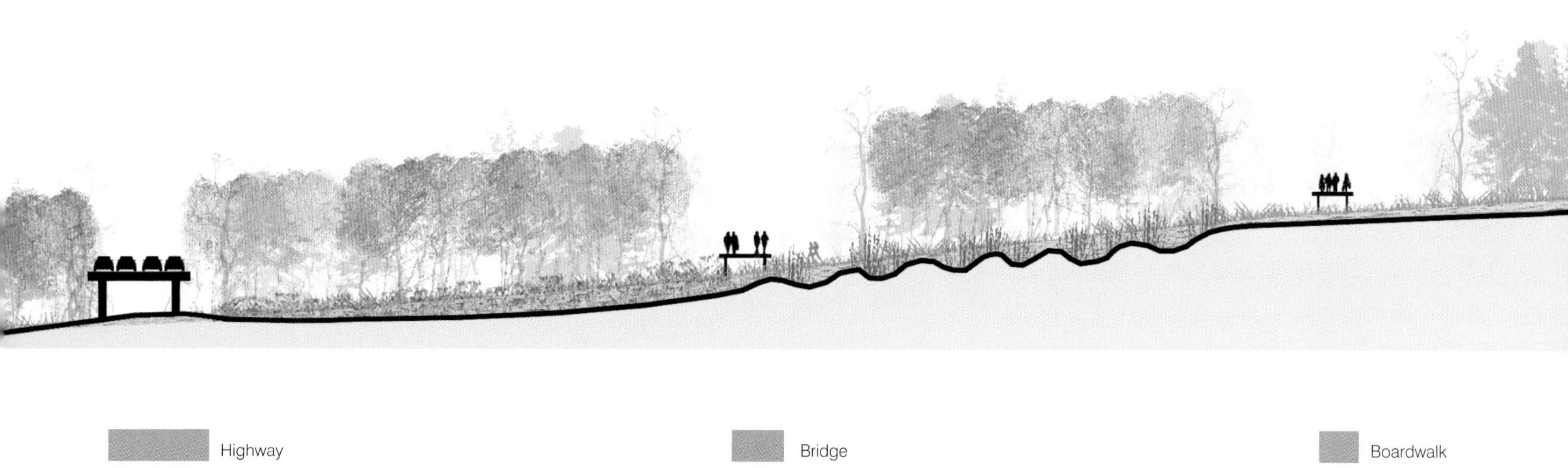

Rendered conceptual plan

1 Transit center (bus station, bike rental)
2 Bio-swales
3 Stewardship and Sustainability Center
4 Nursery areas
5 Cafe overlook
6 Wildlife center
7 Treatment wetlands
8 Ponds/spring/fountain
9 Upland scrub shrub planting
10 Riparian corridor
11 Meandering streams threading through landscape
12 Bridge (pedestrian with vehicular access)
13 Potential Iactical Retreat Center
14 Parking with water storage
15 Redwood grove
16 Wet meadow
17 Historic garden
18 Raised boardwalk
19 Path and drainage channel
20 Historic and community garden
21 Historic forest

Concept
To repair and restore natural processes and functions of a river and wetland system damaged by human activity

Context
Lake and river watershed/alpine

Upper Truckee River and Marsh Restoration Project, California, USA.

Human activity in and around Lake Tahoe and the Upper Truckee River watershed has taken its toll on the landscape. A programme of restoration and management is being established to repair the natural processes and functions of the river and wetlands; preserve and enhance habitat for wildlife and endangered plants; improve water quality and maintain the world-renowned clarity of Lake Tahoe; and provide public access, recreation and environmental education opportunities.

Opposite
Marsh meets the shore

Once a landscape of natural wetlands fringing Lake Tahoe, development has been extensive in this highly desirable location and includes the creation of residential projects such as the Tahoe Keys community and marina seen at the top of this aerial photo.

Environmental Systems

Upper Truckee River and Marsh Restoration Project, California, USA

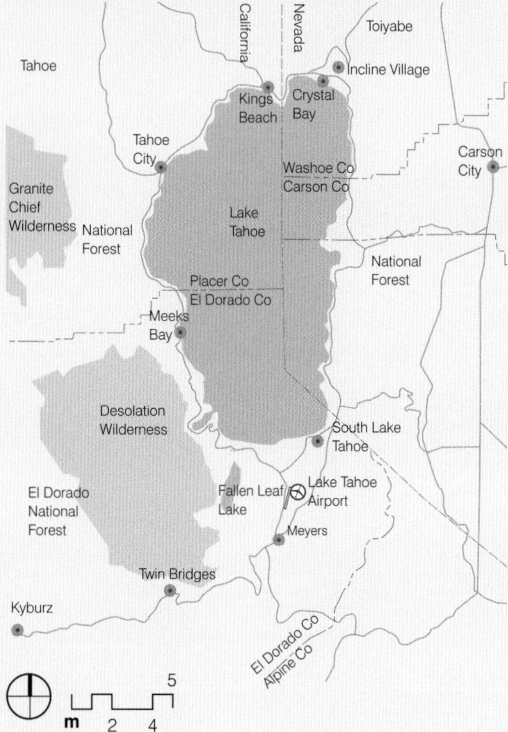

Context

The project area, top, and bottom, the project site shown at the south of Lake Tahoe.

Typical spring snowmelt flows range from 5.66 to 14.1cubic metres per second (cms) and the low flows in the autumn can typically drop to 0.71 cms. Maximum flood flows, often associated with warm spring rains on snowpack, can reach up to over 85 cms. Water levels of Lake Tahoe have a substantial influence on the river's lower reaches. The natural rim elevation of the lake is 1,897 metres and approximately 1.8 metres of additional lake stand is controlled by a dam at the outlet. With operation of the dam, the maximum legal limit is approximately 1,899 metres. When the lake is at or near its upper limit, lake waters will extend nearly two kilometres up the river.

Since the Gold Rush of the 1850s, the Upper Truckee River watershed and Lake Tahoe region have undergone extensive change. For generations people have taken advantage of the natural resources from gold prospecting and logging to fishing, cattle grazing and playing golf. Development in the watershed has been extensive, including commercial and industrial schemes and an airport. Residential projects include the Tahoe Keys, a marina surrounded by a canal-style housing development occupying more than 200 hectares in the centre of the Upper Truckee Marsh, on the southern shore of the lake, which was the largest wetland in the basin. This involved substantial excavation to create the canals and marina, and fill material was pumped into the marsh to create building platforms for the scheme.

The human impact has been costly to the environment with the Tahoe basin losing 75 per cent of its marshes, 50 per cent of its meadows and 30 per cent of its riverside (riparian) habitat. In addition, the famous clarity of Lake Tahoe has been compromised by the runoff of fine sediment and nutrients fed into the lake by rivers, including the Upper Truckee River. And there have been deposits carried in the air. The volume of sediment has been exacerbated by historic logging practices and changes in the environmental systems. The sediment's arrival into the lake waters has been made easy, because remaining marshes have become disconnected from the incised, over-deep river and no longer perform their filtering function.

Concern about the extent of change and impact on natural systems, has led a group of local agencies to seek ways of restoring the wetlands and natural habitat. Since the 1990s, the California Tahoe Conservancy, California Department of General Services' Real Estate Services Division (RESD), Tahoe Regional Planning Agency (TRPA), and US Bureau of Reclamation have been involved in the planning and implementing restoration of the Upper Truckee River, including the lowest reach and surrounding marsh next to Lake Tahoe.

13 project objectives and design directives were identified to help guide planning for restoration of the Upper Truckee River and marsh. These ranged from restoring the natural process of the river and floodplain and restoring and enhancing habitat quality to implementing a mosquito monitoring and control programme for public health and safety.

To realise these objectives and directives, a team of planners and scientists has been preparing and implementing plans for river and wetland restoration, wildlife protection and management, rare plant protection, and trail and interpretive facility development compatible with the area's valuable natural resources. The planning process has included an extensive program of public involvement and an interagency co-ordination process, involving local people and an agency advisory group. In addition, the conservancy assembled a science advisory team to help in investigating key technical issues. Public and agency input has been sought through design charettes and other small group meetings and workshops.

The first phase of work was called the Lower West Side (LWS) Wetland Restoration. This involved the restoration of a marsh area into a functioning floodplain and wetland at the Cove East site near the lake. Here, wetland had been filled during the Tahoe Keys development, but planned homes were never built. The project encompassed a 9.23 hectare portion of the historic Upper Truckee Marsh. Work involved the removal of approximately 67,800 cubic metres of fill to lower the land to the original marsh level, re-contouring and re-vegetation using native plants to restore natural wetland, and reconnection to the river to return to natural hydrologic functions on the site. More than 61,000 cubic metres of sandy fill removed from the site were used to restore a second, former quarry site in the nearby Washoe Meadows State Park. Studies of naturally functioning wetland east of the river produced three target plant community and topographic analogs (i.e. comparison sites) to guide the restoration actions: willow-wet meadow, transitional meadow and wiregrass wetland.

Left
Pollution plume

Sediment washed into the lake's water reduces its clarity.

Project objectives and design directives

A set of project objectives and design directives were identified to help guide planning for restoration of the Upper Truckee River and marsh.

Project objectives

- Restore natural and self-sustaining river and floodplain processes and functions.
- Protect, enhance, and restore naturally functioning habitats.
- Restore and enhance fish and wildlife habitat quality.
- Improve water quality through enhancement of natural physical and biological processes.
- Protect and, where feasible, expand *Rorippa* populations.
- Enhance the quality of public access, access to vistas, and environmental education at the Lower West Side and Cove East Beach.

Design directives

- Avoid increasing flood hazard on adjacent private property.
- Protect natural scenic qualities.
- Design with sensitivity to the site's history and cultural heritage.
- Design the wetland/urban interface to benefit resource needs.
- Take actions that are compatible with upper watershed conditions and activities.
- Recognise and plan, through adaptive management, for change over time.
- Implement a mosquito monitoring and control programme for public health and safety.

At the completion of the works large rubber water bladders, set across the openings of the site to the Upper Truckee River during construction, were kept in place until wetland vegetation had been sufficiently reestablished to stabilise site soils and to avoid a surge of sediment into Lake Tahoe once river flow entered the site. The bladders were removed after a couple of years allowing the high flows of water into the restored wetland over the river banks and from the lake.

Monitoring of the site has shown the success of the Lower West Side fill removal and re-vegetation approach, using nearby analog sites as guidance. The lowering of the site to the target elevation was also refined in the field when organic soils were encountered during excavation, indicating that the surface of the covered former wetland had been reached. The restored elevation placed the landscape in proper relationship with the depth of groundwater, its frequency of river flows, and the extent of lake water backup to reestablish a functioning wetland habitat. The rapid rate of re-vegetation has exceeded pre-project expectations.

The second phase of restoration is planned for a conservancy-owned site of almost 250 hectares comprising the Upper Truckee Marsh, Upper Truckee River and Trout Creek, running from US Highway 50 to the lake. This lowest reach of the river was straightened and moved in the 1800s from its historic meandering route and placed in a linear, constructed channel. As a result, the river no longer overtops its banks at a frequency that would enhance the wetland habitat functions of the adjacent marsh. Additionally, the area has experienced considerable undirected public access and recreation, which has disturbed wildlife and damaged the landscape.

Above
Wetlands

Looking south from the lake inland, the beauty of the wetlands fringed by development and mountains.

Opposite
Restoring marshland

Restoration works in the marshlands, top left and right, have included removing topsoil to lower the land to original marsh levels, re-contouring and re-vegetation using native plants, and reconnection to the river to return the natural hydrologic functions on the site.

Centre left and right, Lake Tahoe is the only location in the US for the Tahoe yellow cress (*Rorippa subumbellata*), which is a candidate for listing under the US Endangered Species Act. The diminutive ground cover plant, with yellow flowers is located on Tahoe's beaches and other nearby sandy soil areas that dot the lake's margins.

Bottom left and right, lakeside wetlands. With headwaters in the granite-dominated High Sierra, the Upper Truckee River flows through forests, grazing land, a golf course, and the urban areas of Meyers and the City of South Lake Tahoe before reaching the lake. The river drains the largest watershed of Lake Tahoe, covering over 90 square kilometres, providing the largest volume of runoff to the lake, averaging 110 million cubic metres annually. River flow originates from snowmelt, direct rainfall, runoff, and groundwater sources. The river conveys sediment and nutrients from the single largest watershed.

Overleaf
Jewel of the Sierra

Lake Tahoe is one of the deepest and largest alpine lakes in the world, and is known as the Jewel of the Sierra. At more than 500 metres deep, Tahoe is the second deepest lake in the United States, and the tenth deepest in the world. Its surface area is 495 square kilometres. Lake Tahoe is located on the borders of the states of California and Nevada, bound on the west by the Sierra Nevada and in the east by two mountain chains that are part of the Carson Range. The Upper Truckee River is critically important to the clarity and water quality of the lake. Its famous clarity reached a peak depth of up to 30.5 metres, but has since deteriorated to 22.8 metres in recent years. This has been attributed to fine sediment and excessive nutrient discharges.

A multifaceted restoration and natural resources management plan is being developed to address project objectives and alternative restoration approaches are undergoing environmental review. The range of river and wetland improvements under consideration include the reestablishment of the natural river morphology and increased wetting of the floodplain meadow in appropriate locations. Narrowing the channel and elevating the bed through channel aggradation is one approach under consideration. Grade-control structures (i.e. hard points to stabilise the riverbed elevation) would be used to accumulate sediment in the proper locations. Reconstructing a new channel alignment at the proper elevation using historic channel patterns and the evaluation of soil conditions as guides is also being considered. Diverting the channelised river into the central portion of the marsh using a short pilot channel without complete reconstruction of the river is a third option that would allow the streamflow to find its own path in an area where traces of the old channel still exist. The final option involves the excavation of a lowered terrace around the current river alignment for construction of an inset floodplain. Other restoration features in the plan include adjustment of the bed elevation at the river's mouth, which became over deep because of incision by the straightened river. The re-vegetation and re-contouring of the site's dune and forest areas and the re-establishment of a lagoon connected to the river behind the barrier beach on the lakeshore are also planned. These physical restoration actions are being supplemented by a natural resources management plan that includes maintenance, monitoring, and adaptive management responses.

The restoration plan area includes an important, existing public access route to Lake Tahoe at Cove East Beach and other portions of property that contain significant sensitive resources where public access can be detrimental. The plan calls for improved trails, interpretive facilities, and observation viewpoints to maintain and enhance public access to Cove East Beach. Elsewhere, wildlife protection is proposed by managing and directing public use away from sensitive resources. These facilities could include a trail-end and viewpoint destination in a non-sensitive location while discouraging trails into wildlife habitats or sensitive plant species locations. These protection features are also being used to discourage public access to portions of the project beach that supports the largest populations of the Tahoe yellow cress, a rare plant that only occurs around the margins of Lake Tahoe. The twin goal is to diminish the public's desire to access areas where important resources can be harmed and, instead, provide a high-quality user experience in less sensitive areas.

Following the completion of the environmental review process, the second phase of the river and wetland restoration will undergo detailed design development and construction. Because of the short construction season in this alpine setting (May to October), implementation of the second phase of the restoration plan is expected to require up to four years.

Concept

Planning long-range water supply in response to global climate change

Context

Rural, urban/Mediterranean

Water Supply Management Program 2040, California, USA.

The twin pressures of increased demand for water and climate change are creating the need for more innovative water supply planning. In California, the East Bay Municipal Utility District (EBMUD) has taken a unique approach to providing clean water to more than 20 cities in the years to 2040.

Opposite
The East Bay

Innovative solutions are sought to answer increased customer demand for water and the challenges of a changing climate. This image shows the Oakland waterfront, part of the extensive urban area, with a population of more than 1.3 million, served by the water and wastewater services supplier, the East Bay Municipal Utility District.

Water Supply Management Program 2040, California, USA

Above
Delivery system

Shown in its context, EBMUD Mokelumne aqueducts crossing the delta.

Opposite

A water-demand study of the EBMUD in 2040 depicting land use descriptions including the range of residential densities, schools, offices and commercial uses, petroleum refineries and parks.

Traditionally, water utilities have responded to growing demands for water by increasing supplies. But recognising that water shortages are likely to increase in future years, the regional agency, East Bay Municipal Utility District (EBMUD), wanted to explore its options by reviewing its water supply management programme. The work included projecting the future demand for water and assessing the effectiveness of water conservation programmes, recycled water opportunities, using groundwater storage, water transfers, enlarging existing reservoirs or building new ones, and desalination. The plan for the future was to be designed as a package of solutions that would encourage careful water use, identify new water sources, and increase storage opportunities. Throughout the review process, community liaison and public meetings played a key role in helping to identify future programme objectives and solutions.

EBMUD is a regional agency providing water supply and wastewater services to an estimated 1.3 million people along with industrial, commercial, and institutional water users in the East Bay region of the San Francisco Bay Area. The service area of approximately 85,700 hectares and its water system serves 20 cities and 15 unincorporated communities in Alameda and Contra Costa counties. The district supplies an average of 833 million litres per day of potable water in non-drought years. The principal raw water source of these supplies is the Mokelumne River in the Sierra Nevada, with a diversion point at Pardee Reservoir in Calaveras and Amador counties. In an average year, approximately 90 per cent of the water used by EBMUD customers comes from the Mokelumne River watershed. EBMUD has water rights that allow for delivery of a maximum of 1,230 million litres per day from the river, subject to the availability of river runoff and the senior water rights of other users.

Over the long term, approximately ten per cent of EBMUD's water supply is provided by runoff into its local reservoirs located in the East Bay. However, during dry years, evaporation can be equal to runoff, resulting in no yield from this local supply.

EBMUD's existing water supply management programme was prepared by EDAW and adopted in 1993. However, in the light of new pressures, primarily climate change and increasing water demands, the 1993 programme required updating. The primary purpose of the Water Supply Management Program 2040 is to identify and recommend solutions to meet dry-year water needs through to 2040. Carried out in a number of stages, the work has been based on a broad review of existing supply and demand, including a projection of increasing demand; an assessment of the district's drought management programme; an assessment of the potential for groundwater storage and recovery programmes; integration of new water supply connections; and an assessment of the security of aqueducts that cross the Sacramento/San Joaquin Delta. An assessment of the impacts of global climate change on the district's water supply and demand has also been included in this work.

Having built up an understanding of the existing situation and the available supply options, work began on compiling a variety of water supply portfolios. The idea was that each portfolio would meet the anticipated dry-year water demand, but that it would be achieved in different ways. The development of a range of portfolios provided the opportunity to explore different types of solutions. Each portfolio was composed of a collection of component parts, or building blocks, such as drought-year rationing (this is usually voluntary and includes not watering lawns or washing cars and cutting back on frequent use of appliances such as dishwashers), conservation, recycled water, and various supplemental supply components. Recycled water can be used in place of potable water to reduce demand for applications such as irrigation and industrial processes. Drought-year rationing (or water-use restrictions) is a policy matter that, when implemented, results in the short-term reduction of water use by district customers.

More than a dozen portfolios were assessed for operational feasibility, the volume of water delivered during the worst-case drought, the frequency and severity of required drought-year rationing, the resulting cost of such rationing, and the cost of each portfolio in terms of capital outlay, operations and maintenance. Results from this stage of assessment were used to refine the portfolios to five primary portfolios, each with a different emphasis. For example, Portfolio A emphasised a reliance on the use of groundwater basins for storage in wet years which could be drawn on in dry periods, while Portfolio B emphasised the development of a diverse range of regional partnership projects. Other primary portfolio themes included local system reliance, lower carbon footprint and heavy reliance on recycled water and transfers. All five primary portfolios were taken forward for analysis in the Water Supply Management Program 2040.

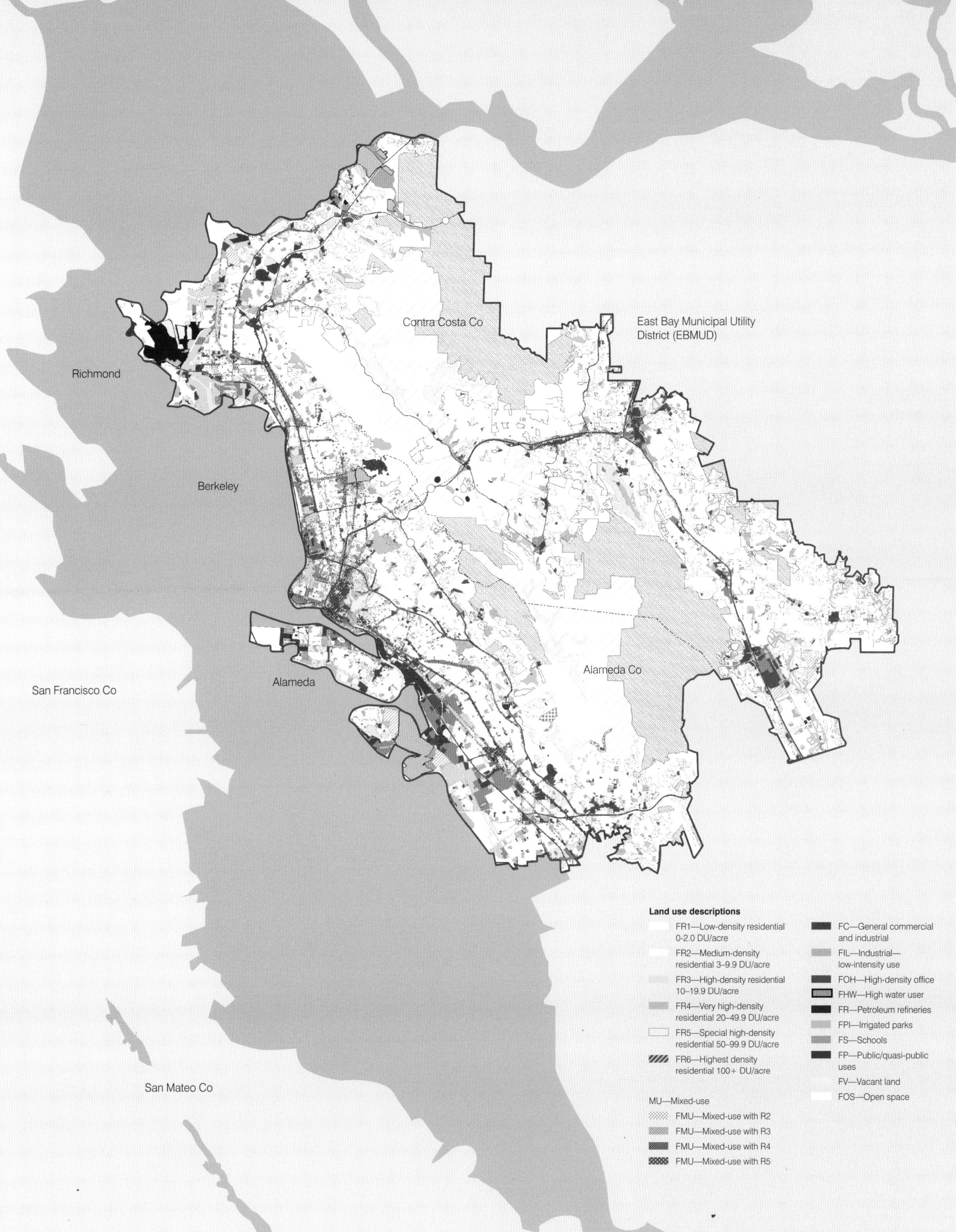
Contra Costa Co
East Bay Municipal Utility District (EBMUD)
Richmond
Berkeley
Alameda
Alameda Co
San Francisco Co
San Mateo Co
Land use descriptions
FR1—Low-density residential 0-2.0 DU/acre
FR2—Medium-density residential 3–9.9 DU/acre
FR3—High-density residential 10–19.9 DU/acre
FR4—Very high-density residential 20–49.9 DU/acre
FR5—Special high-density residential 50–99.9 DU/acre
FR6—Highest density residential 100+ DU/acre
MU—Mixed-use
FMU—Mixed-use with R2
FMU—Mixed-use with R3
FMU—Mixed-use with R4
FMU—Mixed-use with R5
FC—General commercial and industrial
FIL—Industrial—low-intensity use
FOH—High-density office
FHW—High water user
FR—Petroleum refineries
FPI—Irrigated parks
FS—Schools
FP—Public/quasi-public uses
FV—Vacant land
FOS—Open space

Table of supplemental supply scoring. This technique was used to translate the district goals into performance criteria in four categories: Operations, Engineering, Legal and Institutional; Economic; Public Health, Safety and Community; and Environmental. The darker the colour, the better response the component had to the criteria (dark blue = good). Any component that scored low on more than two criteria was eliminated from further consideration. Nine supplemental supply components were brought forward for inclusion in the portfolios as indicated by the arrows on the right.

Ability to meet the criteria	
H	High
H/M	High/Medium
M	Medium
M/L	Medium/Low
L	Low
[L]	Hold from further consideration

Operations, Engineering, Legal, and Institutional Criteria

- 1. Provide water supply reliability.
  - 1. Minimize the vulnerability and risk of disruptions.
  - 2. Minimize disruptions in water service during construction.
  - 3. Maximize the system's operational flexibility.
  - 4. Maximize implementation and phasing flexibility.
  - 5. Minimize the institutional and legal complexities and barriers.
- 2. Optimize current water right entitlements.
  - 1. Maximize efficient use of current water right entitlements.
- 3. Promote District involvement in regional, sustainable solutions.
  - 1. Maximize partnerships and regional solutions.

Economic Criteria

- 1. Minimize cost to District customers.
  - 1. Maximize use of lowest cost water supply options.
  - 2. Minimize the financial cost to the District of meeting customer demands for given level of system reliability.
- 2. Minimize drought impact to District customers.
  - 3. Minimize customer water shortage costs and District supply augmentation costs.
- 3. Maximize positive impact to local economy.
  - 4. Maximize local water supply options.

Location	Code	Component Name\Criteria	OE 1.1	OE 1.2	OE 1.3	OE 1.4	OE 1.5	OE 2.1	OE 3.1	Econ 1.1	Econ 1.2	Econ 2.3	Econ 3.4
State	SUP-04	Semitropic Groundwater Bank	M	H/M	H/M	M	[L]		M	See Dry Year Unit Cost ($/AF) Cost Column	Utilize at Portfolio Level	Utilize at Portfolio Level	L
Central Valley	SUP-05	Bixler/Delta Diversion	L	H/M	L	M	[L]		L				M/L
	SUP-06	Duck Creek Reservoir	M/L	M	M	L	[L]		M				L
	SUP-07	Groundwater Banking/Exchange (Sacramento Basin)	M	H/M	H	H	M		H				L
	SUP-08	Groundwater Banking/Exchange (San Joaquin Basin)	M/L	M	H/M	H	M/L		H				L
	SUP-25	Northern California Water Transfers	M/L	H	H	H	H		M				L
Local — East Bay Service Area	SUP-09	Bayside Groundwater Project	H	H/M	H	H/M	H/M		L				H
	SUP-10	Bollinger Canyon Reservoir	H	H/M	H	L	[L]		L				H
	SUP-11	Buckhorn Canyon Reservoir	H	H/M	H	L	M/L		L				H
	SUP-12	Cull Canyon Reservoir	H	H/M	H	L	[L]		L				H
	SUP-13	Curry Canyon Reservoir	H	H/M	H	L	[L]		L				H
	SUP-16	Low Energy Application for Desalination (LEAD) at C&H Sugar	M	H	L	L	H/M		M				H/M
	SUP-18	Regional Desalination Project	H/M	H/M	H	M	M/L		H				H/M
Upcountry	SUP-20	Enlarged Camanche Reservoir	M/L	M/L	M	L	M/L		M/L				L
	SUP-21	Inter-Regional Conjunctive Use Project (IRCUP)	M/L	M	H/M	H/M	M/L		H				L
	SUP-22	Enlarge Lower Bear Reservoir	M/L	H	M/L	L	M		H				L
	SUP-23	Middle Bar Reservoir	M/L	M	M	L	[L]		M/L				L
	SUP-24	Enlarged Pardee Reservoir	M/L	M	H/M	L	M		M/L				L

Criteria	Objective	Sub-objectives																			
	EBMUD Dry Year Unit Cost ($/AF)		Cost				1,900		630	890		710			2,600	1,900		1,200	840		730
	EBMUD Dry Year Yield (MGD)		Yield				4.2		45	9		42			1.5	20		17	2.2		51
Environmental Criteria	4. Promote recreational opportunities.	1. Minimize adverse impacts to recreation resources, designated parklands, designated wilderness areas, or lands permanently dedicated to open space, particularly rare opportunities and ADA access that are not found in other parts of the region. 2. Provide recreational benefits.		M/L	L	M/L	M/L	M/L	M/L	M/L	L	L	L	L	L	L	H/M	M/L	H/M	L	H/M
	3. Minimize carbon footprint.	4. Maximize CO2-efficient and renewable energy use. (+/- CO2 tons/year)		M	M	L	M	M	M	M	M	M	M	M	M	M	H	M	H	H	H
		1. Minimize short term and long term greenhouse gas emissions from construction. 2. Maximize energy efficiency associated with operations & maintenance. 3. Maximize contributions to AB 32 goals.		L	M	M	M/L	M/L	M	M	M	H/M	H/M	H/M	H	L	H/M	M/L	H/M	H/M	H/M
	2. Preserve and protect biological resources.	1. Minimize adverse impacts on the environment. 2. Minimize construction and operation effects on environmentally sensitive resources. 3. Maintain populations or known habitat of state or federally listed plant or wildlife species at or above sustaining levels. 4. Minimize the reduction of riverine habitat of listed fish species and adverse affects to native fish and other native aquatic organisms. 5. Minimize impacts to wetlands & other jurisdictional waters of the United States; alterations to water flow in waterways and reservoirs/lakes, and habitat loss for sensitive species, pristine areas and special habitat features. 6. Maximize benefits to fish, including natural production of anadromous fish; and the likelihood of meeting federal and state ambient water quality standards to protect natural resources.		[L]	[L]	[L]	H/M	H/M	H/M	H/M	M/L	M/L	M/L	M/L	M/L	M/L	[L]	H/M	M	[L]	M
	1. Preserve and protect the environment for future generations.	1. Maximize long-term sustainability by applying best management and sustainability principles.		H	M/L	M/L	H	H	H	H/M	M	M	M	M	M	M/L	H/M	H	H/M	M	H/M
Public Health, Safety & Community Criteria	4. Maximize security of infrastructure and water supply.	1. Minimize the risk of death or injury from the failure of a program component in an earthquake or flood or from other causes. 2. Maximize the protection of supply sources and associated infrastructure. [Portfolio]		Utilize at Portfolio Level																	
	3. Minimize risks to public health and safety.	1. Minimize disproportionate public health or economic impact to minority or low-income populations.		H/M	H	M	H	H	M	M	M	H/M	M/L	[L]	H/M	M	[L]	H/M	M	M	H/M
	2. Minimize adverse sociocultural impacts.	1. Minimize adverse impacts to cultural resources, including important archaeological, historical, & other cultural sites. 2. Minimize short-term community impacts. 3. Minimize long-term adverse community impacts 4. Minimize adverse social effects 5. Minimize conflicts with existing and planned facilities, utilities and transportation facilities.		H/M	H/M	M	H/M	H/M	H/M	H/M	[L]	M/L	[L]	[L]	H/M	M	M	H/M	M/L	M/L	M
	1. Ensure the high quality of the District's water supply.	1. Minimize potential adverse impacts to the public health of District customers. 2. Maximize use of water from the best available source.		M	L	M/L	M	H/M	H/M	M	H/M	H/M	H/M	H/M	H	H/M	H	H/M	H	H	H

Water supply portfolios

Building a portfolio from project components

Components			
Conservation level	Rationing	Recycling level	Supp. supply
A	0%	1	1
B	10%	2	2
C	15%	3	3
D	20%		4
E	25%		5
			6
			25

—— Example portfolio 1

The five primary portfolios were then examined more closely. Results from integrated water supply computer modelling highlighted the strengths and weaknesses of each portfolio and this information contributed to the development of the final preferred portfolio as a robust and flexible plan for EBMUD's 2040 water supply reliability needs. The preferred portfolio is a flexible programme that:

- Meets projected growth in customer demand through aggressive water conservation and recycled water development.
- Lowers customer drought-year rationing burdens during an extended drought significantly from the district's current policies through development of new supplementary water supply initiatives.

Under the preferred portfolio, rationing, conservation, and recycled water use combined would provide sufficient water to meet normal demands through to the year 2040. However, those programmes alone would not be sufficient to meet year 2040 water demands during a prolonged drought. Supplemental water sources, beyond those already planned or constructed, must be developed to ensure reliability during a multiple-year drought.

The components that comprise the preferred portfolio include ten per cent drought-year rationing, high levels of recycled water and conservation, as well as a selection of possible supplemental supply components which could include groundwater banking, water transfers from northern California, desalination, and enlarging the Lower Bear and/or Pardee reservoirs. Maximum levels of conservation (39 MGD) and recycled water (11 MGD) were chosen to maintain EBMUD's aggressive policies for overall demand management. Meanwhile, the drought-year rationing level of ten per cent was chosen to allow flexibility in an emergency or to respond to the many unknown factors in the future. Supplementary supply components will also be needed to keep drought-year rationing at a lower level and to meet the need for water in drought years.

The next step for the preferred portfolio was to develop a series of different scenarios for how and when the components could be implemented to ensure that the need for water is met over the planning period. EBMUD's approach to carrying out the preferred portfolio is to develop the supplemental water supply components that are most feasible and environmentally responsible according to the circumstances that arise during the 2010–2040 planning period. Many of these circumstances—impacts of long-term climate change, funding availability, political will and success, legal and institutional hurdles, and resolution of technical issues—cannot be predicted with certainty. The district's supplemental water project planning response must remain flexible so that if a project were to encounter a development hurdle that prevents its advancement, an alternative would need to be found.

The strategy is based on being open and flexible to pursue different components based on which are the most feasible for implementation. For example, if short-term Northern California water transfers are obtained early in the planning period, this will provide time for conservation, recycled water, and other supplementary supply components to be developed. In addition, pushing the pursuit of recycled water projects and conservation to the maximum will offset the need for supplementary supply projects.

High levels of conservation and recycled water will also offer the benefit of taking pressure off of the Mokelumne River, providing continued opportunity for preserving and enhancing downstream aquatic habitat and recreation opportunities on the river. This flexible strategy for water management planning will enable EBMUD to adapt to unknown future conditions including global climate change, pursue the components that are gaining the best results, and respond to emergency conditions.

Left
Pardee Reservoir and spillway

Pardee Dam and Reservoir provides storage for municipal water supply, hydropower generation, and public recreation. EBMUD stores water in Pardee Reservoir before it is transported to the service area.

Above
Pardee Reservoir

Aerial image, top, showing the existing Pardee Reservoir, and below, showing the proposed new increased inundation area marked in light blue. One possible supplemental supply source is enlarging the Pardee Reservoir.

Overleaf
Water supply system map and the Preferred Portfolio

This map geographically depicts where the preferred portfolio components are located throughout the EBMUD service area and Sierra Nevada. The preferred portfolio is designed to be robust, flexible, diverse, and to pursue projects on multiple, parallel tracks in order to respond flexibly to an uncertain water future. The EBMUD area, shown left, in the wider context of the Mokelumne River watershed and supply system. On average, approximately 90 per cent of the water used by the district customers comes from the Mokelumne River watershed where EBMUD has water rights for delivery of up to 325 MGD (1,230 million litres per day) from the river, subject to the availability of river runoff and the senior water rights of other users. Water travels approximately 145 kilometres through an aqueduct system to the service area.

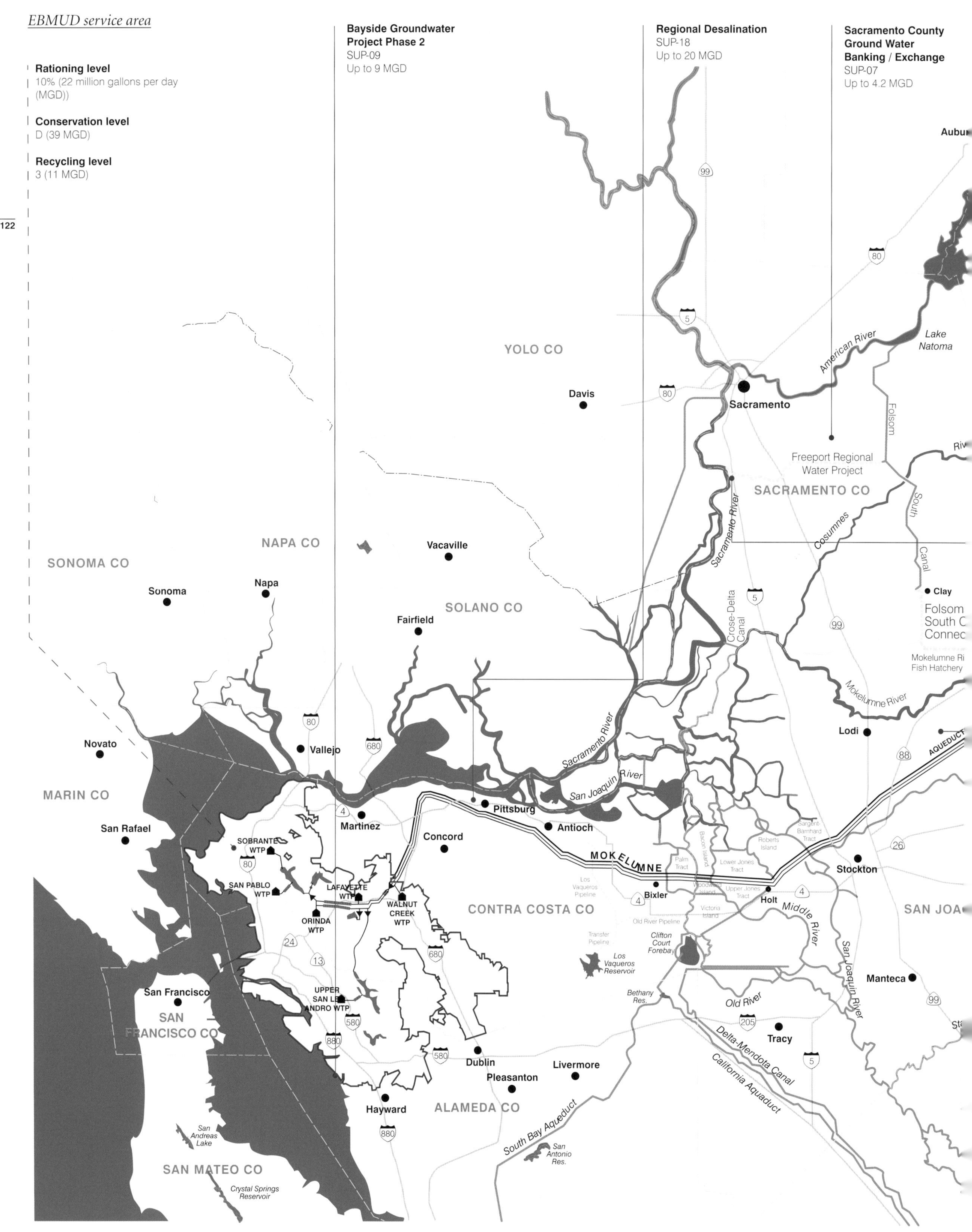
EBMUD service area
Rationing level
10% (22 million gallons per day (MGD))
Conservation level
D (39 MGD)
Recycling level
3 (11 MGD)
Bayside Groundwater Project Phase 2
SUP-09
Up to 9 MGD
Regional Desalination
SUP-18
Up to 20 MGD
Sacramento County Ground Water Banking / Exchange
SUP-07
Up to 4.2 MGD
Freeport Regional Water Project
YOLO CO
SACRAMENTO CO
NAPA CO
SONOMA CO
SOLANO CO
MARIN CO
CONTRA COSTA CO
SAN FRANCISCO CO
ALAMEDA CO
SAN MATEO CO
Davis
Sacramento
Lake Natoma
American River
Folsom
South Canal
Cosumnes
Sacramento River
Cross-Delta Canal
Clay
Mokelumne River Fish Hatchery
Mokelumne River
Lodi
Vacaville
Fairfield
Sonoma
Napa
Novato
Vallejo
San Rafael
Martinez
Pittsburg
Antioch
Concord
San Joaquin River
MOKELUMNE
AQUEDUCT
SOBRANTE WTP
SAN PABLO WTP
LAFAYETTE WTP
ORINDA WTP
WALNUT CREEK WTP
UPPER SAN LEANDRO WTP
San Francisco
Bixler
Holt
Stockton
Middle River
Old River Pipeline
Transfer Pipeline
Clifton Court Forebay
Los Vaqueros Reservoir
Bethany Res.
Old River
Tracy
Manteca
Delta-Mendota Canal
California Aqueduct
South Bay Aqueduct
San Antonio Res.
Dublin
Pleasanton
Livermore
Hayward
San Andreas Lake
Crystal Springs Reservoir

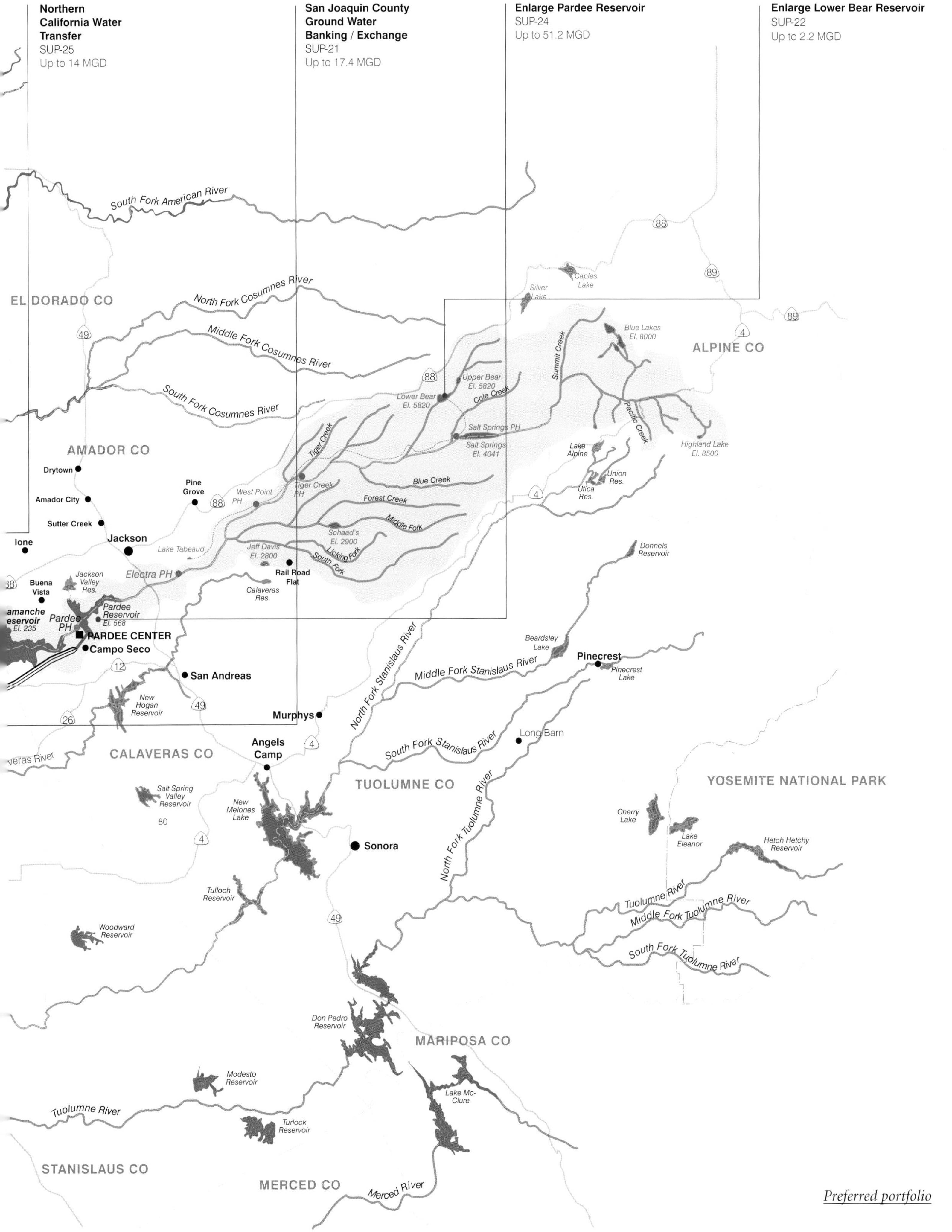

Northern California Water Transfer
SUP-25
Up to 14 MGD

San Joaquin County Ground Water Banking / Exchange
SUP-21
Up to 17.4 MGD

Enlarge Pardee Reservoir
SUP-24
Up to 51.2 MGD

Enlarge Lower Bear Reservoir
SUP-22
Up to 2.2 MGD

South Fork American River
EL DORADO CO
North Fork Cosumnes River
Middle Fork Cosumnes River
South Fork Cosumnes River
AMADOR CO
ALPINE CO
Blue Lakes El. 8000
Upper Bear El. 5820
Lower Bear El. 5820
Salt Springs PH
Salt Springs El. 4041
Pacific Creek
Highland Lake El. 8500
Union Res.
Blue Creek
Forest Creek
Middle Fork
Schaad's El. 2900
Licking Fork
South Fork
Jeff Davis El. 2800
Rail Road Flat
Calaveras Res.
Drytown
Amador City
Sutter Creek
Pine Grove
West Point PH
Tiger Creek PH
Jackson
Ione
Lake Tabeaud
Electra PH
Buena Vista
Jackson Valley Res.
Pardee Reservoir El. 568
Pardee PH
Camanche Reservoir El. 235
PARDEE CENTER
Campo Seco
San Andreas
New Hogan Reservoir
Murphys
Angels Camp
CALAVERAS CO
Calaveras River
Donnels Reservoir
Beardsley Lake
Pinecrest
Pinecrest Lake
Middle Fork Stanislaus River
North Fork Stanislaus River
South Fork Stanislaus River
Long Barn
TUOLUMNE CO
YOSEMITE NATIONAL PARK
North Fork Tuolumne River
Cherry Lake
Lake Eleanor
Hetch Hetchy Reservoir
Salt Spring Valley Reservoir
New Melones Lake
Sonora
Tulloch Reservoir
Woodward Reservoir
Tuolumne River
Middle Fork Tuolumne River
South Fork Tuolumne River
Don Pedro Reservoir
MARIPOSA CO
Modesto Reservoir
Lake McClure
Turlock Reservoir
Tuolumne River
STANISLAUS CO
MERCED CO
Merced River

Concept
Ancient technology given a new life

Context
Cedar Creek: Rural/arid
Black Law: Rural/temperate

Cedar Creek Wind Farm, Colorado, USA and Black Law Wind Farm, Scotland, UK.

With their majestic presence and impressive capacity to produce clean energy, wind turbines are the preferred choice for many governments and energy producers in the drive to reduce carbon emissions. However, to maximise production potential and minimise local opposition, the siting and design of wind farms requires increasingly careful assessment and planning.

Opposite
Epic scale

Elegant turbines standing on their 80 metres tall posts at the Cedar Creek Wind Farm on the broad, open plains of northern Colorado, a site selected because this was the most windy area in the state.

In context

In its spectacular ridge-top setting, the wind farm when running at full production is estimated to reduce carbon emissions by 900,000 tonnes per annum compared with fossil-fuel based energy generation. Along with promoting wind farms, the state's New Energy Economy also includes encouragement for solar-power facilities along with untapped geothermal and biomass resources.

Witn increasing interest in the generation of clean energy, wind farms are being developed around the world. Here, examples from the USA and UK demonstrate how installations can be made in very different locations.

Cedar Creek Wind Farm, Colorado, USA

Set in the wide open plains of northern Colorado, and occupying a site of 13,000 hectares outside the town of Grover, the Cedar Creek Wind Farm is built on an epic scale. One of the largest single wind-powered facilities in the USA when it was completed, it comprises almost 300 turbines striding across the flatlands with the capacity to produce 300 megawatts of electricity to serve the needs of 90,000 homes.

The expansive site for the Cedar Creek development in northern Colorado was selected after research revealed this location was distinguished by the fact that it has the highest average annual wind speed in the entire state. The winds, predominantly from the north-west, accelerate in speed as they encounter the terrain of the project area. Settlers in the area have for generations made good use of the wind power with an assortment of windmills, some of which can still be seen in the landscape. As the eleventh most windy state in the USA, and with the goal of producing 20 per cent renewable energy by 2020, Colorado has a policy of capitalising on this free resource and has evolved a renewable energy policy called the New Energy Economy.

At the outset of the project, proposals for the Cedar Creek Wind Farm were for a clean energy facility including 300 turbines, up to three substations and an operations and maintenance facility along with a 120 kilometres, 230 kilovolt electric transmission system, and new switching system that enabled the facility to connect with the existing transmission system and deliver power into the electric grid. The preferred choice of turbine was a three-blade version, in a mix of 1,000 and 1,500 kilowatt capacity machines standing on 80 metre tubular steel posts and spaced almost 230 metres apart to catch the best of the wind.

To accommodate the complex requirements of the proposed scheme work began with site assessments and an opportunities and constraints analysis to prepare a comprehensive application for the client. To determine the best site for the turbines and route for the transmission line, the opportunities and constraints analysis included detailed resource evaluation and mapping. This process also evaluated the potential impacts of the project including land use and natural resources, cultural resources and effects on the environment. A wildlife habitat assessment was also completed for the wind farm site and the transmission line corridor. Among the benefits to arise from this analysis is that it produces a thorough understanding of the site and conditions which helps in answering questions raised during the consultation and approvals process. Additional work at this stage also includes developing visual simulations and materials for the consultation phase.

Public consultation was extensive and along with meetings and workshops to discuss plans, explanatory materials were produced to explain clearly how the wind farm would work and contribute significant environmental benefits for the state. At full production it was estimated that the wind farm could reduce carbon emissions by 900,000 tonnes per annum compared with fossil-fuel based energy generation.

Site planning

GIS image showing the locations of turbines as black dots. The green boundary shows the extent of the planning area.

Hagshaw Hill (27,836m)
Nutberry Hill (27,502m)
Hagshaw Hill Extension (27,275m)
Dungavel (30,913m)
Bogside (7,425r
Black Law (1,064m)

Above
In situ

A cross-section of the landscape of Black Law and its environs with turbines. In red is the proposed extension to the wind farm.

Right
Repairing the scars

The 1,400 hectare wind farm site included a large area of land disturbed and disfigured by open-cast coal mining. Remediation of the land and natural habitats was an important element in securing planning permission.

Bottom left and right
Landforms

Two visualisations showing the undulating topography of the hilltop site and proposed turbine positions.

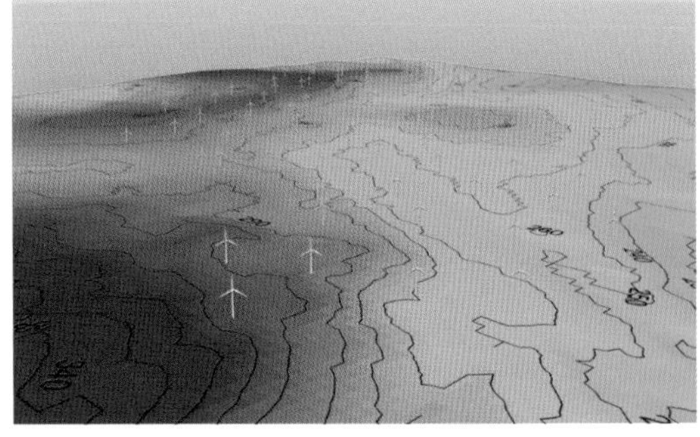

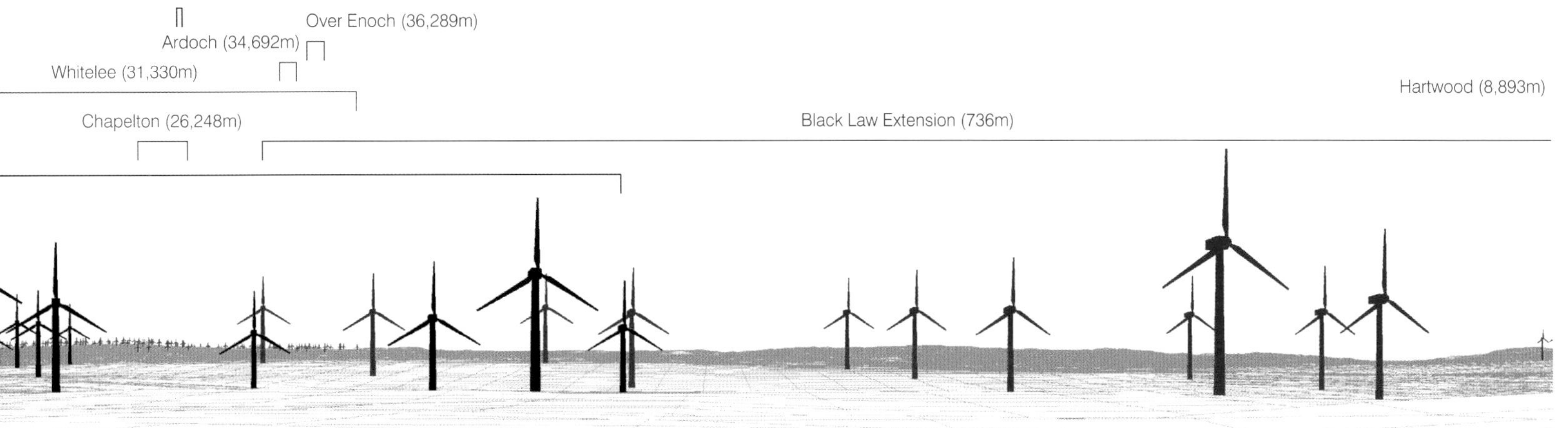

Black Law Wind Farm, Scotland, UK

Meanwhile, in the UK, and set in an exposed moorland area of the central Scottish plateau just over 30 kilometres west of Edinburgh, the Black Law Wind Farm has been completed. Its 42 turbines have the capacity to produce 97 megawatts of energy and meet the energy needs of 70,000 homes. It is anticipated that the facility saves 200,000 tonnes of carbon dioxide emissions a year. When complete it was the largest onshore wind farm of its kind in the UK. Here the additional challenge was to construct a wind farm on the site of a former open-cast coal mine, along with moorland, forest and pasture.

Work on proposals included a capacity assessment to gauge the suitability of the 1,400 hectare site, contribution to the layout design of the wind farm, a landscape and visual impact assessment to provide accurate visualisations of how the completed project would be viewed in the landscape and its potential impacts, a restoration plan for the disused coal mine, wildlife habitat surveys and enhancement and extensive public consultation.

The success of the proposals achieving planning permission was rooted in the work involving remediation of the land and improving local wildlife habitat for indigenous species including badgers, otter, water vole, curlew, lapwing, snipe, black grouse and the long-eared owl. Working closely with organisations including Scotland's Royal Society for the Protection of Birds, Scottish Natural Heritage, the local authorities and landowners, work on the land has included transforming the open-cast mine site as shallow wetlands, replacing conifer plantations with deciduous woodland, grassland and blanket bog. Within a year of regeneration it was possible to see the establishment of typical upland plant species including cotton grass, heather, blaeberry and bog cranberry.

The success of the original wind farm has led to permission being sought for an extension comprising a further 12 turbines bringing total energy production capacity to just over 142 megawatts.

3 Regeneration

“Cities and their surrounding regions are now widely recognised

as important economic drivers—vital to future prosperity.

In the UK, the Manchester city region has been recognised by the government as a national economic powerhouse. City regions contain the major centres of business, high-value employment and opportunities for wealth creation. They sit at the heart of travel networks, provide a rich source of creativity and innovation, and are home to many top educational institutions and cultural assets. There is, however, much more we can do to unlock their economic potential and to ensure that the benefits of wealth creation are shared more widely among our communities.

Sir Howard Bernstein
Chief Executive, Manchester City Council

Concept
Improved public realm as a catalyst for regeneration

Context
Urban/temperate

Manchester City Centre Masterplan and Piccadilly Gardens Masterplan and Landscape Design, Manchester, UK.

Following a devastating terrorist bomb attack in Manchester's centre, the city turned adversity into an opportunity to transform its urban core, and refocus the place as a major European city and regional economic hub for business and retailing.

Opposite
Vision

Sketch showing the area of the city centre most damaged by the bomb blast along with early ideas on how to re-energise and reconnect the public spaces.

CULTURAL DESTINATION
SPECIAL EVENT
MAJOR OPEN SPACE / SCULPTURE
WESTERN GATEWAY
MAJOR RETAIL STREET
"NEW CATHEDRAL" STREET
EXTEND ENERGY

Manchester City Centre Masterplan and Piccadilly Gardens Masterplan and Landscape Design, Manchester, UK

The bomb blast

The billowing dust and debris of the blast photographed seconds after the bomb exploded.

Causing widespread destruction, the IRA bomb blast injured more than 200 people and destroyed almost 100,000 square metres of retail and office space. Almost 700 businesses had to relocate from their damaged premises. The explosion also wrecked two multi-storey car parks and the city's biggest bus terminus along with historic buildings including the famous Royal Exchange and Corn Exchange. This immense physical, economic and social damage became the catalyst for revitalising the industrial city's historic centre.

Before the bomb, Manchester's city centre economy and environment had been at a low ebb. The monolithic 1960s and 70s Brutalist-style shopping centres were run down, increasing traffic congestion was a blight and streets were unwelcoming after dark. In addition, retailers were anticipating a further slow down in trade as they became vulnerable to competition from a large new out-of-town shopping centre.

After the bomb, the period of clearing up and starting repair was accompanied by action to look to the future. Extensive public consultation was accompanied by a competition to find a plan for the future through an international competition which attracted almost 30 entries.

The brief was to look beyond just repairing the physical damage caused by the bomb, and to create an ambitious and aspirational vision for the long-term future. The aim was to rebuild and regenerate the place as a major European city with a liveable centre and reinforce its role as a regional retail and business destination. Key requirements included the following:

- To create interesting and active streets together with new and enhanced civic spaces.
- To secure strong and diverse development.
- To provide for an integrated transport system.
- To recreate and reinforce the relationship, including physical and economic linkages, with surrounding areas.

Renewal of the city centre began with establishing six strategic objectives, these were:

- Restoration and enhancement of the retail core.
- Stimulation and diversification of the city's economic base.
- Development of an integrated transport strategy.
- Creation of a quality city core fit for the twenty-first century.
- Creation of a living city.
- Creation of a distinctive Millennium Quarter.

From these objectives a masterplan team was selected and the plans evolved further. Not intended as a prescriptive blueprint, the masterplan was conceived as a flexible framework to guide public and private development.

Achieving transformation was rooted in revitalising the public realm to make the city an appealing and safe place to work, shop, live and visit. By restoring confidence in the old industrial city it would be possible to move forward.

Based on the goals of creating greater permeability, unity and sensitivity, the concept focused on re-energising the city centre by unpicking some of the townplanning weaknesses of the 1960s and 70s. The new city centre needed clear routes, safe streets, reduced traffic and clutter, new parks and public spaces and more cultural venues. It was also hoped to encourage residential development to bring more activity to the centre, which at the time was home to no more than a few hundred people. All of this would combine to expand the economy from eight hours a day to 18. Along with opening up routes, it was the intention to break down some of the large blocks of post-war development such as the big shopping centres where blank concrete walls created a hostile environment. The nineteenth century Royal Exchange building was identified as the model for the maximum size block in the new scheme. This building and the Corn Exchange were among a cluster of prominent historic buildings badly damaged in the bomb blast and their restoration was carried out as one of the first priorities in the regeneration programme.

Manchester's city centre showing the large area at the centre of the bomb blast at the left of this image, and Piccadilly Gardens to the right nearby. Improvements to the public realm have been a powerful catalyst for wider regeneration.

Opposite and left
Making connections

A central part of the regeneration plans were to upgrade and create public spaces, improve routes and connections throughout the city centre, open up vistas and encourage new and vibrant street life extending the use of the centre beyond traditional shop opening hours.

At the heart of the plan was the improved street structure and pedestrian routes connecting the Saxon core around the cathedral to the surrounding Georgian, Victorian and modern development. This linking of the central areas was intended to open up and identify opportunities for the northward expansion of retailing and for significant increases in the scale, density and quality within the whole area. A cruciform-shape of streets was identified in the heart of the city to open up views, improve accessibility and create destinations. The cruciform shape is anchored by mainline railway stations, in the north by Victoria Station and in the south by Piccadilly Station.

Along these spines, new public spaces were created. At the north end a former 500 space car park was transformed into a green oasis called Cathedral Gardens. Along with replacing tarmac with grass, the design includes earth sculpture, extensive tree planting and art installations. Surrounding the Medieval cathedral, this tranquil and contemplative space is linked with the nearby River Irwell and is also the setting for the historic Chetham's School of Music along with a new exhibition centre called Urbis. With its competition-winning design by Ian Simpson Architects, this building was completed as part of the regeneration programme.

Right
Gathering places

A former four-lane road interchange close to the heart of the blast has been transformed into one of Manchester's most popular gathering places. Called Exchange Square and designed by leading landscape architect Martha Schwartz, this new space incorporates connections with the past through its distinctive curved water feature on the site of the ancient Hanging Ditch water course. Among the historic buildings overlooking the square is the refurbished Victorian Corn Exchange, renamed The Triangle, which has become a modern shopping centre.

Opposite
The Shambles

Before the bomb, these ancient, timber-framed pubs—the Old Wellington Inn and Sinclair's Oyster Bar, known together as The Shambles—were surrounded by modern city centre development. During rebuilding works, the structures were dismantled and moved to their new location on the edge of Exchange Square where long views have now been opened up to the early Georgian St Ann's Church. New Cathedral Street was created too, completing the vista from church to cathedral.

South of the cathedral, and close to the heart of the bomb blast, a former four-lane road interchange has become Exchange Square. Designed by landscape architect Martha Schwartz, this is a high-energy, modern space. Among the features which resonate with the past is a curved water feature on the site of the ancient Hanging Ditch watercourse. Overlooking the square is the refurbished Victorian Corn Exchange, renamed The Triangle, which has been transformed from a market hall to a modern shopping centre. Close by stand two ancient and extremely popular timber-beamed pubs, the Old Wellington Inn and Sinclair's Oyster Bar, known together as The Shambles. Formerly surrounded by poor quality modern buildings, these were badly damaged in the blast, dismantled and shifted sideways to be rebuilt in a different location to open up views to the early Georgian St Ann's Church. New Cathedral Street was created too, completing the vista from church to cathedral.

Also looking onto Exchange Square is the 1970s Arndale Centre shopping complex where former imposing, fortress-like walls have been pierced by new entrances relating to the local street pattern for greater permeability and shops have been incorporated at street level. A multimillion pound refurbishment and extension to the entire shopping centre has since been carried out. Completing the sides of Exchange Square is a large new department store.

Throughout the scheme, all decisions were underpinned by integrating economic, social and environmental sustainability for an improved quality of inner city life. The masterplan was supported by proposals for an integrated transport network with the primary objective of striking the appropriate balance between good public transport and private car, delivery and emergency vehicles access.

The improvements to the public realm have re-energised the city centre boosting its popularity and prosperity. The work has also stimulated regeneration of surrounding areas including large developments such as the Printworks. A former newspaper printing works, this has been reinvented as an entertainment centre with cinemas, restaurants, a gym, clubs and bars. Further south, the complete reworking of Piccadilly Gardens and public transport infrastructure has created a contemporary-style park and new meeting place in the city.

Piccadilly Gardens

One of the largest public spaces in the city centre, Piccadilly Gardens had long been run down and uninviting. Created as the result of demolishing an old hospital, it was an unresolved space. Plans to reinvent the area involved improving the relationships between the gardens and local streets and buildings. The road system and public transport routes were also simplified to remove the blight of constant traffic which had turned the gardens into a huge roundabout.

Piccadilly Gardens

One of the unexpected consequences of the intense focus of regeneration around the bomb site was that some surrounding areas suffered a downturn from a lack of attention. It even seemed that the success of the new works accelerated their decline. Although just a few streets east of the core regeneration area, Piccadilly Gardens, central Manchester's largest open space, was one such place to suffer. The deterioration was marked by the inner-city blight of poverty and crime. Inevitably the downward spiral saw the place become increasingly desolate and local businesses started to move out.

As part of the regeneration strategy, it became clear that rejuvenating Piccadilly Gardens was an essential component in the economic and social success of the wider city centre. With work underway to strengthen the north–south route through the city, rethinking Piccadilly Gardens provided an opportunity to repair the east–west axis. One of the central challenges was to resolve the design of this open space which had become a public gardens by default early in the twentieth century when it occupied the gap left by the demolition of the old Royal Infirmary hospital. For the first time, here was the opportunity to make the space relate to surrounding buildings and realise its full potential.

When design work began, the environment was hostile and under heavy pressure of use. At the centre of a major transport interchange of buses, trams, taxis and cars, close to main railway stations and on a busy pedestrian route, the sunken gardens had become badly neglected; they were scruffy by day and dangerous at night. To add to the challenge, technical restraints on the project included a warren of underground infrastructure including the city's largest electricity substation located directly beneath the gardens. The new design had to accommodate this infrastructure below ground, while above, it also had to re-incorporate a number of historic statues. And local aspirations were high, consultation revealed that people wanted a place they could be proud of and a great civic space where crowds could gather for citywide celebrations.

By closing roads and rebuilding the bus system, the design set about streamlining the complex flow of public transport and reclaiming the gardens for the public. Key to reducing traffic impact on the open space, two buildings were added between the park and the road, one, an award-winning office by Allies and Morrison, the other a graceful curved concrete pavilion and wall by Tadao Ando. To further banish traffic, sections of carriageway were removed on the north and west edges, enabling the gardens to run up to building frontages. The central focus of the new contemporary-style park is a fountain.

A huge elliptical disc in black granite, it features inset water jets and misting units with coloured fibre-optic lighting activated in a programme of computer-generated displays. Around this, the new gardens are open, light, simple and flexible, with plenty of versatility for walking or picnics, meeting friends and children's play. These areas include large open lawns and generous paved terraces finished in slate, granite and York stone with precast concrete edges.

Since connections across the gardens were critical to wider regeneration in the city, two main pedestrian links were established; a curving axis that echoes the flowing shape of Ando's pavilion and a north–south 'catwalk' through one side of the elliptical fountain linking Manchester's Northern Quarter to China Town in the south. Planting includes areas of mature trees including oaks and magnolias, meanwhile the lawn holds surprises—in spring, half of it is entirely covered in dark blue crocuses, while in the other half, crocuses grow in circles beneath the trees.

Along with incorporating the electricity substation and an underground plant room for the fountain, the design work also included bespoke street furniture, planters and collaboration with English Heritage to relocate the area's historic statues. A high-quality contemporary lighting scheme adds interest, colour and drama and ensures the place is accessible and safe at night.

The gardens have become a popular, vibrant and dynamic space with places to walk, rest and play, along with cafes, a flower shop, a regular farmers' market and flexible areas for one-off events. Upgrading the gardens has led to considerable revitalisation of the area including the redevelopment of one side of the historic square to provide new office accommodation. This scheme also helped to generate revenue for the gardens.

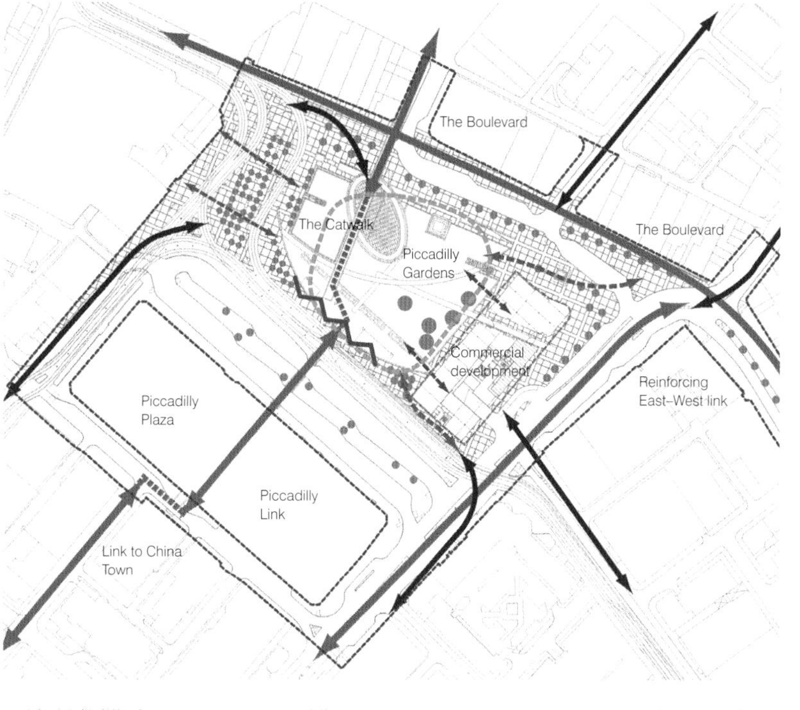

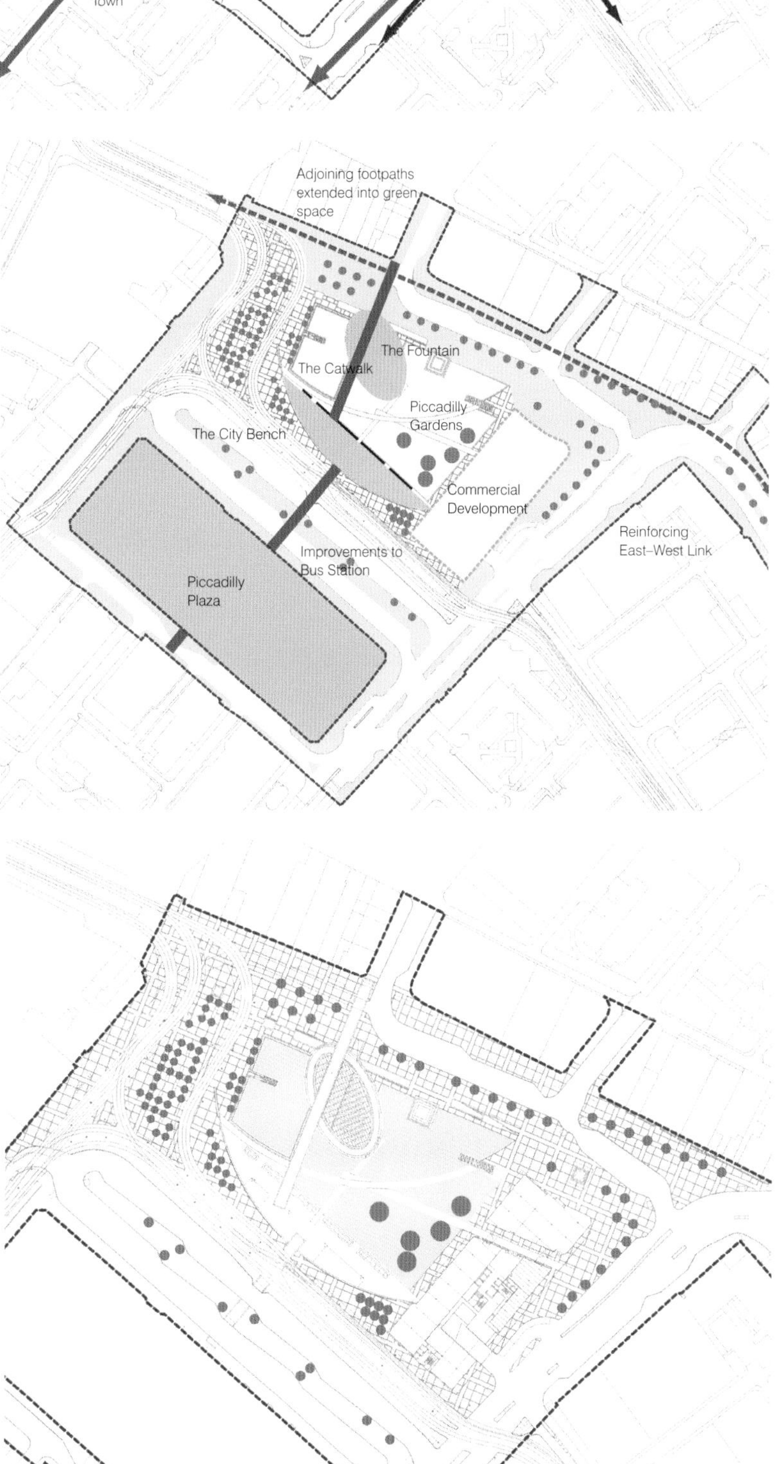

Evolution

Drawings showing circulation routes, the layout of key elements including the elliptical fountain and the planting scheme including numerous new trees.

Right
A space for all

Far removed from the days when Piccadilly Gardens was a hostile place, the space has become extremely popular with families, local office workers and shoppers and as a welcome place to rest and as a gathering place for major city events. The design, with its large expanses of lawn, elliptical fountain and intersecting walkways, appears simple, but in fact, out of sight, it incorporates great technical complexity including the fact that below ground is a network of infrastructure including Manchester's largest electricity substation. The new design also had to re-incorporate a number of historic statues including the substantial Queen Victoria Monument.

Opposite

Aerial view of the wedge-shaped gardens showing the Queen Victoria Monument placed to the side of the fountain.

Overleaf

On any sunny day, one of the most popular features of Piccadilly Gardens is the fountain where water jets set into the paving act like a magnet to young children who love dashing in and out of the spurting jets.

ONE
150,000 SQ FT
FICES TO LET
www.onepiccadillygardens.com
GVA Grimley
0161 834 7187
ONE

prime offices
GVA Grimley

Concept

Creating a world-class modern Islamic city that respects local culture and history

Context

Urban centre/arid desert

The Heart of Doha Masterplan, Doha, Qatar.

Following the discovery of oil and gas in the 1930s, Doha's growth has been rapid and impressive. From a simple village where fishing and pearl diving formed the core of the economy, Qatar's capital city is now a large modern metropolis.

Opposite

Density and complexity

The capital city of Doha shown in an aerial photograph from 1952. The Masterplan site is close to Souk Waqif.

Al Rayyan Road
Al Kahraba Street
Eid Ground
Souk Waqif
Old Fort
Burial Ground

The Heart of Doha
Masterplan, Doha, Qatar

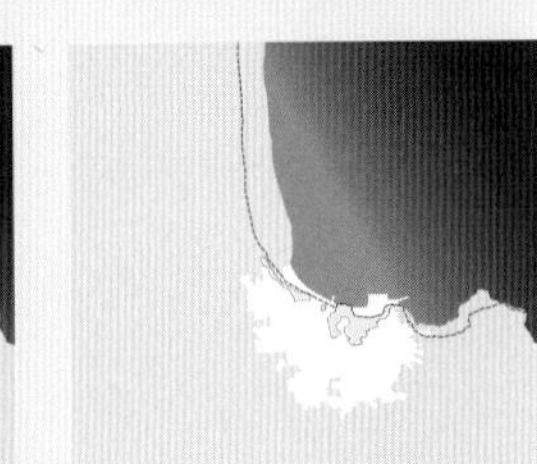

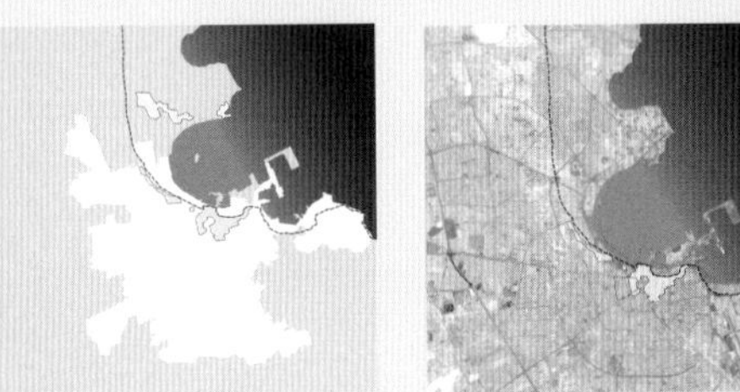

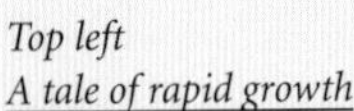

Top left
A tale of rapid growth

The old wadi was an important part of the city fabric, it was a welcome watering hole for local animals and a place for people to meet and share their news.

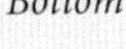

Bottom

The growth of the city has been accompanied by significant change in the shape of the coastline, the progression shown here moves from 1947 to 1959, 1973 and 1988.

Centre

The red outline marks out the central Doha area that was the focus of the masterplan. On the left is the city in 1947, and on the right, the results after 60 years of rapid expansion.

Top right

The contemporary city with its forest of towers.

In just half a century, old Doha's low skyline of traditional adobe courtyard houses pierced with the domes and minarets of mosques has given way to new building and is now dominated by pristine skyscrapers. The rapid expansion of this city has been fuelled by oil and gas revenues and made possible by the private car and Western-style urbanisation.

But the speed of change has been at a cost. The city's heart has been rebuilt and forfeited much of its beauty and charm; traditional climate-sensitive architecture has given way to modern buildings, many of which are undistinguished in style and energy hungry. The private car has brought congestion and pollution to the streets and widespread suburban development has weakened the city's centre of gravity as well as causing social networks to become fragmented with the inevitable loss of community spirit.

Seizing the opportunity to establish Qatar as a centre of contemporary urban excellence, Dohaland, a subsidiary of the Qatar Foundation has helped set new and exemplary benchmarks for creating environmentally, socially and economically sustainable cities in the Gulf region. The Qatar Foundation for education, science and community development is a private, chartered and non-profit organisation, founded in 1995 by His Highness Sheikh Hamad Bin Khalifa Al-Thani, Emir of Qatar. Guided by the principle that a nation's greatest resource is the potential of its people, the foundation aims to develop that potential through a network of centres devoted to progressive education, research and community welfare. Guided by this same principle, a blueprint for the future has evolved for a 35 hectare site in the city centre which is to be regenerated based on local traditions and culture. This is the Heart of Doha, where an inspiring and sustainable urban environment will be created as a place for future generations to flourish and prosper.

The brief for regeneration of the city centre was to bring Qatari families back into the heart of Doha, to restore a sense of community, and to improve the environment and boost the economy by creating a safe, well-served and thriving centre with schools, shops, small businesses, health services, mosques and public spaces all within easy walking distance of where people live. As part of this work, new buildings will take inspiration from traditional structures, road traffic will be better managed and the quality of the environment will be improved.

Doha is on the east coast of the Qatar peninsular which reaches into the Arabian Gulf. The capital city has a long curving coastline and harbour. Set back from the sea, close to the seat of government at the Emiri Diwan, is the site identified for regeneration in the Heart of Doha Masterplan.

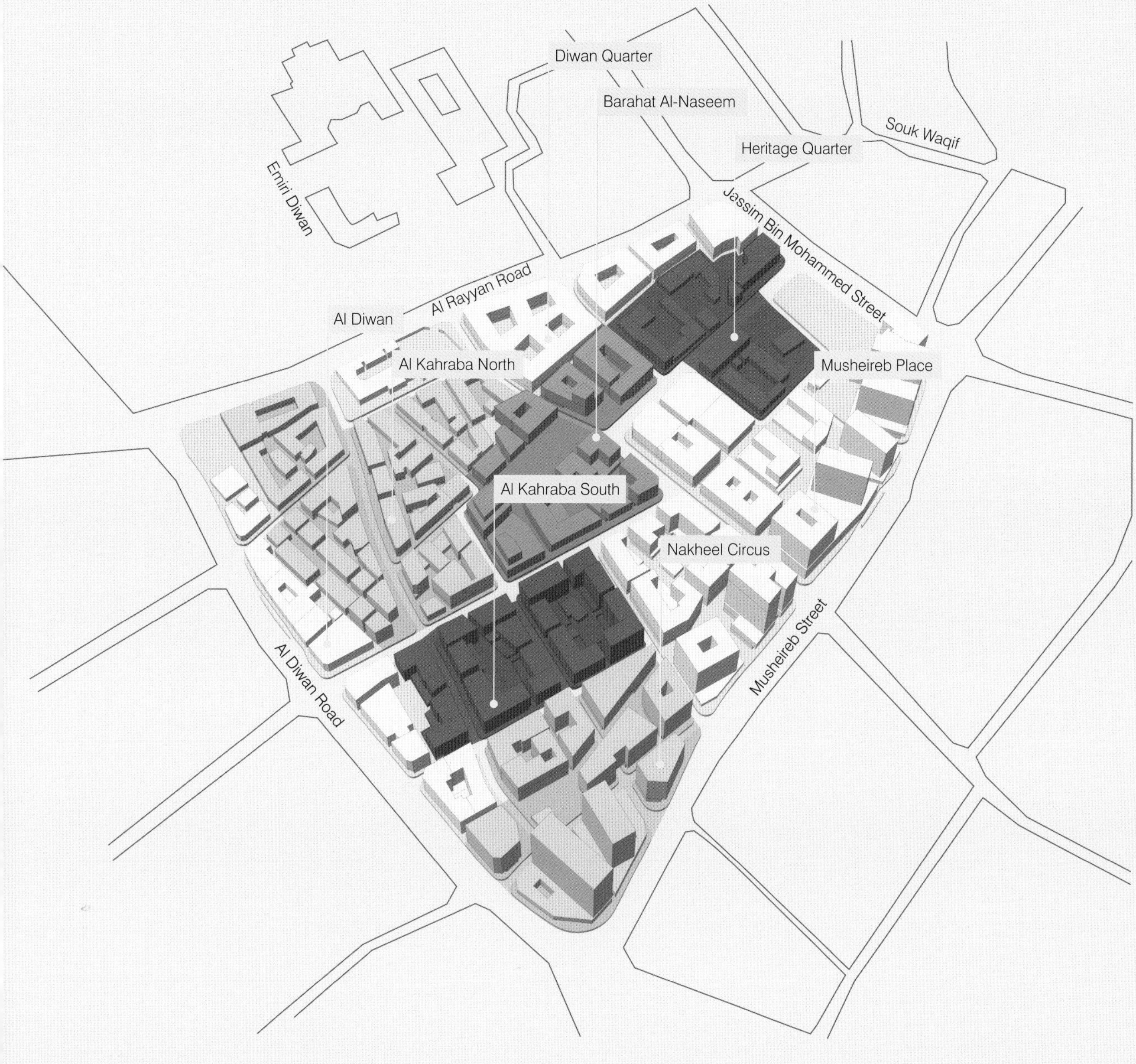

Diwan Quarter
Barahat Al-Naseem
Heritage Quarter
Souk Waqif
Emiri Diwan
Jassim Bin Mohammed Street
Al Rayyan Road
Al Diwan
Al Kahraba North
Musheireb Place
Al Kahraba South
Nakheel Circus
Musheireb Street
Al Diwan Road

Left
Character and distinctiveness

Delivering interest and diversity to the revived Heart of Doha, the site is perceived as a sequence of different character areas. These include Musheireb Place which follows the line of the old wadi Musheireb and forms part of the retail core, and the Al Kahraba North neighbourhood which will be primarily residential.

Below
Layers of the city

Understanding and analysis of the city centre site revealed layers of uses which have evolved over generations.

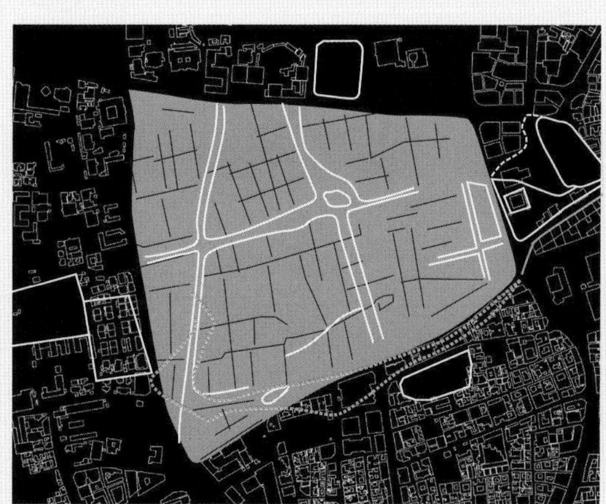

Historic urban grain and the wadi route as a reference framework for the masterplan.

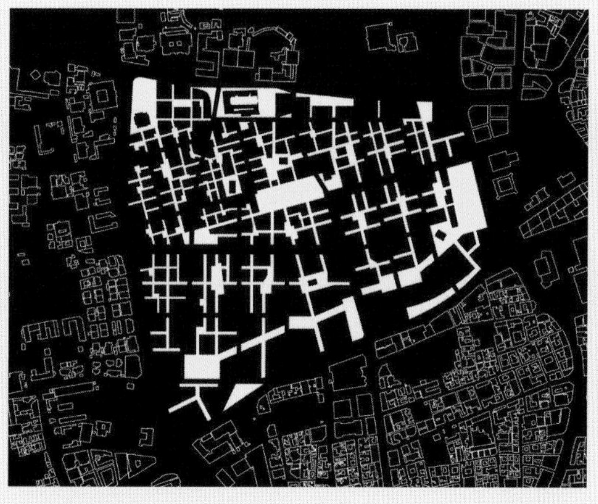

The lattice creates intimate *sikkats* for people.

The street grid captures north/ south wind and caters for road traffic.

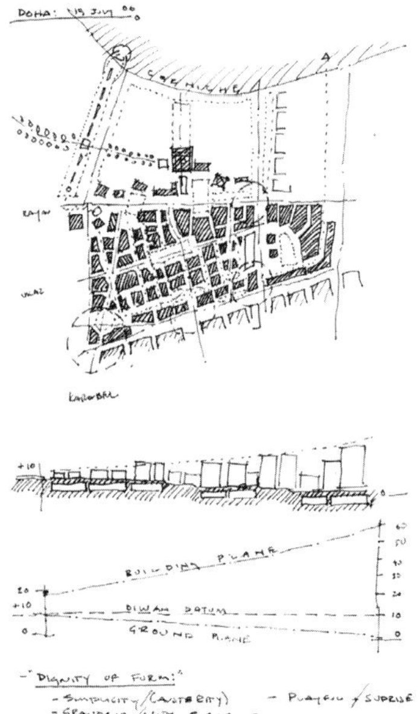

Early stages of the work concentrated on understanding the essence of the place by rediscovering its poetry, exploring its history and learning how the city had evolved. Using historic maps and photography it was possible to identify the key elements of the old city's fabric. These included the alignment of the main thoroughfares, the lattice of narrow and shady pedestrian lanes which criss-crossed the city, the position of the souk and the route of the ancient and important fresh-water wadi which flowed through the town to the sea. Along with exploring the historic urban grain, it became clear that the climate was also written in the street patterns with many lanes and roads positioned on a north–south axis to channel the cooling sea breeze, and with the lattice of pedestrian lanes oriented to maximise shade from the hot and bright sun. Understanding the past provided an invaluable intellectual reference for the masterplan. Important historical streets and structures were retained and integrated with a north–south oriented street grid for car access. This Western-style gridded city-paradigm is combined with an intricate lattice of *sikkats* (informal lanes), drawing references from Islamic street patterns and vernacular building types.

The re-creation of a dense and intricate urban neighbourhood also helps to address concerns about the loss of community spirit in the city. It was clear that the lack of residential accommodation and amenities in the centre had contributed to people moving to villa-type developments in outlying suburbs. Here families enjoy living in large homes on large plots of land, however this suburban style of living has seen people-led increasingly insular lives which are dominated by the necessity to drive everywhere.

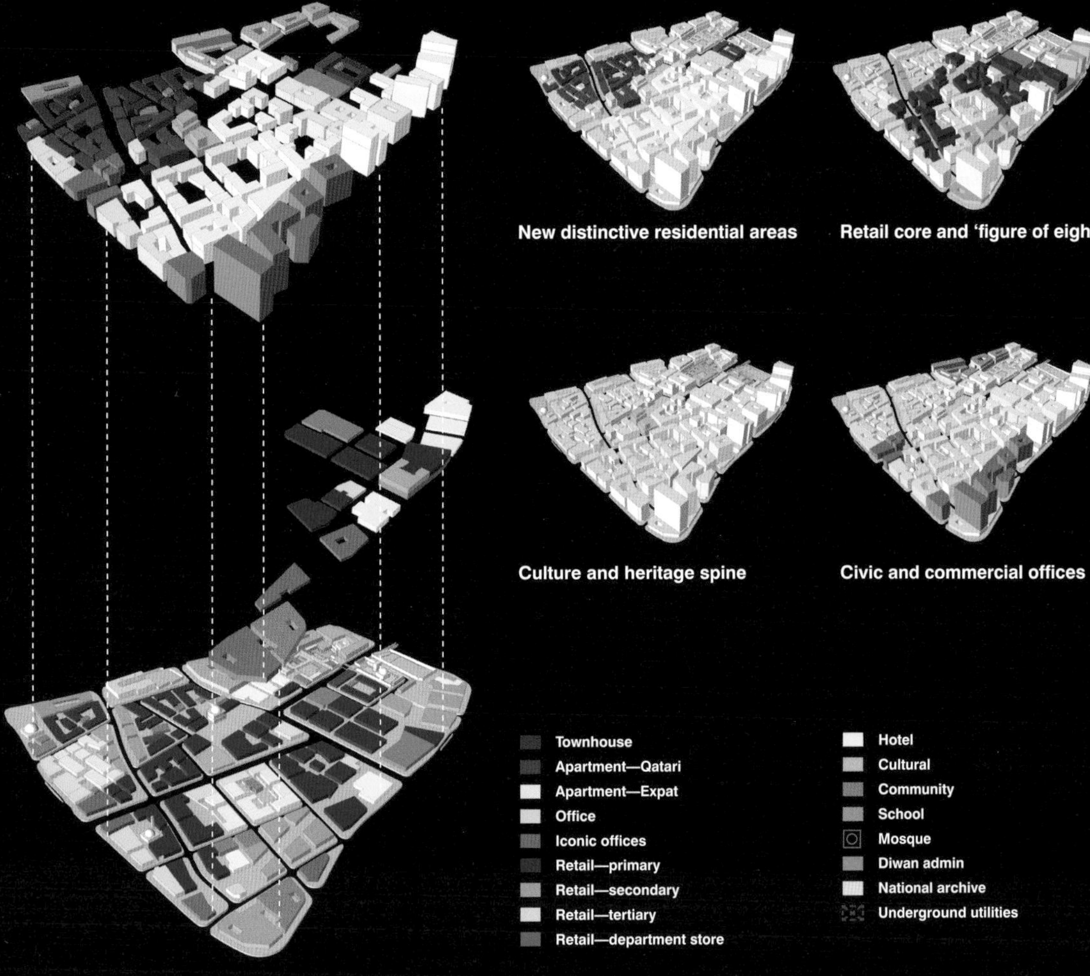

Left
Complexity and diversity

The plan incorporates a diverse mix of uses and character areas to ensure social and economic vibrancy. While some areas are predominantly residential, others have a predominance of retail or commercial offices, but all incorporate a range of uses to ensure they are well served at a local level.

Opposite
Barahat Al-Naseem

A visualisation of the heart of the future city, above, and below, sketches exploring building height and massing.

As a result precious and traditional community and family networks have begun to disintegrate.

The solution incorporated into the Masterplan has been to create a sequence of mixed-use and densely planned urban neighbourhoods with beautiful and generous-sized homes which have easy access to all the services and amenities required by the new urban population. The heart area has been divided into eight distinctive districts, each with its own identity these include Musheireb Place which follows the line of the old wadi Musheireb and forms part of the retail core, the Heritage Quarter with its historic Eid Ground and adobe houses, the Diwan Quarter adjacent to the great Emiri Diwan government building which contains a large proportion of civic and commercial offices. By contrast, at the Al Kahraba North neighbourhood, new family homes of generous size and contemporary style are proposed. Providing important layers of privacy, the townhouses will be arranged as a *fareej* or cluster around courtyards which form the nucleus of the family network and help strengthen the sense of community.

Revitalised public space will be the key to success in this dense part of the city. Plans include new squares and courtyards where people can gather in cafes or shops and stroll in shade and comfort along streets and *sikkats*. Features in the new streetscape will have strong resonance with the past, incorporating many different styles of colonnades, shading canopies and water features reminiscent of the old wadi. Not only will they help craft beautiful places, they will also create a microclimate and provide welcome respite from the intense light and heat. These high quality public spaces will weave together the eight mixed-use districts and contribute to the sustainability goals of the Masterplan by reducing car use, promoting social interaction, boosting the city-centre economy, and improving the built environment.

Surrounding these public spaces will be beautiful buildings that draw inspiration from the past. A new language of architecture is to be evolved by architects selected by a panel of judges, including Aga Khan professors of Islamic architecture, through a process of international competition. Collectively, the architects will engage in a creative dialogue to find a new language that addresses the tensions between history and modernity; unity and diversity and public and private realms.

Opposite, top and bottom left
A place for living

A reinterpretation of the traditional courtyard house, opposite and top left, by Allies and Morrison. Generous townhouses will provide flexible internal layouts to suit different family needs and each dwelling will feature a beautiful and shady *iwan*, the traditional reception space. Respecting traditions, public spaces will give way gracefully to the privacy of the family home. Bottom left, the townhouses will be arranged as *hara*—clusters of family homes which form the nucleus of the community.

Overleaf
A blueprint for the future

A vision demonstrating that the masterplan is a culmination of understanding the history, climate and distinctiveness of Doha.

The vision of Doha by Her Highness Sheikha Mozah bint Nasser Al-Missned

- A culture of quality firmly rooted in the infrastructure of our country.
- A rising homeland that confidently embraces modernisation and proudly observes tradition.
- A modern state in the context of Arab culture, tradition and religious beliefs.
- A meeting, not a melting, of cultures.
- An environment of freedom, creativity, innovation, communication, meeting and interacting.
- As the mother is the centre of the family, the family is the centre of the community and the state.
- Islam has always guaranteed the full rights of women, and women have always occupied a central role in Islamic civilisations.

Concept
Finding the balance between supply and demand

Context
Urban/temperate

Social Infrastructure Frameworks, UK.

Knowing that the most successful and sustainable communities are those that are well served with schools, healthcare and leisure facilities, it has become essential to find ways to target and calculate the appropriate levels of services to meet the needs of individual neighbourhoods.

Opposite
Successful and sustainable

Creating successful communities means ensuring they are well-served with the appropriate and adequate provision of services including schools, libraries, sports facilities and healthcare.

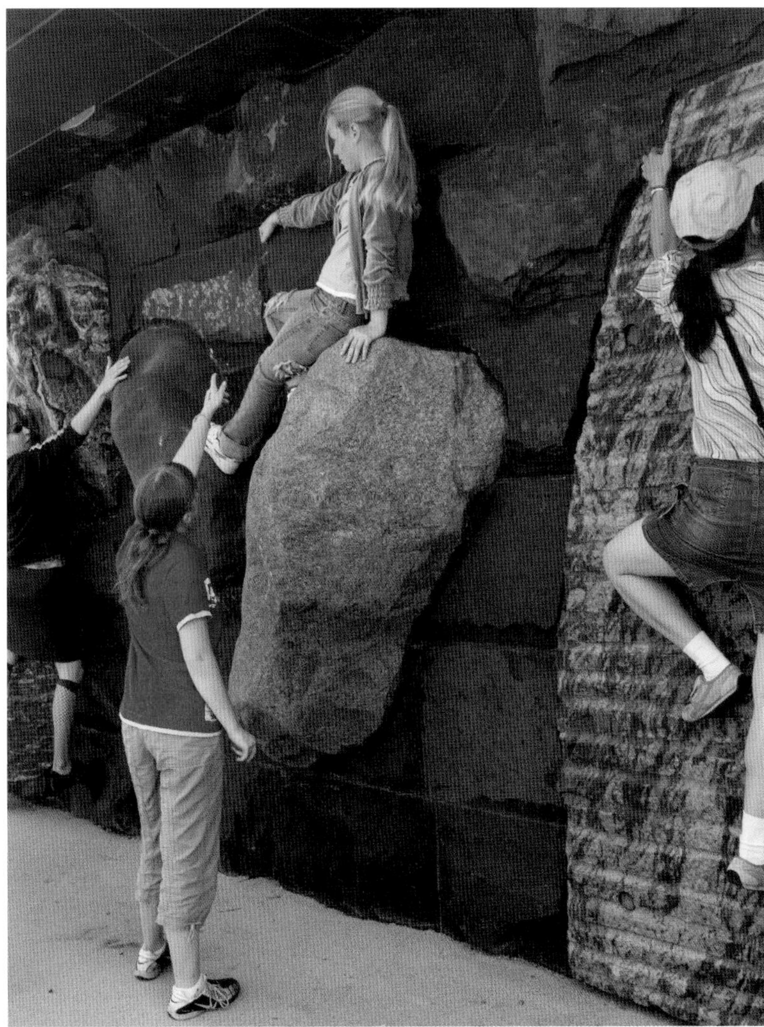

SIF benefits

The benefits of Social Infrastructure Frameworks include:

- The iterative and multi-sector project approach which breaks down the barriers between different providers and presents a unique opportunity to identify opportunities for co-ordination and co-operation.
- Significant financial benefits to the government by delivering social infrastructure in a co-ordinated, co-located and integrated way.
- Results have demonstrated a need to challenge the legal and regulatory basis of existing funding and delivery regimes so that future facilities represent value for money and can adapt to changing needs over time.
- It provides a clear evidence base for planning policy and service delivery strategies and inputs to corporate performance assessments, comprehensive spending reviews, corporate strategies, local area agreements and planning contribution strategies.

Identifying the balance between supply and demand, the Social Infrastructure Framework (SIF) is a sophisticated planning tool for making sure that communities have the right quantity and mix of public services. It is designed to work as an integral part of planning for sustainable communities. The SIF recognises that every community has different needs; for example towns and neighbourhoods with lots of young families will need schools, healthcare and other services that are quite different from a place with a predominantly elderly population or an urban area with flats for young professionals. However, the SIF's scope is much broader than examining just existing supply and demand.

The computer-based tool has the flexibility to be used in almost any geographical area. It is programmed with a wide spectrum of data relating to the type of local population, existing homes and the numbers, types and locations of proposed new homes along with existing schools, health centres, libraries and so on. With all data in place, the tool is designed to look in a comprehensive and simplified manner across services to provide a base for initial discussions. This broad picture is created to help service providers work together towards solutions. The five broad sectors it encapsulates are education, health and social care, libraries and community services, recreation and leisure services, and emergency and essential services.

Along with looking at existing provision, and whether it is in surplus or deficit, the tool can also be used to calculate future demand. This is based on assumptions about whether communities will be growing or contracting. In a growth area, it can ensure that new homes and social infrastructure are built simultaneously. It determines when and where new facilities will be required, how much land they will occupy, and the associated costs of acquiring land, designing and constructing facilities and the ongoing revenue implications.

The tool can also be used to identify ways of gaining efficiency. Through the database and spatial mapping, the SIF works out how future needs can be met through maximising the use of existing facilities and/or the phased delivery of new single-use, co-located or integrated facilities and services. For example it might be possible to combine health and social care services under one roof instead of needing two buildings. In a significant development from previous approaches the SIF estimates are analysed using geographical information systems (GIS) to apply accessibility, choice and quality factors and provide a spatial picture of future needs. By overlapping maps, the scope for co-location or integration emerges. The approach is highly interactive to ensure that representatives of the various services can take part in testing the SIF proposals and making sure that recommendations fit with best practice to serve the community.

The evolution of the SIF toolkit came in response to the UK's nationwide programme for the construction of new homes and communities, setting the goal for three million new homes by 2020. Anticipating that the influx of new populations into any area would have an impact on local services, the SIF was developed to provide a method of calculating how to best serve these communities with the services and amenities they need at the time of the study, and what they may need in the future.

The data is drawn from carefully selected sources including the government statistics—for information on demographics, central and local government—for housing, planning and local service information, the National Health Service—for GP and other healthcare services and Sports England—for information on provision of indoor and outdoor facilities. With this detailed information, it is possible to make predictions about future population numbers, the age mix, and family sizes so that the type and range of social amenities meet local needs.

There are five stages in a SIF. Having established a study area, the first step is to define the baseline and establish a picture of the place, its population and services as they exist. The second step looks at local policy and plans. The third calculates future needs for the existing and future populations. The fourth explores the potential to adapt what exists and to create bespoke solutions. And finally, proposals are tested with representatives of interested parties and plans for new services are devised in a co-ordinated approach.

A primary objective of the SIF partnership approach involving all interested parties is to ensure that policy objectives are delivered, turning aspirations for sustainable communities into reality.

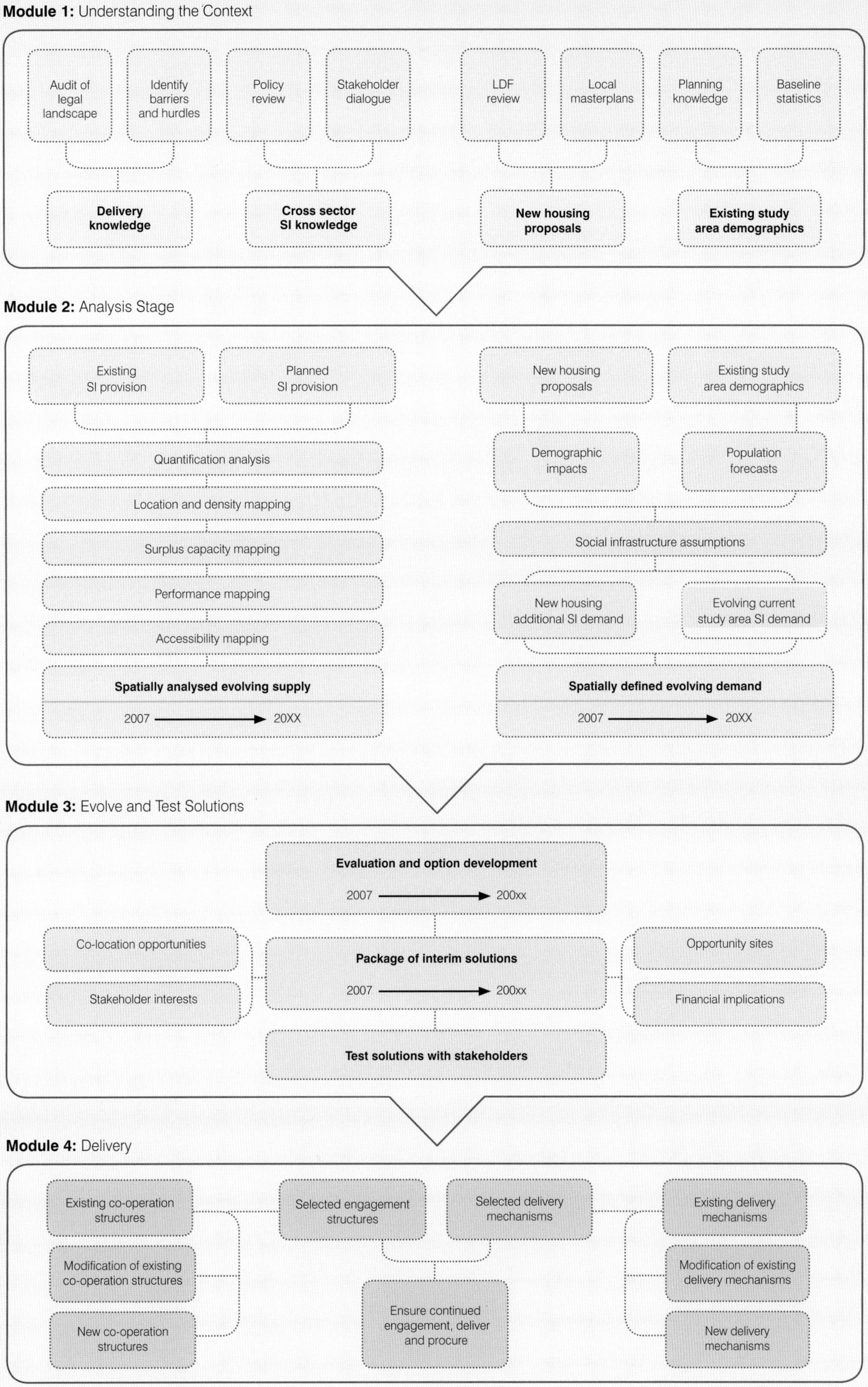

A tool for joined-up delivery, putting services where and when they are needed, there are five stages in a SIF:

- Establishing the characteristics of the existing population, quantifying the nature of existing social infrastructure (SI) provision and identifying areas of greatest need.
- Reviewing existing social infrastructure policy and plans and auditing the existing legal delivery landscape for effectiveness.
- Detailed modelling to establish future needs from the existing and new population and their cumulative social infrastructure service and facility needs. These are analysed for the scope for co-location or integration.
- Adapting existing delivery mechanisms and developing tailored delivery solutions.
- The spatial and delivery solutions are then tested with key stakeholders to secure a co-ordinated delivery strategy.

Right and opposite
The London Borough of Barking and Dagenham Pilot SIF

This work looked at future population growth and the associated social infrastructure needs. Analysis of data explored existing and future demand against the current and planned supply of social infrastructure. It also explored costs for provision, and the potential for co-location/integration of facilities and services. The LBBD-SIF involved significant stakeholder consultation to audit existing delivery mechanisms and develop innovative methods of future delivery.

The project for Barking and Dagenham analysed the current policy and legal landscape and ensured that existing delivery proposals were bedded into the SIF process.

Results included:

- Reviewing NHS LIFT and Building Schools for the Future strategies to provide multiple-service facilities.
- Asset management strategies for money programmes and site acquisition and disposal plans.
- A planning strategy for contributions from new development to be established.
- A number of new public/private and public/private mechanisms that allow the public sector to share any value uplift from new facilities and respond to changing circumstances.
- A community-led mechanism to manage facilities and spaces.

Dentist surgeries
Not available
1–2
3–4
5–6

Potential required no. of dentists
0
1
>1

Dentist supply, demand and accessibilty

Open space by hectare
0.8–2.0
2.1–8.0
20.1–40.0
40.1–70.0

Potential required open space (m^2)
-0.1–0.0
0.1–2.0
2.1–8.0
8.1–20.0

Open space supply, demand and accessibilty

Primary education supply, demand and accessibilty
London Borough of Barking and Dagenham Social Infrastructure Framework

The SIF toolkit involves a detailed evaluation of existing policies, service and facility provision, different population projection methods within the existing and planned communities and a wide range of national, regional and local standards and targets for social infrastructure provision. In a significant development from previous approaches, the toolkit estimates are analysed using GIS tools to apply accessibility, choice and quality factors and provide a spatial analysis of future needs and the scope for co-location or integration.

In assessing local healthcare provision for example, it is possible to use local or national standards against forecasts of the future population profile to estimate the requirements for GPs, how many consultation rooms are required, how many dentists, and how many acute hospital beds are required.

Nursery, primary and secondary school provision can also be calculated by understanding the local population profile and the likely profile of families moving into new homes. For example, areas with many young families will have greater demand for schools than an area with an older population.

Concept
New life for a World Heritage Site and derelict former docks

Context
Inner city/temperate

Pier Head Public Realm Design and Kings Waterfront Masterplan and Public Realm Design, Liverpool, UK.

Built on a majestic scale, Liverpool's famous waterfront grew to reflect the city's role as one of the world's largest and busiest ports. Since the seventeenth century, the docks helped Britain forge powerful links with the rest of the globe bringing in exotic shipments of tobacco and cotton, cocoa and sugar. More recently, however, as shipping trade has relocated, the Merseyside docks are being reinvented.

Opposite
Pier Head

The exuberant waterfront buildings at Liverpool's Pier Head overlook a transformed public space which incorporates a new stretch of canal. This is the first UK urban canal extension in a generation and links a sequence of dock basins to bring new vitality to the famous Merseyside waterfront.

Pier Head Public Realm Design and Kings Waterfront Masterplan and Public Realm Design, Liverpool, UK

Above and below
Making plans

At the heart of Liverpool's World Heritage Site, the Pier Head area is shown, top, in context with the adjacent Kings Waterfront.

Below, the masterplan of the area showing the famous Three Graces—the Royal Liver, Cunard and Port of Liverpool (formerly Dock Office) buildings, and the route of the new canal threaded through the public square.

Work in this area also included masterplanning Mann Island to the south, which is the site of the new Museum of Liverpool, the continuation of the new canal and mixed-use development including homes, offices and shops.

Along with the pilgrimages made by Beatles' fans, and visitors to Tate Liverpool and the historic docks, the ebb and flow of tourists in Liverpool have come to replace the shipping. However, despite its global renown, the famous Merseyside waterfront had become neglected and degraded. The expansive public space at Pier Head in front of the famous Three Graces dockside buildings was run down, and just a short distance to the south, the prime site at Kings Dock was being used as a car park. Elsewhere, the once-thriving dockland water basins, originally the focus of the city's wealth creation, had become largely abandoned and lifeless.

The catalyst for this latest phase of regeneration was when Liverpool won the coveted award to become European Capital of Culture for 2008. As a centrepiece for the year-long calendar of events, the Pier Head and nearby docks were transformed in a bold and confident regeneration programme on a scale to match the waterfront architecture of the exuberant Royal Liver, Cunard and Port of Liverpool buildings. The focus of this work was a new canal extension, linking the Leeds and Liverpool Canal to the north with disused dockland water basins adjacent to Kings Dock to the south. This bold move was to revitalise the existing water spaces with tourist-based boating activity and enliven the Pier Head area on route. The work at Pier Head has transformed a windswept square into an attractive public space intended to attract more residents and tourists to the area, to provide better connections between the docks along the Merseyside waterfront and to make places for people to linger and enjoy the views.

Instantly recognisable as one of the city's main postcard shots, Pier Head is key to Liverpool's sense of identity and became part of the UNESCO World Heritage Site for Liverpool's Maritime Mercantile City in 2004. In common with the whole dockside area, Pier Head has a long history of different uses and reinvention and the recent work is a continuation of that story. Even the land it stands on is artificial, having been constructed as an extension to the river wall in the nineteenth century during a period of docks expansion. In the intervening years mooring basins were filled or modified, making way for the construction of the Three Graces, the site was the point from which emigrants set sail to the New World, and where their descendants returned to on their way to fight in the two world wars. More recently it became used as a bus terminal with ferry landing stage, and most recently a public square. The canal link can be seen as part of this continuum of change, as the space once again adapts to new needs.

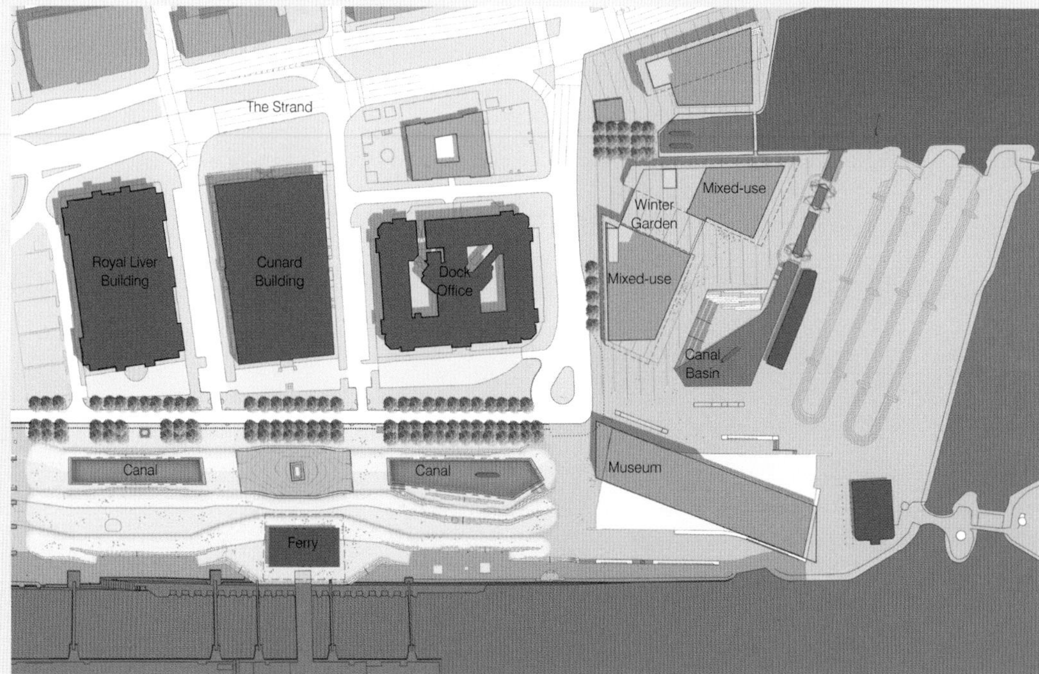

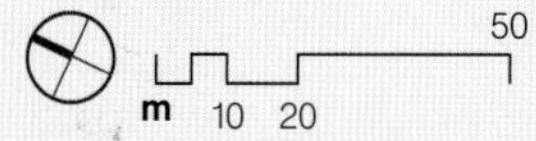

In an epic feat of engineering, the canal extension has been excavated through the public space in front of the Three Graces. While a large portion of the new waterway runs beneath the plaza, it becomes visible at two large open basins, separated by an expansive lawn. These three elements echo the scale and presence of the Three Graces. This stretch of busy waterway brings movement and interest to the waterfront and provides sheltered places to sit, watch the passing narrowboats and enjoy the views. At 650 metres in length, this is the first major urban canal extension in the UK in a generation. The mixed-use scheme also includes the construction of the new Museum of Liverpool, homes, shops and offices around a third canal basin on Mann Island at the southern end of the site.

For navigational reasons the canal's water level needed to be several metres below the surface of the public realm itself. To deal with the changing levels and provide close access to the water, seating and steps connect the upper and lower spaces. The seating and steps are a feature used throughout the expansive 2.5 hectares of public space where the surface has acquired numerous level changes during its many different phases and types of use. The creases or folds in the surface are constructed in a stone that is paler in colour than the main paving material. These bands of lighter colour flow north–south through the site and are splayed open in places to form steps or areas of seating.

Revived and revitalised

A visualisation looking south past the Port of Liverpool Building on the left and towards the new Museum of Liverpool in the distance. As the result of a tremendous feat of engineering, the canal link forms a 650 metre extension to the British Waterways Leeds and Liverpool Canal enabling it to terminate at Canning Dock within the South Docks bringing boats into the heart of the docks and enhancing visitor destinations including Tate Liverpool at Albert Dock and the Echo Arena at Kings Waterfront.

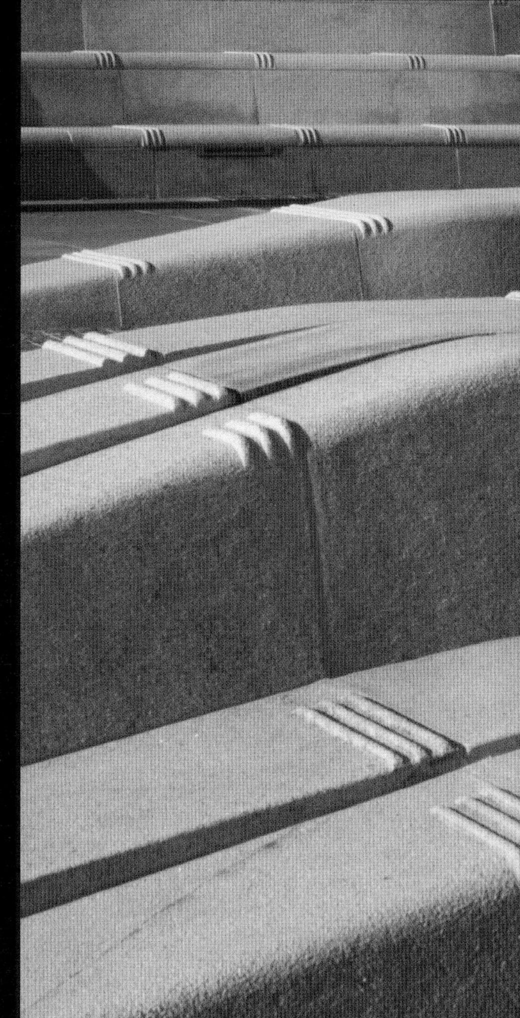

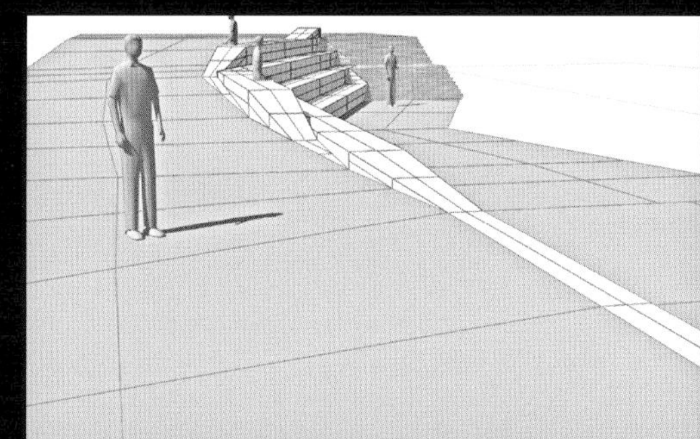

Opposite and above
Under foot

Overleaf
From vision to reality

The crease lines that create the paving folds run the length of Pier Head, and are highlighted with a pale, warm-toned natural stone chosen to complement the facades of the Three Graces. They are used to guide rainwater collection through much of the space. However, as they approach the barges and enjoy the views.

In addition to being sculpturally attractive, and embodying a high degree of refinement and craftsmanship, this integrated seating is robust and much less vulnerable to vandalism than relate to their surface use and loading. For example, small stones are used in areas where heavy cranes are used and large flag stones appear in open expanses of paving.

A subtlety varied colour palette of mid-grey granite, highlights these stone

3-D computer modelling and computer numerically controlled (CNC) cutting were used extensively. Through this process the 3-D models created during the design phases were directly used as templates to cut the finished stone, forming a seamless link from design through to

The public space at Pier Head provides a rich and varied experience for enjoying city and riverside views or simply watching boats float past.

MUSEUM OF LIVERPOOL

2010

Kings Waterfront in the context of the docks with the River Mersey, at bottom, and Pier Head to the left. Landmark buildings on the site are the Echo Arena and BT Conference Centre. The Echo Arena was completed in time to host *The Musical* a song and dance spectacular which was one of the main opening events of Liverpool's 2008 City of Culture celebrations. The masterplan for the 15 hectare site also includes mixed-use development integrating homes, offices, shops and hotels.

Kings Waterfront

South of Pier Head, and beyond Albert Dock, the area now called Kings Waterfront had lain derelict for years. Originally called Kings Dock, it ceased to be used for shipping in the 1970s, was filled in and subsequently became a car park. Despite its prime riverside position, it remained empty for years and has been transformed from the largest area of derelict land in the city centre, to the largest new development.

The masterplan for the long-abandoned 15 hectare site evolved with the focus on a new 11,000 seat Echo Arena and adjoining convention/exhibition centre, both designed by Wilkinson Eyre Architects. The mixed-use scheme also includes hotels, homes and shops. Another distinctive feature of the project is the 500 metre waterfront promenade.

Contributing to the strong identity of this new development, the promenade combines an innovative street and paving treatment with new seating. Addressing issues of safety, but also an integral part of the design, a sequence of bollards has been incorporated into the scheme to ensure that vehicles are kept away from the water's edge. Distributed along the promenade, these sculptural forms take their inspiration from the shapes of cast-iron mooring bollards or capstans found on the docks. Made in a family of different sizes, the bollards have a dual use as seating. The components can be assembled in a variety of clusters and configurations to create different types of seating for people sitting alone, for couples or for larger groups. Their staggered arrangement discourages abuse from skateboarders.

Model homes

A sequence of visualisations for homes integrated in the new communities at Kings Waterfront. Proposals include high-density development of energy-efficient buildings which are well served with local schools, parks, shops and other amenities.

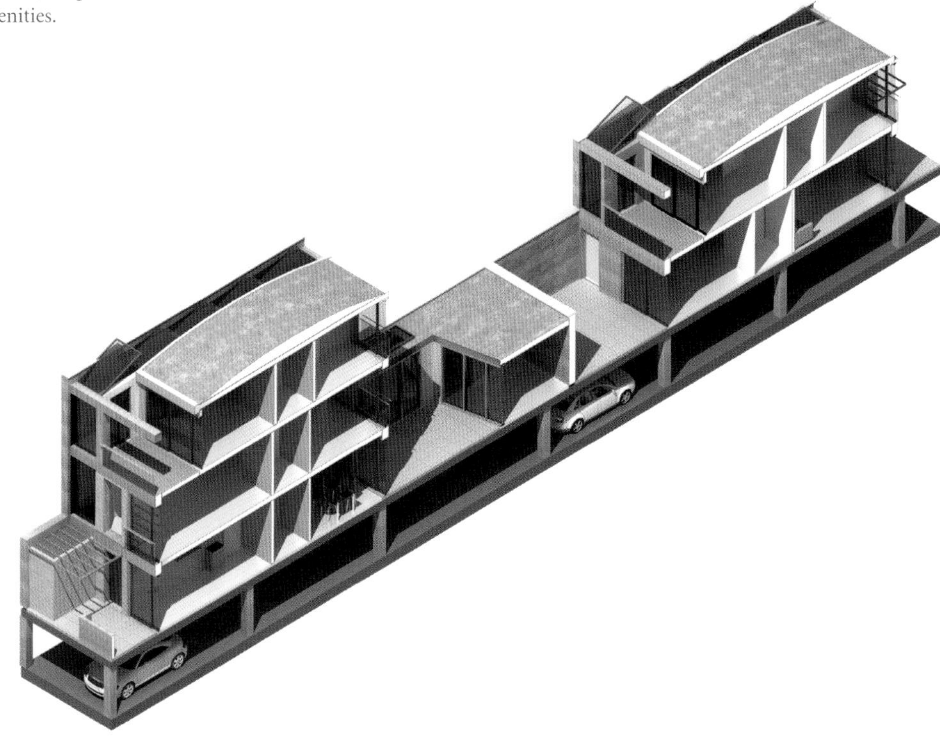

On a wider scale, the seating units directly relate to paving striped bands of dark and light grey, along the length of this ribbon site. Three sizes of paving unit have been used to define pedestrian areas and the roadway. Long rectangular slabs form the promenade and are set to draw the eye to the water's edge and beyond, small setts are used for the roadway and medium-sized blocks link the two at a shallow kerb. While the stripes appear random, they relate directly to the adjacent new buildings and create a barcode-style interpretation of the site. This visual device also creates the optical illusion of giving the linear site greater width and acts as a form of traffic calming.

Opposite
The promenade

While the placing of seating along the promenade may appear random, the pattern is directly related to the masterplan of the Kings Waterfront site. Where pedestrian traffic is heaviest close to the arena and conference centre, the seating is used in clusters, while adjacent to pocket parks they are more sparsely spaced, enabling a fluid connection to the river's edge. The barcode-style stripes in the paving also correspond to the buildings and open spaces, and the banded pattern acts as a form of traffic calming and creates the optical illusion of giving the promenade greater width.

Above
Sit back and enjoy

Dockside mooring bollards or capstans provided the inspiration for the seating which lines the new promenade at Kings Waterfront. The rounded shapes were adapted to form the basis of the modular seating system which also doubles as a safety barrier to prevent vehicles falling into the water. Using 3-D computer modelling, a family of module designs was created in different sizes to be used singly or grouped in a variety of configurations.

Concept
A blueprint for two decades of sustainable economic growth

Context
Urban/temperate

Sheffield Economic Masterplan, Sheffield, UK.

With its goals of creating 30,000 jobs, a new business district and world-class business school, boosting the local economy and raising earnings, an ambitious 20 year economic plan has set out to build on Sheffield's strengths, improve its economic performance and return it to being a major European city.

Opposite
Steel city

Sheaf Square by the railway station at the heart of the industrial city of Sheffield, famous for centuries of steel production and as Britain's centre for the manufacture of cutlery. With growing competition from overseas and manufacturing in decline, the city was in need of a new economic vision and commissioned the UK's first economic masterplan combining economic strategy with physical development.

Sheffield Economic Masterplan, Sheffield, UK

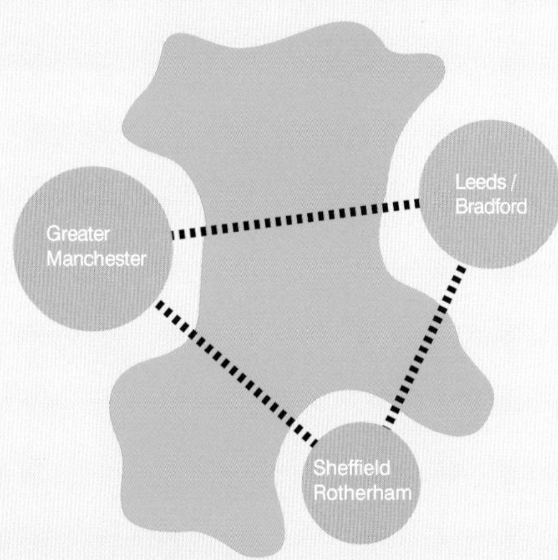

Regional relationships

Administrative boundaries rarely match the economic reality of labour markets and investment flows. The Sheffield economy impacts upon, and is directly influenced by, neighbouring locations and as such the future success of the City Region economy requires all areas to work collaboratively. The masterplan also recognises the importance of connectivity to national markets, particularly the City Region economies of Leeds, Manchester and London, as well as further afield, international connectivity through the airports at Manchester, Doncaster and Sheffield, and the ports of Liverpool and the Humber.

The masterplan created a distinctive, inspirational and deliverable blueprint for the city's spatial and economic development over the coming 15 to 20 years, and has become recognised as an example of national and international best practice.

One of the seats of the Industrial Revolution, the northern English city of Sheffield had experienced economic decline through the second half of the twentieth century. Work to upgrade the city centre, install a tram system and encourage new business produced impressive results with an improved infrastructure and the generation of more than 75,000 new jobs in the decade to 2005. To keep up the momentum and in line with urban policy that sees cities as engines of economic growth, the UK's first city development company, called Creative Sheffield, commissioned an economic masterplan that would drive the next phase of growth to 2020.

Work on the masterplan took its inspiration from the city's history. It explored some of the highlights from the centuries of manufacturing and Sheffield's rich cultural heritage. As far back as the Middle Ages, the city was widely known for its production and use of metals, particularly in making knives. It became a world-renowned centre for cutlery production and is still associated with high-quality tableware. With the Industrial Revolution, the place saw the growth of manufacturing on a large scale and mechanised factories along the River Don produced a stream of metals and steel and products made with these materials. Continuing in its role as a centre for excellence and innovation, at the start of the twentieth century Sheffield was the birthplace of stainless steel. And in the following decades wartime armaments were made here. However, by the end of the twentieth century, new centres of steel production around the world combined with highly competitive pricing saw the collapse of the British steel industry and more than 50,000 jobs were lost in the city.

In recent years, the manufacturing base has survived by moving into areas of specialism including making medical instruments and parts for the aerospace and motor industries. Sheffield has also established a reputation for its creative industries, not least in music as the birthplace of successful musicians including Jarvis Cocker and the Arctic Monkeys. As home to two universities, the city also has an unusually high proportion of young residents with more than 40 per cent of the population aged between 20 and 34—twice the national average.

The masterplan was created as the result of a three-stage process. The first was an extensive review of existing demographic, economic and physical conditions to identify the critical issues which needed to be addressed in the masterplan. Having agreed the overall direction and main priorities, the second step was to undertake a wide-ranging dialogue with stakeholders. This involved key thinkers and organisations at the local, sub-regional, regional and national levels to consider the critical questions and interventions which would help shape and strengthen the Sheffield economy. A range of techniques was used in the dialogue phase from one-to-one interviews through to thematic seminars around the UK and as far afield as Detroit, as well as a conference to test and develop the initial masterplan content. The third and final stage of the process was the development of the masterplan document, with accompanying spatial strategy and delivery framework to help guide implementation and provide a mechanism for monitoring progress.

As part of the detailed analysis within the masterplan preparation it was acknowledged that the successes of the previous decade had been remarkable, but that significant challenges remained. The masterplan presented the case for accelerating the pace of change based on the following factors:

- Evidence showed that many full-time jobs in manufacturing had been replaced by lower paid and often part-time jobs in the service sector.
- Research into the manufacturing sector showed that if current trends continued manufacturing employment would halve by 2020.
- The city lagged behind others in the UK in terms of banking and finance-related employment as well as other business and professional services—these sectors could help in delivering a higher-value economy.
- The city was constrained by a relatively small hinterland, with limited labour demand and supply, and only narrowly based trading opportunities.
- Increasing educational standards with greater numbers of young people entering higher education would increase the demand for better paid and higher skilled jobs.
- Need to respond to the shift towards a more knowledge-intensive UK economy as it responds to increasingly global competitive pressures.
- Sheffield's recent progress involved very high levels of public investment coupled with the use of spare capacity (e.g. in city centre land). These two factors would reach a natural conclusion in the short-term and must be replaced by a more productive economic base.

Sheffield Manufacturing and Service Sector Employment

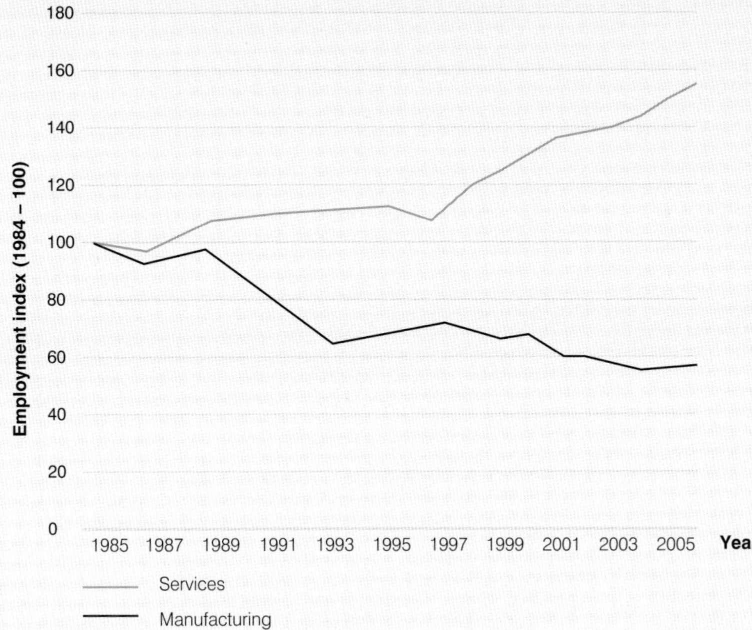

Private Sector Services Employing over 2,000

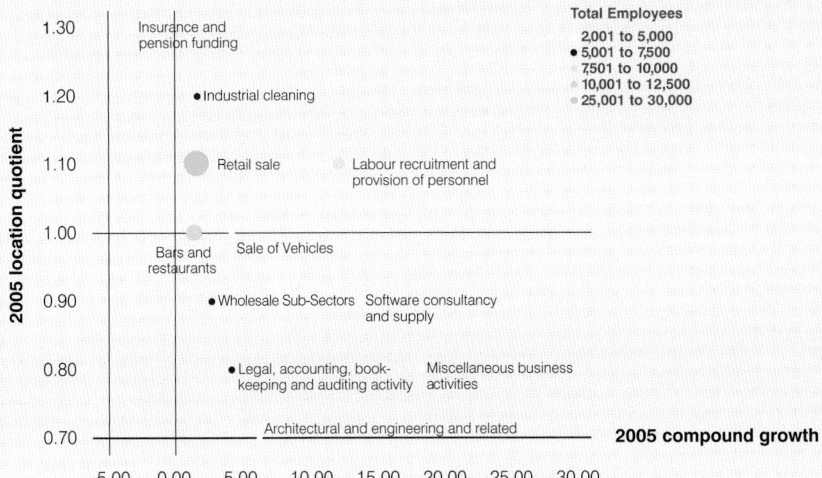

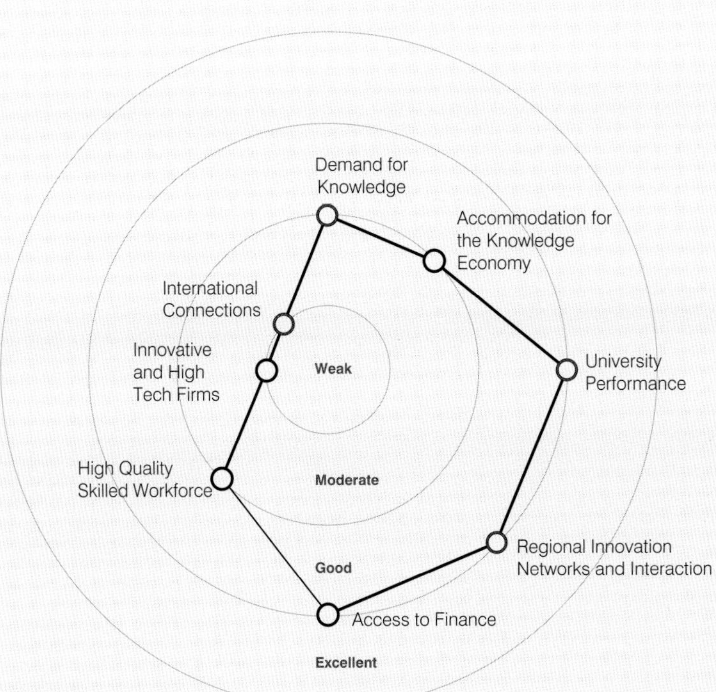

Approach to economic transformation

Sheffield's recent success in reversing decline has been remarkable by the standards of any city, but significant challenges remain. The economic masterplan presents the case for accelerating the pace of change in the economy.

There are three stages in preparing the masterplan.

Stage 1: In-depth analysis of the city's existing demographic, economic and physical conditions.

Stage 2: A wide-ranging dialogue with local people, key national thinkers, and leaders of other international post-industrial cities.

Stage 3: The development of a long-term economic vision and strategy for the city.

The graph, top, shows Sheffield's manufacturing and service sector employment, where the top line denotes services and the lower line denotes manufacturing. Evidence showed that many full-time jobs in manufacturing have been replaced by lower paid and often part-time jobs in the service sector. Recent research on the manufacturing sector shows that if current trends continue, manufacturing employment will halve by 2020.

Centre, graph showing private sector services employing more than 2000 people. The city lags behind others in the UK in terms of banking and finance-related employment and other business and professional services. These are the sectors identified to help deliver a higher value economy.

Bottom, SWOT analysis—strengths, weaknesses, opportunities and threats. Increasing educational standards with greater numbers of young people entering higher education will increase the demand for better paid and higher skilled jobs and also increase the mobility of young workers who will leave to find work if necessary.

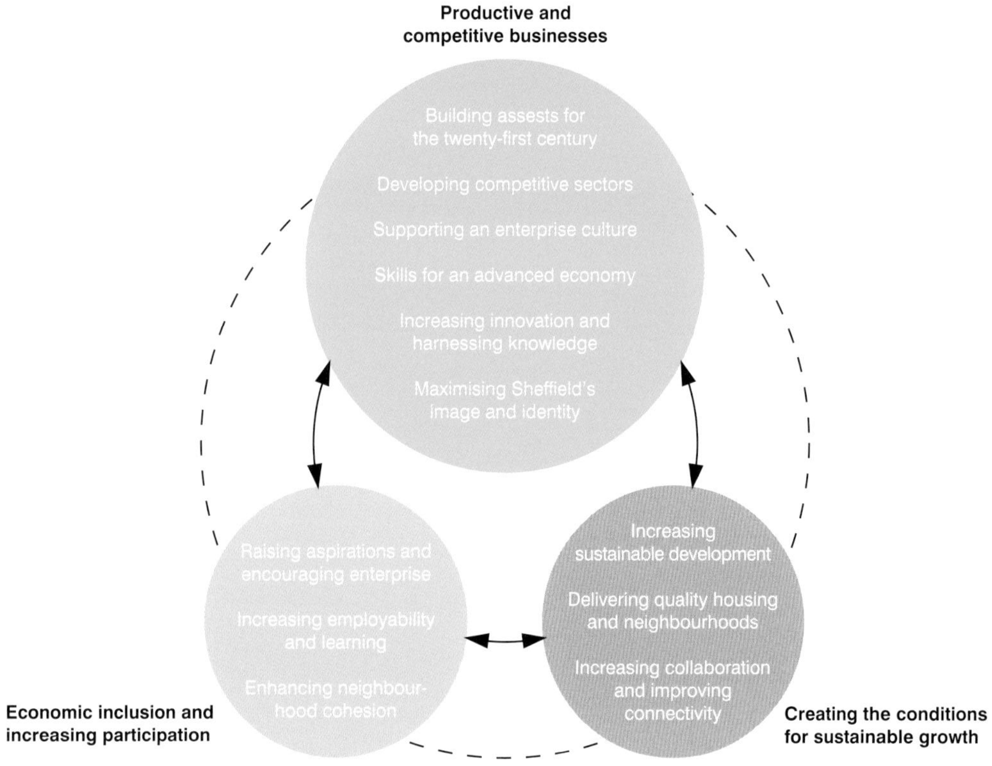

Productive and competitive businesses

Building assests for the twenty-first century

Developing competitive sectors

Supporting an enterprise culture

Skills for an advanced economy

Increasing innovation and harnessing knowledge

Maximising Sheffield's image and identity

Raising aspirations and encouraging enterprise

Increasing employability and learning

Enhancing neighbour-hood cohesion

Economic inclusion and increasing participation

Increasing sustainable development

Delivering quality housing and neighbourhoods

Increasing collaboration and improving connectivity

Creating the conditions for sustainable growth

Development of a three-dimensional strategy

There are three elements to addressing the prosperity gap in Sheffield. These are expressed as three themes which provide the strategic rationale underpinning the economic masterplan and its corresponding programmes and projects.

These are:

- Productive and competitive businesses.
- Economic inclusion and increasing participation.
- Creating the conditions for sustainable growth.

Economic success is not a static objective, and the UK economy is shifting towards a more knowledge-intensive economy as it responds to increasingly global competitive pressures. Sheffield's recent progress has involved very high levels of public investment coupled with the utilisation of spare capacity, for example, in city-centre land. These two factors will reach a natural conclusion in the short-term and must be replaced by a more productive economic base.

The research also identified Sheffield's prosperity gap as a concern. Analysis showed a £1.1 billion shortfall between the city's economic potential and its actual production. The combined factors of too few people in employment and low levels of productivity showed that the per capita growth per annum in Sheffield was only 87 per cent of the English average.

The strategy for change was expressed as three key themes in the masterplan as follows:

- Productive and competitive businesses: Increasing enterprise, innovation, employment and productivity to levels which return the city to a high productivity, high-earning economy.
- Economic inclusion and increasing participation: realising potential and increasing employment to bring 16,000 existing Sheffield residents back into employment.
- Creating the conditions for sustainable growth: providing the capacity for growth through better transport and higher quality neighbourhoods. Ensuring that ambitious economic growth is also sustainable in environmental terms.

With clear goals established in the masterplan, the city development company Creative Sheffield acting as a leader in the new phase of growth has already seen new ideas evolving. Planned innovations include:

- A business district creating a new economic driver in the heart of the city.
- A world-class business school to help employers make small and medium-sized businesses the best in their field.
- A radical internship programme placing the best undergraduate students and recent graduates with local employers.
- A Sheffield brand to be created and used across the city and replace the plethora of confusing logos.
- A local investment fund, set up to assemble development sites and prepare them for development.
- Improving collaboration between centres within the region, and with Manchester and Leeds, to create a regional economy to rival London.
- A city events programme building on headline events and developing an early evening economy to keep people in the city between 5pm and 8pm.
- An initiative to reduce the amount of business going outside Sheffield by encouraging the use of local suppliers.

The main objective of the project was to produce a compelling long-term economic strategy to drive investment and growth within Sheffield. The masterplan has been officially endorsed and approved by Creative Sheffield, Sheffield City Council and Yorkshire Forward. Activities within the masterplan currently under way include a new retail quarter, new business district, the Sheffield Digital Campus for high-tech industries and a programme of strategic marketing.

Components of Sheffield's Prosperity Gap

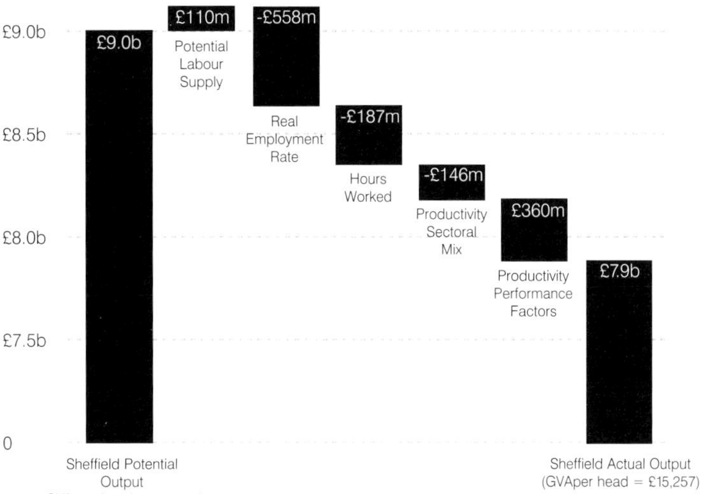

Top
Prosperity gap

The Sheffield Economic Masterplan has identified that there is a £1.1 billion shortfall between what the Sheffield economy could produce and what it does produce. The combined effect of too few people in employment and low levels of productivity in the economy produces a wide gap in prosperity for Sheffield compared to other UK cities. The city has performed very well in recent years with relatively strong levels of GVA (Gross Value Added) per capita growth of five per cent per annum, 1999–2004.

Despite these improvements, an output gap persists between Sheffield and the England average and in 2004 GVA per capita in Sheffield was only 87 per cent of the overall English figure. This works out at almost £2,000 per person.

Strong
Improving
Strong
Strong
Strong
Improving
Sheffield
Meadow Hall
Rotherham

Middle
Housing potential

There is a broad consensus that neighbourhood environments have a major impact on economic mobility and Sheffield's deprived neighbourhoods are in danger of undermining future efforts to increase economic participation. The masterplan supports a series of existing strategies across the city aimed at improving neighbourhood cohesion, in particular the Housing Market Renewal Area Development Frameworks, the Successful Neighbourhoods Partnership which is driving the 'Closing the Gap' strategy and the City Strategy which aims to transform the city's most deprived areas.

Bottom
Regional context and potential

Areas of settlement
Green spaces
Roads
Lower Don Valley city employment location
Sheffield Rotherham economic zone
Upper Don Valleycity employment location
Contributory economic centres/catalysts
Areas of relative housingmarket strength
Housing-led regeneration focus areas
Regeneration/development activity
Spreading market strength
City centre—regional economic driver
City fringe regeneration activity/catalysts
Area wide economic/ employment centres
District centres—local economic activity focii

Below
Welcome to the city

Taking its name from the River Sheaf which was the reason for Sheffield's existence and location of early settlement, Sheaf Square provides an upbeat welcome to the city for those arriving by train. The River Sheaf and the River Don provided the city with an excellent source of clean water and water power for its early industries. The site of the new public square was previously a run-down open car park and congested roundabout.

Opposite

The square looking towards the mainline railway station at night, features an animated stepped waterfall and fountains. And below, one of the largest elements in the space is a huge serpentine stainless-steel sculpture by local artists.

Sheaf Square

As part of Sheffield's reinvention, but separate from the economic masterplan, a programme of enhancing public spaces included the area in front of the mainline railway station. An important gateway to the city, this had been a run-down car park and a traffic-congested roundabout. To provide an upbeat welcome Sheaf Square was created to celebrate arrival in the city. With its huge sculptures and water features and colourful nighttime lighting, the new public space also provides a direct and safe pedestrian route to the city centre. Called the Gold Route, this is a sequence of linked public spaces between the railway station and the centre. Linking with the city's wider regeneration, the work was completed as part of the major refurbishment of the railway station and its environs.

The square, in fact triangular in shape, was created by re-routing a road and demolishing a former office building. Taking inspiration from Sheffield's past as a world leading steel-producing city, one of the central art installations is Cutting Edge. Like a great blade of steel, this is an 85 metre long stainless-steel wall with water flowing down its surface created by local artists Brett Payne, Chris Knight and Keith Tyssen, with glass details designed by Keiko Mukade.

Along with being a striking horizontal element that directs pedestrians between the centre and station, this also marks part of the perimeter of the square and acts as a noise baffle to the ring road. Meanwhile, in the centre of the square, a great snaking water feature made with Pennine gritstone incorporates stepped cascades for flowing water. At night the place is charged with the drama of blistering red and electric blue coloured lighting.

In addition to providing an upbeat arrival and valuable new public space, Sheaf Square's role has been to:

- Create a gateway to the city centre that reinforces Sheffield's reputation as a European city of technological innovation and learning with a lively cultural and artistic life.
- Create a prestigious setting for major investment in almost 46,500 square metres of new commercial and mixed-use development.
- Offer clear and safe integration between train, tram, bus, taxis and cycle transport with inclusive access.
- Create a lively square with potential for active frontages and event space together with opportunities to rest.

Concept

Waterfront revitalisation to upgrade Tianjin's global image and reposition it as a state-of-the-art international port city

Context

Inner city/temperate continental monsoon climate

Hai River Masterplan, Environmental Design Masterplan, and Cultural Heritage District Landscape Design, Tianjin, China.

After centuries as one of China's major trading centres, the city of Tianjin wanted to expand its role in the global marketplace and identified the need to update its image. Along with raising its profile and positioning it as a modern business-friendly environment, the aim was to upgrade the heart of the city around the river and attract more international investment.

Opposite
Changing perceptions

Reconnecting the city with its river, this high-quality public promenade has become an extremely popular destination and has played a significant role in transforming perceptions of this huge and ambitious trading city.

Regeneration

Hai River Masterplan, Environmental Design Masterplan, and Cultural Heritage District Landscape Design, Tianjin, China

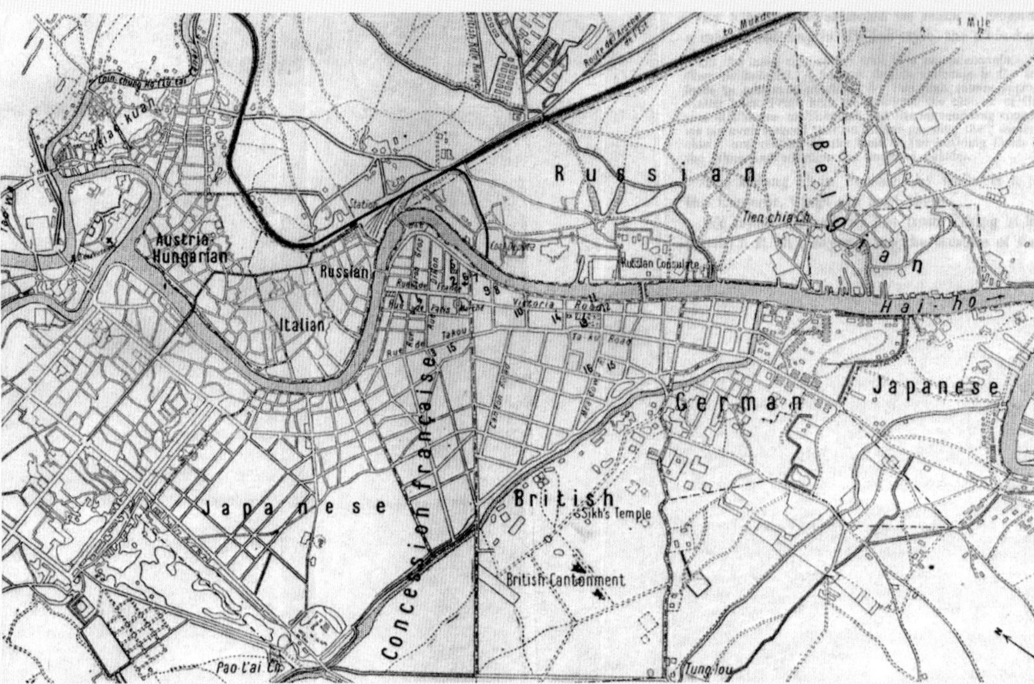

Historic context

The river has always played a prominent role in Tianjin's past and is celebrated in beautiful historic paintings and maps. The map here also shows the colonial districts. Opened for navigation more than 1,800 years ago, the Hai River is part of the largest water system in northern China and it flows more than 1,000 kilometres through eight provinces. However, most recently, its banks were overrun with an accumulation of poor-quality buildings and rubbish and effluent from local industry impaired the water quality.

Six objectives

To unify the masterplan and its four phased development districts, Tianjin's development plan sets out six objectives.

These are to:

- Highlight the long and varied history and culture of the city.
- Attract high-tech industry to the waterfront area.
- Identify city landmarks near the river.
- Protect the ecological environment of the watershed.
- Improve accessibility to the river.
- Develop tourism and recreation along the river.

A major commercial and industrial centre since the twelfth century, Tianjin has an unbroken history of trading not just throughout China, but also with the rest of the world. Its strategic position just under 140 kilometres from Beijing on China's Grand Canal and close to the east coast and Pacific Ocean, has made it an ideal location for business and commerce. As one of the four cities under the direct jurisdiction of China's central government, Tianjin has steadily grown in reputation as an international port city, helped by the establishment of the Binhai New Area, a major Special Economic Zone, which has further strengthened its ties with international markets.

With a population of almost 12 million, Tianjin is China's sixth largest city in terms of urban population and the third largest city in terms of urban land area after Beijing and Shanghai. As part of its legacy as an international centre, the city has an impressive collection of handsome colonial-era buildings constructed by European merchants who built homes from English Victorian mansions and French chateaux to Bavarian villas and Romanesque palaces. The trade with Europe has not always run smoothly, and skirmishes in the mid-nineteenth century led to British and French troops attacking the city. Eventually differences were settled and in 1858 the Treaty of Tianjin was signed to facilitate foreign business.

In addition to the rich character and unusual architecture, another focal feature of the city is the Hai River. Opened for navigation more than 1,800 years ago and part of the largest water system in northern China, it flows more than 1,000 kilometres through eight provinces. The river and its many tributaries are prone to flood and drought and in recent years have become heavily polluted. The city turned its back on the waterway and its banks subsequently became run-down and neglected, and clogged with factories, ad-hoc buildings and refuse.

As part of China's economic revival and new global confidence, the city authorities set about revitalising the urban fabric with the goal of upgrading Tianjin's international image and reviving its great trading past to reposition it as a state-of-the-art international port city. To reverse the trend of neglect, pollution and decay, part of Tianjin's regeneration has been focused on its river, to turn the banks into a beautiful waterfront with a promenade that creates public space by the river. Work also included cleaning up the river to create an environmental resource.

A masterplan evolved to revitalise a vast stretch of the Haihe (meaning Sea River) which winds its way through the metropolis on route to the Bohai Sea. A key feature in the landscape, the waterway is being given back to the people in a scheme that transforms its banks into a continuous green corridor of accessible, linked public space. Focal open spaces of varying sizes, characters and usages have been injected with new landscape features inspired by the city's identity and cultural heritage. Local historical materials juxtaposed with a brighter colour palette emphasise a scale and texture that resonates with the traditional city fabric while also creating a vibrant and contemporary ambiance. Extending more than 20 kilometres, the regenerated area will provide a framework structure for cohesive yet diverse future development. In addition to upgrading and transforming the physical environment of the core river area, work on the future vision also included an economic assessment and analysis for financial modelling to forecast the roles of commerce, foreign trade, science, and technology in bringing Tianjin into full play as part of northern China's economic hub. Traffic circulation was also addressed to combat congestion and improve travel conditions in this growing international logistics centre.

Clearing a path

With the removal of the random and poor-quality development along the river's edge, the opportunity was created to make a broad band of new public space. This entailed an impressive feat of engineering. Regeneration has been focused on the river to transform the banks into a high-quality waterfront with a green spine of public space, opening up accessibility to the river. Work has also included cleaning up the river. This uplifting new space has become premium-value land and is the focus for new development which will grow from the embankment back into the fabric of the city.

The masterplan framework for this scheme aimed to redefine the city's identity and liveability, and to guide its development strategy by placing the river at the nexus of its urban revitalisation efforts. Work on this extensive scheme has been divided into four phases, each with a distinct district identity, starting with a five kilometre stretch in the Cultural Heritage District. On both Hai River banks, the upgrading is concentrated along a ribbon of waterfront around 50 metres deep previously occupied by old factories, ad-hoc development and roads. Old buildings were moved and the road relocated to a position set back from the river's edge. This created long bands of new public space flanking the river. The completed scheme provides contemporary-style, broad, stone-paved promenades, trees and green open spaces with river and city views. The positive impact of the new-style public realm was almost immediate—stimulating land values, increasing tourism and triggering new development in adjacent neighbourhoods including the construction of 30,000 homes, retail centres and cultural facilities. Weaving together spaces and developments of varied scale—from large to pedestrian—has created a complex waterfront environment at the heart of the city that attracts people and activity to the river.

Following completion of the Cultural Heritage District, the remaining phases are the Urban Entertainment District which passes through more than two kilometres of the historical shopping and recreation areas; and the Central Business District, extending almost three kilometres and encompassing colonial architecture. The final stretch is called the Smart Town District, which spans ten kilometres through an undeveloped part of the city where plans have been set to accommodate high-tech businesses and create a sustainable community with impressive environmental credentials. Throughout the works are key elements of public infrastructure requiring special attention including roads, bridges, water transport, water purification, embankment renovation, lighting, greenery and landscape, environmental arts, and public buildings.

The second phase of the project has been completed and planning of the middle section of the development is currently underway. The Hai River mid-stream section is located between two of Tianjin's major urban areas: the Tianjin Central District and the Binhai New District. With 18 kilometres of riverfront, this project serves and connects these existing urban cores. With an area of nearly 100 square kilometres, the site provides the opportunity to define major city functions. Envisioned as an international-standard eco-city encouraging innovative industries and business, this area will become a modern urban service core of the future Tianjin.

Strategy diagram

This diagram shows a range of development opportunities inspired by the site's historic and cultural character and its relationship with the river. The success of new schemes will be rooted in their careful relationships with future land uses and transportation networks.

The urban design framework comprises the following;

1 Hai Memorial Park at the head of the river will complement existing and future cultural and commercial developments.

2 A new commercial area incorporating existing cultural heritage resources adjacent to the centre of the old city.

3 Maximising the rear connections to Tianjin railway station to alleviate traffic issues at the front.

4 A new front door to Hai River by reinvigorating the historic Italian cultural district and water plaza.

5 Replanning of the commercial area to improve connections between Heping Road pedestrianised street and the river.

6 A new multimedia performance centre as a focal point at the curve of the river.

7 Balanced commercial development on east and west sides of the river to enhance the central business district.

8 Reuse old warehouses to create an artists' village, contemporary art centre and outdoor sculpture park.

9 Reuse the old steel factory to create multipurpose exhibition and recreation centre called Discovery Park.

10 Create a Smart Town as a new commercial centre based on high-tech industries and business.

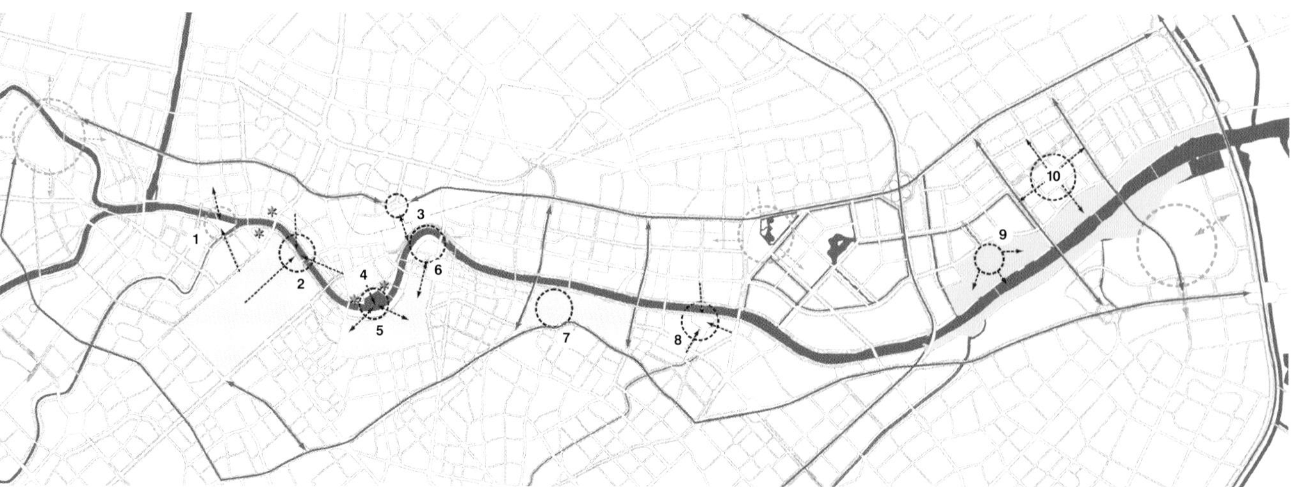

Study area showing developable and non-developable land

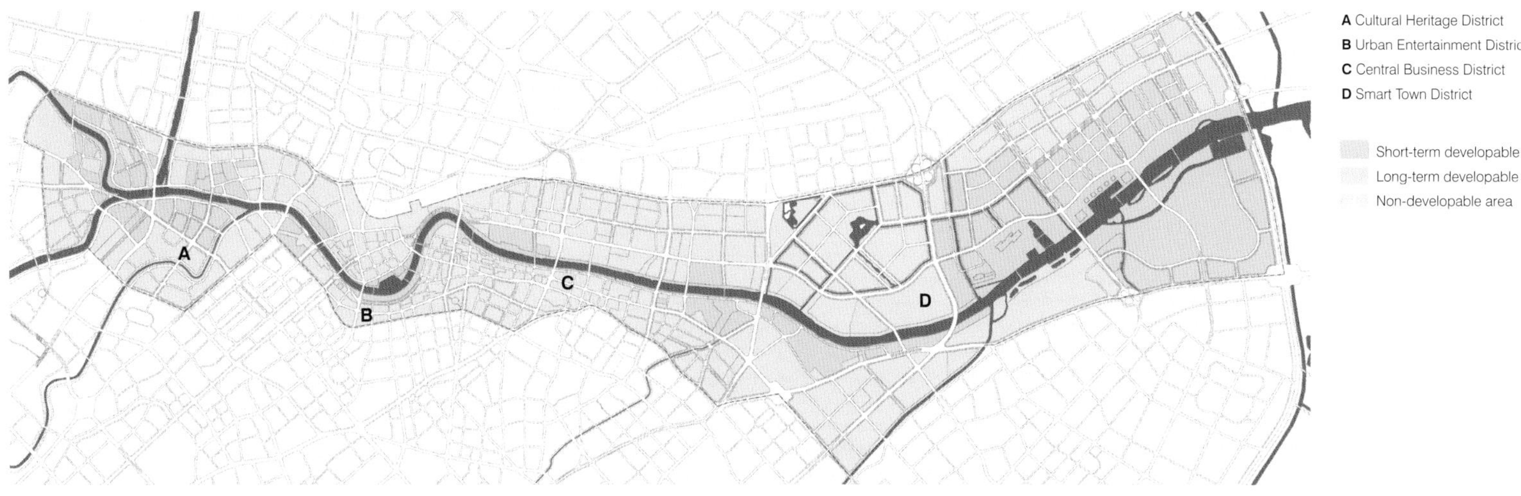

A Cultural Heritage District
B Urban Entertainment District
C Central Business District
D Smart Town District

Short-term developable
Long-term developable
Non-developable area

Study area showing accessibility by walking distance from stations

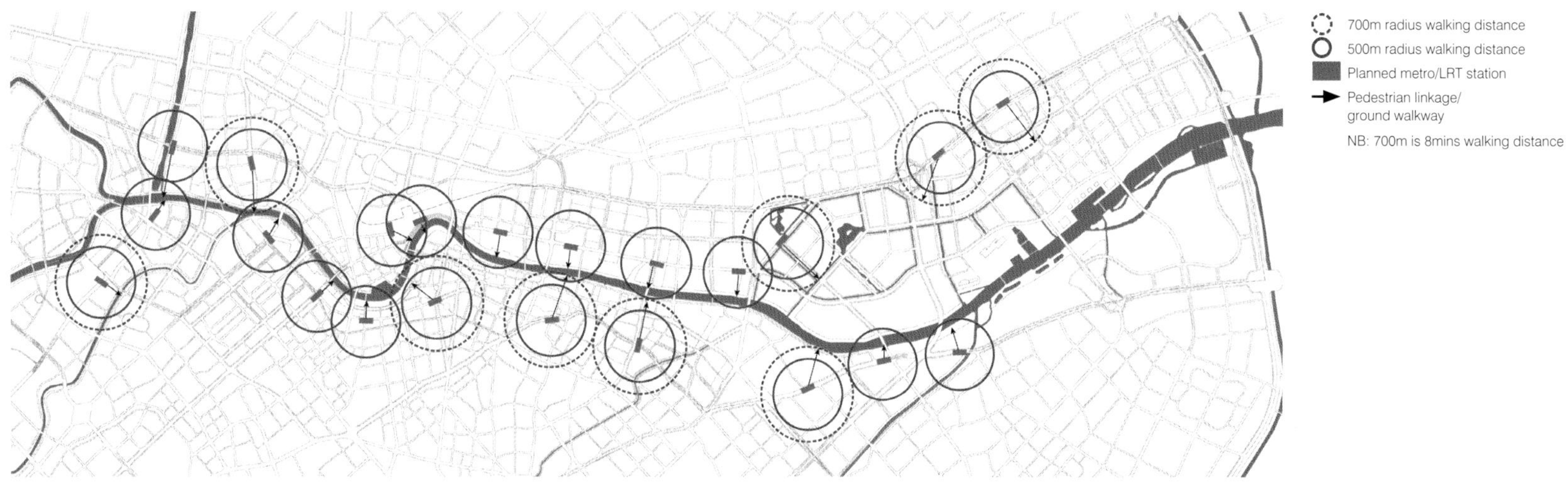

700m radius walking distance
500m radius walking distance
Planned metro/LRT station
Pedestrian linkage/ground walkway
NB: 700m is 8mins walking distance

Study area showing open spaces and waterways

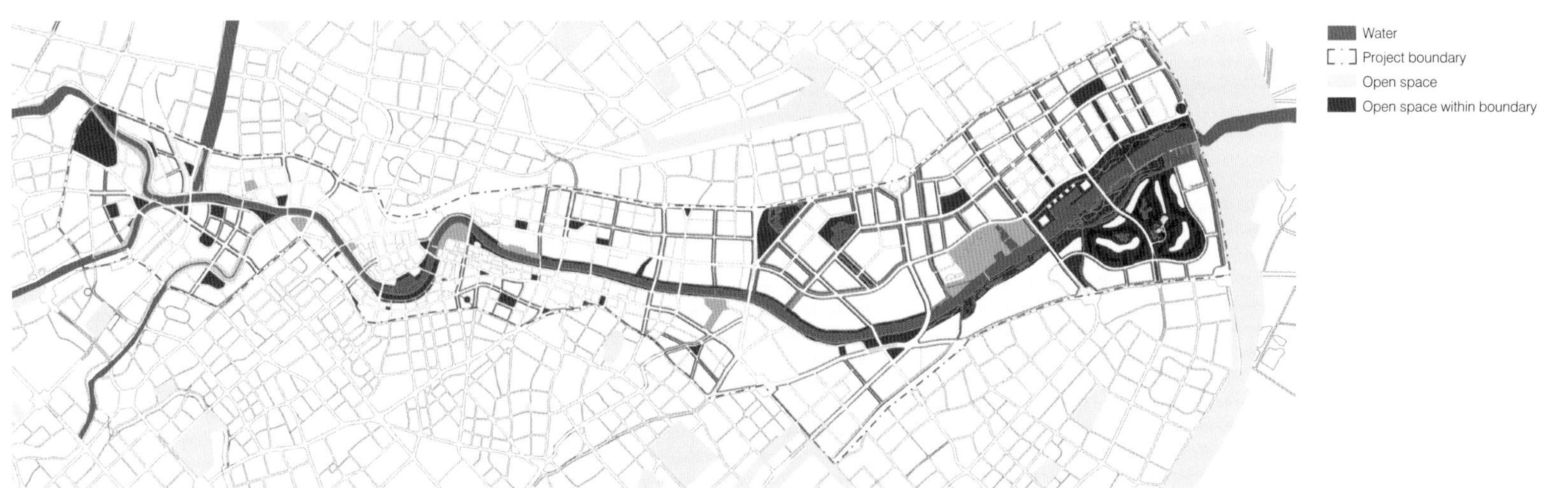

Water
Project boundary
Open space
Open space within boundary

Good quality public spaces used to be a premium in the city; the new embankment has become a popular public stage and a vibrant space with day-long activities—people strolling and cycling, fishing, meeting with friends and even enjoying dancing lessons.

Improved public spaces are not just beneficial to the local community, they are good for the economy making the city more appealing to investors. They are also an important factor for businesses who may want to relocate here and be confident that their staff will be happy in the new environment.

Round the clock

Along with being attractive during the day, the riverside promenade is beautiful at night. The great attention to detail includes high-quality lighting which helps create safe places. It also enables city dwellers to enjoy the experience of strolling by the river and feeling pride in their city resplendent in its colourful lights against a backdrop of huge buildings symbolic of economic confidence. Features such as lighting masts are inspired by industrial design and echo the shapes of the huge cranes at work in the port.

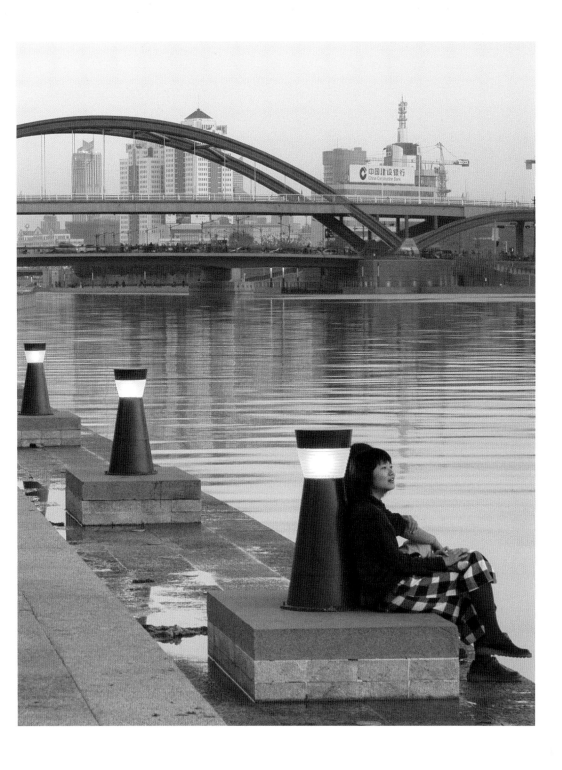

By transforming the river banks into a new public space, the river has been given back to the people. To provide variety and interest along the stretch of promenade, the landscape is broken into open spaces of varying sizes, characters and uses inspired by the city's identity and cultural heritage. Local historical materials are juxtaposed with a bright colour palette for scale and texture that resonates with the city fabric while also creating a vibrant and cosmopolitan atmosphere.

4 Community

"In this age of hasty urban expansion and trite, homogenising globalisation, planning new

communities has become the real testing ground for sensitive design.

People react positively to comfortable homes, safe and friendly neighbourhoods with local shops and services, rich cultural life, and beautiful open spaces. Our design principles are thus simple but thoughtful and effective and include understanding lifestyle, heritage, and culture and respecting topography, ecology and climate. This is how we create communities that we can be proud of and which will be enjoyed for generations to come.

Professor Nasser Rabbat
Aga Khan Professor of Islamic Architecture, MIT

Concept
Benchmark development in native bushland

Context
Pacific coastal bushland/temperate

Murrays Beach, Wallarah Peninsula, Australia.

Finding the balance between environmental protection and development, Murrays Beach at Australia's Wallarah Peninsula sets new benchmarks in sensitive and sustainable community living.

Opposite
Bushland community

The Murrays Beach development is integrated with its natural setting and its buildings sit lightly in the landscape. Studies of the site's natural qualities have included a survey of more than 100,000 trees.

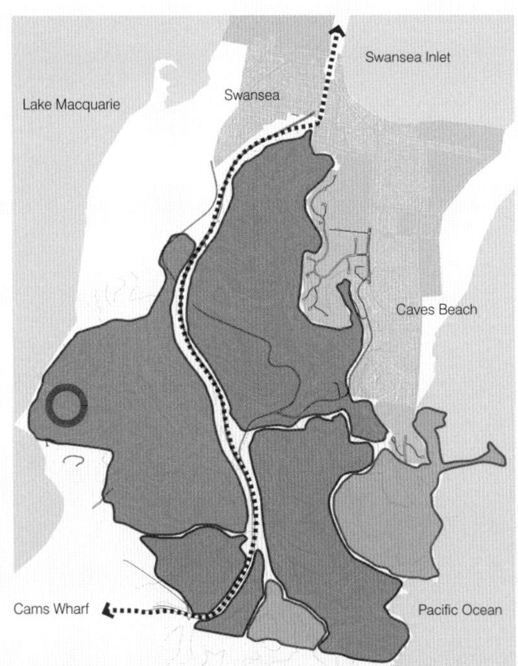

Above
Masterplan

On the eastern shore of Lake Macquarie, Murrays Beach is within easy reach of the lakeside amenities, the Pacific coast and the ecologically rich Wallarah National Park.

Opposite
Lightly in the landscape

To preserve the character of the site, its undulating topography has been retained and residential building plots and building envelopes are planned around existing trees. Utilities are accommodated in shared trenches and service corridors to minimise the disturbance of vegetation root systems.

With its long stretches of beach, rocky outcrops, native forests and rich variety of wildlife, the 600 hectare Wallarah Peninsula forms a long and narrow stretch of land bounded by Lake Macquarie on the west and the Pacific Ocean on the east. Just over 100 kilometres north of Sydney, the area was the traditional land of the Awabakal people, and archaeological investigations indicate signs of habitation dating from 11,000 years ago. With its spectacular setting and impressive range of leisure amenities, the location is highly desirable and the brief for development was to ensure the site's natural assets and bushland character were protected and celebrated.

One of the first tasks undertaken by the developer was to dedicate 178 hectares of the peninsula to the state government to form Wallarah National Park. A masterplan, with supporting management plans, was then established to set an environmental and design framework for development of the remaining land.

Murrays Beach, on the eastern shore of Lake Macquarie, has been the focus of the first phase of development. Early work on the 200 hectare area included extensive surveying to understand the qualities of the site's topography, water courses, wildlife and vegetation, which culminated in a comprehensive survey of more than 100,000 trees. This information was then analysed and used to inform the evolution of the site plan by guiding the location of roads and other infrastructure, building plots and landscape design.

In terms of the natural environment, the development is designed to integrate with the landscape, with buildings sitting lightly on the land, avoiding sensitive areas along the foreshore, wildlife corridors, creeklines and critical flora and fauna habitats. All vegetation communities were mapped and more than six million seeds were collected within the site to ensure the supply of local plants; more than 250,000 plants were propagated in a dedicated offsite nursery. In addition, the site's undulating topography was retained and residential building plots and building envelopes were planned around existing trees. Utilities for homes were designed to be accommodated in shared trenches and service corridors to minimise the disturbance of vegetation root systems.

Below
Learning landscape

Along with making the site easily accessible, boardwalks help to prevent sensitive areas from disturbance by large numbers of walkers. Information panels help residents and visitors understand and appreciate the qualities of the landscape.

Opposite
Retain, reuse and recycle

The distinctive character of this peninsula landscape has been carefully retained and new landscape features are carefully integrated. Rock recovered from the site is reused for retaining walls, driveways, paths and carparks; logs are reused for seating, fencing and steps where appropriate; hollow logs are relocated to wildlife corridors; and vegetation mulch is reused in landscaping.

Water management has been integrated from the outset. The site lies within the Sydney Basin Bioregion and is dominated by a temperate climate characterised by warm summers with no dry season. Rainfall occurs throughout the year, but varies across the bioregion depending on altitude and distance from the coast, with wetter areas being closer to the coast or in higher altitudes. The area's highest recorded rainfall is 246 millimetres in one day, so to manage sudden and extensive rainfall, the landscape design includes water detention basins, swales along the roadsides where appropriate and permeable paving materials. To promote water conservation, each home has its own rain collecting tank and the use of native planting and retention of natural vegetation has dispensed with the need for irrigation.

The sensitive reuse of materials has also been emphasised. Rock recovered from the site is reused for retaining walls, driveways, paths and carparks; logs are reused for seating, fencing and steps where appropriate; hollow logs are relocated to wildlife corridors; and vegetation mulch is reused in landscaping.

Social sustainability has been considered throughout, with homes grouped in small neighbourhoods around amenities such as a local village green, cafe, sports facilities, play areas and community centre. In addition, the networks of pathways and cycleways provide safe and easy movement around the site and help encourage exchanges between neighbours. The cycleways also form part of the site's economic sustainability, by providing easy routes to the local retail centre at nearby Swansea.

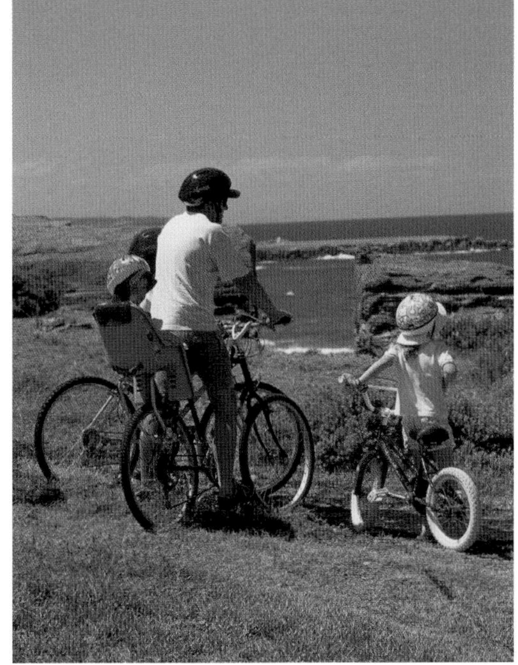

Concept
From airport to community

Context
Prairie/temperate

Stapleton Central Park, Greenways and Community, Denver, USA.

When planes first flew from Denver in 1929, the new municipal airport, which would eventually become known as Stapleton Airport, was located on the city's far-flung north-eastern edge. In the intervening decades, a booming economy and rapid population growth have seen the city expand and gradually absorb the airport into its urban context.

Opposite
Hard top

Hard and hostile, the former airport's site looked unpromising, but was in an ideal location within easy reach of the city centre.

Stapleton Central Park, Greenways and Community, Denver, USA

Echoes of the past

Fragments of the old airport, including this control tower, have been retained as features of the new landscape which are evocative of the site's history. Occupying a vast swathe of land close to the centre of the expanding city, Stapleton Airport's scale echoed that of the surrounding landscape characterised by mountains and prairies.

By the 1990s, Denver's continuing economic growth drove demand for a new and bigger international airport that, once completed, would be the third largest in the world. With the new airport located east of the city, the vacated site of the abandoned airport presented a prime opportunity for redevelopment. The city's response to this opportunity was to create a new community called Stapleton.

The Stapleton vision was to create a modern, mixed-use and sustainable urban development for 30,000 people which would be just ten minutes from downtown Denver. The plan features the ideals of urban life—a network of walkable neighbourhoods, offices and retail areas with an integrated system of parks and open space, including a large central park. The largest urban infill project of its kind, Stapleton has become a national model for environmentally responsible urban redevelopment.

The development plan for Stapleton began to evolve shortly after the airport's closure in the mid-1990s. The site was large, having contained an airport with six runways and five terminals. Two years of extensive research and community consultation revealed that there was demand for a sustainable community based on traditional neighbourhoods with a mix of homes, shops and workplaces, walkable tree-lined streets, diverse and distinctive homes, schools, green spaces and environmental conservation. This vision was enshrined in the development plan called "The Green Book".

The Stapleton Central Park features prominently in the community's masterplan. This park has become a community centrepiece and a regional destination. With its links to the city's existing open spaces and with the creation of new trails, the Stapleton community will have access to the first greenway trail loop around a major US city. The design of the park also acknowledges Denver's Victorian city plan and ensures that Stapleton is integrated into the existing urban fabric by following the street, block, park and parkway pattern.

The goal of creating an environmentally responsible development was a prime consideration from the beginning of the development process. Along with promoting walking and cycling, other environmentally sustainable features including native and drought-tolerant planting, careful water management and construction methods that contribute to sustainability.

At a detailed level, homes are laid out in dense neighbourhoods of around 25 properties per hectare. Homes are mostly in traditional pitch-roof style with porches in the front and garages around the back. This design responds to the surrounding historic neighbourhood's architectural precedents. However, while they reflect the historical homes, they achieve modern performance standards by meeting the independently assessed Energy Star rating, which creates homes that are at least 15 per cent more energy efficient than regular properties. Meanwhile, the main shopping centre, Northfield Stapleton, was granted a LEED Silver certification in autumn 2006 making it one of the US's first retail complexes to achieve this high standard.

Masterplan

Occupying the full footprint of the airport site, the development of a new community has been planned as a series of networked, walkable neighbourhoods, plus offices and retail destinations along with a system of parks and open spaces. One of the most prominent features is the grand Central Park.

The neighbourhoods are created for a variety of income levels and demographics and the parks and open-space systems are designed as an amenity for the new communities and for the wider region.

Right
Building communities

As soon as the first residents moved in to this development, it was clear that the place was going to engender a strong sense of community. The provision of amenities and services is impressive including playschools, work clubs, car-share pools, children's after-school activities, centres for the older residents, sports clubs, cycle clubs, a popular neighbourhood newsletter and more. The landscape design encourages people to explore, take part in healthy activities and enjoy time with neighbours and friends. Many of the older residents say Stapleton has the feel of the places they grew up in where neighbourliness was the norm.

Opposite
Recycling

One of the goals of the Stapleton redevelopment project was to enhance the sense of place by retaining and reusing some of the unique features of the old airport. Airplane hangars and outbuildings have been refurbished to accommodate a variety of businesses including Colorado Studios, a television and film complex. The former terminal's 5,000-car garage has become one of the busiest transit hubs in the Denver area and expanses of the terminal's carpet have found new life as carpet backing in commercial and residential installations. Even the runways have been recycled. Around 5.5 million tonnes of concrete and asphalt have found new uses as foundations, road and pathway aggregate while large, rugged blocks of concrete—nicknamed 'Staplestone'—have been used in walls, bridges and rough-paved areas.

Bavarian Sausages

Below
Stapleton Central Park

Generous public parks and open spaces, including the 32 hectare Central Park, are an important feature of the quality of life for the new community and have boosted the city of Denver's green areas by around 20 per cent.

Opposite
From concrete to creek

Once smothered in concrete and forming part of the runway, the removal of the hard cover made it possible to open up the landscape and reveal features including this beautiful creek which runs through the core of the site.

Forming the heart of Stapleton is the grand Central Park. This 32 hectare park is conceived on a large scale which not only provides a resonance with the size of the former airport but also relates to the nearby prairie landscape. An elongated rectangular shape, the park incorporates a broad promenade slicing diagonally through the green space, along with a large amphitheatre, a woodland area in the west and reinstated, sculpted prairie mounds and dune systems in the north and east. More intimate features include a play pond, sports fields, children's play areas, cafes, trails and pathways.

The park forms part of the open-space system throughout the city and links with the ecologically restored Westerly Creek in the east and Sand Creek in the north. Westerly Creek has been one of the development's great successes. In the days of the airport, the broad creek was buried under the runways in a concrete culvert, but has now been opened and restored with planting including native Colorado riparian tall grasses and short prairie grass.

It now performs the dual function of contributing to the area's stormwater management system and providing valuable wetland wildlife habitat to the likes of racoon, wildfowl and deer. Trails along the creek provide Stapleton's residents with hiking, horseback riding, biking, dog walking and bird watching opportunities.

Concept
An economically, socially and environmentally sustainable urban extension

Context
Edge of town/temperate

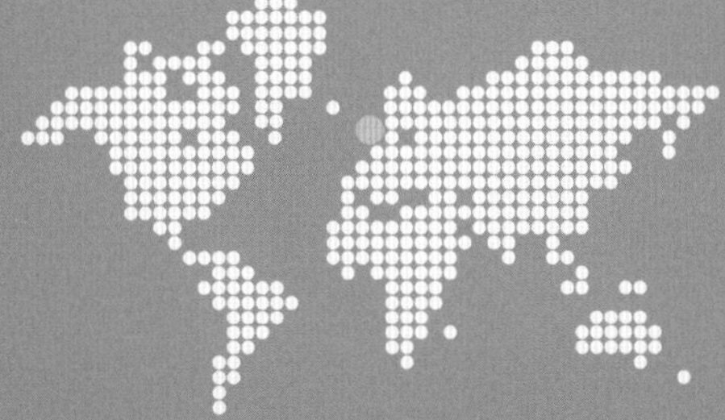

Upton Sustainable Urban Extension Masterplan, Upton, UK.

Originally part of the post-war vision to create new communities, Upton has waited half a century to realise its full potential as a prototype for innovative ways of living.

Opposite
Sustainable new community

Set in a mature landscape and with generous public opens spaces, Upton is a model of sustainable urban growth with a strong environmental, social and economic agenda. Bulrushes, in the foreground, are not just aesthetically pleasing, they provide wildlife habitat and form part of the development's water-management system.

Upton Sustainable Urban Extension Masterplan, Upton, UK

Streetscape

As an integrated extension of Northampton, the design of Upton's urban fabric including the hierarchy of road widths, types of street frontage and prominent buildings all take inspiration from the existing town.

Opposite
In context

Aerial image, top, shows the proposed Upton extension in its setting to the south-west of Northampton. Images below, show from left to right, a close-up of the scheme, the structure of development around a hierarchy of roads, and a network of open spaces.

On the south-west edge of Northampton in central England, the Upton site had been intended in the 1960s to be part of the strategic growth of the town to accommodate people and businesses moving out of London. However, with those plans unrealised, the land remained part of the rural hinterland. Its development was eventually triggered when a new phase of growth was initiated in the late 1990s under the stewardship of the site owner and the government regeneration organisation English Partnerships (now the Homes and Communities Agency). Upton formed part of an area identified for strategic expansion and presented an opportunity for the government to create a model for twenty-first century greenfield development... a sustainable urban extension.

A 44 hectare site, Upton is bounded on the north and east by roads, and on the west by a site for further expansion. To the south is the Upton Country Park. In 2000, outline planning permission was secured on the site for a major extension to Northampton. The approval was for a conventional type of scheme with homes located around a community centre and a school, it was car oriented and the affordable housing was to be concentrated in clusters. Along with the transfer of ownership came the decision to update the plan. With a new sustainable growth agenda from central government, a partnership was set up between English Partnerships, Northampton Borough Council and The Prince's Foundation—a built environment charity, to take on the challenge.

Responding to the proliferation of uninspiring, car-centred housing schemes, the revised plans for Upton were created to set new high-quality benchmarks for housing schemes. Revisions were made during an Enquiry by Design public consultation process. Engaging the local community was a fundamental aspect of the project. The Upton Working Group and Steering Committee set up by the project partners comprised local residents and members of the Upton Parish Council, plus representatives from consultants including masterplanners and engineers. An ongoing dialogue between partners, consultants and local residents informed the design of the development and ensured that the community would take pride in its environment.

In a distinct move away from the conventional proposals, the consultation process embraced a more innovative, sustainable approach. The number of residential units was increased by 35 per cent to almost 1,400 homes to create a critical mass of population able to support local facilities including the school, shops and public transportation. The affordable housing was to be integrated throughout the scheme rather than being segregated. Public spaces were to be generous and varied and pedestrian-friendly street design was incorporated, as was a sustainable approach to stormwater management. Overall, the plan aspired to a socially cohesive, environmentally sustainable community. The idea was to promote healthy lifestyles, reduce reliance on cars and provide a safe and enjoyable, family-oriented place to live. In addition to the high-quality environment, there were ambitions for the buildings to exceed expectations with well-designed and built homes achieving the highest eco ratings by being energy and water efficient.

Guided by these principles, the masterplan evolved as a distinctive mixed-use scheme which has been designed as an integrated part of Northampton. A local centre, including doctors' surgery, shops, offices, a pub, nursery and live/work units are placed at the north of the site, a country park is at the south, and in the centre is the new local school and public square forming the heart of the community. The three are linked by the high street which acts as the anchor of the development. Homes are grouped close by within easy walking distance. Achieving a high average density of 45 homes per hectare, the compact residential areas are constructed in patterns of terraces, streets and mews with properties in a variety of sizes and styles from modest and traditionally inspired two-storey brick homes to grand town houses along with some contemporary-style designs. The rich palette of materials includes a variety of coloured bricks, timber cladding and locally-sourced ironstone. Almost a quarter of the properties are affordable homes which have been integrated throughout the site with the aim of supporting social integration.

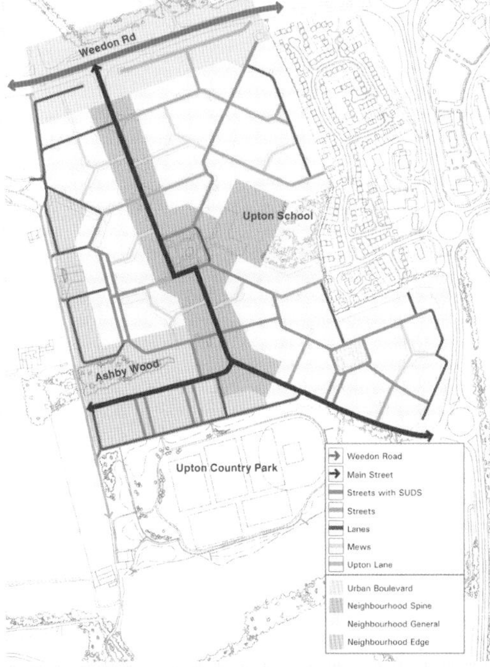
Weedon Rd
Upton School
Ashby Wood
Upton Country Park
Weedon Road
Main Street
Streets with SUDS
Streets
Lanes
Mews
Upton Lane
Urban Boulevard
Neighbourhood Spine
Neighbourhood General
Neighbourhood Edge

Weedon Rd
Upton School
Ashby Wood
Upton Country Park
SUD System
Existing Natural Features
School Grounds
Public Squares
Diverted Nene Way

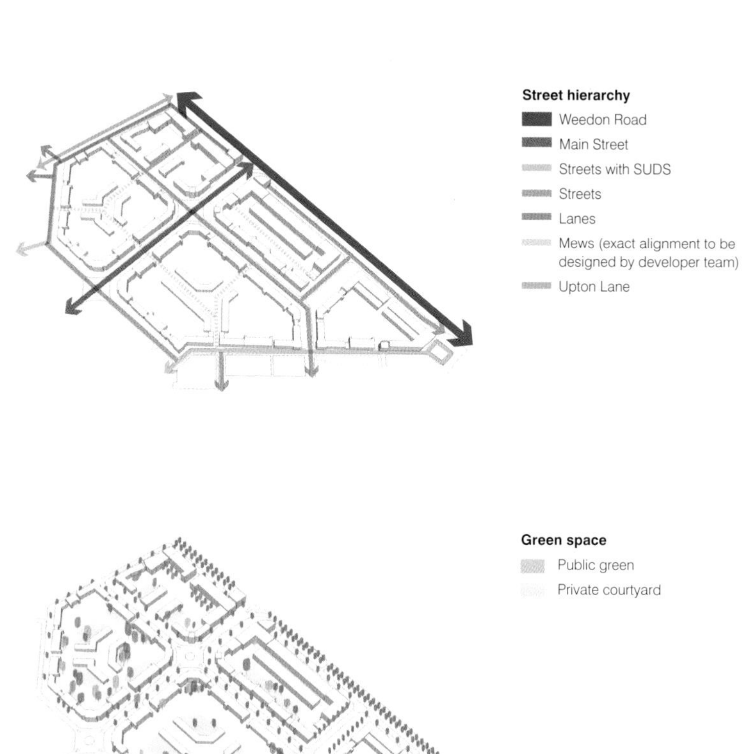

Green space
Public green
Private courtyard

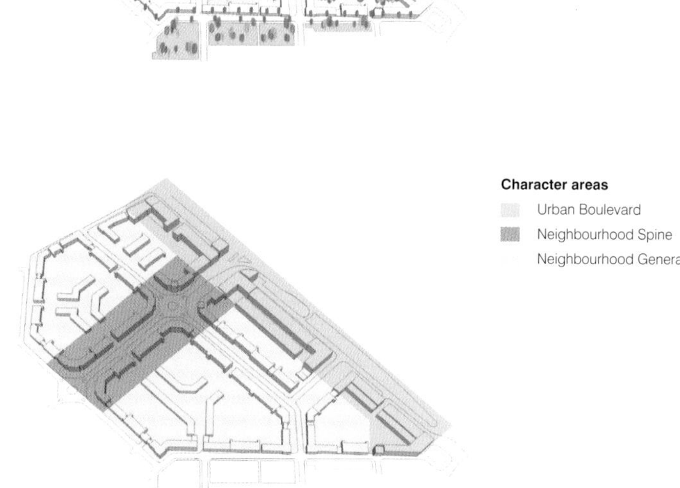

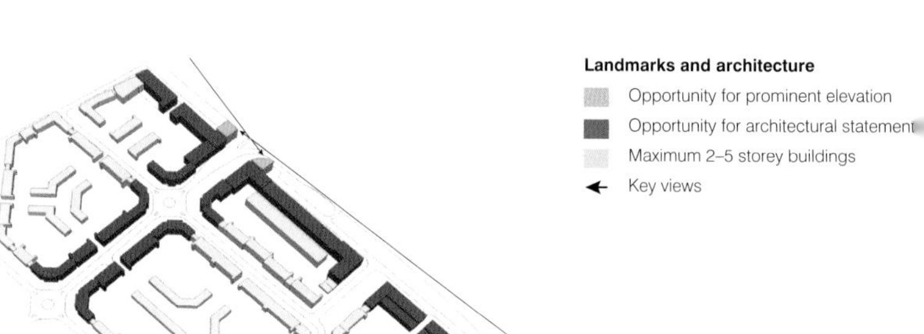

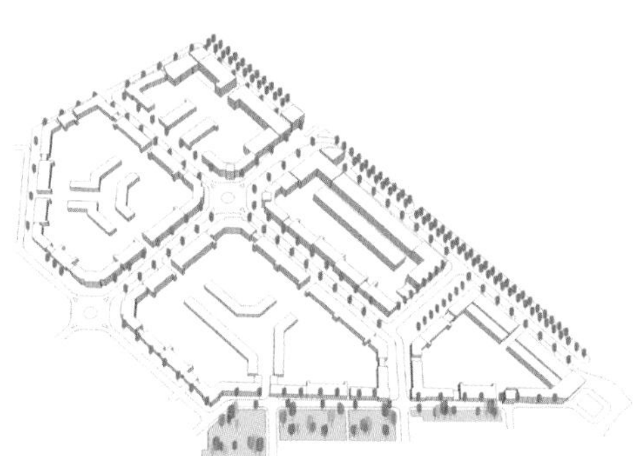

Above, right and opposite
Design guidelines

Visualisations of potential street scenes, above, and right, a sequence of the composite layers incorporated into the masterplan from street hierarchies to green spaces. Upton was one of the first schemes in the UK where a design code has delivered a sustainable community. The code sets out the aspirations for the development based on traditional placemaking principles. Without prescribing a particular design style, the code identified key elements in the character of Northampton's streets and open spaces from street patterns to building materials. By taking inspiration from Northampton it has been possible to ensure that Upton looks and feels like a natural extension to the place.

A high level of energy- and water-efficiency was a major aim of the scheme with all homes achieving the Building Research Establishment Environmental Assessment Method (BREEAM) Excellent rating and some the even higher award of Level 6 for the UK Code for Sustainable Homes. Setting impressive benchmarks for efficiency, buildings are oriented to make the most of sunlight and solar warmth. All south-facing homes are equipped with solar water-heating systems. Around 85 per cent of all homes employ new energy and water technologies, and many incorporate photovoltaic tiles capable of providing a third of a typical family's electricity demand. All homes are designed to harvest rainwater, and some will feature green roofs, while others will have heat recovery ventilation. Also featured in the mix are ground source heat pumps, communal biomass boilers, and water-efficient appliances. These measures have exceeded the scores necessary to achieve the BREEAM Excellent rating.

The visual cohesion of the scheme has stemmed from the production of the Upton Design Code. This was one of the first schemes in the UK to use a design code as a tool to ensure that aspirations contained in the framework plan would be translated into the built development. The Upton Code contained a set of detailed design guides which address spatial planning, masterplan and urban design issues. It was established to guide developers and help the extensive new development evolve in a way that responded to the surroundings, to look and feel like a part of Northampton. Without prescribing a particular design style, the code's success was in identifying elements of Northampton's unique character, especially in its streets and buildings, as a basis for the new scheme. Details include street patterns, the scale of buildings, building types, architectural detail, open spaces and the palette of local materials. The code also defines the strict environmental standards that apply across the development. While Upton has become one of the first schemes in the UK where a design code has delivered a sustainable community, the concept has gained support and has since been implemented in a number of projects.

In another unusual move, much of the infrastructure was completed in the early stages of work on site to help set high standards for the public realm. Much has been learned from the Upton experience, for example the use of collaborative design workshops and design codes have been adapted for subsequent projects. House builders have been able to evolve the use of new eco-technologies and non-standard home designs created for Upton and many of the consultants involved have taken part in conferences to share the experiences of working on such a groundbreaking project.

Opposite
Sustainability

Sustainability has been a key theme throughout the evolution of Upton from concept to construction and maintenance. Social sustainability has been promoted through the inclusive design process where people have been encouraged to share their local knowledge and explain their needs and aspirations. Social interaction is promoted in the built environment which has been designed with opportunities for people to meet as they walk to school, the shops or in the parks. Environmental sustainability includes features such as promoting public transport, cycling and walking, reducing car use, the water-management systems and construction of buildings to very high eco ratings. All buildings must achieve exemplary levels with the national BREEAM Eco Homes Excellent rating and some have gone yet further in achieving zero-carbon status. Developers have been encouraged to incorporate innovative technologies such as photovoltaic cells, wool insulation, solar hot water systems, green roofs and rainwater harvesting systems. Where possible, building materials have been sourced locally.

Economic sustainability has been addressed in numerous ways including providing a dense community to ensure the viability of amenities and services such as local shops and public transport. There are good connections to the whole Northampton employment area and live/work units have been provided locally. In addition, the high quality standards maintained throughout the scheme ensure the place retains its value and remains a good investment.

Left
Water management

Integrated stormwater management was one of the objectives to emerge from the Enquiry by Design process. Overlaid with Upton's street network is a sustainable drainage system (SUDS), known in the US as low impact development (LID) or best management practices (BMP) and in Australia as WSUD, water sensitive urban design. Because Upton sits on the edge of a flood plain, the SUDS provides an efficient and visually attractive way to alleviate the burden of the pipe system especially during short, sharp and intense downpours, which are increasingly common in the UK. This comprises vegetation-filled swales at the roadsides that will collect, convey, and naturally process stormwater runoff, while relieving the watershed of contaminants which are trapped in the soil beds of the swales. This hydrological system discharges water cleansed of pollution into the River Nene to the south, integrating Upton into its local ecology. Filled with attractive reed beds and grasses, these green corridors combine effective management of surface water while also boosting local biodiversity by creating new wildlife habitats.

Concept

A world-class lakeside community designed to demonstrate that what is good for the environment is also good for business

Context

Urban lakeside/mildly temperate

Jinji Lake Waterfront Masterplan and Landscape Design, Suzhou, China.

The Jinji Lake masterplan helps to transform a large swathe of a semi-rural lakeside into a showcase community for 600,000 people and international corporations. The work involved a fusion of urban planning, landscape architecture, environmental expertise and economic strategies that together make one of the world's largest community plans.

Opposite
Sunset on Suzhou

The impressive expanse of Jinji Lake is the focus of a new community development incorporating homes, commercial and retail accommodation along with generous high-quality public space and improvements to the water quality and surrounding natural environment.

Jinji Lake Waterfront Masterplan and Landscape Design, Suzhou, China

Key masterplanning principles

Looking towards the old city, new lakeside development and sculptures have their own distinctive characters.

To ensure the long-term economic, social and environmental sustainability of the project, eight key principles were developed. These were to:

- Develop the hierarchy of public open spaces integrated with the urban design framework.
- Design a dynamic waterfront for different uses and functions that respond to the natural condition of the lakefront.
- Incorporate active commercial and civic uses into, or with close proximity to, open space to ensure socio-economic vitality.
- Provide a variety of recreational and educational opportunities.
- Create a unique identity for each neighbourhood.
- Establish a cohesive visual and physical connection around the lake.
- Implement short- and long-term strategies for improving the lake's water quality.
- Orient residential streets to provide views of the waterfront.

With its World Heritage-status historic gardens, beautiful pagodas, ancient temples and canals, the city of Suzhou has long been a popular tourist destination. In recent years, however, the economy has shown signs of flagging. To provide a catalyst for reinvigorating the city, it was designated one of China's five special development areas with the mission to attract Fortune 500 investors from the USA and Europe into the industrial park, originally a joint venture with Singapore investors.

Key to its strategy of appealing to major corporations and international investors, the city has created a showpiece community around Jinji (Golden Rooster) Lake. This provides an exemplary setting for local and foreign residents and visitors, and is within easy reach of the new industrial park where international corporations will be based. To maximise enjoyment of the waterside, and foster a high quality of life, the development of more than 550 hectares forms a green garland around the shoreline. It incorporates parks and public squares, promenades and boardwalks, cafes and tea houses, fishing piers and viewing platforms, a harbour and marina interwoven with development for homes, offices, a cultural district and shops serving an anticipated population of 600,000. The scheme has also been designed to integrate water-quality measures to protect this scenic lake.

Founded more than 2,500 years ago, Suzhou is on the lower reaches of the Yangtze River, and forms part of the Jiangsu province west of Shanghai. In addition to its architecture and gardens, the city is also famous for its opera and city centre with its ancient history of research, design and production of silk garments and accessories. Suzhou has a population of more than eight million. However, along with taking pride in its past, the city has a vision of a future energised with contemporary buildings and the high-tech economies of its new industrial park. Together, the Jinji Lake project and industrial park will provide opportunities for injecting the metropolis with new life, stimulating investment and development for the larger region.

On the eastern outskirts of the city, Jinji Lake had been part of a semi-rural area and until recently its coastline was fringed by fish farms. Close enough to share the benefits of urban life and far enough away to have a distinctive character, the lake provided an ideal setting for an exemplary water-based development scheme.

The design process included case studies of successful waterside developments around the world, including the popular waterfront promenades of Boston, Sydney and Singapore, full of a variety of promenades, markets, cafes and restaurants, parks and water sports, all drawing people to the waterside activities.

Understanding of these great places included exploring the relationships between architecture and open space, between pedestrians and vehicular traffic and between the waterfront and surrounding neighbourhoods.

As the masterplan evolved, it became clear that the lake's size demanded that a varied rhythm and pace should be incorporated into the landscape and community design. As a result, the plan incorporates eight district neighbourhoods around the lakeside including an arts and entertainment village, a discovery island and a harbour neighbourhood. Each place has its own distinct identity, responding to the lake, taking full advantage of the views and amenities with plenty of opportunities for exploration and interaction with the water from strolling along its shores to sailing.

District 7
Mirror's Crossing
Neighbourhood

District 6
Arts and Entertainment Village

District 1
Harbor Plaza

District 8
Discovered Island

District 2
Grand Promenade

District 5
Reflection
Gardens

District 4
Reflection Point

District 3
Marina Cove
Neighbourhood

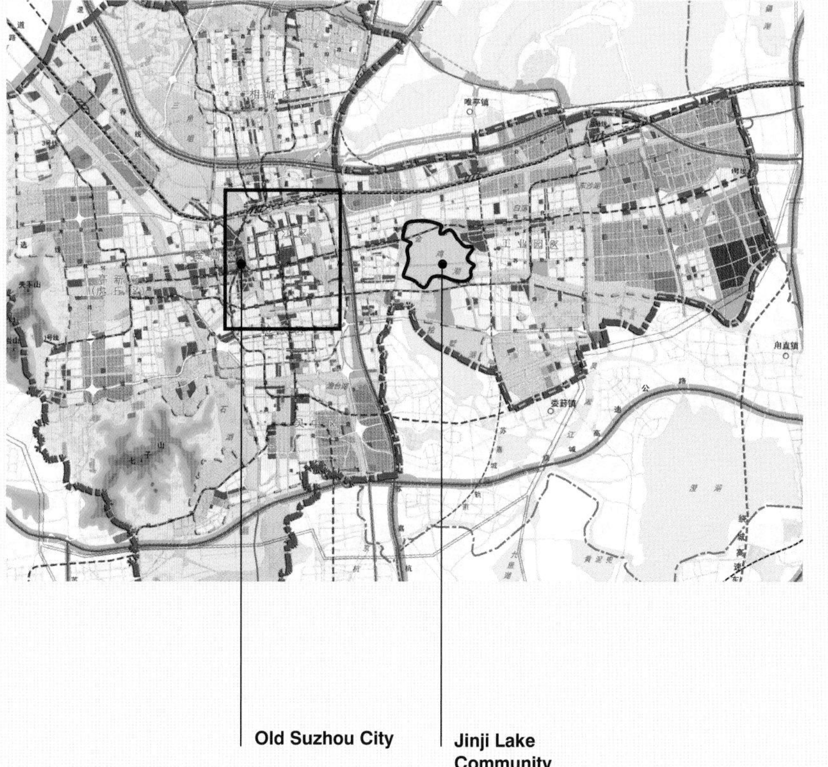

Above
Masterplan

The masterplan framework showing the eight district neighbourhoods, each with its own distinct character ranging from the upbeat Harbor Plaza which is the venue for spectacular light, water and music shows, to the tranquillity of Reflection Point. As part of the commitment to sustainable design practices, careful attention was paid to water quality and interactions with natural ecological systems. Natural and created wetlands along receiving streams are used to filter pollutants found in water from nearby agricultural land and in urban stormwater runoff.

Left
Context

Jinji Lake and new community shown in their regional context to the east of Suzhou.

Above left, middle and right
Relishing the public realm

The challenge of the open space design was to respect the historic traditions of Suzhou while also creating a modern environment for the new community. It is clear from the enthusiastic crowds, that local people have no hesitation in enjoying their new waterside walkways and parks. Suzhou has a reputation as one of China's most desirable cities to live and work in, and so there were high ambitions for the new development. The quality of the built landscape has exceeded expectations by attracting high standards of developments and land values have increased more than fourfold since the conception of the project.

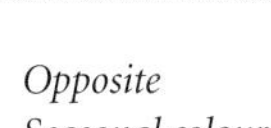

Opposite
Seasonal colour

Creating a composition of texture and colour, strong horizontals and verticals, this area of Millennium Park at Harbor Plaza combines beds of vivid red seasonal flowers with the strong vertical trunks of ginko trees which are encouraged to grow tall and straight with their intricate bamboo scaffolding.

Overleaf
Peace and tranquility

In the Water Plaza, the simple horizontal boardwalks and limited palette of materials deliver an air of tranquillity. This water garden is a contemporary version of the traditional Chinese notion of "borrowed landscape" and the boulders mark the original lake shoreline.

To add a further layer of distinction, the lake is divided into two zones. The north-western section is described as being active with a marina and a variety of water sports facilities, a man-made pleasure island, arts and entertainment amenities and high-density development including high-rise apartment complexes and offices. The main entrance area called Millennium Plaza offers a platform for stunning views and underlining the theme of time it features a massive clock inset into the paving. Close by is Harbor Plaza, a new gathering place for the city, where routinely at weekends, crowds of more than 10,000 people gather for the spectacular light and music show which is based around an impressive sequence of high-powered, water-jet fountains.

Also in this area is a contemporary interpretation of the traditional water garden, a serene place featuring boardwalks, pavilions and pergolas which lead people to the water's edge. Boulders set into the lake's edge to encourage interaction with the water inviting people to paddle, sit on the rocks and contemplate the views.

Meanwhile, the south-eastern section of the lake is more tranquil with Reflection Point Park, Reflection Gardens, natural wetlands and canals, trails, a bird sanctuary, an education area and low-density building.

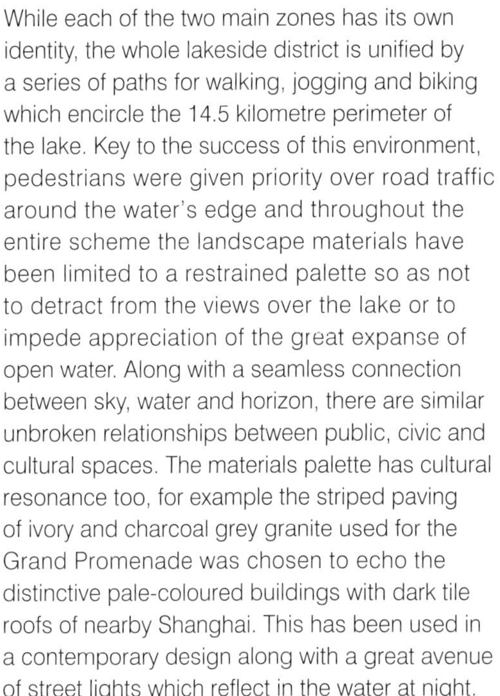

While each of the two main zones has its own identity, the whole lakeside district is unified by a series of paths for walking, jogging and biking which encircle the 14.5 kilometre perimeter of the lake. Key to the success of this environment, pedestrians were given priority over road traffic around the water's edge and throughout the entire scheme the landscape materials have been limited to a restrained palette so as not to detract from the views over the lake or to impede appreciation of the great expanse of open water. Along with a seamless connection between sky, water and horizon, there are similar unbroken relationships between public, civic and cultural spaces. The materials palette has cultural resonance too, for example the striped paving of ivory and charcoal grey granite used for the Grand Promenade was chosen to echo the distinctive pale-coloured buildings with dark tile roofs of nearby Shanghai. This has been used in a contemporary design along with a great avenue of street lights which reflect in the water at night.

Landscaped public spaces are highly varied in style, some taking inspiration from ancient designs, others entirely modern. They range from formal gardens with brightly coloured flower beds to small woodlands where thousands of new trees have been planted including camphor trees and stands of red maple and willow. Unusually for China, where public spaces tend to be highly regulated and controlled, there is generous public access.

In the detail of the public space design, one of the challenges was in combining respect for the historic traditions of Suzhou and looking to the future. The goals were to weave together the old and new worlds, business and recreation uses, everyday living and education about the environment. The dynamic nature of the high-quality public realm was conceived to appeal to local residents and also to display confidence to international investors. Even in the early stages of the development, investment in the public realm had already paid dividends by seeing land values increase at an impressive rate.

Opposite
Grand Promenade

Along a great stretch of the western bank of the lake, the Grand Promenade provides a broad walkway for enjoying views. The minimal materials palette ensures that all attention is focused on the water and sky. The success of this new community lies in the continuous pedestrian-oriented waterfront which links and runs through all eight neighbourhoods and provides the seamless integration of public spaces with civic and cultural areas and the private realm.

Top left
Arts and Entertainment Village

Design solutions are contemporary expressions of vernacular traditions and this formal pool surrounded by residential development demonstrates how landscape design becomes an integral part of the community's infrastructure.

Top right
Mirror's Crossing Neighbourhood

A shallow-arch bridge with colourful flower planting along its edges and through the middle which forms a continuous link between gardens flanking this waterway.

Above
Green and pleasant

Planted areas have a great richness and intensity combining trees with areas of lawn and waterside planting, and unlike many formal Chinese gardens, people are encouraged not just to admire but to interact with the landscape.

Above
A lake for all seasons

Local people have acknowledged that the open spaces around Jinji Lake have added to their quality of life and are enjoyed all year round. Flaming red maple trees in the snow, and the sense of being transported to a different place and time is part of the philosophy of traditional Chinese gardens.

Opposite
Reflection Gardens

The scheme's sustainable approach includes establishing natural wetlands such as these gardens at Reflection Point. The exemplary environmental design has ensured that many of China's mayors have made Jinji Lake a permanent stop on their annual national tours of significant new public works.

A key element of the plan is maintaining the water quality of Jinji Lake. One of the cleanest lakes in the country, it was anticipated that new development might increase pollution. Design guidelines outline a stormwater runoff management programme with a proposal for incorporating a high-quality waste water management system. Natural water-system management is also proposed, with the expansion of existing wetlands along with the creation of new wetlands and 'bio-swales' within close proximity to the lake's edge, where canals criss-crossing the region enter the lake. By reducing suspended solid matter in the water, reeds and grasses perform the function of natural filters. The process also reduces the quantity of nutrients and heavy metal pollutants entering the lake. The masterplan also addresses recommendations for cleaning up existing pollution.

Not only have the parks and gardens provided the city with unusually generous public open space, encouraging interaction with water and promoting an active lifestyle, the creation of a contemporary garden style has been identified as a bold move in a city noted for more than 2,000 years of gardening history. The Jinji Lake scheme's sleek and contemporary styling in architecture and park planning has become a tourist destination in its own right, and has attracted developers from around the world.

Concept
Redefining suburban new community design and sustainability

Context
Rural/temperate

Ladera Ranch New Community Masterplan, California, USA.

Responding to the challenges of California's increasingly tough environmental legislation, the Ladera Ranch development is recognised as a breakthrough model for sustainable green building practices, and has established new high standards for the development of masterplanned communities in Southern California.

Opposite
Close-knit communities

High-density housing ensures that people have a great sense of belonging to a community and that they are close to the amenities and services they enjoy and need.

Community

Ladera Ranch New Community Masterplan, California, USA

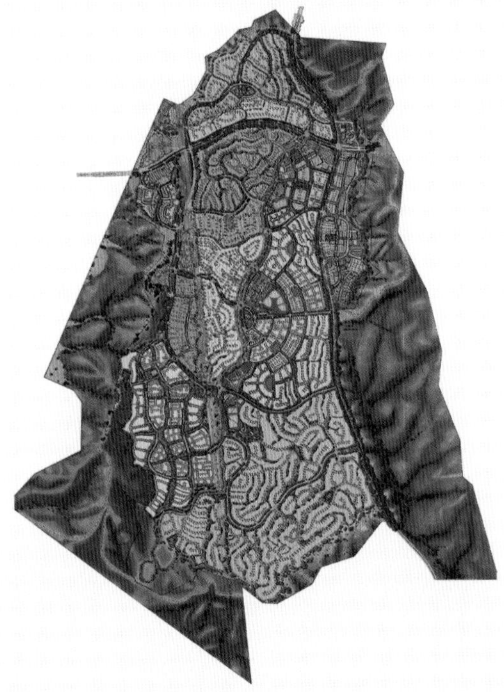

Above
Masterplan

The Ladera masterplan evolved from four key ideas; to respect the legacy of the land, to ensure that each village design was distinctive, to give neighbourhoods a fresh, authentic character and to integrate an emphasis on social interaction.

Opposite
Green and pleasant

Generous green spaces create a beautiful setting, and also provide natural water management with swales to capture storm water and enable it to soak slowly back into the land. Site planning features such as street patterns, curb-separated sidewalks, street-width restrictions, roundabouts and pocket parks were required of all builders. In addition, architectural requirements such as reduced garage emphasis, front porches, varied massing and the achievement of an authentic style were set out in the guidelines.

A robust design review process was established to guide individual builders in implementation.

Set in a historic ranchland setting, this substantial new community is surrounded on three sides by open landscape and strikes a careful balance between providing much-needed housing and preserving precious natural habitat and resources. Creating strong market demand, the scheme became one of the fastest selling masterplanned developments in the USA.

On the historic Rancho Mission Viejo, a vast working cattle ranch in Orange County, a site of more than 1,600 hectares was designated for the creation of a new, environmentally responsible and well-served community of around 30,000 people in more than 8,000 homes.

The masterplan evolved from four cornerstone ideas; to respect the legacy of the land, to ensure that each village design was distinctive, to give neighbourhoods a fresh, authentic character and to integrate an emphasis on social interaction. In achieving the desire to protect the landscape and natural habitats, around 650 hectares of sensitive habitat has been set aside from development land to be preserved in a perpetual land trust. A conservation and management programme is integrated with features such as the careful use of water, native and drought-resistant planting, and the limited use of turfed areas. To achieve the goal of distinctive neighbourhoods which foster a strong sense of community the mixed-use design arranges homes in a cluster of six villages each provided with local amenities. Along with high-quality and energy- and water-efficient homes, the scheme also includes commercial and retail centres within easy reach of homes. The two main town centres are East and West Mercantile; East Mercantile offers a mix of retail, office and multi-tenant commercial space along a pedestrianised street and West Mercantile offers smaller-scale neighbourhood services.

The housing meets the needs of a mixed-economy community with a range of properties from large family villas to rental apartments. To reduce car use and encourage people to enjoy the outdoor spaces, most homes are within walking distance of local amenities including shops, offices and restaurants, playgrounds, schools, nurseries and libraries. Fulfilling the social and cultural aspirations of the plan, a community service organisation was established to promote activities to reflect the interests of residents and as a result the community spirit is thriving with the founding of more than 150 groups and clubs which organise a year-round programme of events.

To encourage healthy lifestyles, open space is easily accessible too and includes walking and cycling trails with connections to the regional trail system, more than a dozen parks, and sports facilities including soccer, baseball and swimming. All homes are within two blocks of a neighbourhood park or other open space.

Homes have been built in smaller than typical builder parcels to enhance the architectural and housing type diversity. To ensure that design and construction were completed to the highest possible standards, builders were subjected to a competitive selection process. At the local scale, each village is carefully sized (900–1,400 dwellings) to allow all residents to be within a seven minute walk of a central area comprising schools, child care, live/work housing, parks and, in most cases, a village green. Also included is a social and leisure club; typically 1.5 hectares in size with a 500 square metre building, the club provides swimming, a children's play area, meeting rooms and places for weddings and other special events. The home association offices are also based here, so residents can come for serious as well as leisure-oriented business.

Around these village cores, can be found the highest density housing enabling large numbers of people to be close to services and amenities. A unique housing type, called Home-Based Business, was developed in two of the villages which combined living and working space, so that small businesses could exist in the same building as their proprietors. Not previously built in Southern California, this housing type required substantial work in code and zoning adaptation to achieve planning permission. Now built, this housing type has proved especially successful and has added to the list of project innovations.

All village cores, schools, child-care centres, major parks and retail services are located on a central multi-modal movement, or activity corridor, so that all facilities can be available to all residents with the greatest level of convenience and least use of the car.

Above and opposite
New ways of living

Arranged around open spaces and pedestrian walkways, the layout of neighbourhoods provides plenty of opportunities for social exchange and enjoying public spaces. The presence of cars is downplayed, with most traffic dispatched to the edge of the development and to reduce speeds, traffic-calming measures include narrow roads and roundabouts. Meanwhile, walking is encouraged and pathways make it easy and pleasurable for residents to walk to other neighbourhoods or amenities without crossing a major street. In Terramor all homes are within just a few minutes of open space including the water park with its open-air pool and children's play area. There are also paths leading to the Ladera Ranch community trail which encircles the whole community.

The success of the project has been its ability to appeal to residents who are attracted to the new ways of living. It addresses the three tenets of sustainability, environmental, social and economic. In environmental terms the energy and potable water demand reduction, high-quality landscape and habitat protection provides a beautiful and healthy setting. In social terms the work on community interaction has paid dividends with the growing numbers of clubs and groups catering for a broad range of interests. In economic terms, the shift of focus to creating great neighbourhoods has seen land values rise substantially compared with nearby by communities.

At the neighbourhood level, a strong emphasis was placed on delivering visual appeal and distinctiveness to avoid the monotony of many previous developments. Detailed historical research was completed by the planning and architectural team to identify the key elements of walkable and popular neighbourhoods elsewhere in the region. Specific architectural principles, street characteristics, neighbourhood size and landscape details were identified. Each neighbourhood was accompanied by design guidelines which defined these important elements.

One of the last villages to be completed was Terramor in the south-western area of the site. With rapid advances in environmentally responsible design and construction and with local building legislation becoming ever tougher, Terramor benefited most from the latest thinking in sustainable development.

From the outset, this village was designed with an innovative approach tailored specifically to environmentally aware buyers. This focus was generated through surveying people who had expressed an interest in Ladera Ranch; it asked them to describe what sort of homes they would find most appealing. Respondents said they dreamed of a home that was part of a community and where there was a strong sense of place. Many people were town dwellers, often living in older homes, who were considering a move to suburbia. They were identified as a new type of buyer for Ladera.

The scheme of just over 1,200 homes was designed with a particularly broad market appeal featuring detached family houses and terraces of townhouses along with condominiums, courtyard homes and live/work units. Green building elements include water and energy efficiency through features such as formaldehyde-free insulation, fluorescent lighting, energy-efficient appliances, instant hot-water systems and low-flow water fixtures along with low VOC paints and carpets, and optional natural finishes such as certified wood, bamboo and cork. The mandatory programme for recycling ensured that two thirds of construction waste materials were reused. Among the most popular green features are the roof-fixed photovoltaic panels which are fitted to almost 40 per cent of homes. The result is that the average home at the development uses 20 per cent less energy and water than comparable homes in Orange County. At the time of its completion, Terramor's installation of photovoltaic panels made it the largest solar-power generating community in the USA. In the broader landscape, drought-tolerant planting, reduced turf areas and weather-responsive, centrally controlled irrigation systems form part of the water-conservation measures.

Ladera Ranch green features

- A 6.5 kilometre long central bio-filtration system which runs through the core of the site has been engineered to collect and naturally treat low-flow stormwater runoff.
- This green spine also accommodates an activity corridor for walking, cycling and running that links all villages.
- A centralised computer system provides close control of the irrigation system.
- The villages of Terramor and Covenant Hills adopted green building programmes.
- The development at completion had the largest concentration of homes with photovoltaic energy generation in the nation.
- Ladera's average home energy use is 20 per cent lower than the national average.
- Over 20 per cent potable water demand reduction was achieved including almost 50 per cent irrigation water reduction.
- An impressive 70 per cent of construction waste was recycled.
- Improvements in Indoor Environmental Quality with low off-gassing materials and natural lighting and ventilation guidelines.

5 Public Realm

“Architecture, landscape architecture and urban planning

interweave to mutually define the contemporary city.

Animated, even electrified, by human need and habitation, comprised of modulated, three-dimensional space, and complemented by naturalistic elements, the public realm shapes the city's public face as a roof creates privacy. One demands the other.

Robert Ivy
FAIA, editor-in-chief, Architectural Record

Concept

High-quality public spaces make places, create distinctiveness and add value

Context

Urban landscape plaza, park and streetscape/temperate

Tokyo Midtown Landscape Design, Tokyo, Japan.

When Japan's Defense Agency relocated its headquarters out of central Tokyo, the move created a rare inner-city redevelopment opportunity. In an unusual move, the scheme dedicated half of its precious land area to the creation of public open space. The landscape design of this large mixed-use complex marks a significant cultural shift in the approach to creating public space and designing landscapes in Japan.

Opposite
Tokyo Midtown

Unlike other recent large-scale developments in Tokyo which are raised on a podium, this project is explicit in its desire to plug in to the wider city and connects at ground level to the surrounding urban context on each edge.

Midtown Tower
Plaza
Midtown East
Galleria
Design Wing
Hinokicho Park
Ritz Carlton Residences

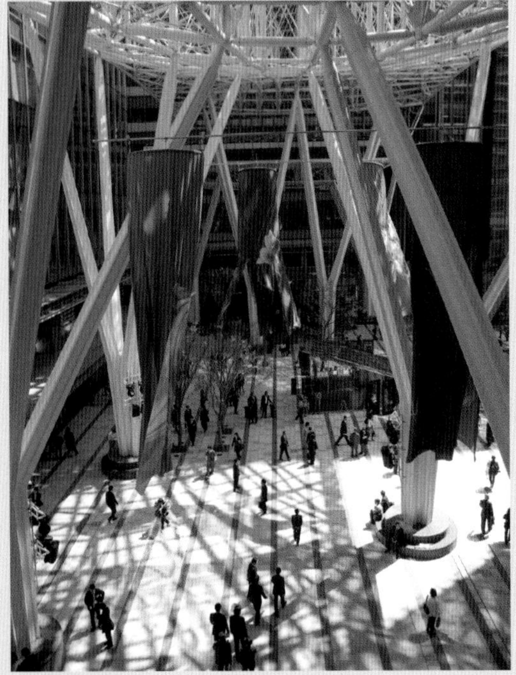

Above
Round-the-clock landmark

Known for its clubs and bars, Tokyo Midtown joins the city's frenetic nightlife.

Bottom

The new buildings are on an impressive scale with this supersize galleria like the set from a futuristic film. From the south, pedestrians are drawn through the densely built portion of the site and led through to the beautiful open spaces beyond. The dynamic scheme derives exciting tensions from the contrasts of hard and soft landscaping.

Opposite
Masterplan

Buildings in the south and south-eastern part of the site are wrapped round with the sequence of gardens which range from the intimate and detailed scale of the Garden Terrace to large expanses of lawn.

In the heart of Tokyo's Roppongi District, noted for its nightlife and cosmopolitan population, plans for the ten hectare former military site were to transform it from an introverted and enclosed enclave to an extravert and well-connected piece of city. Most radically, around half the site was to become a significant public park and gardens.

Called Tokyo Midtown, the development has become an extremely popular destination attracting more than 35 million people in its first two years. The scheme incorporates a cluster of five mid- and high-rise towers containing a mix of uses including commercial, retail, residential, a hotel and cultural amenities. Grouped asymmetrically, the buildings sit in southern and western portions of the site and are wrapped round with green spaces including the Hinokicho Park to the east.

In a city which is largely comprised of a patchwork of small and irregular parcels of land, the fact that the Midtown site was so large and had been intact for centuries presented a rare opportunity to create an entire new district. The roughly square-shaped plot was once a feudal estate, and throughout the seventeenth and eighteenth centuries was the villa residence for the feudal lord of the Mouri family. In the Meiji Period, from 1868–1912, the area became an army post. Following World War Two it was used for US military housing, the era when Roppongi became known for nighttime entertainment. Most recently, the site served as Japan's Defense Agency headquarters. The agency's vacated site was offered at auction in a sale that made headlines and achieved renown as one of the city's most expensive real estate transactions. Part of the reason for disposing of the land was to encourage development that would energise this area and provide a boost to the sluggish economy.

A fusion of traditional and modern design, Tokyo Midtown also combines Western and Japanese influences. The concept of *wa* translates as "the essence of Japanese-ness" and the project team's goal was to capture *wa* in a new way. For example, the landscape design incorporates particular forms, relationships and materials familiar to Japanese sensibilities, but which have been romanticised and abstracted.

The landscape design has two distinct characters, predominantly hard surfaces close to the buildings and a softer treatment for the park and gardens space. The main entry plaza and retail frontage connect directly to the street where new tree-lined sidewalks ring the site. Here the pedestrian traffic is high, with people heading to and from offices, shops, homes, galleries and subway stations across the expansive main plaza. These hard landscaped areas are finished in cream stone paving with a decorative banding in black. The pattern, colouring, and proportions are based on tatami mats, Japan's traditional woven rice-straw floor covering. The striking black bands echo the mat's cloth hem and reflect elements of the building facades. At intervals, the paved surface is broken open and glazed to provide natural light, filtered through shimmering water, into the retail areas and subway routes below ground. The surface is also pierced and planted with trees and bamboo-filled planters that rise up to create intimate gathering areas finished with timber decking.

In contrast to the intense and controlled hard-landscaped areas, the north and west edges of the site burst open into a generous swathe of public space. To the west, the linear gardens with meandering paving lead visitors through a compact and intimate sequence of spaces to reach a low-rise pavilion which accommodates the 21_21 Design Sight Museum. A key feature is the serpentine waterway, which recalls a natural stream that once flowed through the site. The historic stream is reinterpreted as a contemporary, romanticised water feature including active jets and terraced pools. The stream and pathways weave through areas of flower gardens which provide a programme of year-round changing colour.

Eastwards from the pavilion, the site opens up on a grand scale to form the central lawn, a large and simple expanse of grass. The shape of the lawn is a continuation of the building lines at the heart of the scheme. Unfamiliar in Japan where landscapes are usually spaces for contemplation and are intended to be viewed from a distance, the lawn is a distinctive Western element where people are invited to walk on the grass or simply sit and rest.

Hinokicho Park
Grass square
21-21 Design Sight
Garden Terrace
The Park residences at The Ritz Carlton, Toyko
Midtown Tower
Galleria
Plaza
Midtown East
MINATO-KU ROAD
Midtown West
GAIEN-HIGASHI STREET
100
m
50

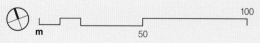

Right
Connection and reflection

With good access and views through the site, the development is an inviting place to visit. Glazing inset into the paved surface lets light into the retail below. Seating areas are denoted by timber decking and softened by planting.

Below and opposite

Attention to detail is a hallmark of this high-quality scheme. The sculptural shape of the benches, is created as an integrated but raised extension of the timber used for decking. Meanwhile, lighting is provided by elegant lamps and the striped patterns in paving are inspired by traditional tatami mats which were woven from rice straw and finished with a dark cloth hem.

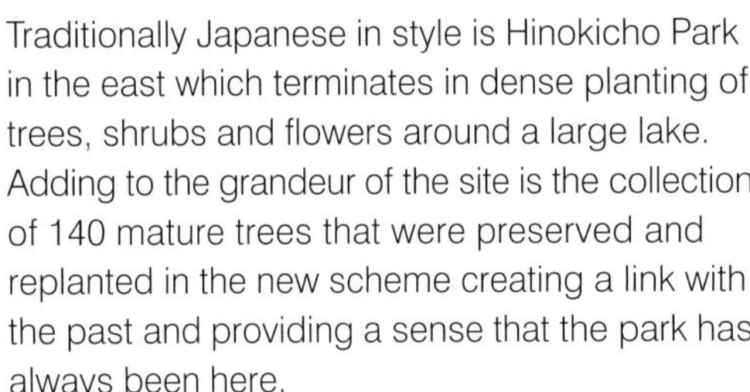

Traditionally Japanese in style is Hinokicho Park in the east which terminates in dense planting of trees, shrubs and flowers around a large lake. Adding to the grandeur of the site is the collection of 140 mature trees that were preserved and replanted in the new scheme creating a link with the past and providing a sense that the park has always been here.

Taking advantage of the rare opportunity to create significant new open space in the city, Tokyo Midtown has an inclusive quality which is communicated through the landscape. It has become a popular destination and its elegant design sets new high standards for Japanese open space, encouraging social interaction alongside splendour and sustainability.

- Tokyo Midtown covers a 10.1 hectare site.
- 50 per cent of the project area is dedicated to open space.
- 140 mature, existing trees were preserved on site.
- Tokyo Midtown has a total floor area of 563,800 square metres.
- Archaeological exploration turned up two Edo Period gold coins that were returned to the government and valued at over US$40,000 each, as well as utensils and more than 50,000 pieces of pottery, all displayed at the Suntory Museum within the development.

Opposite and above
Walk, rest and play

The landscape provides the setting for a range of activities and is designed with an interesting rhythm and contrasts from the extremes of the simple expanses of lawn to the highly intricate garden areas with meandering paving, flower beds and the sculptural mature cherry trees.

Sustainability

The design incorporates practical innovations, including solutions marked by a variety of sustainable features and advances in resource conservation. All park pathways are constructed of poured-in-place permeable paving, reducing runoff and pollution to the local water table. Rain water is harvested and stored in cisterns for irrigation. In addition to covering four hectares with luxuriant greenery, some building roofs are also planted with a diverse range of foliage, reducing runoff and heat.

The landscaping of such lush green garden space also heralds the emergence of an eco- and people-friendly realm, ideal for rest and relaxation. Solar panels were also installed, and all outdoor lighting is LED.

Pedestrian bridges jut out to meet the park spaces, reinforcing the connectedness of the public realm.

Above and opposite
A stroll in the park

After the hard landscaping of the areas around the towers, Tokyo Midtown's gardens have a feminine quality combining great delicacy and a lightness of touch.

With predominant colours of pink, green and grey, the place is full of variety, richness and incident including walkways, water, lawns and flower beds.

Overleaf
Harmony and geometry

At the top of this image, the gallery, designed by Tadao Ando, is integrated into the landscape with the straight pathways echoing the geometries of the building. These straight lines are intersected by the softer meandering paths whose graceful curves flow through the site and are picked up in the design of the roadway.

Concept

A public park in a flood-prone zone reconnects a city's centre to its river

Context

Urban river/sub-tropical

River Heart Parklands, Ipswich, Australia.

Expecting to treble its population by the 2020s, the city of Ipswich in eastern Australia is experiencing rapid growth coupled with an extensive urban regeneration programme. Acting as a catalyst for renewal and providing a focus for the centre of the city is the River Heart Parklands, which has transformed a neglected, unsightly and flood-prone riverbank into a high-quality and popular public space.

Opposite

Down to the river

Uniting the city with its river, and acting as a catalyst for high-quality development, the new terraced parklands step down to the waterside and provide a multi-use public space with spaces for picnics and enjoying the views as well as strolling and learning about the area's industrial past.

River Heart Parklands, Ipswich, Australia

Below
Fast-growing city

Anticipating rapid population growth, the parklands have been created to provide additional amenity space and also to set benchmarks for new development in this city noted for its high quality of life.

Opposite
New views

Terraces, boardwalks, jetties and walkways are threaded through a replanted and rejuvenated river's edge. Boardwalks over the flowing River Bremer create a fresh perspective of the water and the city, they provide a close experience of the river and extend the accessible area of parklands.

With terraces and boardwalks, lookouts, public barbecues and picnic facilities, the banks of the Bremer River have been reclaimed for the city's growing population. The area used to be overgrown and derelict; a heavily vandalised and hostile environment. But these extensive works have helped shape the city's reconnection with the river and made the water its central focal point.

With a population of more than 150,000, and with ambitions to achieve close to 500,000, Ipswich is the oldest provincial city in Queensland and is just 40 kilometres west of Brisbane. During the past century and a half its industries were rooted in mining and mineral extraction, and it became a railway centre—the Workshops Rail Museum is one of the area's most popular tourist attractions. By creating this new slice of riverside public realm, the city has established a benchmark for future work that will help promote its reputation as an attractive place offering a high quality of life. In 2007, Ipswich won an international award as "most liveable mid-size city in the world".

The creation of the new parklands is expected to have a wide impact. Along with providing inspiration and the impetus to upgrade Ipswich's central business district and shopping areas, it sets new standards for developments that follow. In addition, by interpreting the site's history, this public space is helping to reinforce the powerful sense of place.

The parklands project began with extensive local consultation which included the indigenous Yuggera community. The resultant cultural heritage report describes the site's historical context, including its past use as a wharf. To ensure precious historical items were not lost during the works, an archaeological 'spotter' was engaged to watch for articles of significance during the demolition and construction stages. The found items, such as old glass bottles, were secured in display cases and embedded in walls around the parklands to provide visual references to the site's past.

Growing from this understanding, the masterplan for the area evolved with key objectives including improving access to and enjoyment of the river; incorporating jetties and boardwalks in robust, industrial materials to reflect the site's past uses; opening up views; introducing shelters and picnic facilities; and interpreting the site's history.

The site itself proved a major design and engineering challenge, not just because most of the area is set on steep slopes of at least 40 per cent, but also because the river is prone to occasional but serious flooding. Some 95 per cent of the park area has been inundated in past floods and even minor flooding can submerge large areas. The multidisciplinary team decided on a design approach to work with the site and minimise the need for extensive land modelling, to create maximum accessibility with walkways, some of which stretch out into the water, and provide robust, industrial-style handrails, balustrades and shelters. In the event of a flood, these handrails and balustrades are designed to fold away and collapse to reduce the possibility of damage caused by river debris or large objects in the water such as trees. Once the water has subsided, all surfaces and finishes are designed to be washed down quickly and easily. Within the first few months of the parklands' completion, the area was subject to a flood of five metres and survived unscathed.

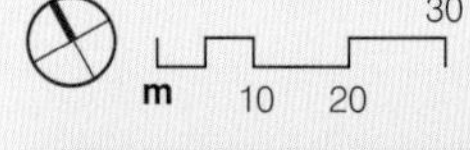

1 Park entry signage
2 Reconfigured carpark
3 Distinctive signage to Ellenborough Street axis
4 Existing embankment to remain
5 Vehicle drop off and toilets
6 Existing rail bridge
7 Future pedestrian bridge
8 Future lift structure to pedestrian bridge
9 Informal grassed terraces
10 Ramp to water edge (1:7 approx.)
11 Possible future cafe location
12 Water plaza
13 Feature 'light stick' to line up with mall axis
14 Interactive cascading water feature
15 Future path to park edge along Bremer Street
16 Wetland water feature
17 Path at three per cent providing 'access for all' to water edge through rainforest
18 Created rainforest utilising existing planting
19 Possible future jetty
20 Boardwalk along river edge
21 Timber shelter
22 Feature on Bell Street access
23 Existing retaining walls
24 Seating/resting area with shelter in the rainforest
25 Ecological terraces to river edge

Right and opposite
Prone to flood

Occasional flooding is a feature of this landscape and as much as 95 per cent of the park area has been inundated in the past. Even minor flooding can submerge large areas of the bank. The parklands are designed to accommodate flooding with collapsible and removable handrails along sections of boardwalk to reduce damage to structures during flooding.

Integrated sustainability

Environmental, economic and social sustainability were designed into the project from the start

- Much of the construction work was undertaken by Ipswich City Council employees, increasing the opportunity for skills development in the local community and supporting local employment.
- Recycled water was used wherever possible, while working within health requirements.
- An existing set of sculptures by Rhyl Hinwood was relocated from the city centre to a more intimate waterside location within the parklands.
- Existing heritage structures, including bridges, were integrated into the design.
- Recycled timber was used for the signage.
- Preservation of existing site trees was important not only for habitat, but for bank stabilisation, and all boardwalks and landscape items were designed to avoid disturbance.
- A local indigenous species palette was used and the site's original riparian flora zones were replicated on the banks.
- A wetland system was designed into the base of the steep bank to pick up stormwater runoff and to encourage localised opportunities, such as fauna access to freshwater and educational opportunities.
- Biodiversity is promoted and local ecosystems are supported.
- Existing natural vegetation was retained and enhanced.
- More than 100 species of the plants used were native to the site and there was diligent removal of noxious weeds.
- All timber used for signage was recycled and at all times heritage issues were 'top of mind' in every decision made.
- The site contains a historic railway along with an abutment from a former road bridge crossing. Wharf piers, sandstone blocks and artefacts from previous maritime uses of the site were also uncovered and preserved.

Overleaf
Working with the site

The parklands are set on a steeply sloping site which presented a major design and engineering challenge. However, by basing the design on a series of terraces, it has been possible to provide high levels of accessibility and give the place a distinctive character. Interpreting the site's history has also helped to create a powerful sense of place.

Concept

New parklands to create interactive, sustainable and beautiful public spaces, that inspire environmental restoration and investment in a new extension to an historic city

Context

Alluvial plain/monsoon maritime

Wuxi Li Hu New City and Waterfront Parklands Masterplans, Wuxi, China.

For centuries the ancient Chinese city of Wuxi relied on water for its livelihood. Canals were used for transporting raw materials and finished goods to and from its factories and Li Lake (also known as Five Mile Lake) was home to its fishing industry. But by the end of the twentieth century the city's relationship with water had become estranged.

Opposite
Lakeside promenade

Extremely beautiful at night, this boardwalk features a sculptural structure inspired by the sails of local boats. A historic temple is seen across the water in the distance.

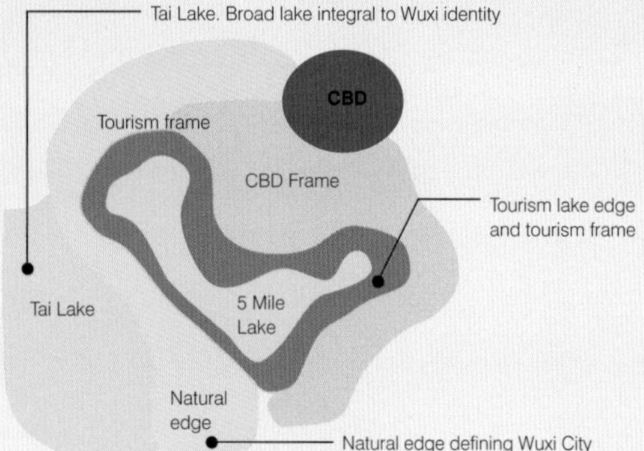

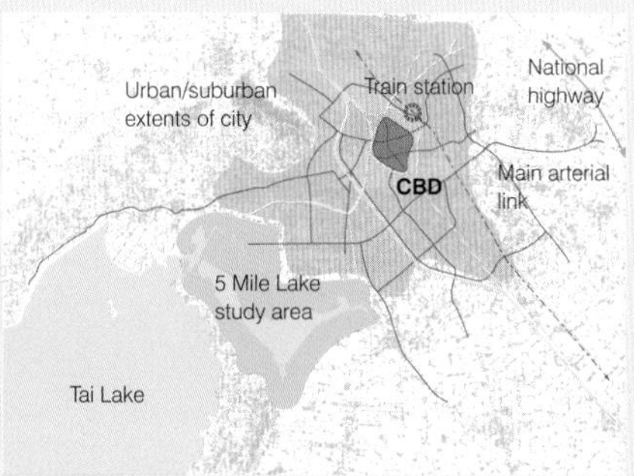

Above
In context

A framework diagram, showing the lake, new city and parklands area in context with the existing city and the larger Tai Lake. Also, the project is seen in its wider regional landscape. Key to the economy is agriculture and manufacturing. It is also one of China's top tourist destinations.

Opposite
Wuxi Li Hu New City plan

The extensive new development proposals encircle the entire lake. This structure plan shows general land uses, major roads and public transport routes and the main elements of the new district including landmarks, axes, activity centres and gateways. There will be six new precincts each with its own distinctive character, The Esplanade in the north, followed by the Lake Centre area to the east, The Quay, Lakeside Village, South Bank and Turtle Head. Waterside parklands will help to reconnect the city of more than four million people with its lake, to provide a new high-quality playground, to enhance the local landscape and water quality and provide a boost to the tourist industry. Below, a sequence of diagrams showing the new city plan's major structural elements, the land uses, urban design and proposed building heights.

Around 130 kilometres north-west of Shanghai and close to the Yangtze River and the East China Sea, Wuxi's economy had reached a slow ebb and was clearly in need of a boost. To help revive its fortunes, the place was designated by government as an investment city and started to explore ways of diversifying its economic base to promote future growth. With a population of more than 4.5 million, the city had expanded fast in recent years and looked once again to its relationship with water to carry it into the future.

To manage growth and create a framework for development, a future vision and masterplan were commissioned to explore the potential of the extensive Li Lake edge and adjoining hinterland. As the result of site assessments, understanding the cultural and economic context and a series of on-site workshops, a number of options for future growth emerged. From these it was possible to identify the strengths of each proposal and draw together a preferred vision for a new lakeside city to maximise the potential of the area's spectacular landscape, its mild climate and good transport connections.

The plan was for a new urban area, Li Hu New City, to be built on the south-western edge of Wuxi on the banks of Li Lake. The crescent-shaped waterway is on the eastern edge of the massive Tai Lake, one of the country's largest lake environments. Based on a sequence of six districts each with its own distinctive character, this city extension would be intended to make the most of opportunities for tourism and recreation. Having established itself as a tourism area in the early 1900s, Wuxi has become one of China's top ten visitor destinations with more than 16 million visitors a year. Most trips are made by day visitors, with just 400,000 tourists from outside China. The city government also wanted to foster greater local community connections with the lake and mountains.

To encourage development and to stimulate regeneration and environmental protection, a plan was created for waterside parklands around Wuxi Li Lake noted for its stunning mountain backdrop and pretty towers. The proposed new city is approximately 24 square kilometres comprising the lake (40 per cent), existing fish farms (eight per cent), mountain fringes (eight per cent) and mainland (44 per cent). The goals of the Waterfront Parkland Masterplan were to create public open space, and community attractions and amenities that were sensitive to local culture the environment.

Because the waterfront parklands area is so extensive, the plans and work have been divided into phases. The first phase included the Gateway Plaza, the Waterfront and Fishing Dragon Island. Incorporating traditional and contemporary design ideas, visitors are invited on a journey of exploration. Variety and changes of pace are provided by a mix of open and enclosed spaces, formal and informal areas, places for contemplation and others for picnics and playing on the beach. There are cafes and restaurants, places to fish, broad stone-paved boulevards and timber boardwalks stretching out over the water. Every aspect of the design invites interaction with the water from enjoying lake views and taking a ferry to paddling on the beach.

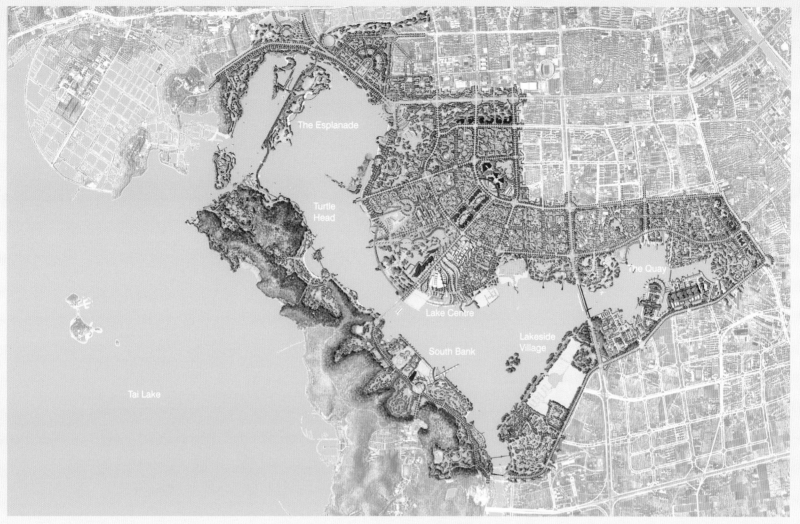

The Esplanade
Turtle Head
The Quay
Lake Centre
Lakeside Village
South Bank
Tai Lake

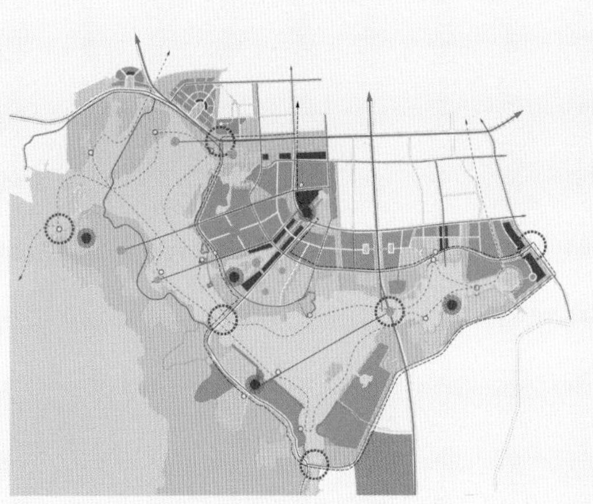

Structure Plan

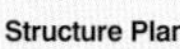

- Activity centres
- Landmarks
- Axes
- Gateways

- Tourism and recreation
- Commercial
- Institutional
- Residential
- Open space

- Highway
- Major and minor roads
- Light rail vehicle route
- Ferry route
- Ferry terminal
- Public transport interchange

Land Use Plan
Major city zones

The plan of major city zones illustrates the detailed allocation of land uses throughout the New Lake City including:

- Tourism and recreation
- Commercial
- Institutional
- Residential
- Open space

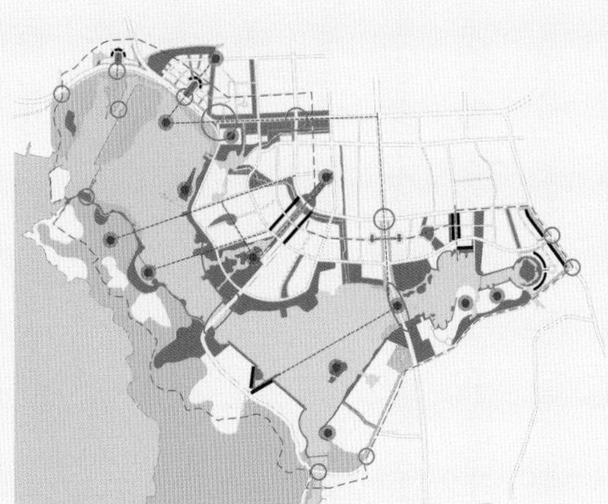

Urban Design Plan

- Landmarks
- Axes
- Gateways
- Building edges
- Major open spaces

Building Height Plan

- 1–2 storey (>9m)
- 3–4 storey (9–15m)
- 5–6 storey (15–21m)
- 7–15 storey (21–50m)
- 16–30 storey (50–100m)
- Central lakes

Gateway Plaza

Stretching out across the lake and forging new connections with the water, this shaded boardwalk features iconic and graceful architectural elements which take their inspiration from the sails of local Tai Lake fishing boats.

Starting in the north-west corner of the lake, the Gateway Plaza forms the main entrance to the broad ribbon of waterside parklands which extend along more than five kilometres of coast. The old and run-down fish farms which occupied this area were flooded and taken out of use; a move which immediately helped to improve local water quality. The visitor's arrival is marked by a soaring sculpture inspired by the elegant sails of the local Tai Lake fishing boats. At night this iconic structure is transformed with light shows. And now the sculpture is also recognised as the logo of the new Wuxi city representing the integration of traditional and contemporary styles. To the north of here are forest walks, open parkland and beaches, while to the south is Flame Plaza.

With its network of walkways and boardwalks and a viewing platform looking south across the lake to the mountaintop Luding tower this area has a more urban feel. Flame Plaza will form the gateway to the lake from the new city. Halfway between the plazas is Fish Dragon Island. Linked by a walkway from the mainland, this island was formerly used by fish farmers, but has now been transformed into an appealing playground with a man-made beach and gardens, a favourite spot for picnics and weddings. A neglected stand of handsome camphor trees has been preserved and transplanted to form a grand shady avenue and old buildings on site including a former hotel have become a museum to the area's fishing heritage.

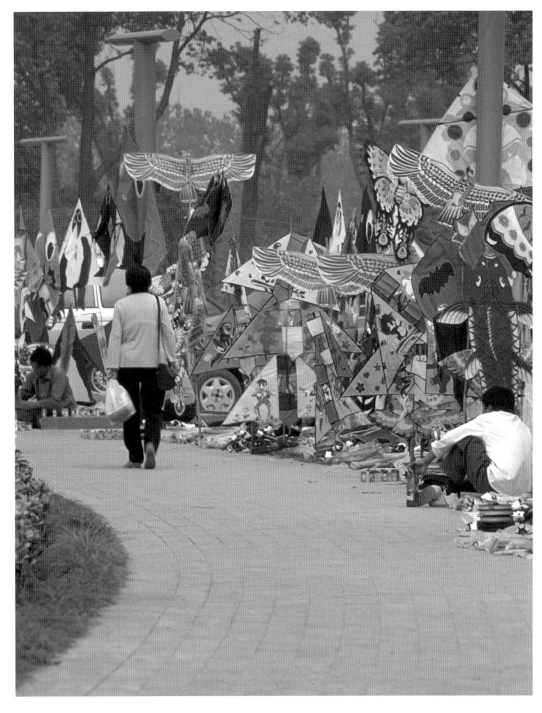

Pleasure principle

The public spaces, particularly the open lawn areas, have become enlivened with colour with this dazzling array of kites for sale, and activities such as families and friends enjoying picnics. The parklands have become a popular weekend destination and a new meeting ground for the community.

Wetland boardwalks

In contrast with the stone-paved promenades, the boardwalks meandering out over the water offer a softer and more natural setting. Wetlands have been installed in several locations to raise awareness of their beauty and environmental value which includes natural water filtration.

Right and below
Surprise and delight

The highly varied landscape includes moments of pure delight such as these colourful flower beds set into the water. And, below, once a poorly maintained service road, this grand pedestrian avenue has been created with mature camphor trees which were retained and transplanted.

Opposite
To infinity

The boardwalks are a romantic element in the landscape and have helped bring the community into close contact with the lake once again.

On the east side of the lake is Wuxi Bridge Park, a green space focused on a small lake surrounded by a traditionally-inspired shade walk which doubles as a place for displaying local photography and artworks. Around this circular central hub, there are four seasonal gardens and a ferry terminal, which form a strong view axis to the Great Wuxi Bridge over the Li Lake.

The Great Wuxi Bridge from which the park takes its name provides a new connection to the south where plans for future phases of work include the creation of an extensive Environment Park with a conservation and protection theme. This will include educational and research facilities, a seed and spore bank and protected habitats for rare medical and culturally significant plants, including fungi. This southern area will also include a ten kilometre long wetland corridor to manage stormwater entering the lake. One of the long-term aims is to isolate the smaller Li Lake from Tai Lake to protect the water quality and environment. Also in the future will be the creation of a grand central park for the new city and an arts park.

More than just creating beautiful public space, the parklands are key to the transformation of the area. Along with improving quality of life in the city, they are conceived to enhance Wuxi's image as an attractive place to live and work—encouraging more investment, particularly from high-tech industries. Enhancing the natural beauty, the parklands are also intended to boost the tourism industry and set high-quality benchmarks for the developments that follow in Wuxi and beyond. Even with just the initial phases of parklands complete, the transformative effects of the work are clear. Local response to the new public spaces has been positive and enthusiastic with the city dwellers enjoying their new playground and renewing connections with the water, land values are rising, investment continues to flow into the area and tourism figures are increasing.

睡莲

Concept

A high-quality business environment for a world-class organisation

Context

Rural/temperate

The Royal Bank of Scotland Landscape Masterplan, Edinburgh, UK.

With recruiting and retaining the best staff always a prime concern of employers, creating new premises presents the opportunity to design a workplace with strong employee appeal. When the Royal Bank of Scotland needed a world headquarters to accommodate its rapidly growing workforce, it selected Edinburgh as its global hub and consolidated its executive management team in one purpose-built location on the edge of the city.

Opposite
Restored and revived

The restored historic parklands and newly sculpted landscape provide the setting for the bank's headquarters which sits, Acropolis-like, on a raised platform with views to the south.

The Royal Bank of Scotland Landscape Masterplan, Edinburgh, UK

The vision

A conceptual sketch looking out from the new headquarters and across the formal courtyards. Also forming part of the design, close to the new building, are proposals for a sunken garden shown here in east–west and north–south cross-sections.

In a parkland estate west of Edinburgh, the bank's ambitious plans were to create world-class facilities to match its status as a global bank and Scotland's largest employer.

Along with the restoration of a neglected and densely wooded parkland, created more than a century ago as the grounds of a grand country house, the project involved the careful landscape management of the existing site, together with planting significant new specimen and woodland trees and hedges. This was combined with contemporary earth modelling incorporating a fully integrated water management system to provide a beautiful setting for the new headquarters. Accommodating more than 3,000 staff, the main headquarters building was designed as a series of business units or houses linked by a glazed street. In addition, the Listed 1890s Gogarburn House was redeveloped to provide restaurant facilities and a health and leisure club, stables were converted into a nursery and a new conference centre and executive business school was created.

The focus of the site is the award-winning headquarters building by Michael Laird Architects. Placed in an elevated clearing, the elegant contemporary-style building, wrapped in glass and sandstone, is designed as a low-rise structure. It sits within generous boundary woodland belts and below the tree line to help reduce its impact when seen from the city and from Edinburgh Airport to the north. Its great outward-curving crescent shape maximises the sweeping green views to the south. The orientation also contributes to the structure's energy-efficient design. In a campus-style arrangement, the sequence of blocks is linked by a glazed 300 metre-long central street. In this space, members of staff can stroll between restaurants, coffee shops and informal break-out meeting spaces, and make use of services including a bank, pharmacy, supermarket and hairdresser.

To retain and improve the best features of the estate grounds and accommodate the new structures, initial landscape work involved surveys to identify the most precious areas of established parkland and mature specimen trees. Once these areas were defined, parts of the original garden design and plantings were recreated, while in other areas, contemporary interpretations of the original themes were extended. Major earthworks were required to sculpt the land and create a platform for the new building helping to open up views of the Pentland Hills. Leading from the building, a series of grassed terraces step down to connect with the realigned Gogar Burn, the waterway from which the site takes its name, and the wider parkland beyond.

Because it was anticipated that the new building could potentially have an impact on the local hydrology, the landscape design incorporated ways of dealing with possible changes such as an increase in rain and stormwater runoff from the main building. To address these hydrology issues, sensitive earthworks included redirecting the course of the Gogar Burn. Work was also carried out to improve natural habitats close to the water course to encourage greater biodiversity. In addition, two large reed-beds were created as part of the extensive site-wide sustainable drainage system. The site's proximity to the city's airport meant that close collaboration was required with the Civil Aviation Authority. One direct result of these discussions was the avoidance of open water which could encourage flocking birds. Instead reed beds were designed to perform a dual function of collecting and filtering water.

To restore a sense of historic grandeur to the parklands, a large number of semi-mature trees were imported, including oaks and limes to form new avenues and to expand the attractive woodland areas. In addition, a living green screen of almost one kilometre in length was created four-metre-high pre-clipped conifer hedge to screen the site's 1,600-space car park.

Along with the large-scale work, details were important too. Smaller scale interventions included hard and soft, contemporary-style landscaping of the forecourt areas and courtyards within the new office wings. Interior planting formed part of the scheme too with full-sized trees including weeping fig close to seating areas and lining the internal high-street walkway.

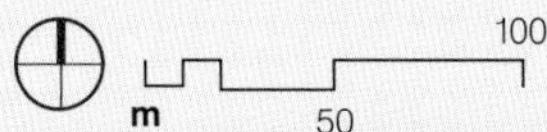

1 Main entrance
2 Main site access
3 Site access
4 Bridge access
5 Surface car parking
6 Deck car park
7 Water feature
8 Service yard
9 Energy centre
10 Sculptural flood plain
11 Executive garden
12 Main terrace
13 Southern courtyards
14 Linkage spaces
15 Restaurant terrace
16 Northern courtyards
17 Main staff drop-off
18 Formal parkland
19 Managed woodland / grassland
20 Interventions
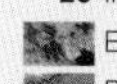 Existing trees / woodland
Proposed trees / woodland

Above
Landscape masterplan

The headquarters is shown in the context of its restored and new landscape with features including managed woodland and a sculpted floodplain.

Overleaf
Landscape contrasts

Looking north towards the headquarters building, in the foreground are the grasses of the naturalistic flood plain while the building is raised in a formal setting on a series of made terraces.

Right and below
Picturesque and pragmatic

Views from the building include seasonal wildflowers, which provide colour and variety in the southern areas of the parklands. Sculpted serpentine terraces create beautiful land forms which step down to the waterways.

Opposite

Reached by a meandering pathway with bridges over waterways, the renovated Gogarburn House is now used as a staff restaurant and health and leisure club.

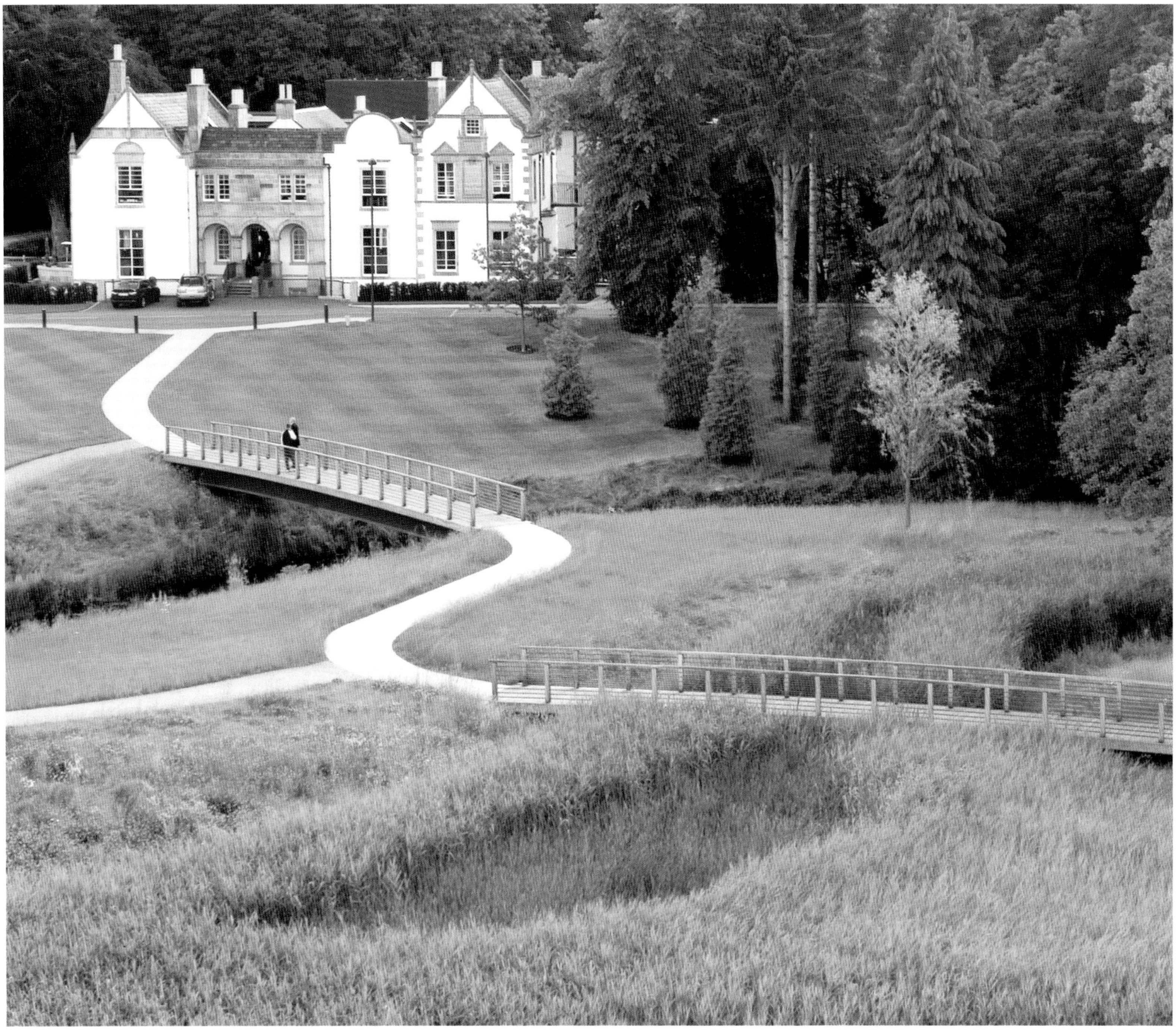

Concept

A new public park and mixed-use scheme to regenerate one of the final undeveloped pieces of Barcelona's beachfront

Context

Coastal urban/Mediterranean

Parc Diagonal Mar, Barcelona, Spain.

With sandy beaches, cafes and restaurants, marina and promenade, a triumphant feature of Barcelona's Olympic legacy from 1992, has been the transformation of its Mediterranean coast. One of the last pieces for redevelopment was at the eastern extremity of the major thoroughfare called Avinguda Diagonal, the site of this playful, contemporary art-inspired public park, which connects directly to the beach.

Opposite

Fresh perspective

Formerly a run-down industrial area, the new park is an exuberant place with extensive water at its heart and with views of the sea. Development of this piece of land completes the long-term and successful revitalisation of a long stretch of beachfront which began in the lead up to the Barcelona Olympics of 1992. The area is now hugely popular with locals and visitors and has attracted large-scale investment in new developments.

Parc Diagonal Mar, Barcelona, Spain

Above
Context

The park shown in context with the great Avinguda Diagonal slicing across the city to meet the sea.

Overleaf
Water features

Water is handled in a variety of different ways. Among the most exquisite features are the cool and calming jade-coloured pools.

Opposite
Masterplan

Full of surprise and delight, the park design uses a restrained palette of materials—water, stone, steel, grass and trees—but in a rich composition of irregular shapes, meandering walkways, and level changes which include a sequence of hills created to provide views over the city and the sea.

Once a dangerous and run-down strip of industrial wasteland, Barcelona's beachfront now stands as a model of successful regeneration and has become one of the most popular areas of the city where locals and tourists congregate. Northwards along the coast, and as a continuation of the residential area formerly used as the Olympic Village, Diagonal Mar is a large mixed-use development of homes, offices, hotels and shopping set in a new public park. This scheme provides a gateway to the sea, has contributed to the continued revitalisation of the seafront and has also acted as a catalyst for new investment and development in the wider area. At the centre of the Diagonal Mar scheme the contemporary-style park is the first in Spain to be designed using sustainable principles with a strong environmental agenda. The park provides a green link between the famous Avinguda Diagonal which slices through the centre of the city, and the sea. While built with private investment, the Parc Diagonal Mar is administered by the municipality and is the city's third largest park after Parc Guell and Parc de la Ciutadella.

Occupying the 16 hectare brownfield site of former rail yards complete with run-down and derelict industrial buildings, the focus of the new park is a large lake with its fountains, waterfalls and sculptural mist sprays made on a huge scale from twisting and swooping shiny steel tubing. Around this water feature is a sequence of shaded resting places, children's play areas, cafes, viewing mounds and sports facilities along with bridges and a network of meandering, tentacle-like pathways which lead from the city's neighbouring residential areas to the sea. The design was completed with the internationally renowned architects Enric Miralles and Benedetta Tagliabue of Barcelona-based practice EMBT.

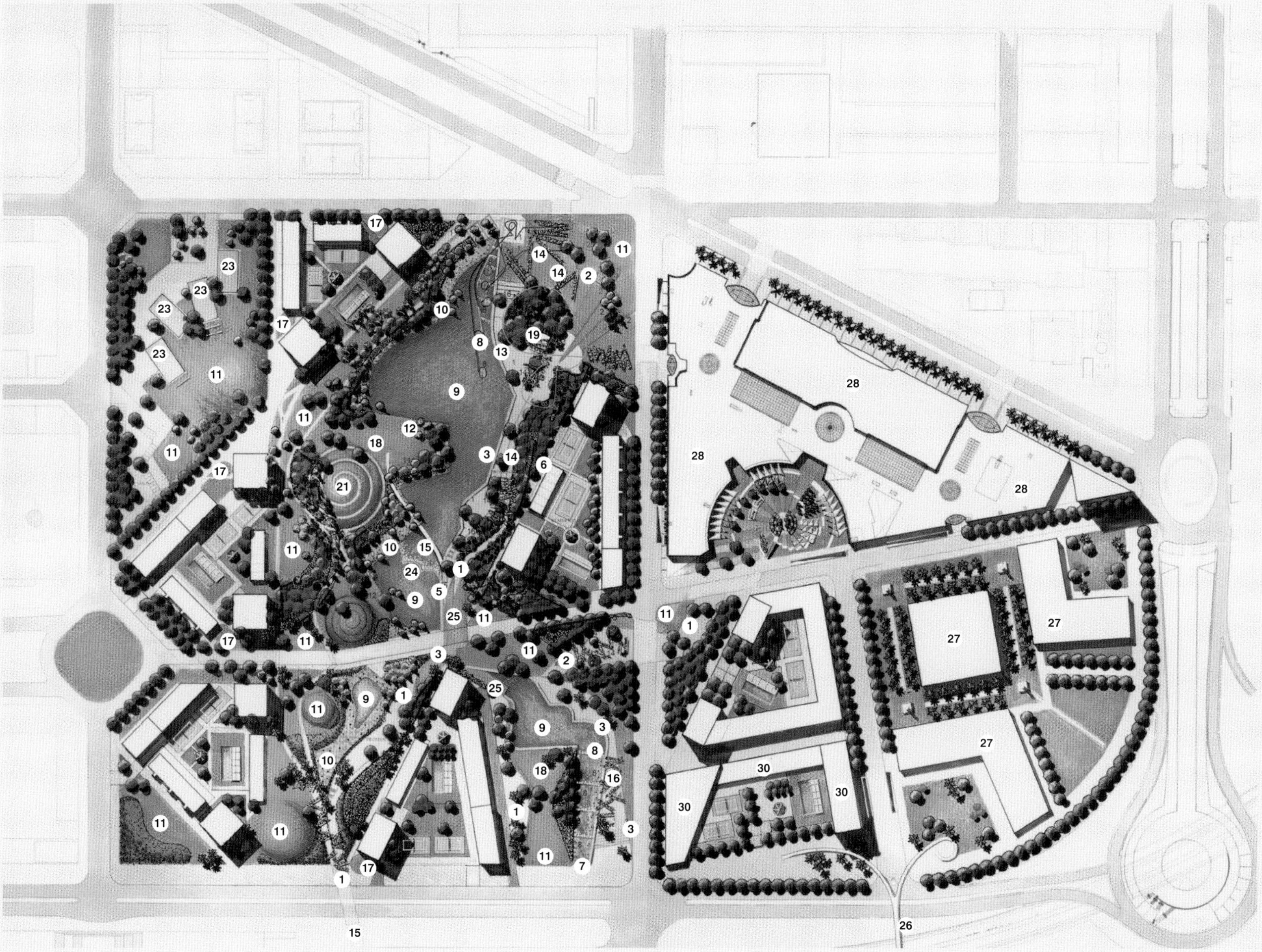

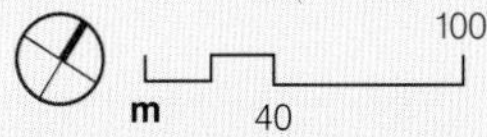

1 Stabilised
2 Pavers
3 Precast concrete border
4 Concrete bench
5 Cast-in-place concrete
6 Concrete skating path
7 Terraced fountain
8 Fountain feature tubing
9 Lake
10 Marsh/aquatic planting
11 Grass
12 Group planting (trees)
13 Linear ramp
14 Pergola
15 Bridge
16 Ramp/stair
17 Car turn-around
18 Playground
19 Cafe
20 Ornamental grass
21 Landscape feature game
22 Paddle tennis courts
23 Sports field
24 Lake overflow step
25 Brick pavers
26 Pedestrian bridge to the beach
27 Proposed conference centre
28 Retail centre
29 Residential phases
30 Hotel, office or other tertiary uses

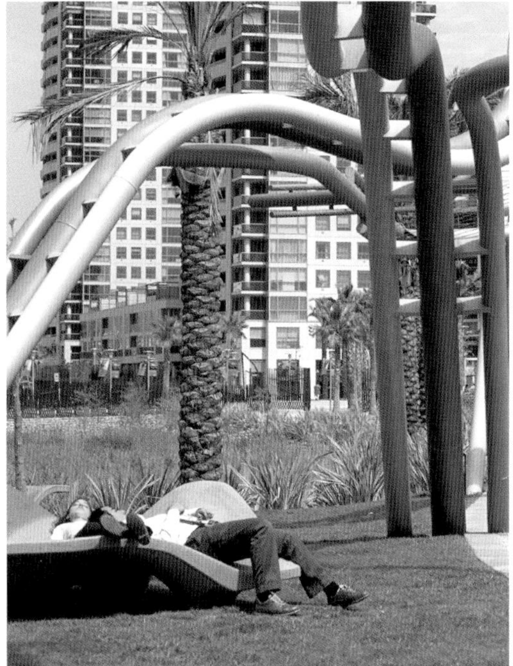

Above and opposite
A day in the park

Even within a relatively small site, the spaces are complex and varied, with places to lie back and relax in the sun, others that appeal to families enjoying the tranquillity of water, and room for running and taking a stroll.

Overleaf
Delight in the detail

Contrasting materials in this hard landscaped area mark a change in levels and potential platforms for outdoor performers or stalls, left.

The style of the park is exuberant and playful with enormous sculptures resembling three-dimensional squiggles in the air, and bespoke seating designs, fountains, gates, giant plant pots and play areas created by local artists. Using a simple palette of stone, steel, concrete, wood, water and plants, the design is packed with inviting detail and colour. Materials were selected for their ability to withstand the harsh salty atmosphere of a seaside area. Clearly reflecting the spirit of the city and Barcelona's strong relationships with modern art and architecture, the design has been conceived not just for enjoyment at ground level, but also to be seen from the surrounding high-rise apartments. It can be perceived as a giant and dynamic abstract work of art. Inverting the traditional idea of the landscape design as a backdrop to buildings, this park is intended as an object in itself with buildings providing the frame. Integrated into the landscape, the development includes 15 residential buildings, three hotels, three office towers and a retail centre.

In a further move away from traditional city parks with their lush lawns and multicoloured flowerbeds, the Parc Diagonal Mar has a strong sustainability agenda which includes lake water provided by rain and a local well, native planting and the reduced use of pesticides, the incorporation of recycled and sustainable materials and porous pavements to minimise storm runoff.

Since its completion, the park has served to inspire more local development with a sequence of new residential, office and retail schemes.

Sustainability

The creation of Parc Diagonal Mar resulted in the first-ever public/private sustainability agreement in Spain, a pact between developer Hines and Barcelona's city council. The agreement governed the park design, construction, and, now, its operation. Hines commissioned the design team to develop a Statement of Environmental Sustainability Report in English and Catalan. The report called for sustainable development principles such as balancing human and natural resources; respecting the interdependence of natural systems; respecting biological and cultural diversity, promoting social equity and economic development; balancing short-term and long-term needs and objectives; and the conservation of natural resources to be incorporated in the design of the park.

Sustainability features

- Porous pavements to minimise stormwater runoff.
- Native planting to curtail irrigation and the use of pesticides.
- A regional retention pond with aquatic plants around the edge for first-flush stormwater cleansing and to provide habitat for marine and bird species.
- Time-controlled fountains and small-scale mist sprays.
- Irrigation water provided by the lake.
- Wetland areas around parts of the lake for stormwater filtration.
- Use of groundwater as the lake's primary source.
- Lake liner protected with a soil cap.
- Recycled soil excavated from adjoining retail development.
- Grass clippings and other harvested vegetation are composted.

Concept

An elegant and secure new public space of national importance and global significance

Context

Urban/temperate

World Trade Center District Public Realm, New York, USA.

Rebuilding New York's World Trade Center district has involved working with a complex, and sometimes conflicting, set of demands creating civic space that is beautiful and fully accessible, while at the same time incorporating high levels of security controls, accommodating a subsurface nest of infrastructure including the utilities and transportation network, and complementing the new iconic buildings.

Opposite

Finding the balance

The exuberant and uplifting design of the new transportation hub by Santiago Calatrava is set in generous public space where, throughout the project, the balance is found between accessibility and security.

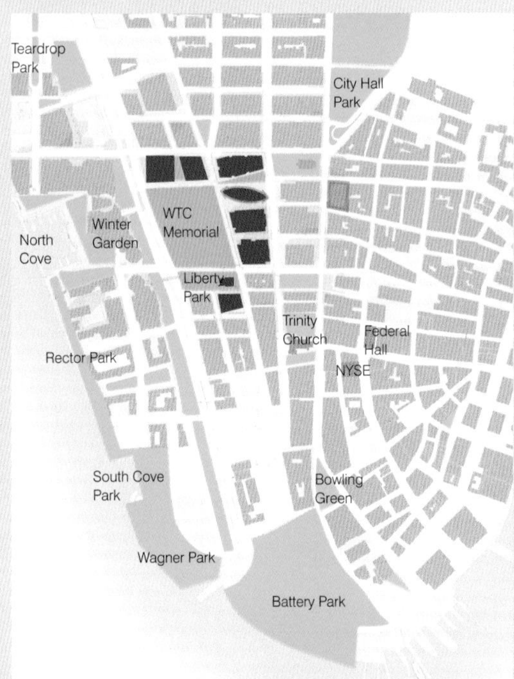

Manhattan rising

The New York skyline as it will look when construction is complete on the new World Trade Center site. The tallest structure will be Tower 1, by David Childs/SOM Architects, which stands at just over 540 metres tall. The plan of the Lower Manhattan area with the World Trade Center site in context and highlighting the green spaces is also shown.

Following the terrorist attacks of 2001, the World Trade Center site became the focus of major new development including a memorial to the two destroyed towers, the construction of five new skyscrapers by high-profile architects including David Childs/SOM Architects, Norman Foster, Richard Rogers, and Fumiko Maki, and an exuberant transport hub by Santiago Calatrava. At the same time extensive work was required on all underground infrastructure from the subway and rail services to sewers, water systems and power lines. To visually unify the entire 6.5 hectare site, the public realm has been designed as an elegant skin. This is the base from which the new buildings rise and it acts as the public face of the scheme.

While appearing effortlessly simple, the restrained palette of materials and contemporary-style street furniture work hard at meeting the varied requirements of a wide spectrum of interested parties from city planners, the police department, city and state transportation departments, the developer and architects to engineers, retailers and the client, the Port Authority of New York and New Jersey. A major component of the work was the challenge to understand the diverse demands on the space and then work with all parties to build consensus.

From the start of the project, the sense of openness and accessibility in this high profile civic space was a key priority. And while security was also extremely important, the approach was to resist turning the site into a fortress. Learning from the experience of other cities such as Washington DC where security measures are often highly visible, designs for this project have been conceived to be effective but also unobtrusive producing a new and intelligent kind of security aesthetic.

To unify the entire district, and create a calm and ordered public space, the expansive area of paving is designed in a simple and complementary palette of dark grey, mid-tone and white stone. Different tonal effects are achieved with different finishes. The white stone incorporates distinctive swirling black lines. The stone pattern moves from the darkest colour at the roadside curb, through the mid-tone and finally to the palest tone at the building face. At the same time, the size of paving moves from smaller modules close to the curb to large and generous stones at the buildings. The white stone was selected because of its synthesis with the colours of the key building lobbies. The Tower 1 lobby has a black floor and the three other key buildings have opted for white. In each case the lobby flooring material, known as the "building carpet", is extended beyond the footprint of the building into the public realm where it is integrated with the white stone. While the memorial area, designed by Michael Arad with Peter Walker and Partners, remains a separate and distinctive space for contemplation and reflection, the district's sidewalk seam edge is wrapped around its perimeter unifying it as part of the district.

This edging band, also referred to as a seam, is the location of a complex range of integrated features. Here, the most visible form of barrier to vehicles is the use of bollards. To integrate trees and bollards, close collaboration with project engineers was necessary to ensure that buried items including the root balls of trees and footings for the bollards were set in positions which were appropriate to meet safety requirements, but which did not interfere with the underground utilities and infrastructure. To reduce their visual impact, bollards were designed as a tapering elliptical form. Also here in the perimeter seam are the lighting poles, signage, ventilation grates and even stormwater collectors for the natural irrigation of street level planting.

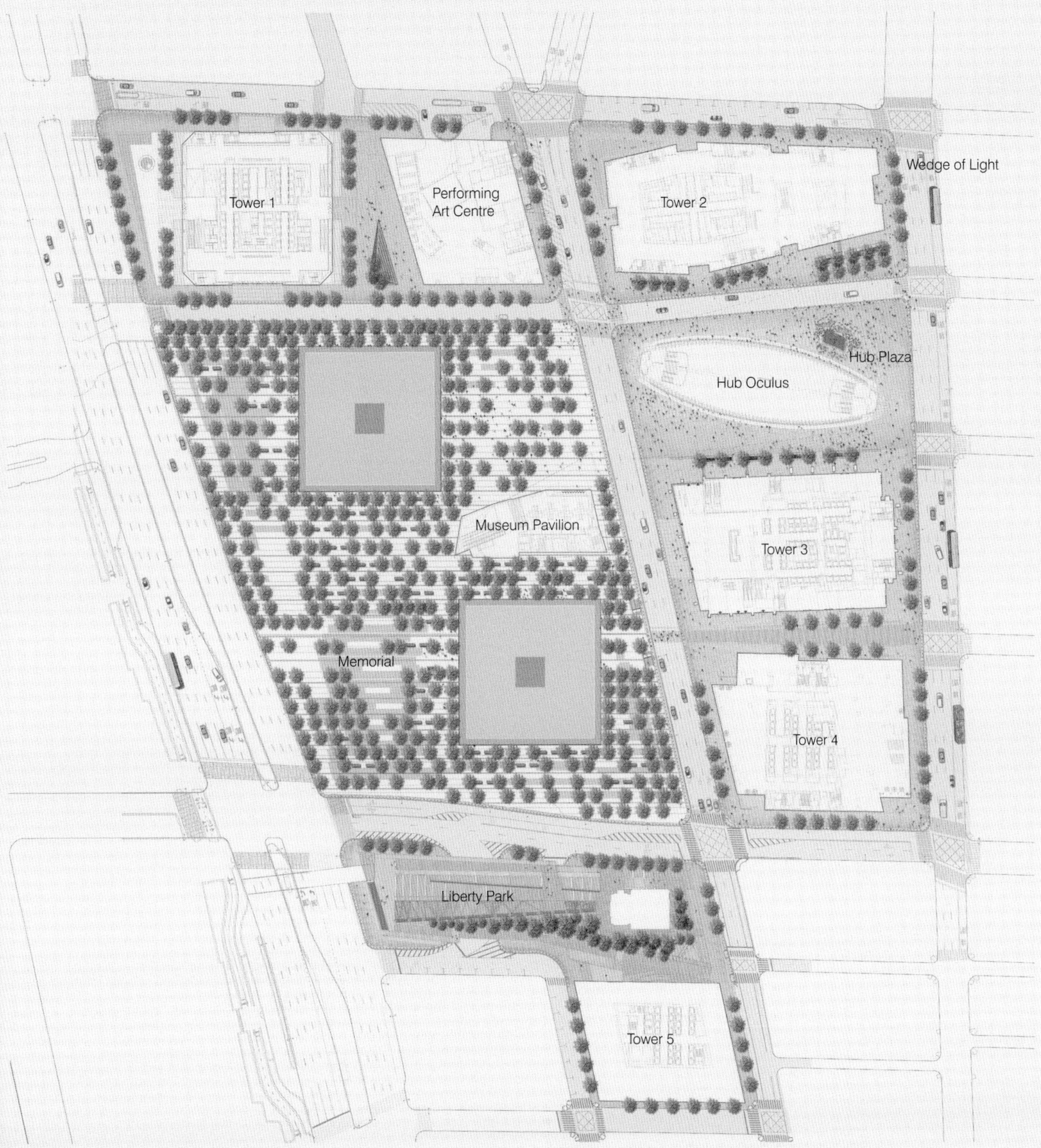

Masterplan

The 6.5 hectare site showing the arrangement of new structures to the north, east and south of the former World Trade Center's "Twin Towers". The buildings destroyed in the terrorist attack and the more than 3,000 people who lost their lives, will be remembered at the National September 11 Memorial and Museum which includes a new public space with two huge pools set within the footprints of the towers. The public space around the new structures provides clear views through the area, generous circulation spaces and places to linger and is unified by the use of high quality stones from US quarries.

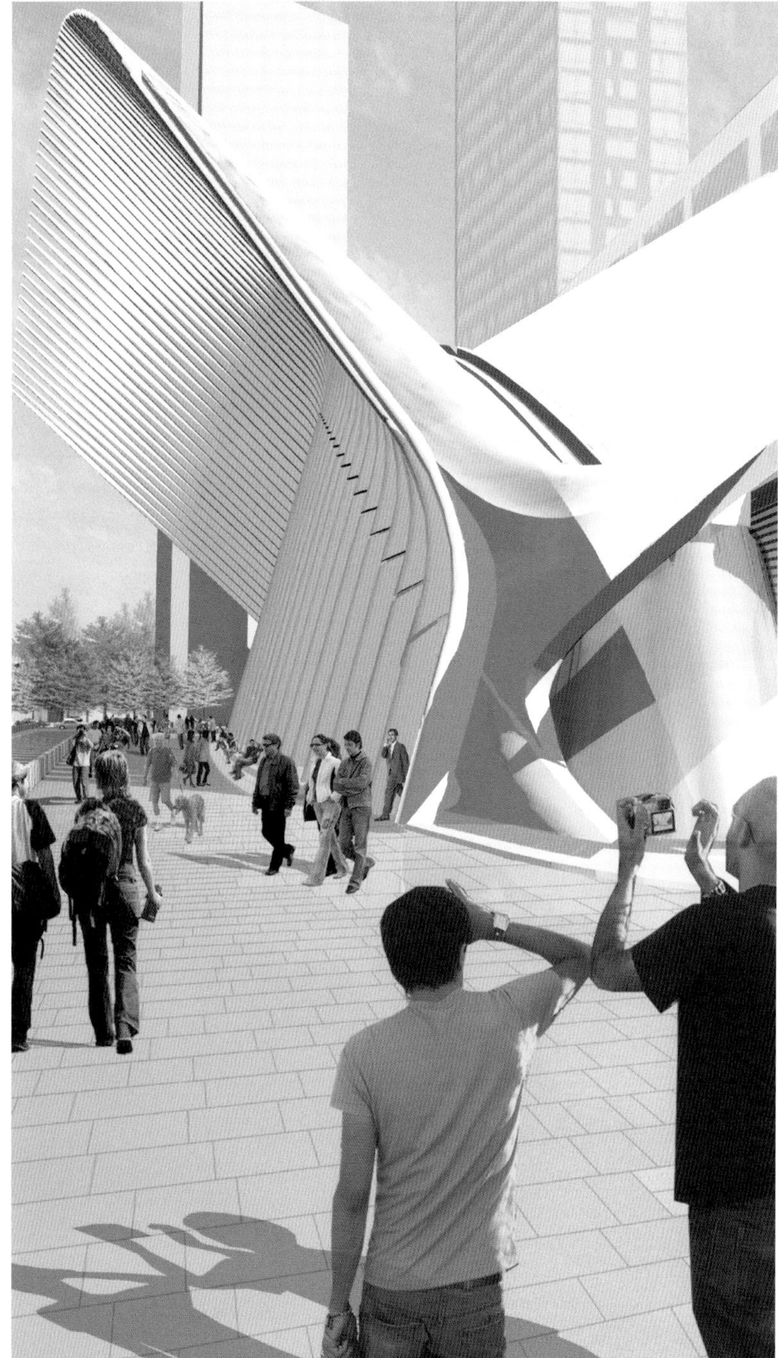

Soaring sculpture

Reminiscent of a huge bird with its wings splayed, the transportation hub by Santiago Calatrava is a freestanding structure set in a landscaped plaza which will be one of the busiest areas within the site. The hub will provide service for the Port Authority Trans-Hudson (PATH) commuter trains, New York city subway trains and a potential rail link to John F Kennedy International Airport as well as seamless indoor pedestrian access to the World Financial Center, adjacent buildings and the Hub transit centre.

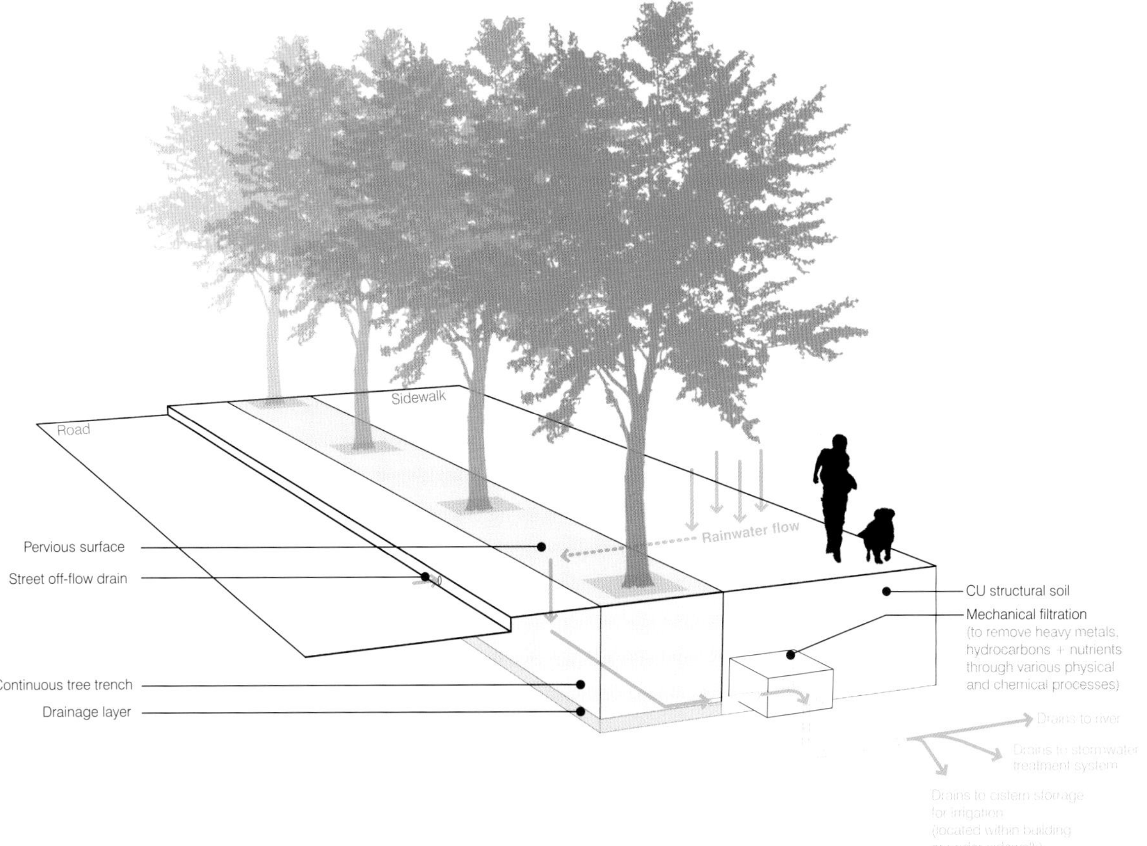

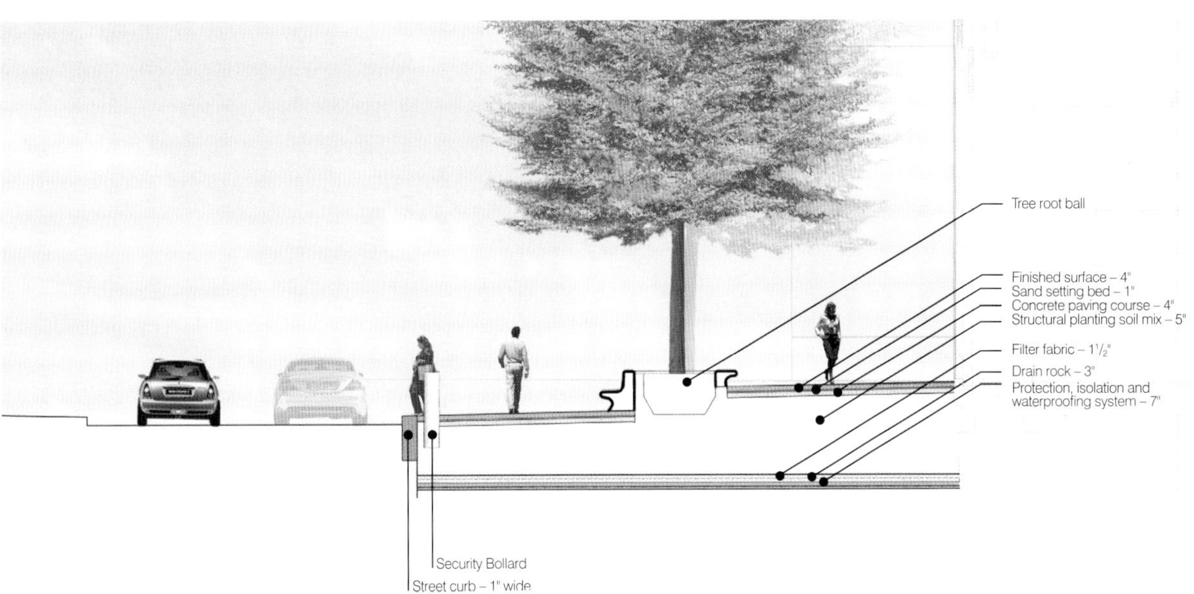

The edges of the site incorporate a complex range of features from security elements including trees and bollards to drainage for handling high volumes of rainwater. The integration of all the elements close to the surface was essential to keep space below clear for subways.

Liberty Park

Along the southern edge of the site, the new screening building is designed to sit beneath a new park which takes its name from the nearby Liberty Street. The security building marks the point at which all vehicles, including buses and lorries, will enter the World Trade Center site.

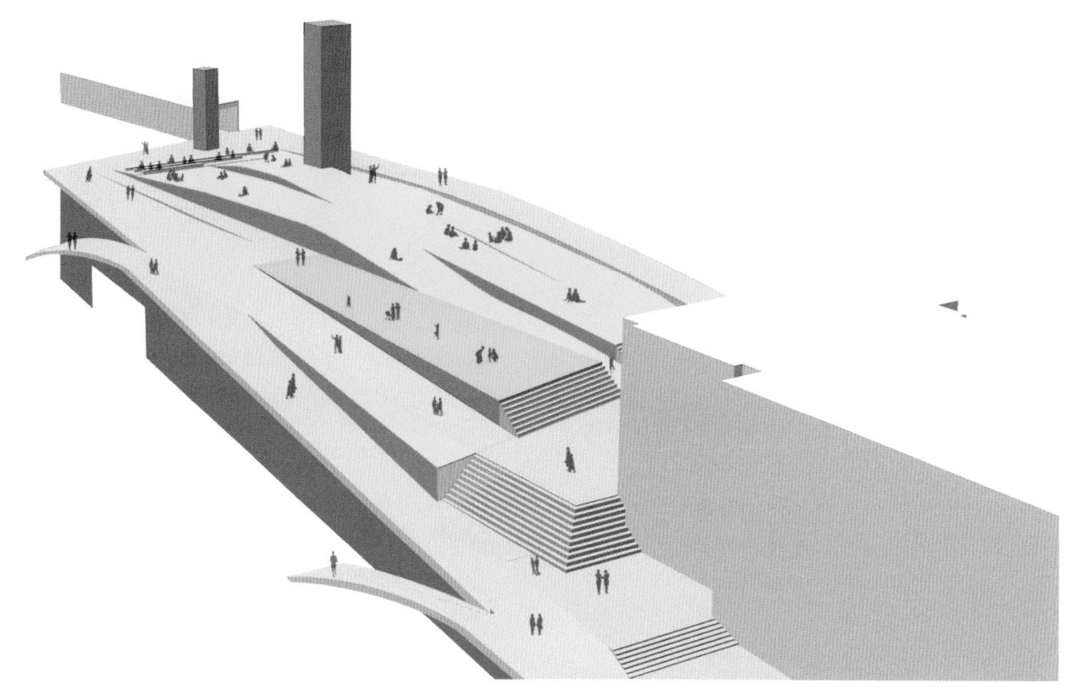

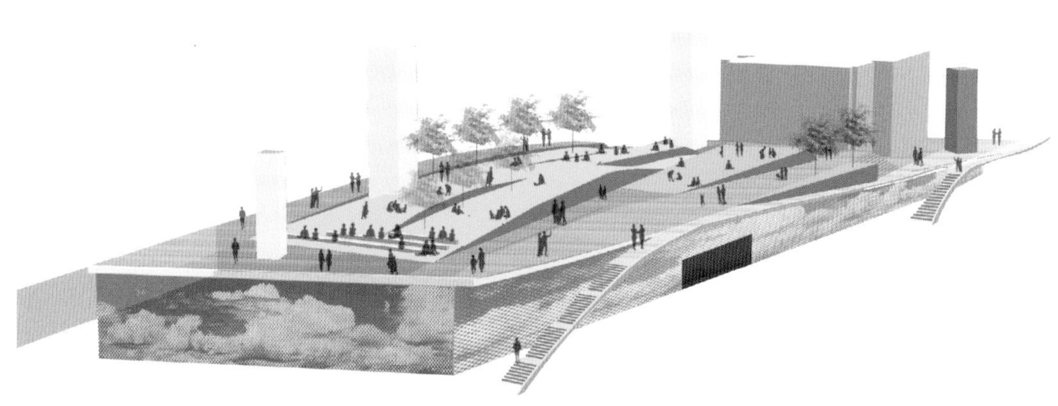

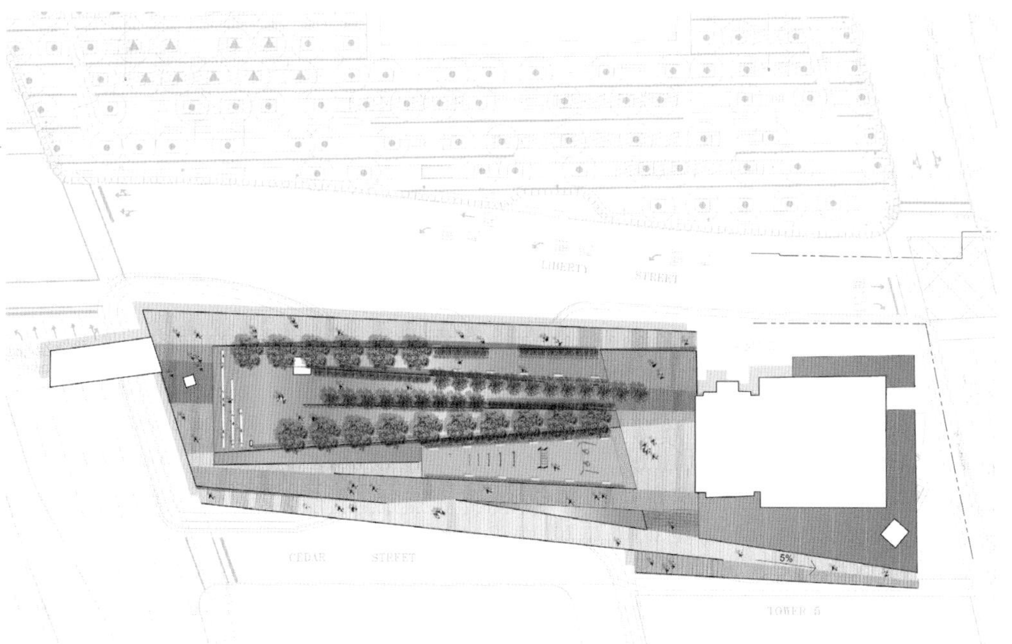

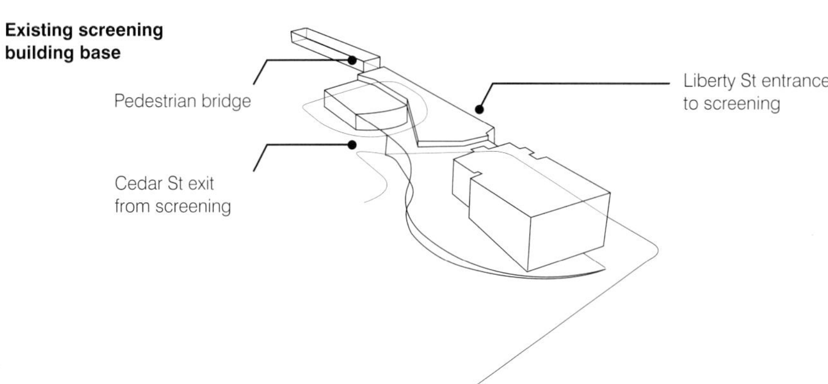

Draping
Liberty Park is a landscape surface draped over the screening building structure. This establishes a simple relationship to the structure underneath and the surrounding streets.

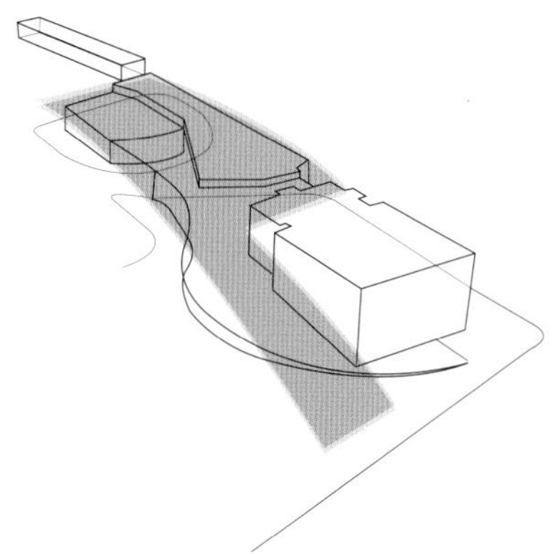

Programme

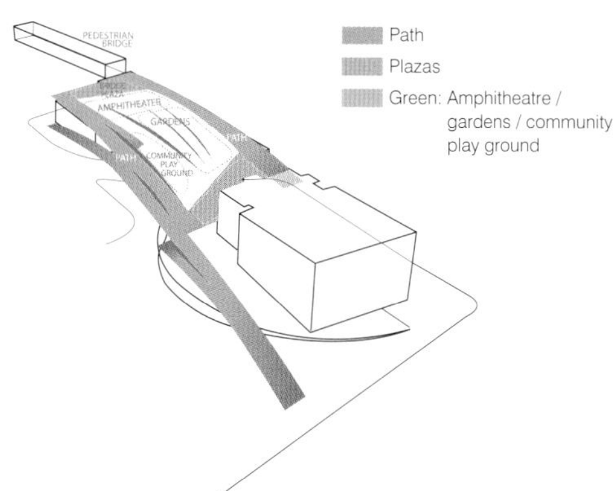

Cutting
The park is cut strategically into a series of spaces that respond to circulation patterns and programmatic requirements.

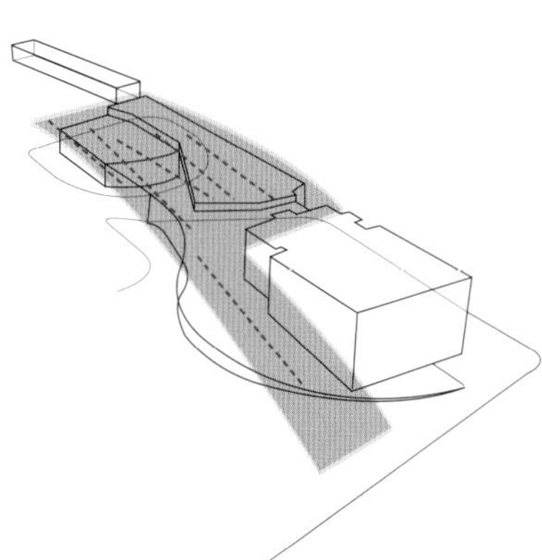

Circulation

Main circulation across the park is provided as ADA accessible path.

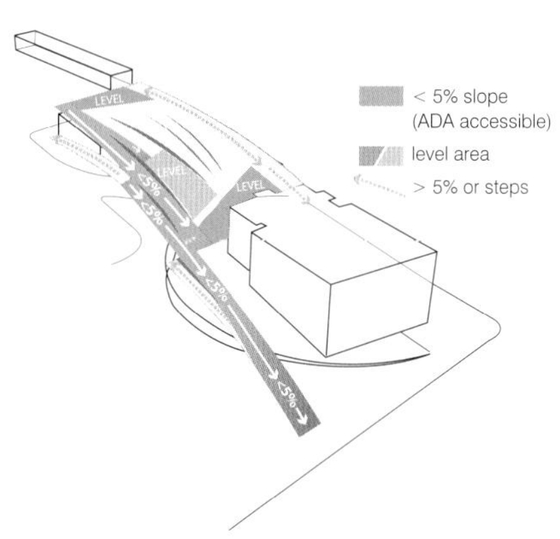

Pealing
The surface is pulled up and down along the cuts to give topography to the park.

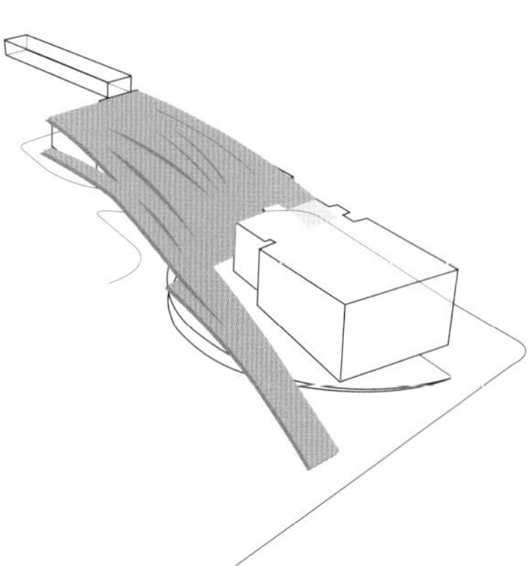

At the southernmost part of the site, there is an opportunity to introduce soft landscaping with a proposed new green space called Liberty Park over the top of the screening building. This is the point at which all vehicles, including buses and lorries, are checked before being allowed to enter the site. Designs are for a gracefully undulating composition of strands of lawn, grasses, and gardens, a new piece of green in the city.

Layered composition

The park will be a new green space composed of strands or ribbons of grass and gardens which undulate as they make their way across the building from east to west. This dynamic design is conceived to be draped over and wrapped around a sequence of buildings.

Concept
The largest waterfront revitalisation scheme in the USA

Context
Pacific port/temperate

LA Waterfront Regeneration, Los Angeles, USA.

Once a small fishing town, San Pedro saw life change dramatically a century ago when the City of Los Angeles annexed a long stretch of its waterfront to accommodate the expanding port. Very soon, tidal marshlands were transformed by development and San Pedro became dwarfed by huge cranes, vast warehouses and the constant traffic of ever-larger ships, trains and trucks. With continued port expansion and the advent of container shipping, the community was progressively cut off from its waterfront.

Opposite
The drama of the docks

Large-scale cranes, buildings and ships provide a dynamic industrial backdrop to extensive new public spaces along the waterfront.

UNIGLORY
KAISEI

LA Waterfront Regeneration, Los Angeles, USA

Above left
The Port of LA

An aerial shot of the port's main channel showing the Vincent Thomas Bridge and to the south, the existing cruise ship dock. As one of the world's busiest seaports, the port encompasses almost 70 kilometres of waterfront and 26 cargo terminals which handle more than 40 per cent of all cargo operations for the United States.

Above right
Long-term plans

Visualisation of the proposed Los Angeles World Cruise Center and the Cruise Ship Promenade and Gateway Plaza.

Opposite top

The Cruise Ship Promenade where timber decking and steamer chairs are reminiscent of being onboard ship while grasses waving in the breeze evoke the rippling sea.

Opposite bottom

The water pools of the Gateway Plaza.

Ranking in the world's top ten largest and busiest, the vast Port of Los Angeles, just over 30 kilometres from downtown, has been vital to the thriving economy of Los Angeles and the Western US. However, while it provides thousands of jobs, the port has also come to dominate the landscape with its super-scale structures forming a barrier between the adjacent community and the harbour. Rebuilding the link between the town of San Pedro and its waterfront has inspired an extensive regeneration and revitalisation programme.

The project's focus is along an 11 kilometre, 162 hectare, stretch of the port's western bank. The scheme stretches from the Vincent Thomas Bridge in the north to the Federal Breakwater, known as Angel's Gate, in the south where the port opens to the Pacific. Building on the historic urban framework and majestic port infrastructure, the plan seeks to integrate the waterfront's history with the needs of the modern community. To accomplish this, the redesigned promenade is divided into a sequence of districts. These incorporate plazas where San Pedro's streets meet the waterside along with event spaces, leisure activities and fountains to enliven the historic waterfront at a human scale and enable people to enjoy and celebrate the drama of the port and its activity. While the scheme is expected to take up to three decades to complete, work carried out since the turn of the century has already delivered significant change to the appearance of the port's working waterfront, bringing fresh energy and activity and new development within San Pedro. The catalyst for this extensive regeneration was a plea from the local community to be able to take a stroll along the waterfront and continued community involvement and consultation has been key to the success of the project. The Port of Los Angeles has embraced the public liaison process and taken on the challenge to transform the epic-scale industrial landscape and make it humane, strengthen the distinctive sense of place, and ensure a relevant, sustainable, organic and long-term revitalisation of the waterside area.

Regeneration plans began by establishing how to balance the needs of the working port with opening up public access to the water and regenerating the San Pedro area. The port management's objective was to provide a range of attractions that would draw people to the water's edge, upgrade San Pedro itself, and strengthen the bond between port and community. At the same time opportunities were identified for creating a new cruise ship terminal, an expansion of the Cabrillo Marina, the regeneration of the Ports O'Call Village (now Ports O'Call Marketplace), the possible inclusion of a hotel/conference centre and maritime museum and an enhanced downtown boat harbour. The vision was to link all of these elements with a waterfront promenade and a revitalised Red Car trolley system, while also including considerations of security and upgraded infrastructure.

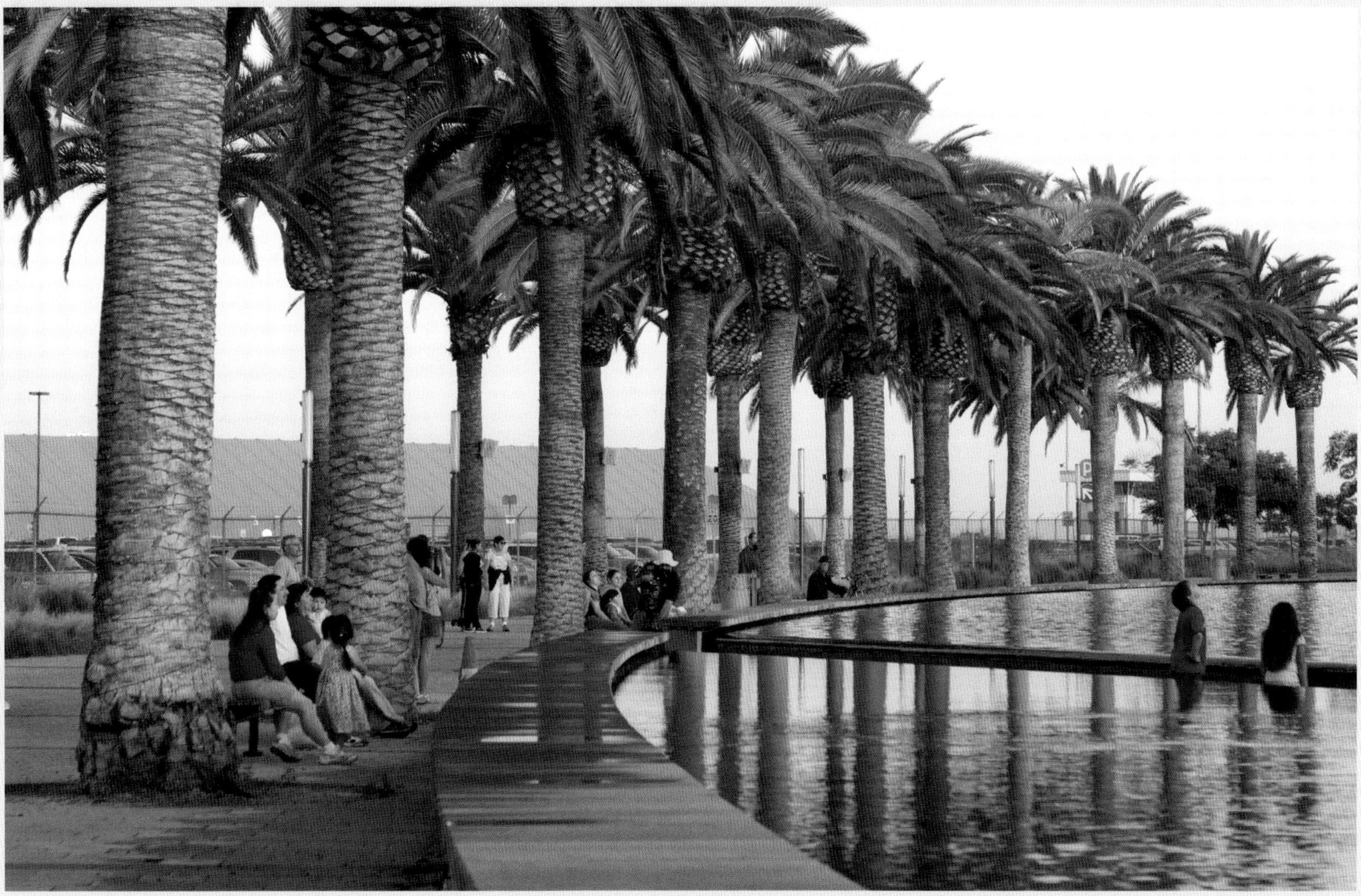

Opposite top
Dramatic landscape

Long excluded from the water's edge, San Pedro's residents have been welcomed back to enjoy the walkways and long vistas through the impressive industrial landscape.

Opposite bottom left

The design of the public realm has a strong nautical flavour. Details include street lighting based on a design with etched-glass angel wings from the 1950s cruise ship terminal.

Opposite bottom middle and right

The Harbor Boulevard Parkway provides a multi-use recreational corridor for the city. It establishes a 1.5 kilometre link between downtown San Pedro in the south with the Cruise Ship Promenade and Gateway Plaza in the north. Designed for pedestrians and cyclists, the parkway includes a broad walkway along with seating and gathering places.

Overleaf
Gateway Plaza

At the northern entrance to the waterfront and the Los Angeles World Cruise Center, and surrounded by significant icons including the Vincent Thomas Bridge, the Gateway Plaza is an impressive civic space which has become the focal point of special events. Rising from black granite pools, the Gateway Fountain celebrates the revitalisation of the waterfront, and provide the setting for spectacular nighttime water, music and light shows. The plaza is also the terminus of the Red Car Line—the last historic remnant of Los Angeles' once extensive streetcar system.

From north to south the work began adjacent to the World Cruise Center, the huge terminal close to the Vincent Thomas Bridge with the capacity to accommodate up to three liners. The first phase of completed regeneration work here was the Cruise Ship Promenade. This former car parking area had been a featureless expanse of asphalt with little visual appeal and limited access for the local community or for the one million cruise passengers arriving and departing here every year. Taking inspiration from the marine environment along with the romance and detailing of luxury liners, the transformation has included installing a boardwalk-style broad promenade, cantilevered look-out points and liner-style railings close to the water's edge. Here, too, is the Bon Voyage Plaza, a place for sitting and enjoying the views, and Recreation Deck with its popular bocce ball courts.

Mature palm trees add height and structure and shade, while, at ground level, swathes of ornamental grasses sway in the breeze resembling ripples of water and recalling the salt marshes that once existed here. Design details include recreated historic street lighting which features etched-glass angel wings which had been part of a 1950s cruise ship terminal. There are deck chairs, chess tables and courts for playing bocce ball, a game popular with Italian and Croatian communities. Nationally known and local artists became involved too and their work has been integrated into the scheme, examples include pictorial ceramic tiling built into the design of concrete bench seating and a major piece of kinetic sculpture with an environmental theme made up of wind-activated stainless steel elements.

The Cruise Ship Promenade went through a year-long design process and at every stage the community contribution was considerable, even in detailed design. Along with access to the waterside, local people wanted to build in small and characterful elements including work by local artists. When it came to selecting lighting, a mock-up site was created to show different light designs in daytime and at night. With no outright favourite, it was decided to incorporate several different designs. The completed projected is rich in texture and colour and full of incident. While clearly rooted in San Pedro's past, this promenade celebrates the drama of the docks, has inspired local confidence and boosted people's pride in their home town while at the same time providing a catalyst for investment.

The second major phase to be completed was the Harbor Boulevard Parkway, a pedestrian walkway that provides a multi-use recreational green corridor for the city.

The parkway establishes a 1.6 kilometre north–south connection between the Cruise Ship Promenade, the Gateway Plaza with its fountains and lights and downtown San Pedro. The 21 metre wide route is designed for pedestrians and cyclists and incorporates a sequence of distinctive plazas for staging community and regional events. Along with custom-designed seating and lighting and clusters of shade trees, there is also a 'story rope', a written tale engraved in granite and set into the paving which relates aspects of the waterfront's history from the earliest native American settlement.

The latest phase to be constructed is the Gateway Plaza and Fountain located at the entry to the waterfront and the Los Angeles World Cruise Center. The spectacular Gateway Fountain with its sequence of 58 massive water jets and choreographed light, music and water displays is designed to herald the revitalisation of the waterfront, provide entertainment for residents, and welcome visitors to San Pedro and the cruise ships. The plaza creates a civic gathering place at this important threshold to the town, surrounded by significant icons such as the Vincent Thomas Bridge and visual attractions of the cruise ships and cranes. It is also the terminus of the Red Car Line—the last historic remnant of Los Angeles' once extensive streetcar system.

Additional segments of waterfront undergoing design and development include the new Downtown Harbor that will be the centrepiece of the waterfront improvements, Cabrillo Beach Park where landforms evoke abstract dunes and create sheltered picnic areas anchoring the vast project's southern terminus.

As the nation's largest waterfront revitalisation project, it is anticipated that the work at San Pedro will generate thousands of permanent new jobs including a large proportion in construction, with the scheme taking as long as a generation to complete.

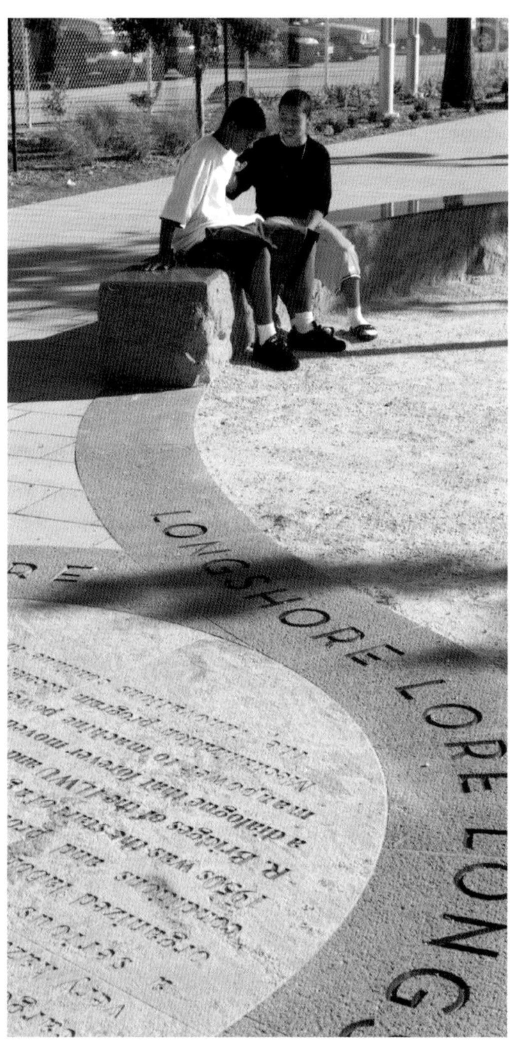

Long story

Water pools provide places of tranquillity, above. While, below, a unifying feature in the Harbor Boulevard Parkway is a 'story rope' set into the paving, this feature in carved stone is engraved with episodes from San Pedro's waterfront history.

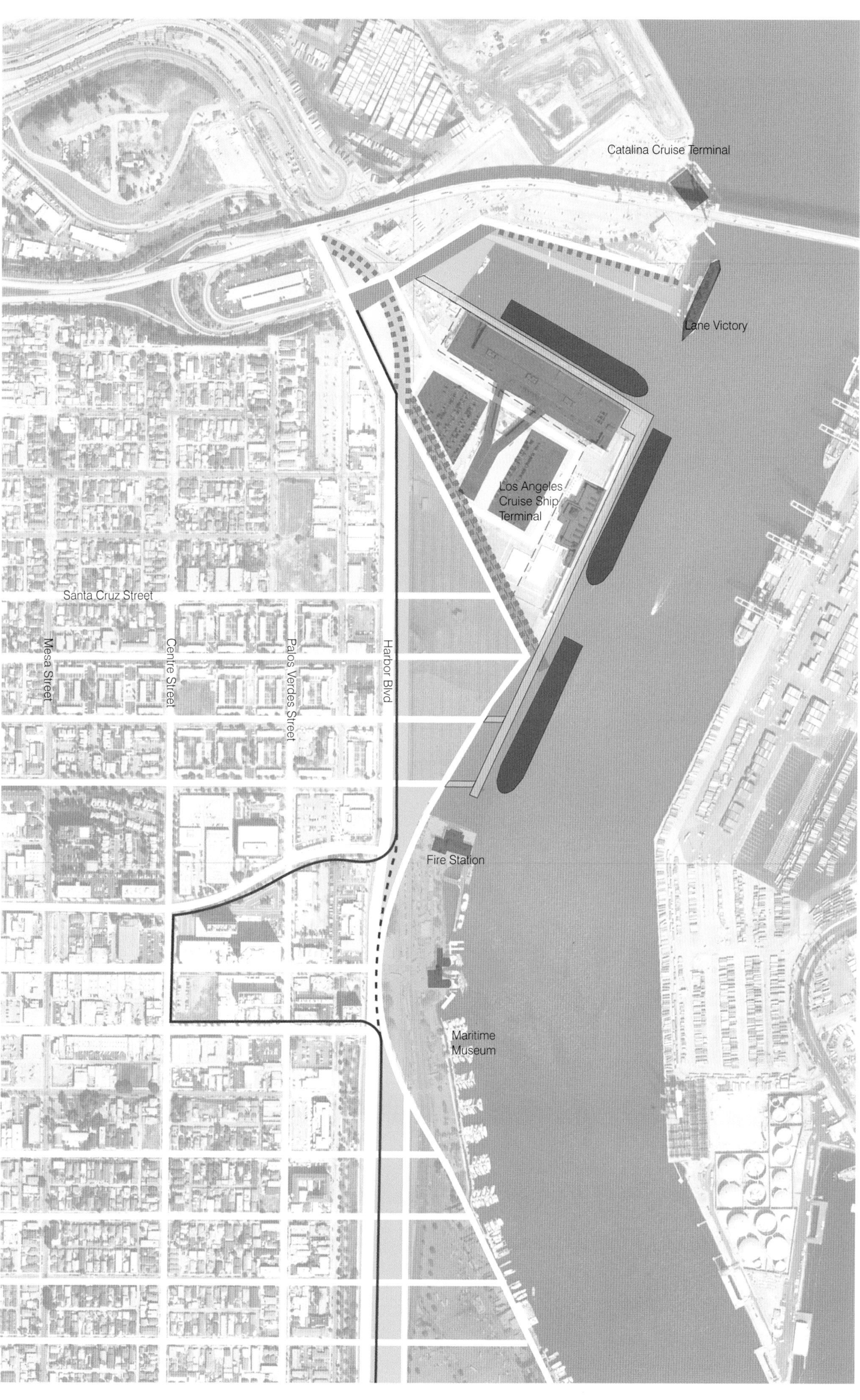

Landscape framework diagram

Key elements in the waterfront regeneration. The revitalisation design principles included:

- Developing a continuous waterfront promenade.
- Creating significant new open spaces.
- Creating a signature address along a grand boulevard.
- Incorporating San Pedro's history in the new design.
- Providing a variety of transportation options.
- Enhancing linkages with downtown.

6 Culture and Leisure

"Landscape architecture is increasingly recognised as a compound inter-

disciplinary phenomenon at the intersection of art, science and utility.

It is an art, but a social art; it is also a way of protecting, restoring or creating natural systems. Unlike painting, sculpture, photography or even architecture, it cannot exist apart from other disciplines. It never seriously flirted with the autonomy that other arts sought in the Modernist era. In that sense, it is the perfect forum for expressing cultural ambitions in a complex, hybrid, global era when the creation and preservation of habitable environments at every scale—and for every income group—are among the most pressing challenges we face.

John Beardsley
Senior Lecturer at Harvard's Department of Landscape Architecture

Concept
Beach resort and community that sits on the land lightly

Context
Coastal/tropical

Anvaya Cove Masterplan and Landscape Architecture, Philippines.

Drawing its inspiration from the location, Anvaya Cove's family-oriented community and beach club has been conceived to sit lightly on the land, minimise alteration to the terrain and vegetation, and protect and enhance local habitat and wildlife.

Opposite
Natural beauty

Key to the appeal of Anvaya Cove is its unspoiled setting, and it was the outstanding natural qualities of the land which became the organising elements. This included working with the undulating topography to preserve as much as possible of the natural landscape and concentrating development on just one third of the site.

Anvaya Cove Masterplan and Landscape Architecture, Philippines

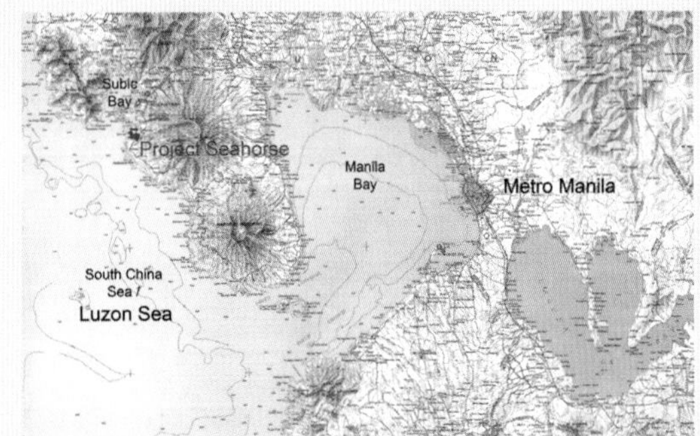

In context

In the Central Luzon region, the Anvaya Cove site is seen, top, and called Project Seahorse, in context with the Philippines capital Manila to the east. The city is within approximately three hours drive of the scheme. At the centre of the image above, the cove is seen in its wider setting of the mountainous landscape of the western Philippines.

Opposite
Site analysis

Top, a site plan including amenities and residential development lots planned to avoid and protect sensitive areas. The masterplan evolved from comprehensive site analysis including the elements shown bottom, from left to right, the description of vegetation ecotypes, vegetation cover and areas not suitable for development.

The masterplan principles

The masterplan's principles include to:

- Protect the natural character of the site, and integrate development with the natural setting.
- Design community spaces and elements to foster family bonding.
- Establish a legible open-space system.
- Provide a variety of residential choices to attract the largest segment of the market.
- Create a safe and convenient circulation system that accommodates automobiles, bicycles and pedestrians.
- Create a community identity by developing a unifying building, landscape and roadway design vocabulary.
- Provide infrastructure in a way that is least intrusive.

In a spectacular natural setting, this 400 hectare coastal site rises from the sea in the west to rugged highlands in the east. Along with cliffs, rolling bluffs and steep hillsides with mature bamboo, mango, cupang, cashew and narra trees, the outstanding natural features of the place include two creeks, called Ilining and Buin, a trio of ridges with plateaus, and dense vegetation fronting onto a 3.5 kilometres coastline of coves and beaches on the South China Sea. The site is around 150 kilometres or three hours drive north-west of Manila, and is just south of Subic Bay, which operated as a large American military base until recently. The area for study and development was a large C-shaped plot. This type of environmentally, economically and socially sustainable scheme has been an innovative development for the Philippines.

The brief was to create a unique, authentic and exceptional development, with the emphasis on second homes where families could enjoy nature and make the most of time together. This was encapsulated in the masterplan vision which stated that the project "is to become the premier resort community in the Philippines offering a variety of luxury neighbourhoods and homes, outstanding and varied recreational amenities for all members of the family, in a setting where development is carefully integrated into the natural landscape".

Sustainability was at the core of the approach where the outstanding natural qualities of the land became the masterplan's organising elements. These were interwoven with strategies to preserve and respect the local culture and village livelihoods, protect environmentally sensitive resources such as the coral reefs and the green sea turtle nesting habitat, and create a viable implementation strategy. This comprehensive approach resulted in a plan that includes a spectacular beach-front resort with water sports, a nature reserve, equestrian centre, a golf course and club house, a wide range of more than 2,200 homes, walking and cycling trails, a conservation programme and international standards of design and service. The scheme preserves more than 60 per cent of the site as natural landscape and limits residential development to compact plots totalling 37 per cent of the land.

Work in the early stages of the masterplanning process began with a comprehensive site analysis. Using geographic information systems (GIS) this range of studies explored numerous aspects of the site such as the elevation range which measured the undulations of the land and elements such as slope categories. Findings revealed that around one quarter of the site comprises slopes above 25 per cent, therefore restricting development opportunities in those areas. Other types of analysis looked at aspect, confirming that the majority of slopes face either north or south. There was work, too, on climate and prevailing winds—the average breeze being from north–north-east, with the monsoon season bringing a complete turnabout with southwesterly winds. Coral cover was logged and while the majority of the fringe reefs have been devastated by the local fishing practice of using dynamite, it was discovered that there remain some patches in fair condition and extensive recovery could take many years. The main vegetation ecotypes were described as including grassland, agricultural, savannah, beach forest, riparian, and wetland, while vegetation cover is a mixture of dense, semi-dense, open and disturbed.

This topographic information was accompanied by analysis of the leisure industry and market factors determining the types and sizes of properties that would be most attractive to buyers. The culmination of this detailed understanding was to act as an inventory of assets. It also helped to identify key opportunities and limitations which would help maximise the best qualities of the site, limit the extent of earthworks, and minimise the risks involved in development.

The next stage of work focused on alternative planning options. This involved creating different scenarios for the site using the same set of main components including the beach club, nature reserve, hotel and spa, golf course, trails, village square with shops, and homes. By placing amenities in different locations on the site, there were impacts on where to best distribute housing, the density concentrations and routes for infrastructure. The options were subjected to evaluation and further market analysis calculating yield and plot values to ensure best use of the site and achieving best value.

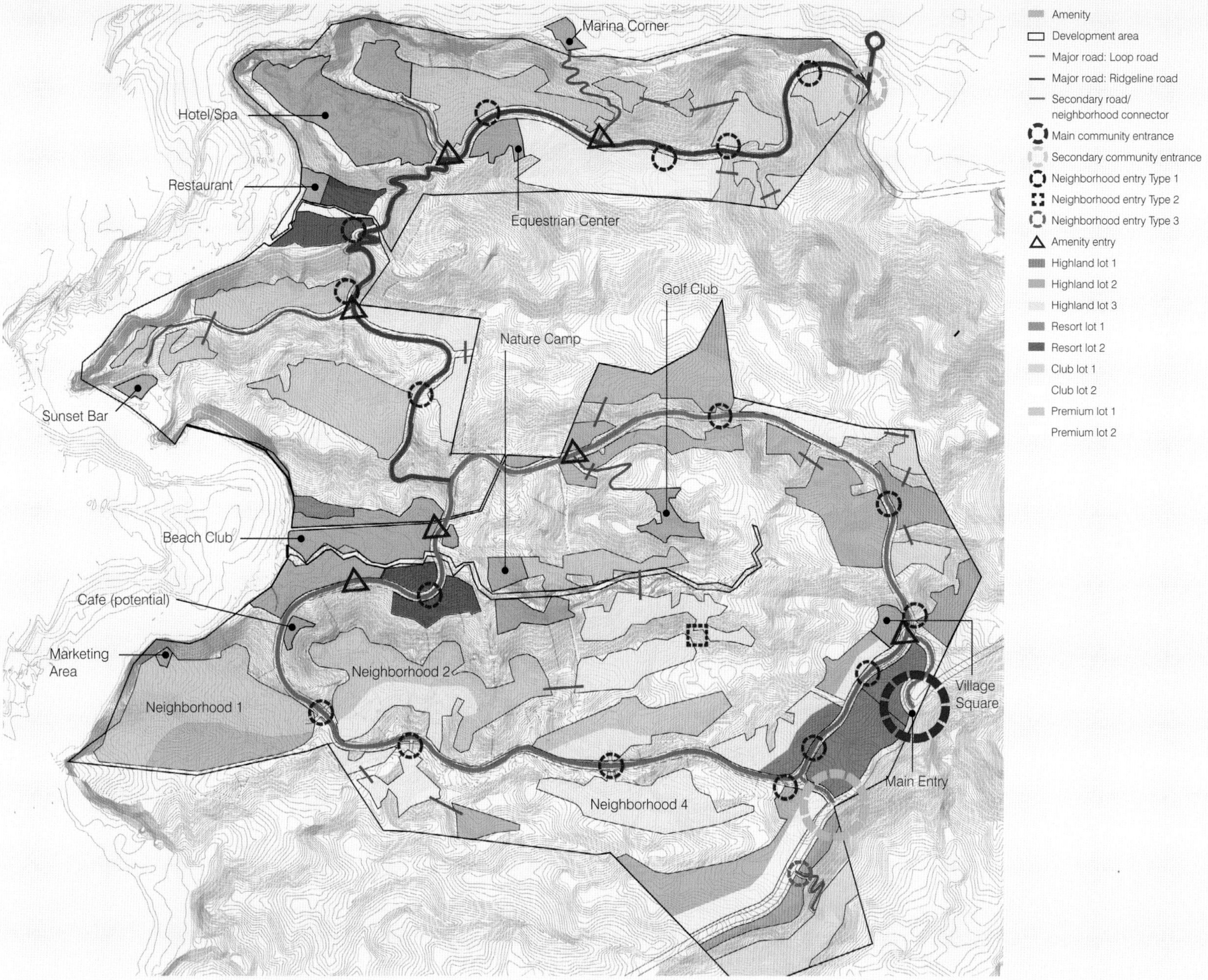

Marina Corner
Hotel/Spa
Restaurant
Equestrian Center
Golf Club
Nature Camp
Sunset Bar
Beach Club
Cafe (potential)
Marketing Area
Neighborhood 2
Neighborhood 1
Village Square
Main Entry
Neighborhood 4

- Amenity
- Development area
- Major road: Loop road
- Major road: Ridgeline road
- Secondary road/ neighborhood connector
- Main community entrance
- Secondary community entrance
- Neighborhood entry Type 1
- Neighborhood entry Type 2
- Neighborhood entry Type 3
- Amenity entry
- Highland lot 1
- Highland lot 2
- Highland lot 3
- Resort lot 1
- Resort lot 2
- Club lot 1
- Club lot 2
- Premium lot 1
- Premium lot 2

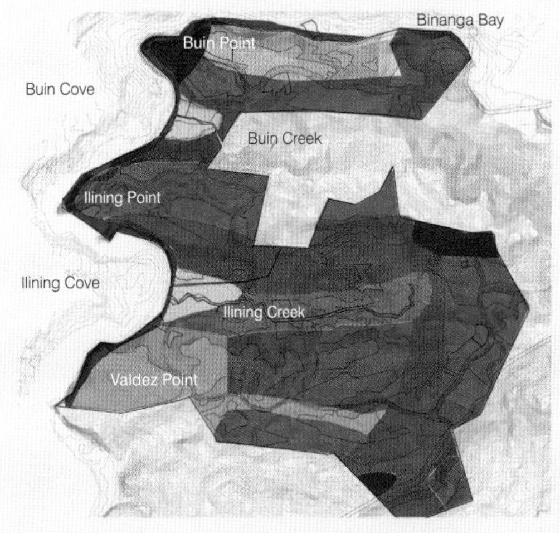

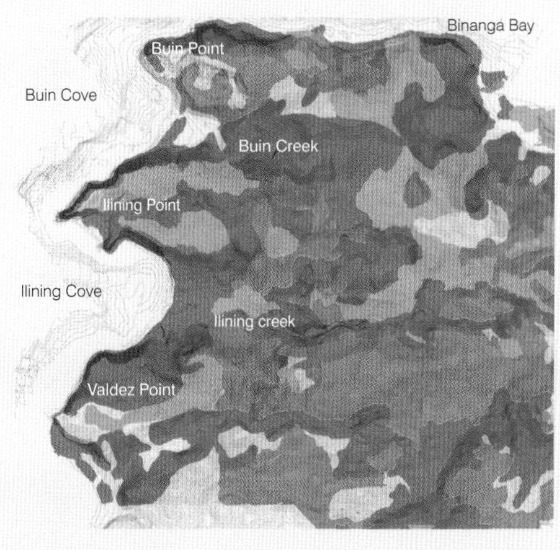

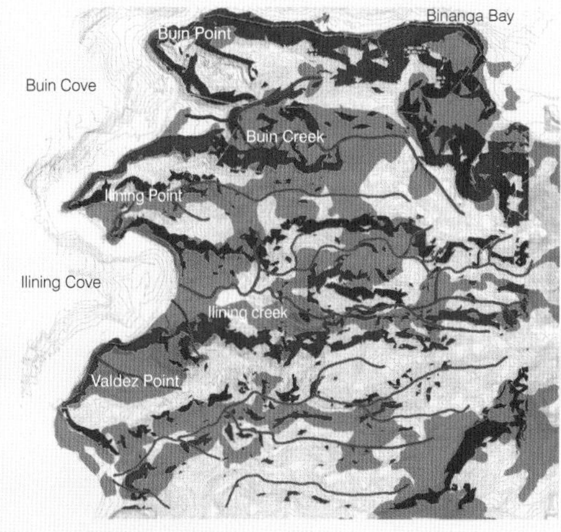

Vegetation ecotypes

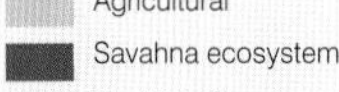

- Grassland
- Agricultural
- Savahna ecosystem
- Banhinia Cogon
- Riparian
- Secondary forest
- Wetland
- Beach forest
- Agroforest plantation

Vegetation cover

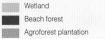

- Dense
- Semi-dense
- Open
- Disturbed

Restrictions for development suitability

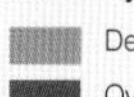
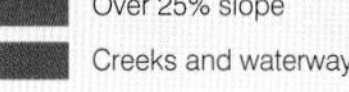

- Dense
- Over 25% slope
- Creeks and waterways

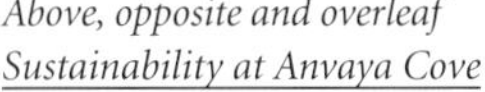

Above, opposite and overleaf
Sustainability at Anvaya Cove

Using a simple palette of natural materials and inspired by local architecture, the beach-side development sits comfortably in the landscape. For environmental, economic and social sustainability throughout the project, the design and development was sensitive to the natural environment and local communities.

A preferred option emerged with the golf course designed around Ilining Cove, into the headland and occupying an area of the eastern highlands at the centre of the site to maximise beach views and views over the golf course.

The detailed masterplan places the grand entrance to the site on its eastern boundary where visitors pass by a stone wall subtly placed into the hillside. Through the entry, the site rises to a high point where a welcome pavilion has great views in all directions, from the mountains to the sea. The main amenities are arranged along the east–west axis, with the golf course and club house west of the village square, followed by the nature camp and then the beach club. A scenic loop road connects these areas and most of the neighbourhoods in the southern portion of the site. In the north, a ridgeline road connects to Buin Cove, the hotel and spa, marina, equestrian centre and additional residential neighbourhoods.

To help deliver the resort's concept and design with consistency, design guidelines were produced including Guidelines for Neighbourhoods and Guidelines for Individual Lots. In the knowledge that the resort will be realised over the course of more than a decade and by a number of different developers, this document provides guidelines for the general style and quality of the place to ensure a degree of consistency, while also encouraging creative freedom within the set parameters. There are suggestions for an architectural style based on the local vernacular and using local material, neighbourhood layouts, a palette of colours and finishes, native planting, designs for trails and roads and suggested materials, streetscape design, measures for privacy and security, and lighting.

Sustainability highlights

The project incorporates social, environmental and economic sustainabilty. Highlights included:

- Preserving more than 60 per cent of the site as open space.
- Emphasising best practice for water sensitive design in design guidelines.
- Planning construction sequencing to ensure protection during mating and nesting for key species such as the green sea turtle.
- Diverting roadways to leave trees in place.
- Hydroseeding of native plants and grasses. This was successfully attempted for the first time as a stabilising measure on steep slopes. Hydroseeding is a planting technique which uses a slurry of seed and mulch which is sprayed evenly over a site.
- A new fishing plan developed with the villagers. Traditionally they have used explosives among the coral as a fishing technique.
- The first comprehensive trail system developed in the Philippines for a second-home resort community, promoting walking and cycling over driving.
- Clustered development. Based on the rigorous site analysis and wanting to avoid large-scale levelling, homes were planned in small clusters, most densely in the highlands, to protect vegetation and trees.
- A stormwater management plan to ensure that water entering the sea was of a high quality and did not include a high sediment load. This was critical to protect the coral and other marine habitats, especially the green sea turtle which nests on the beach.
- Incorporation of traditional building types using local materials and passive solar-energy features to respond to climatic conditions that include heat, humidity and heavy rains.
- Given the year-round hot tropical climate, buildings and landscape were planned carefully to maximise the benefit of cooling sea breezes and to provide shade along paths and in outdoor gathering areas. Shaded structures and covered walkways provide protection from heat and rain.
- Special consideration to preserving the habitats of local flora and fauna including green sea turtles, the Philippine mallard, mangos and figs. Part of the beach is closed seasonally to protect areas where turtles nest. An interpretation programme for natural wildlife and vegetation was also developed.
- Setting resort development back from the beach edge to maintain a buffer during tropical storms and to protect the beach from erosion.

Concept
Creating safe but challenging places where children can play and learn

Context
Public gardens

Children's Gardens, Various Locations, USA.

Children are the toughest critics, so when it comes to places to play, their enthusiasm for imaginative and inspiring gardens is unbridled and unmistakable. This is good news for parents who know their children will enjoy being outside and interacting with nature, and good news for public garden managers and operators who see visitor numbers escalate.

Opposite
Small scale, big fun

At the Red Butte Gardens and Arboretum in Salt Lake City, Utah, the creation of a children's garden was to "provide a special place for children to learn about and experience the uses, sciences and pleasures of plants and horticulture".

Summer Adventures
Summer Adventures

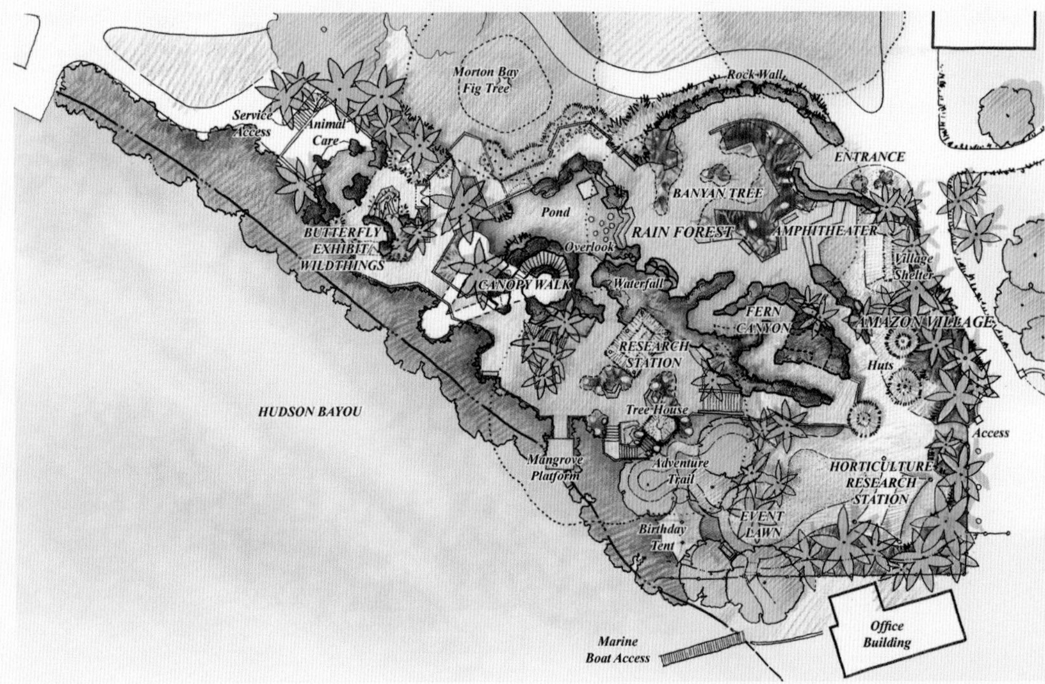

Children's rainforest

Masterplan for the Children's Rainforest at the Marie Selby Botanic Gardens at Sarasota, Florida, fulfilling the legacy of William and Marie Selby by providing an understanding and appreciation of plant life, education and enjoyment to all who visit the garden.

Increasing concern about children being overprotected, underexercised, and out of touch with the natural world has fuelled interest in creating gardens that are designed specifically for the young visitor. The best examples provide opportunities for exploration and discovery that engage all the five senses by climbing, swinging and scrambling, even if that means a few cuts and bruises, and by digging and planting with plenty of mud and water—away from, but allowing, the watchful gaze of grown-ups.

Along with working at a large scale on vast landscape projects, landscape architect Herb Schaal has become renowned for his delightful work at a small scale with more than 20 children's gardens designed across the USA. A recipient of the 2008 Designer of the Year Award from the American Horticultural Society, he believes that today's children have limited opportunities to be themselves because they are so highly controlled in school, at home and when they go out. The result is that there's little room in their lives for simple play and exploring, inventing, creating, contemplating and just being in nature on their own. Schaal's gardens are designed specifically to open up opportunities for safe play and experimentation. The demand for these bespoke places is especially strong in public gardens, such as botanical centres and arboretums, where the addition of a children's garden does not just increase the numbers of young visitors. In many cases, the gardens experience a significant increase in their membership and a steep rise in the numbers of visits.

Taking inspiration from their location and the client's mission, each garden has a powerful theme and is filled with detail to create a stimulating environment that encourages learning and enjoyment of the natural world through play. One of the most inspiring and poignant gardens is Schaal's work at the Olson Family Garden at Children's Hospital, Washington University Medical Center, St Louis, Missouri. This rooftop therapeutic garden is on the eighth floor of the hospital, providing comfort away from stresses of the hospital environment and providing welcome colour, texture and natural elements to delight the senses.

The rectangular rooftop contains a compact design with a hierarchy of spaces, from the most intimate areas where families can quietly be together to the central public area where there is plenty of activity. The design incorporates multiple layers of design and thought.

Through the garden's flowers and trees, the message is about the cycles of life and changing seasons, an opportunity to connect with nature. Research has indicated that many patients are able to make a speedier recovery when they can see the sky and trees and plants. A telescope promontory is provided so children can look out across the city to the world beyond. At a more intimate scale, the garden is about solace for the very sick, a place to converse with caregiving staff or simply reflect in quiet solitude. In very practical terms, the design incorporates clever features such as stepping stones, which are not just fun to walk on, but perform the dual function of helping children regain their balance to walk again. Paving materials are soft to cushion falls. In addition to providing a welcome break to families and children, the garden has also proved popular with medical staff who find respite from the daily stresses inside the hospital.

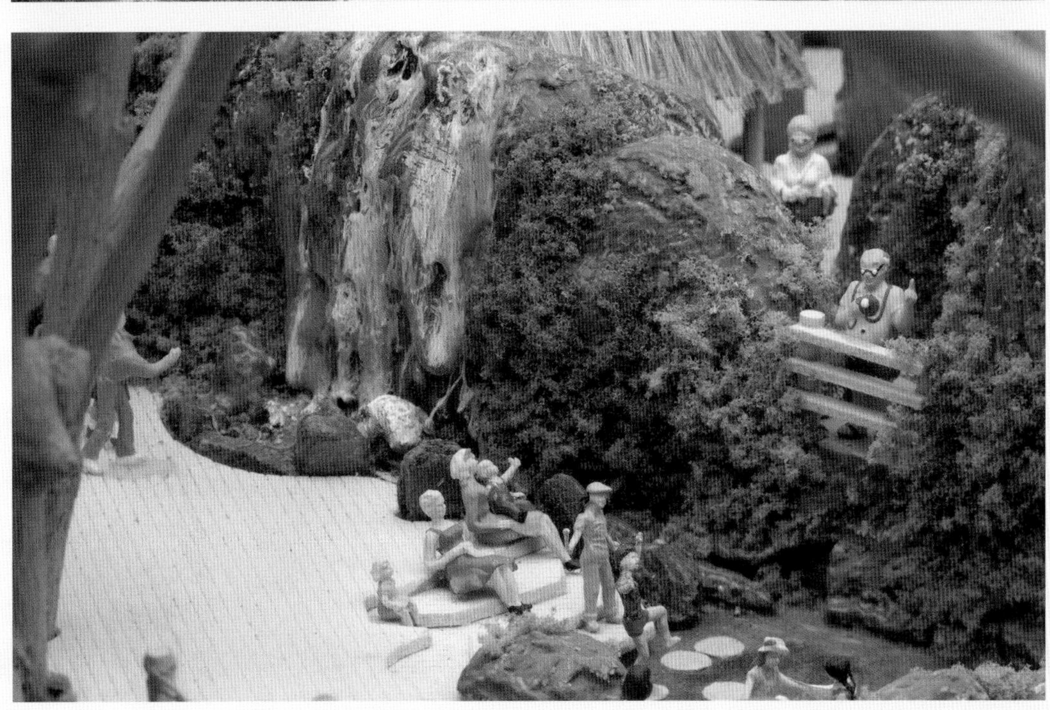

Model environment

Playful model landscapes show clearly how the park at the Selby gardens will fit in and around the characteristic and massive banyan trees which are a feature of the main gardens. The Children's Rainforest is designed as a highly interactive landscape with the emphasis on discovering and learning; features include rope bridges, caves, periscopes to observe underwater sea life, a fern canyon, research station, canopy walk, frog and butterfly exhibit, a pond with a five metre high waterfall, an amphitheatre, event lawn, a mixture of shelters and huts, a horticultural station, a birthday tent and an adventure trail.

Right
Learning through exploring

Children are encouraged to engage with the gardens, to explore, and to use their imaginations. A leader in conservation, captive breeding and animal care, the Cheyenne Mountain Zoo in Colorado Springs has a mission to "connect people with wildlife and wild places".

Opposite
Playing with science

An educational landscape was created for the Gateway Science School, St Louis, Missouri, where every piece of design has an inbuilt educational metaphor, from paving patterns to the sandbox, which help the teaching of mathematics outdoors.

The importance of connecting children with nature is a theme in all of Schaal's gardens. However, this is achieved in a very different way at the Hershey Children's Garden at Cleveland Botanical Garden, Ohio. This garden has become renowned for its hands-on activity, including a trail that leads through various themed gardens based on a scaled-down Ohio landscape, a child-size building, and plenty of play. Meanwhile, in Florida, the Marie Selby Botanical Gardens in Sarasota will have a children's section with a rainforest theme. Aimed at children between the ages of three and 12, this enchanting garden has a mission to connect children to the living planet through play and to teach them about the fragile rainforest environment. From the entrance marked by two vast banyan trees, a trail is created through the landscape where children can explore, enjoy 'safe danger', and learn to respect plants.

The joy of discovery and getting dirty is key to the appeal of the Morton Arboretum Children's Garden, Lisle, Illinois. Part of a historic arboretum, this addition was made possible after a tornado tore through the area and created a clearing. The ten themed areas, with enticing names such as the Curiosity Garden, Adventure Woods and the Backyard Discovery Garden, encourage children to go through the spaces, splash in creeks, swing on rope bridges, visit the wonder pond, and play hide and seek among the trees.

Among the most recent designs is the children's space at the Naples Botanical Garden, Florida. Here Schaal has worked with the topography to create an upper and lower section. The upper section emphasises the horticulture and cultural history of south-western Florida, while the lower area replicates a walk through the Florida ecotones, the transition area between two adjacent ecological communities, in a walk called "from trees to sea". In addition to adding visual variety, the changing levels also make it possible for wheelchairs to access the treehouse by use of a bridge.

Opposite
Flower power

The driving idea behind creating children's gardens at botanic gardens, including the Morton Arboretum in Illinois shown here, was to create a safe and accessible, garden experience for the whole family.

Left
Engaging the senses

From bridges to boardwalks, and from planting compositions to water features, all designs are intended to engage as many of the five senses as possible. In every garden and for each feature a matrix is completed listing how they may be used or played with by children and families. Top left, Children's Garden at Spring Creek Park, where the community helped to build the garden. Top right, small-scale bridge in the children's garden at the Red Butte Gardens and Arboretum at Salt Lake City, Utah. Middle left, high-level rope walks at Morton Arboretum, Lisle, Illinois. Middle right, scarecrow sculptures marking the entrance to Spring Creek's vegetable gardens. Bottom left, oasis and rocky landscape at Red Butte Gardens. Bottom right, a colourful and tranquil place at the Red Butte Gardens.

Concept
Reinventing Britain's greatest seaside resort

Context
Coastal/temperate

Coastal Protection Scheme and Gateway Projects, Blackpool, UK.

With its distinctive serpentine shape, sculptural detailing and massive scale, Blackpool's new seafront has become an iconic feature in the town. It provides a contemporary-style setting for the world-famous Illuminations, an expanded promenade, an enhanced relationship between the town and its beach and improved sea defences.

Opposite
Serpentine Steps

Resolving the dual challenges of improving access to the beach and providing better sea defenses, this serpentine structure combines problem-solving design with engineering for an innovative solution.

Coastal Protection Scheme and Gateway Projects, Blackpool, UK

Above
Time and tide

In its heyday Blackpool was one of the most popular seaside resorts in the world where people from surrounding industrial towns and cities would return in an annual pilgrimage for their family holidays. The advent of package holidays and cheap flights have had a severe impact on the town's tourist trade with the numbers of visitors falling rapidly.

And while the sea has been one of the main attractions, it is also a major threat to the town with great tidal surges sweeping up the beach, washing into the town and damaging sea defences.

Right
Masterplan

An early masterplan showing the potential offered by Blackpool's extensive seafront. The vision to re-energise the resort is focused on the areas around the famous trio of piers and includes hotels shown in blue, a grand casino and entertainment venues in purple, retail areas in brown, new cafes, sports facilities and upgraded public spaces including the promenade and beach. The vision also encompasses improving local neighbourhoods.

With millions of visitors every year, Blackpool has enjoyed more than a century as Britain's most popular seaside resort. However, behind the bright lights and candyfloss, the place has suffered from decline after losing much of its razzmatazz during the post-war boom in cheap package holidays luring British tourists abroad. Fewer holidaymakers led to reduced investment and the place began to look outdated and rundown. To add to the problems of economic decline, the resort also faces the more recent physical threat of rising seas and extreme weather as a result of climate change. To reverse its fortunes, Blackpool initiated a programme of updating and reinventing itself.

In its nineteenth century heyday, as a playground for the working classes, the railways delivered holidaymakers in their thousands to Blackpool's beaches. Here, ordinary people could escape from the harsh reality of their daily lives and enjoy a week or two of fantasy and fun. For glamour there was one of the biggest ballrooms in the world, for excitement there was the Pleasure Beach amusement park and for novelty there were the piers, theatres and the famous night-time Illuminations. As the Las Vegas of its day, Blackpool was always guaranteed to put on a lavish show and it is this distinctive sense of place that provides the basis for future regeneration. As a catalyst for future development, a masterplan was devised incorporating economic and physical strategies to raise the town's profile, stimulate investment and create jobs, provide year-round attractions to extend the visitor season, improve the general environment for residents and visitors alike, and upgrade sea defences to protect the town from the potentially devastating effects of climate change.

To set new high-quality benchmarks and instill confidence in the ambitious new plans, the first phase of projects included the sea defences, creating an upbeat and exciting entrance to the resort and a new public park.

The most prominent feature of the recent work, the serpentine promenade and sea defence structure runs along more than three kilometres of seafront. The challenge was to offer protection from the sea while maintaining the sense of openness and improving connections between the town and its beach.

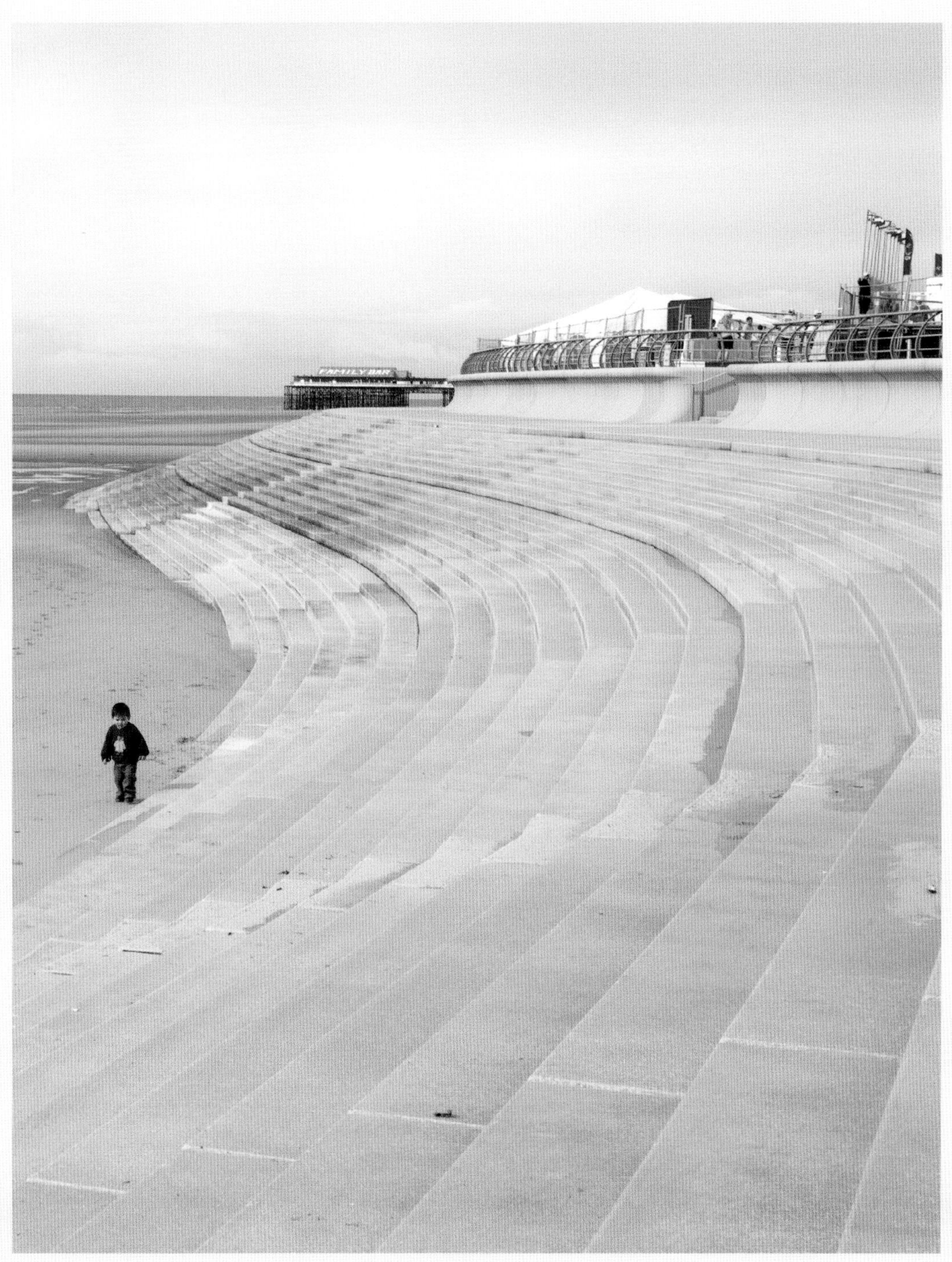

Replacing the imposing Victorian, basalt-faced sea wall which rose steeply from the beach, the new defences have involved radically rethinking the traditional approach to coastal defences. While the old sea wall was a rigid vertical barrier intended to withstand the full force of waves, the new structure takes its inspiration from the organic shapes of local sand dunes. It is designed as a sweeping flight of steps which acts as a massive *revetment* (breakwater) and improves the visual and physical links between beach and town. Its gentle incline make the steps appear as an extension of the beach and its snaking shape has made it possible to expand the promenade and create new headland pockets of public space at the street level. It is anticipated that future development will enliven these headlands with small parks or event spaces encouraging more interaction between the town and its beach.

Work on the structure began by exploring the natural landscape and watching the behaviour of dunes further along the coast. It was noted that the dunes mitigated wave energy with the large surface area of their gently sloping seaward elevation. A design for the new defences evolved which would reduce the energy of the sea hitting the wall by creating the series of steps, each one diffusing the water's force.

Right
Concept images

The natural shapes of sand dunes provided the inspiration for the new sea defences and breakwater. The use of computer modelling created the structure's sequence of serpentine curves and the graceful flight of shallow steps between beach and town evolved with each step acting as a small breakwater. Scale models of the designs were tested in water tanks to watch and record how they responded to waves of varying strengths.

Opposite
Into the curve

Pebble smooth and sculpted into round shapes, these concept images show the evolution of seating designs for the seafront. Integrated into the new promenade and sea defences, the curved shapes make comfortable and sheltered places to sit, and they have the dual function of being designed to redirect seawater away from the town during storms and high tides.

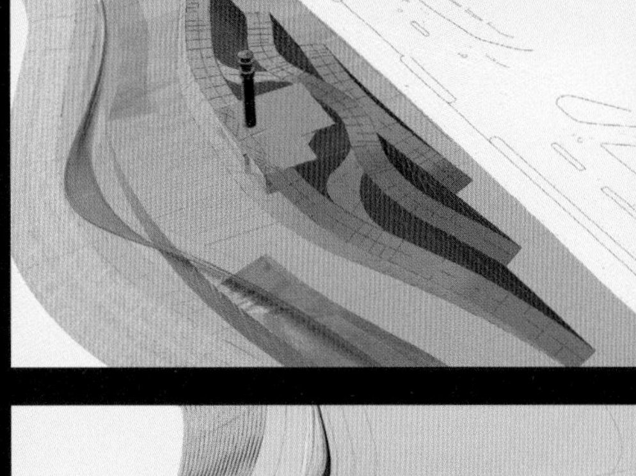

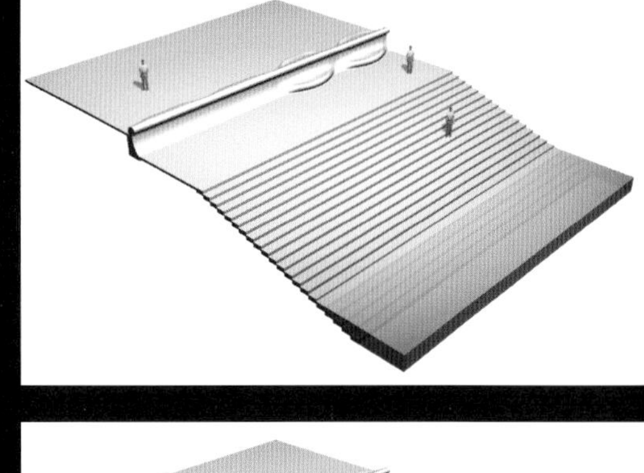

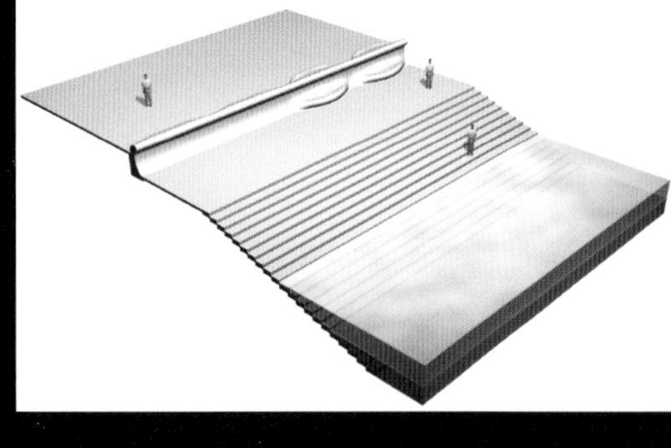

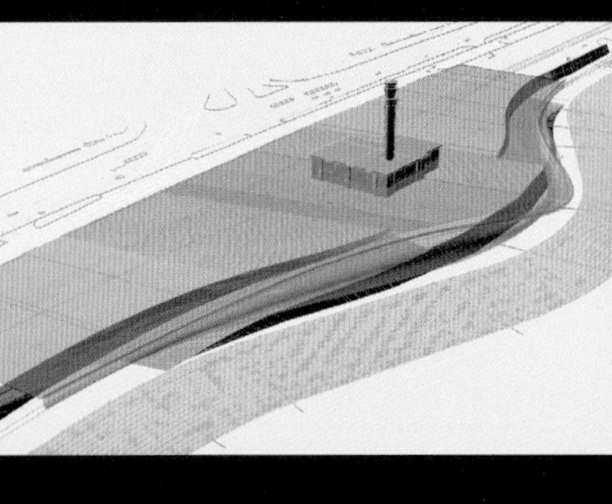

From technical drawings, 3-D scale models of a portion of the wall and headland were constructed directly from the digital models using a computer numerically controlled (CNC) cutting system. The sections were then tested in a water tank with waves of varying strengths up to the force of a one-in-100-year storm event. With the action recorded on video and then analysed, the designs were refined to form the smoothly rounded headlands. It was found that by combining steps with a serpentine shape it was possible to significantly reduce the wave impact. And to cope with even the most ferocious seas, the steps are crowned by a wall with a concave face designed to redirect the waves and turn them back towards the sea. Above here curved railings and sculptural seating details echo the organic design theme.

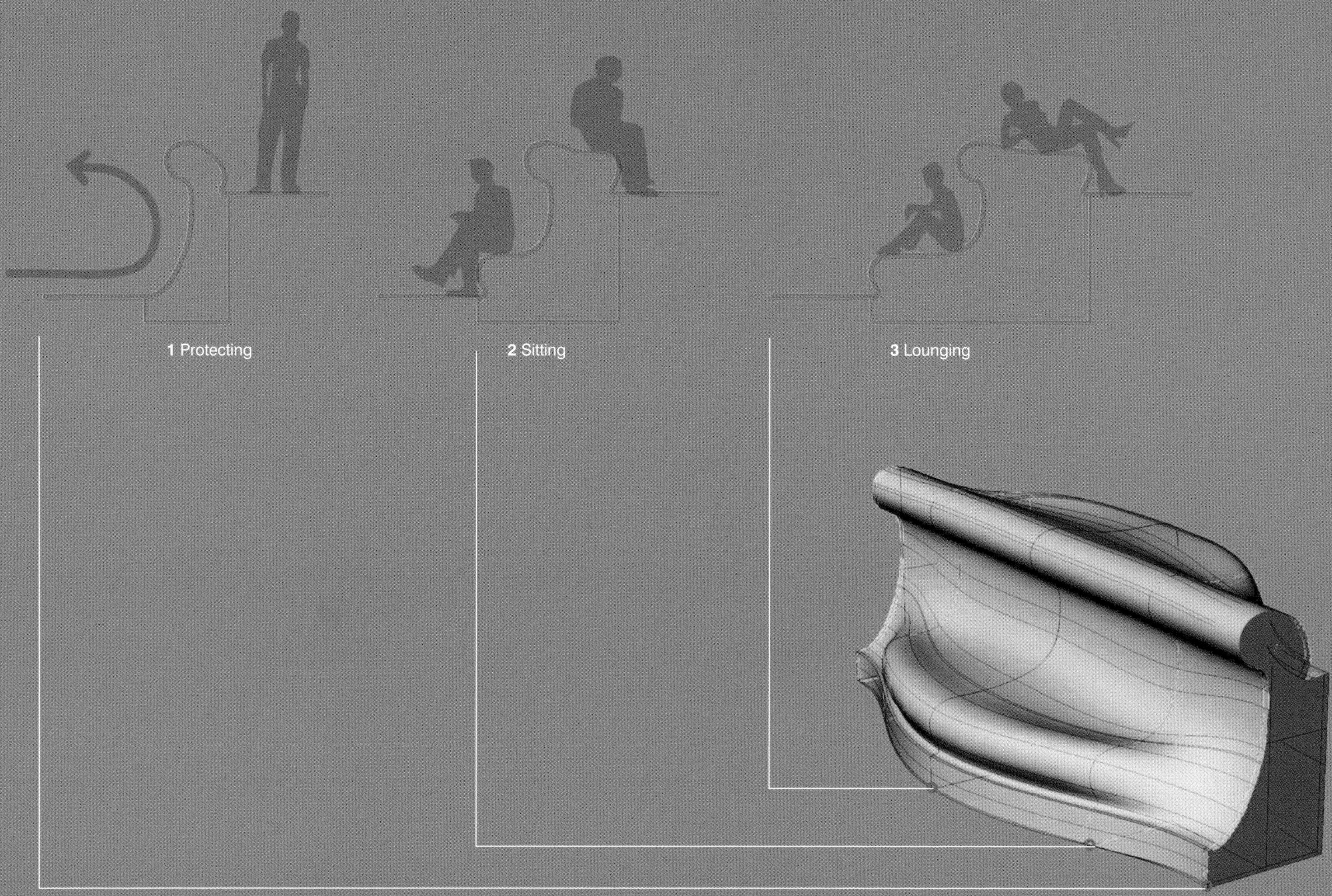

1 Protecting

2 Sitting

3 Lounging

5m pre-cast concrete wall model

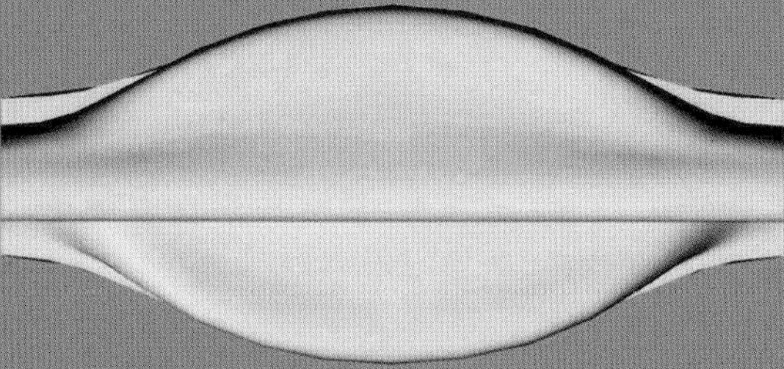

Plan view

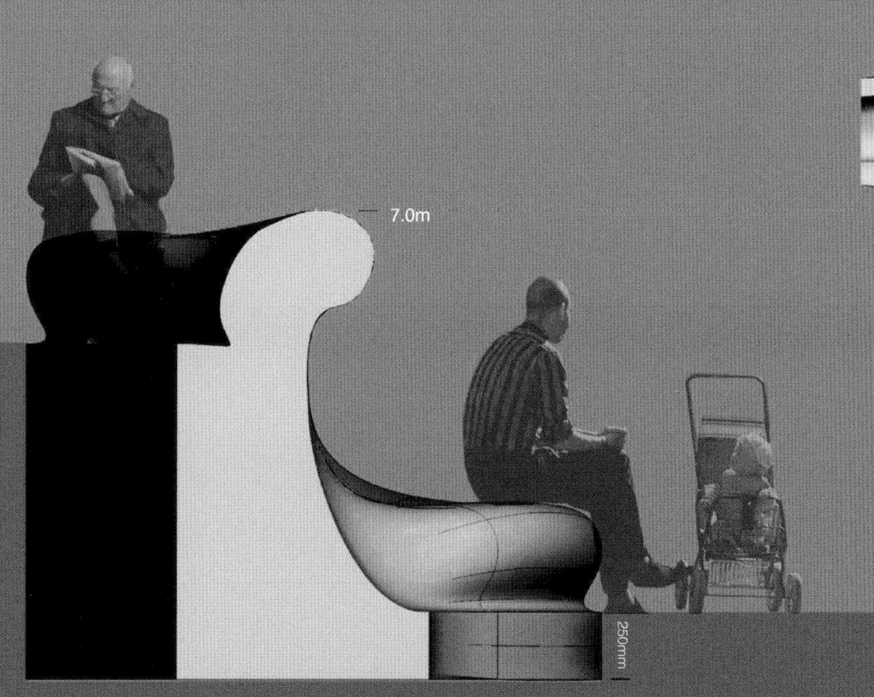

6.5m upper promenade level and elevation

Because of the challenges of pouring concrete in a saline environment, the wall units were precast offsite in a nearby temporary factory and fitted together like a vast three-dimensional jigsaw on site. Computer modelling was used again to calculate the optimum size and weight and shape of each precast unit, some of which weighed more than 16 tonnes. Working between the tides ensured maximum on-site building efficiency using cranes to lift each piece and slot it into place. To complete the attention to detail, and make sure the new structure looked at home on the beach, the concrete was coloured to achieve an exact match with the famous Blackpool sand.

A stroll by the sea

Enjoyed all year round, one of the great pleasures of any visit to Blackpool is a stroll along the seafront and looking out across the enormous expanse of beach and sea to infinity. Coloured to match perfectly the sand on the beach, the curvy sea defence structure becomes an extension of the beach and provides an almost seamless link between the town and the sea.

Blackpool's twin towers

On the site of former railway land which had been used for car parking, the central George Bancroft Park is designed for visitors and local residents. Among the park's most popular features is the pair of 20 metre high climbing towers by sculptor Gordon Young which bear Blackpool's name in huge letters.

In addition to the new seafront, the second major improvement has been upgrading the Southern Gateway to the resort, providing an upbeat and welcoming new entrance to Blackpool's Golden Mile stretch of beach. Bounded by the Irish Sea to the west and the Pleasure Beach to the east, the drama of arrival is heightened with a new-look promenade, colourful gardens and lawn areas, stylish street furniture and, for the evenings, a dazzling state-of-the-art lighting scheme along a one kilometre stretch of promenade. Marking the entrance is a wave-inspired sculpture featuring huge cut-out letters forming the words South Beach. The 400 tonne landmark in precast concrete and decorative recycled glass sparkles with inbuilt LED lighting. The work also included an important new east–west connection between the seafront promenade and the Pleasure Beach complex which is set back from the coast.

A third major innovation is the George Bancroft Park, the first new park for Blackpool since the 1920s. The park takes its name from a well-respected local councilor. Close to the centre of town and occupying former railway land which had been dominated, since the 1980s, by large surface car parks and a busy road, the new park provides a safe, relaxing and enjoyable contemporary-style green space for visitors and for those who live and work in the area. Appealing to a broad cross-section of users, the park incorporates a range of experiences from tranquil community gardens and lawns to playgrounds and games areas. Among the most eyecatching features is a pair of 20 metre high climbing towers, emblazoned with the word Blackpool as a greeting, designed in collaboration with artist Gordon Young which proved an instant hit with climbers and create a powerful visual landmark.

Taking inspiration from these first phases of work, wider regeneration is already taking place with private hoteliers and restaurateurs improving and modernising their premises. Further regeneration projects include improvements to the famous tram system, upgrading the Illuminations and further work on modernising the resort's attractions.

Concept
Transformation through upgraded streetscape and the power of light

Context
Urban/warm-temperate continental monsoon climate

Yingze Boulevard Streetscape and Masterplan, Taiyuan, China.

While Taiyuan's Yingze Boulevard is built at a majestic scale, in recent years it had become run-down and undistinguished. To help transform perceptions of the place, and its fortunes, inspiration was drawn from the past and the future in a project that demonstrates how minimal intervention can have maximum impact.

Opposite
Avenue of light

Disappearing into the distance, the great Yingze Boulevard is an impressive urban thoroughfare.

50

Yingze Boulevard Streetscape and Masterplan, Taiyuan, China

Streetscape

In common with so many Chinese cities, Taiyuan's rapid and ad-hoc growth and modernisation created streets which are lacking in individual character.

The upgraded streetscape has worked as a catalyst for regeneration.

Yingze Boulevard is known as one of China's grandest thoroughfares. For many, it ranks second only to the Chang'an Boulevard (Avenue of Eternal Peace) in Beijing. At more than four kilometres in length, and carrying six to eight lanes of traffic, it forms the main artery through the heart of Taiyuan. This ancient city in north-central China has a population of 3.4 million and is one of the country's great industrial hubs. It is the largest coal-mining centre in the country and an important producer of iron and steel. While the heavy industry has provided jobs and a sound economic base for this city and region, pollution and the widespread destruction of the city's cultural heritage has been a growing concern.

In recent years, pollution, increasing traffic and the rapid spread of modern but nondescript architecture had detracted from the magnificent scale of the street and scarred the city. Following a pattern of degradation that can be seen in countless Chinese cities, the great boulevard had become an anonymous commercial avenue. The sense of one great sweep of promenade had also been lost since the route had become disjointed and fragmented into three sections—one part based around the railway station, and the other two lined with an array of commercial and government buildings.

In a bid to bring unity to the boulevard, and to celebrate the city's grandeur and heritage, a regeneration project was commissioned. With a limited budget, but grand vision, the work has been completed with a delicate touch that has made a huge impression. And while this vision and approach has been created in response to Taiyuan's particular needs, it is a type of solution that could be applied elsewhere.

The main components of the transformation are street sculpture and lighting. The sculpture is based on tall, square-section columns or totems, and shorter bollards constructed in iron with a decorative, geometric filigree pattern. The iron is coloured in a patina of rich reddish brown that is a characteristic colour of the region's vernacular architecture. The consistent use of colour has a profound effect on unifying the landscape and resonating with the area's past. For example, in and around Beijing the bluish grey colour in the built environment is particularly distinctive. The brown colour used in Yingze Boulevard's sculptural totems is the colour that was found in the historic architecture of this region.

By reintroducing the hue into the cityscape, an element of localism and history is reintroduced.

Along with materials and colours, the patterns have been chosen to reflect the city's heritage, both its ancient culture and more recent industrial precedents. Abstract patterns are based on local geometric forms used in traditional design, and subtly reintroduce heritage into the contemporary streetscape. When illuminated at night these columns and bollards have a further local resonance as the warm, glowing light resembles braziers of burning coals. In daylight they are a delight too, with their lacy construction casting beautiful and intricate shadows across the pavement.

The sculptures are installed at key points along the boulevard. The tall columns used in multiples to form a delicate screen between the heavy traffic and pedestrian walkways, and the shorter bollards deployed to separate pedestrians and cyclists. Apart from the impressive scale of the street, the main elements of cityscape are the mature trees which line the walkways at the side of the road. The new iron sculptures work in harmony with the organic outlines of the *Sophora japonica* trees. Existing mature trees were strategically kept as part of an overall tree plan that integrates them with new tree planting groupings.

Above
View from above

Clearly seen as Taiyuan's main artery, Yingze Boulevard, photographed from the air, is shown outlined in red.

Overleaf
The power of light

Past and future symbolised in iron and steel appear as the key materials in the re-energised streetscape. While the pedestrian walkway is given additional texture and colour in the red-brown coloured iron used for illuminated decorative screens and low-level bollards, new 17 metre tall light poles in stainless steel light the roadway.

Taking inspiration from historic patterns and materials used in the local region, the main components in the public space flanking the road are sculptural screens made from a sequence of tall, square-section columns or totems. The same pattern and material are used in the shorter bollards which, when illuminated at night, cast beautiful shadow patterns across the paving.

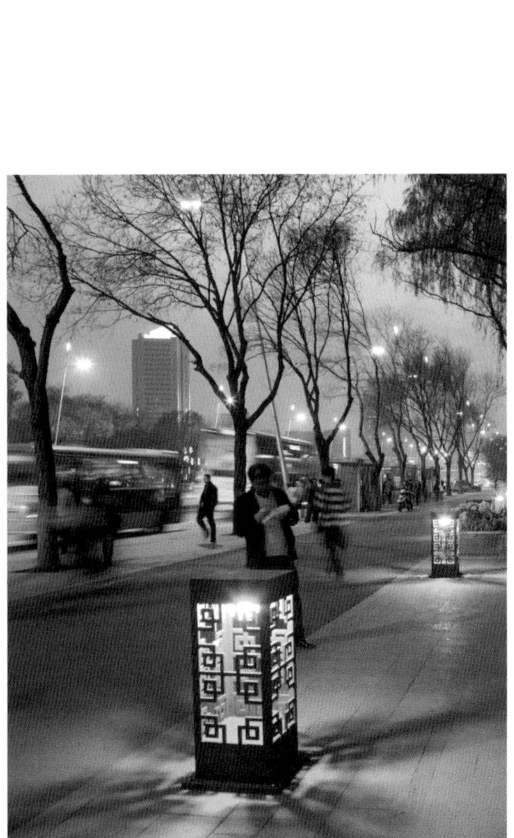

The second major new intervention is the installation of high-level street lighting. This has been achieved with 17 metre tall lamp posts, which are set at an angle inclined over the entire length of the road. Again these have a strong sculptural quality, but this time highly contemporary in style and resembling ethereal wands of light, they are constructed in stainless steel and painted white. These lights unify the length of the boulevard and celebrate its scale, providing a sense of spatial order to the whole road.

The lights also introduce some contemporary drama to contrast with the sculptural totems and playing with the interesting tensions between past and future, local versus cosmopolitan and intimate and grand scale.

These gentle new interventions into the Yingze streetscape took less than three months to install and the project was achieved for a modest budget. Soon after the completion of the boulevard signs of regeneration could be seen including more pedestrian activity along the length of this new civic promenade. Inspired by the success of this project, new work underway includes the design of a new city-centre park and further urban regeneration.

Richness of texture

In addition to the iron sculptures, tree planting has formed an important part of the transformation of the boulevard where new trees stand alongside the existing ones.

The existing trees (first row along the boulevard) are *Sophora japonica* (also known as the scholor tree or Japanese pagoda tree). The new second row of trees include *Fraxinus velutina* (velvet ash or Arizona ash), *Acer truncatum* (shantung maple) and *Salix babylonica* (weeping willow).

With their lovely organic outlines during the winter, these beautiful trees provide welcome shade in the summer. The trees offer a further layer of protection between the road and areas for pedestrians and cyclists.

7 The Future

“Too much of what has been built in the last century is more of a

cautionary tale than an inspiration.

The present generation will deliver a more balanced city, more rational in terms of its use of resources, and more humane than cities of the recent past. It will have to include some of the old, some of the new, some of the big, but also some of the small embroidered bits that make a place unique. There have to be transitions that make sense. Lewis Mumford defined a great city as the maximum number of choices crammed into the smallest possible space; such diversity is what we all want and where most of us hope to live. Overspecialised zoning will have to be dissolved in favour of mixed uses.

Adele Chatfield-Taylor
President of the American Academy in Rome

Rwanda's rising fortunes

Kigali Conceptual Masterplan, Rwanda

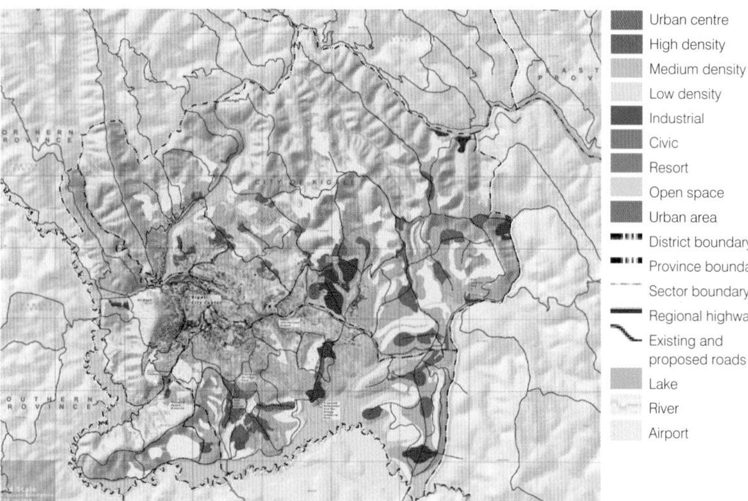

Planning a powerhouse

The Kigali masterplan was developed through public meetings, workshops and seminars, above left. Existing topography showing the undulating rural landscape, top, and the proposed land-use plan, left, which includes high and medium density centres of development in red and orange and industrial areas in purple. Using local materials and traditional skills to build new homes, above, the vision is for sustainable, holistic and locally-based solutions that could transfer to other developing cities.

With its vision of becoming an economic, ideas and skills powerhouse in central Africa, the governments of Rwanda and Kigali sought help in developing a long-range plan for future growth and development. With a projected population increase of more than one million people in the coming 25 years, it was clear that there was a need for unique and innovative urban planning strategies. Among the first steps was the creation of the Kigali Conceptual Masterplan which drew together the skills of a multidisciplinary team including planners, landscape architects, architects, economists, engineers, biologists, ecologists, sustainability experts and GIS specialists. As part of this work there was a series of public workshops, field surveys, information and technical seminars, and stakeholder meetings.

Land-based strategies derived from the natural terrain were developed to affordably promote development that would meet the current needs of a city in which 80 per cent of the population lives on less than $2 a day in areas that lack basic infrastructure and legal rights. Wholesale slum clearance was avoided in favour of increasing the capacity for modernisation, addressing environmental concerns including the need for clean water and developing a flexible strategic plan which will deliver future generations the ability to meet their own needs. The plan's guiding principles included education, training and development as a cornerstone for future growth; equitable solutions for housing, transportation and infrastructure; adoption of environmentally sustainable infrastructure solutions; and the attraction of foreign capital and private investment to underpin future economic, social and physical growth.

This project has been significant because it outlines a vision and an implementable framework centred on sustainable, holistic, and locally-based solutions that, while tailored for Kigali, could be transferred to other developing cities. These solutions directly address issues commonly felt in developing cities including rapid population growth, lack of key infrastructure and services, environmental degradation, lack of economic investment and high unemployment. The second phase of work focuses on capacity building.

Efforts are currently underway to train local planners through the development sub-area plans. With completion of sub-area planning, local staff will be sufficiently trained to carry on the development and implementation of the masterplan. In 2008, the American Planning Association awarded its most prestigious honour, called the Daniel Burnham Award, to EDAW AECOM (now Design + Planning at AECOM) for the Kigali Masterplan. The Daniel Burnham Award honours work which advances the science and art of planning.

Community building

Rawabi Masterplan, West Bank

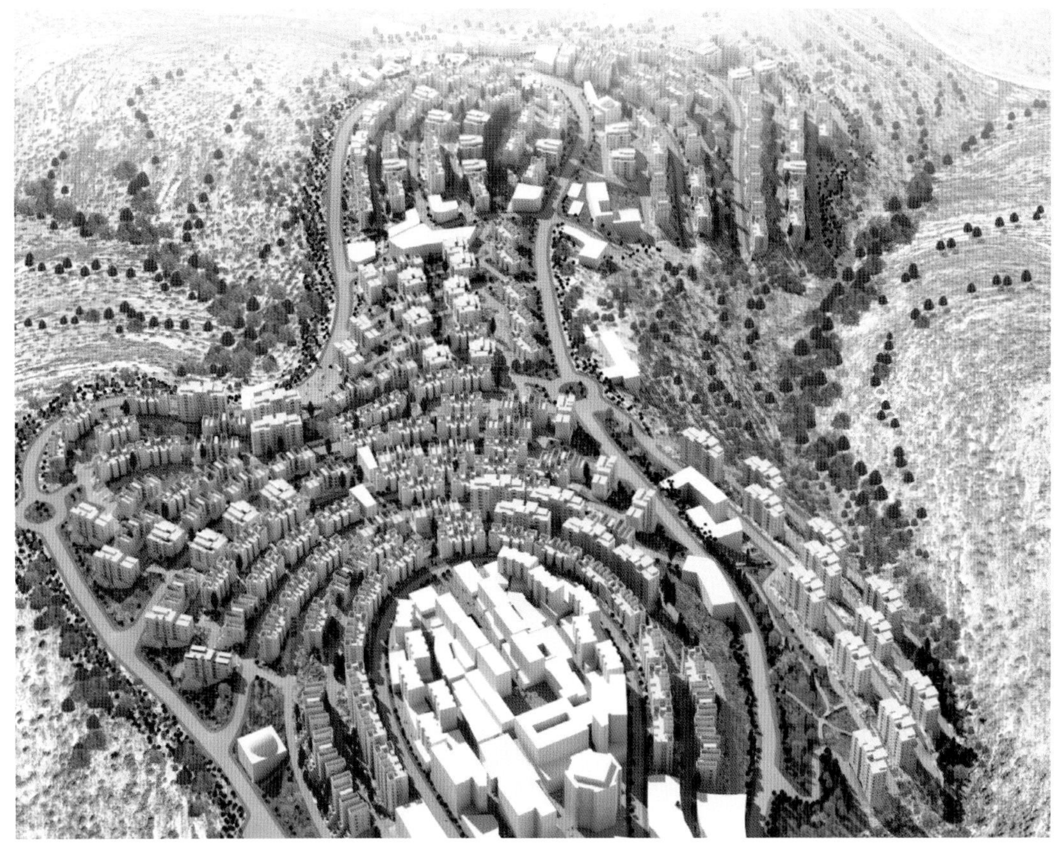

Quality of life

A model new town for Palestinians, Rawabi is planned to respond to the dramatic and distinctive hilly landscape with a central core of development on the highest knoll surrounded by homes arranged in terraces, above left. In Arabic, rawabi means hills. Incorporating homes for as many as 30,000 residents, the new town is designed to appeal to young families who will want to stay and make a life in this beautiful setting.

Rawabi will be the first planned new town for Palestinians in the West Bank and a model of sustainable development for other new towns in the region. Set in olive groves and occupying a spectacular hillside position north of Ramallah, the new town will provide homes for 20,000 people in a mix of apartments and houses. As well as contributing to the ambitious goals of community-building and development of the Palestinian economy, the new town will open up new opportunities for home ownership to young Palestinians. Rawabi integrates exemplary planning principles, sustainable environmental practices, appropriate architectural expressions, a creative public realm and delivery flexibility. The town has been designed around the creation of a number of neighbourhoods and provides access for all residents to a wide range of services and employment opportunities with kindergartens and schools, clinics, cultural centres, places of worship, leisure facilities and a network of parks, playgrounds and open spaces. The town centre provides a strong focus and identity for the town with shops and commercial premises grouped around a central square.

The development also incorporates the provision of necessary infrastructure including new roads, water and electricity supply and sewage treatment and special attention has been given to environmental issues, in particular the conservation of water and other resources and the integration of the development with the surrounding landscape and communities. Rawabi serves as a successful example of collaborative working between the international consultant team and local professionals which will have lasting value. The masterplan provides the framework for the phased development of the town by the private sector with support of the Palestinian authorities and international donor community.

Raising the standards of living and working

Vadarevu and Nizampatnam Ports and Industrial Corridor (VANPIC), Andhra Pradesh, India

Delivering an economic, social and environmental stimulus to what is largely an underdeveloped section of India's south-eastern coastal area, the focus of this project is the creation of a world-class hub driven by a port, airport and industrial corridor. At almost 11,500 hectares in size and set along an expansive 120 kilometre stretch of coast on the Bay of Bengal, this vast mixed-use agglomeration includes the development of one major port, which is envisaged to be the largest along the eastern coastline of the state of Andhra Pradesh. The project also includes a shipyard, a regional airport, an energy park, specialised industrial parks/special economic zones (SEZ), a multi-product economic zone, and resort development that would create direct employment for the population in two revenue districts. Unique to the site will be a mix of industry with tourism and leisure development as well as commercial space and social infrastructure that will set new standards in India for lifestyle communities amid a predominantly industrial land use. Called the Vadarevu and Nizampatnam Ports and Industrial Corridor, or VANPIC, this visionary project is intended to raise the standards of living of the local people, while also protecting and enhancing the beautiful coastal mangroves and reserve forests at the site. The project's end goals include an emphasis on providing training and employment to the local communities beyond traditional industries and towards more high-value industries.

Aspirational Andhra Pradesh

A sequence of mixed-use development including ports, an airport and tourism schemes will act as a catalyst for attracting investment to a long stretch of India's east coast. Currently, a relatively poor and underdeveloped area, left above and below, the new business activity will also stimulate improved training and education for local people.

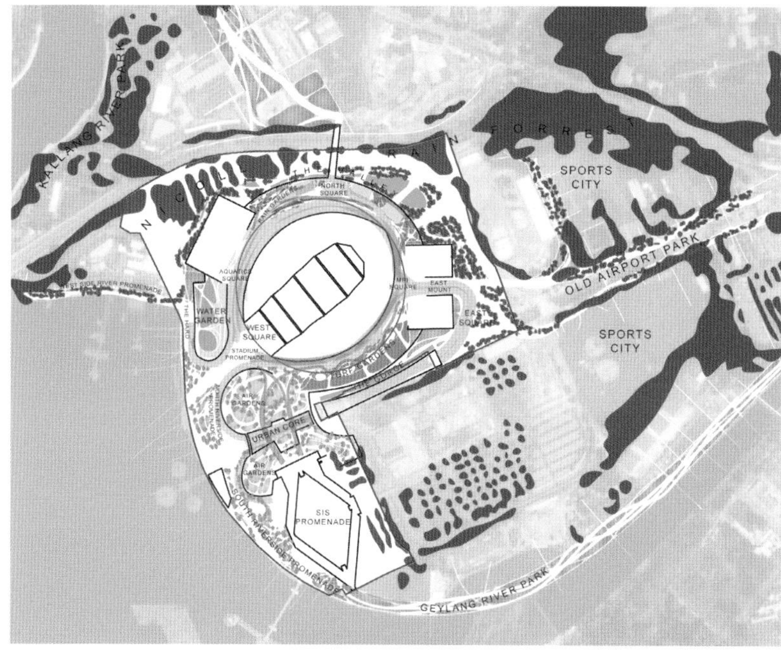

Health, wellbeing and a passion for sports form some of the ambitions for the Singapore Sports Hub on the waterfront of Kallang Basin in the city centre, masterplan and visualisations above.

The landscape design includes extensive planting, including thousands of trees, many grouped in small 'islands' ringed in the lucky colour red, left, and scattered throughout the circulation areas.

State of the art sports district

Singapore Sports Hub, Singapore

As part of Singapore's vision for 2020, population growth and improving quality of life have been identified as key factors in remaining competitive, attracting investment, strengthening the economy and enhancing its regional influence. As part of the plan to grow its population from four million people to six million, a sequence of major development projects is underway. Along with a new national library, university extension, and airport expansion, is the Singapore Sports Hub which is destined to be the region's premier land and sea sports complex. Occupying a prime waterside site of 34 hectares, north-east of the city centre on the Kallang Basin, this high-intensity scheme includes an Olympic-standard 55,000 seat national stadium with retractable roof, a 6,000-capacity indoor aquatic centre that meets world tournament standards, a 3,000-capacity multi-purpose arena, a water sports centre and a mix of commercial, leisure and retail space. In a parkland setting, close to Marina Bay, the complex not only looks inspiring and inviting and makes the most of the waterside views, it also has to work hard bringing life to the waterfront and completing the vision for pedestrian routes along the bay front. Sporting requirements include providing easy and accessible routes into and through the site for the large spectator crowds who will gather for major sports events, good connections with the rest of the city. Innovative stormwater management and sustainable water usage to handle heavy rainfall fulfil the national water agency's Active, Beautiful and Clean initiative. Once complete, the new sports hub will be home to all of Singapore's national sports associations and it will be the region's prime sports destination. Ambitions for the project are that it will encourage a new generation of elite athletes and become home to the first Asian professional football league along with new cricket and rugby tournaments. It will be the stage for the National Day parade and other civic gatherings, and along with fostering a new wave of professional athletes, sporting amenities will be available for the local community. The idea is to promote entertainment and healthy lifestyles, inviting people not just as spectators but also as participants in all sports from lawn bowls to cycling.

The economics of ecology

Fangchengang Mangrove Preservation Planning, GuangXi Province, China

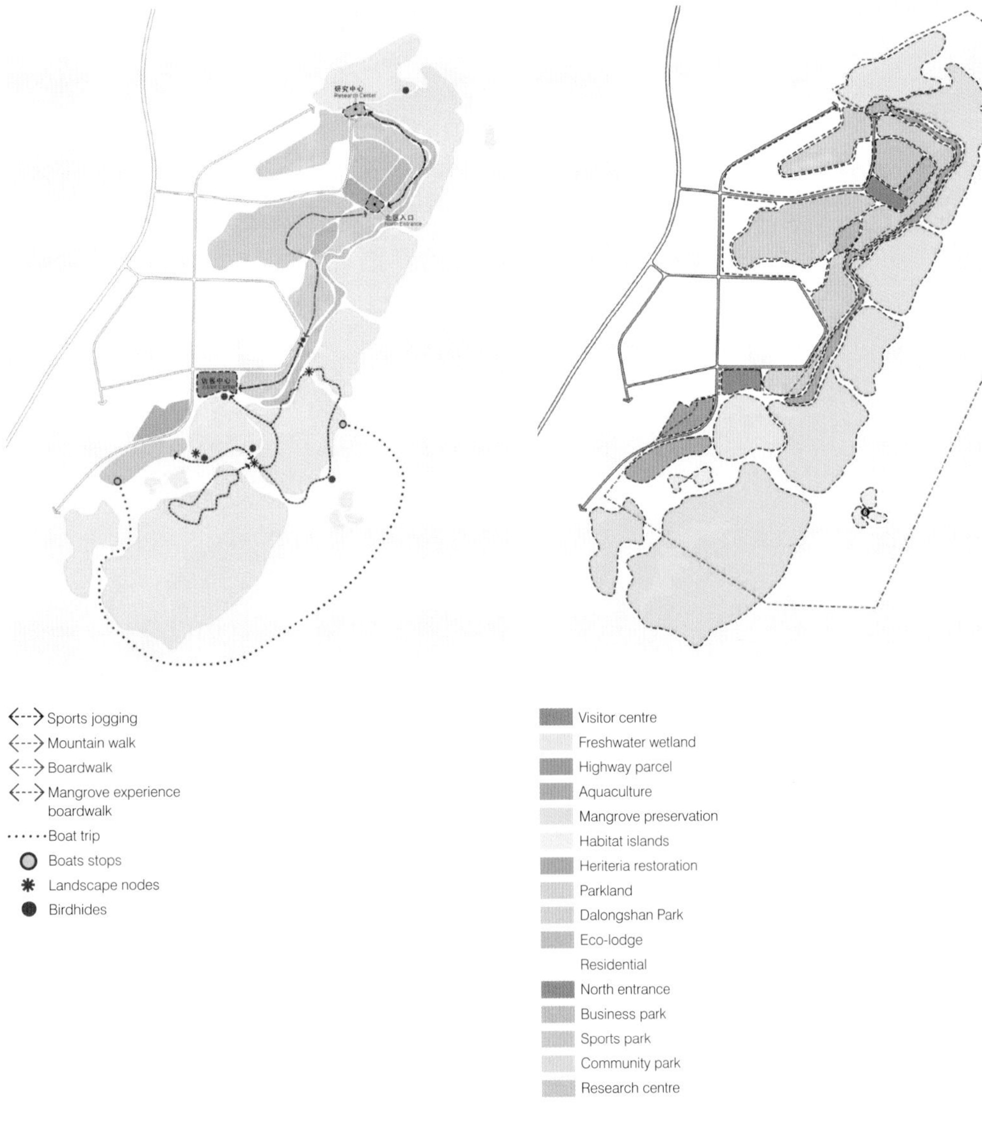

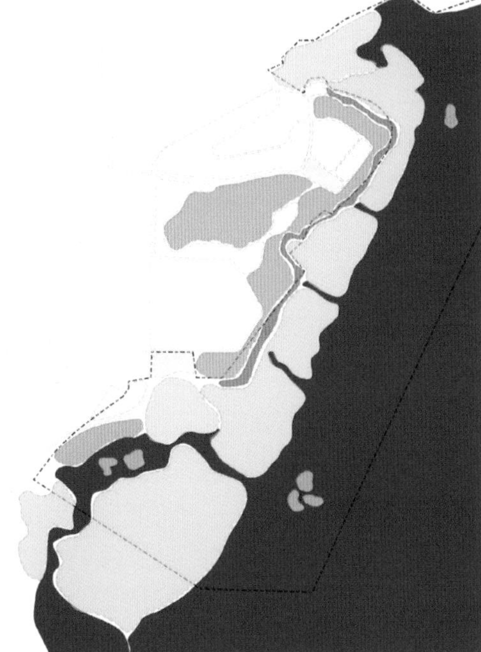

Protect and enhance

Once identified as a site for land reclamation and development, the mangrove forest, above right, is now recognised as a valuable natural asset. Plans, above, show future public uses of the area including jogging trails, waterside boardwalks, birdwatching facilities and boat trips, left. Land uses, centre, include a visitor centre, freshwater wetlands, mangrove preservation, eco lodges and a research centre. And, right, protected areas.

Having long been considered as a site for reclamation and industrialisation, a huge swathe of coastal mangrove forest close to the port city of Fangchenggang, has been established as an ecological park. In south China, close to the border with Vietnam, the area of more than 330 hectares is being transformed into an area for ecotourism, sustainable aquaculture, education and research together with the protection and enhancement of the mangrove. It is also an important route for migratory birds and has become a welcome green space for the city's population of 800,000 and growing. The concept masterplan covered various zoning and management issues for the site including habitat conservation and restoration; water-quality control and stormwater management; mitigation of environmental impacts during construction phase; environmental education and recreational facilities; sustainable management practices. The project is particularly unusual in China since the land is privately owned and has become the first such park in the country to be largely owned and managed by a private developer. The creation of the forest park was prompted by the city being included in the Beibu Gulf Economic Development Zone and its attendant rapid industrialisation including the construction of a steel plant and nuclear power station. It became clear that urban growth was likely to have included the forest. To consider the options of development or preservation, financial analysis and assessment was undertaken and different development scenarios were tested to demonstrate that saving the forest was economically viable. Funding to plan the park was secured from the United Nations Development Programme's Global Environment Facility to create a demonstration site. The programme includes funds for the protection of precious sites including coral reef, seagrass, mangrove and wetland in South-east Asia.

Back to the future

Dragon Lake Bridge Park, Bengbu, China

The city of Bengbu, north-west of Shanghai, has had a long and close relationship with water. The metropolis grew up around activities including freshwater pearl fishing and the name translates into English as clam wharf. However, in recent decades, Bengbu had lost its connection with the waterside because industrial development has hampered access and water pollution made the place uninviting. To improve water quality and local ecology along with encouraging economic growth and accommodating urban expansion, an area of the city's fringe close to Dragon Lake has been identified as a place for new communities and recreational open space. Among the initial phases of development is the creation of the city's first lakefront park. The 25 hectare scheme along one kilometre of shore, called Dragon Lake Bridge Park, is conceived to create a link between the past and the future, and between the city and its waterfront. Its design takes its inspiration from the landscape, local materials and plants and reinterprets them. Among the highlights are the terraces of walkways which work with the existing topography, the Bamboo Garden which takes inspiration from local bamboo forests but is created as a beautiful grove, and the beautiful serpentine boardwalks which meander out across the water and give views back towards the land. Crucial to the success of the new park and future development has been improving the lake's water quality and local ecology. This has been achieved by designing the parklands to include wetlands that reduce and filter stormwater runoff into the lake, incorporating local plant species which thrive with minimal need for irrigation, and creating healthy habitats for fish, birds and insects. It is intended that the park will act as a catalyst for increased tourism, heightened public awareness of the environment, new investment and future development. The park's success has been demonstrated by its popularity with local people and work is underway on other sections of lakeside open space.

Reconnecting with the landscape

Designed to provide a beautiful public space and stimulate economic growth, the park forms the cornerstone of urban regeneration. Contrasting aspects of the park's design range from the intimate Bamboo Garden, top, to the extensive and extremely popular boardwalk bridges which stretch out over the water.

On your bike

CycleCity, Sydney, Australia

Improving health, reducing pollution, saving money, cutting congestion and mitigating climate change, CycleCity offers a new way of thinking about urban transport priorities. Using Sydney, Australia, as a case study, the work explores the feasibility of encouraging more people to cycle to and from the city centre. The study's objective is to initiate and promote a paradigm shift in urban modal transport based on sustainability and health; its method is to design and propose a radical infrastructural intervention which recognises the full potential of the bicycle as a critically important form of urban transportation, and its outcome is to prove and promote the positive possibilities cycling can offer health, the environment and economy. Key to the work was establishing a No Excuses Zone for Sydney. Based on a series of test rides, a zone around the city's Central Business District (CBD) was mapped to measure the distance a healthy person can cycle within half an hour. The map is surprisingly far reaching and provocatively suggests if a person lives within this zone and works in the CBD, they should cycle to work at least a few days a week. The area within the zone contains a population in excess of 750,000 people who currently make almost 50,000 car trips every weekday. In a bid to create improved conditions for cyclists, suggestions for the future include cycle freeways on main routes. These would be a series of radial, fully separated cycle freeways that are safe, fast, efficient, direct and well lit, with potentially a proportion under cover. Designed for cyclists and pedestrians, they would connect Sydney's middle to inner suburbs with the CBD—to get people from home to work and back. Following this pilot study, many other cities have been mapped, with No Excuse Zones established for their urban centres.

Rethinking urban transport priorities

Through rigorous research, the project presents the bicycle as a critically important form of urban transportation in the face of major world issues, including health problems, global warming and peak oil. Our AECOM partner, Maunsell, assisted us in applying our findings into a concise economic argument to justify a radical rethinking of urban transport priorities.

Objective
To initiate and promote a paradigm shift in urban modal transport based on sustainability and health.

Method
To design and propose a radical infrastructural intervention, which recognises the full potential of the bicycle.

Outcome
To prove and provoke, using Sydney as a case study, the positive possibilities cycling can offer health, the environment and economy.

Key drivers for this initiative

Traffic Congestion
It is anticipated that congestion on the roads will cost Australia $30 billion per annum by 2025.

Peak Oil
The "peaking and subsequent decline of world oil production is well documented and widely accepted as fact".

Climate Change
The average car produces 4.36 tonnes of greenhouse gases per year.

Health
Physical inactivity costs Australian tax payers $15 billion a year. Physical inactivity is the second most significant cause of ill health in Australia.

Pollution
Each year, air pollution from cars causes between 900 and 2,000 early deaths and between 900 and 4,500 cases of bronchitis, cardiovascular and respiratory disease, costing between $1.5 and $3.8 billion.

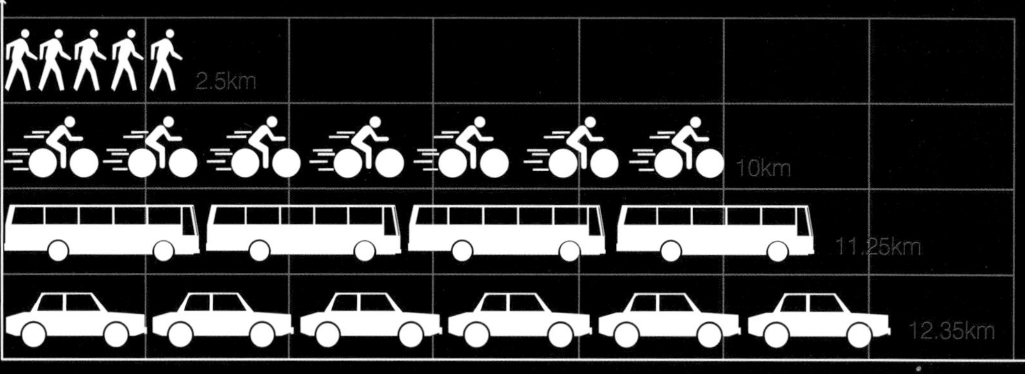

Average kilometres travelled over 30 minutes into Sydney CBD

CycleCity will deliver a

$ 538
Million cost reduction

Summary of Economic Assessment

vehicle operating costs	$69 million
decongestion benefits	$75 million
externality improvements	$26 million
health benefits from cycling	$368 million
total value of benefits	**$538 million**

No excuses

Using Sydney as a case study, the aerial photograph, top right, defines the No Excuses Zone. Orange lines depict potential cycle routes linking the city centre and residential places for widening existing off-road paths in pink and clip-on bridges in turquoise. Field opportunities, opposite right, show major trip generators marked with a

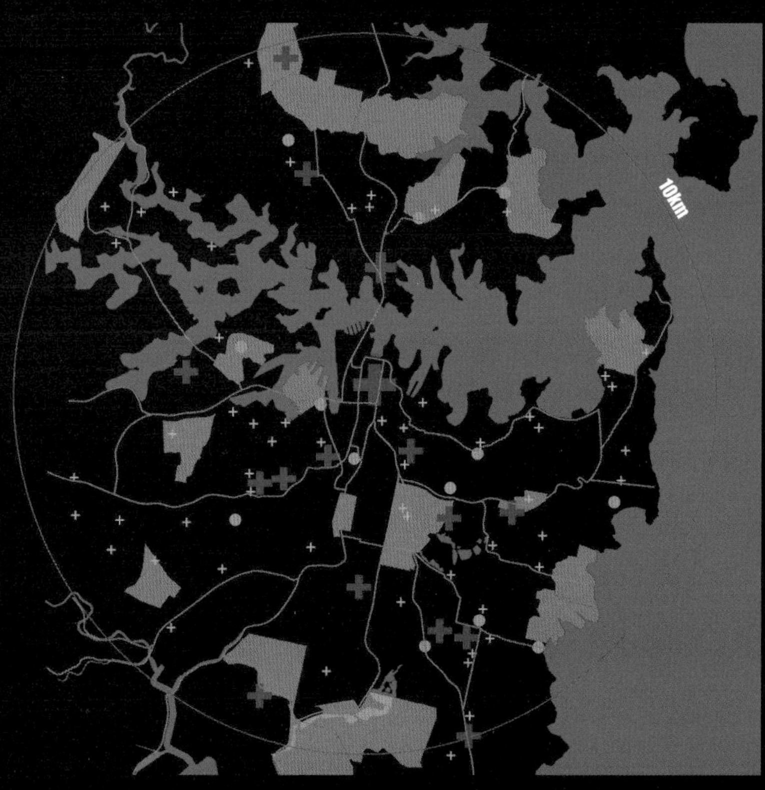

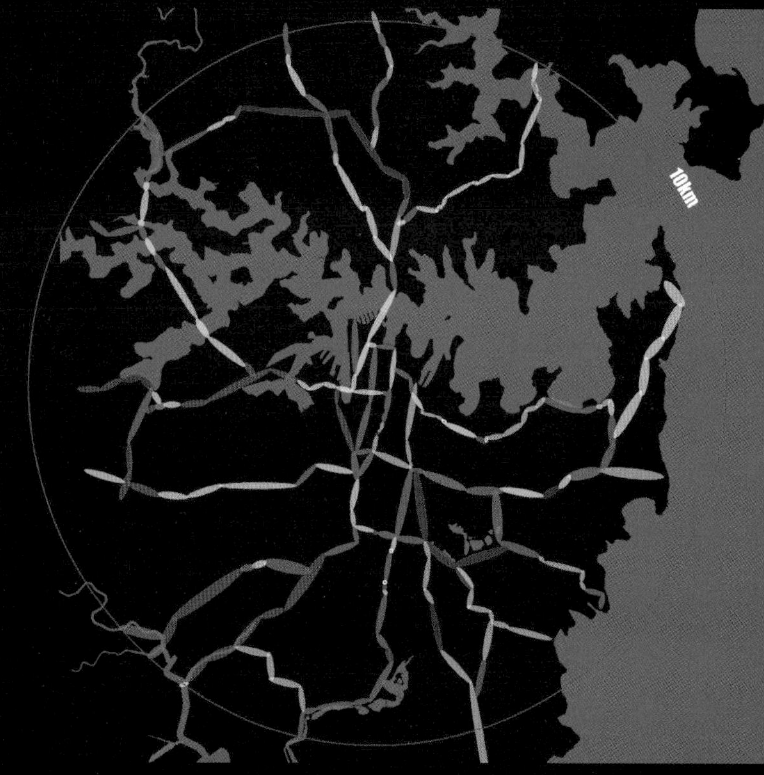

Field opportunities

- major trip generators
- origin zone of +400 car trips
- community centre
- school

Field typologies

- parkland edge
- wide easement
- disused infrastructure
- bridge clip-on
- land encroachment
- road lane seizure
-  widen existing off road path
- proposed urban development
- problematic insertion line

Carbon-neutral in Seattle

Policy Analysis for Energy Efficient Buildings, Seattle, USA

As part of Seattle's continuing work to reduce carbon emissions in its built environment, the city has committed to meet the Architecture 2030 Challenge of all new development to be carbon neutral by 2030. To help meet this ambitious goal, policy analysis was needed to determine the way ahead. The research began with eight policy proposals which were assessed and analysed in the context of factors including the projected growth in emissions from the building sector, and anticipated employment and population growth. Using real estate development projections, and energy model outputs from Design + Planning's proprietary land-planning tool Sustainable Systems Integrated Model (SSIM)™, the performance of each of the eight policies was modelled and quantified. This highlighted benefits—energy savings and/or monetary benefit to the developer, and costs—to city and developer. Using these metrics and qualitative assessments of feasibility relating to Seattle, each policy was rated under the following parameters: cost effectiveness, energy-efficiency potential, economic impact, cost of policy implementation, and administrative feasibility. To help the comparative analysis, these findings were compiled in case study reports, policy scorecards, summary presentations, and visual tools/graphics.

The analysis is being used by the city to determine which new building policies to adopt to meet its greenhouse gas reduction goals.

Transforming Highway 101 to Park 101

Park 101, Los Angeles, USA

Park 101 is an initiative to make Los Angeles a more livable place. The idea is to cap almost one kilometre of the eight-lane Highway 101 running through the heart of the city and turn the area into a vast new public park. The vision was created at an intensive two-week workshop of students taking part in EDAW AECOM's 2008 Intern Programme. The proposal reconnects the city's historic core, north of the freeway, with the civic, cultural, and financial cores of modern LA to the south. The scheme also incorporates underground parking to encourage people out of their cars and into the park and streets above. Benefitting most from Park 101 will be the densely urbanised and park-poor communities of the inner city. Along with new green space they would experience improved connections between neighbourhoods, upgraded public transportation and the potential to reduce the noise and pollution of traffic. Under consideration by the Planning Department of the City of Los Angeles and California Department of Transportation for implementation, the project provides a unique opportunity in the resurrection of downtown LA.

Meeting the 2030 Challenge:
Implementation of green priority and energy code update

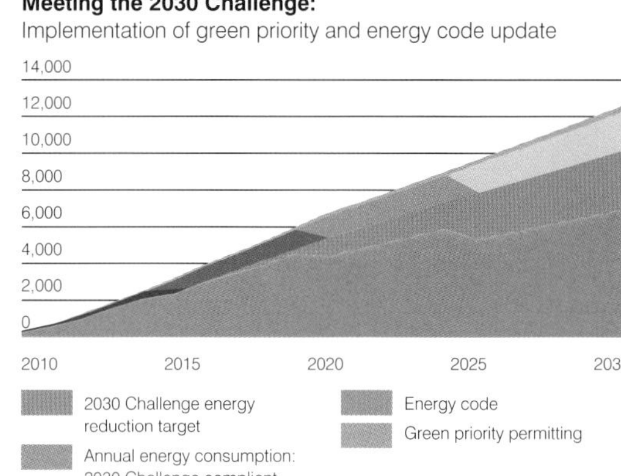

Carbon neutral by 2030

The city of Seattle, left, has an ambitious sustainability agenda and its Architecture Challenge 2030 places particular emphasis on carbon-neutral development. The graph, above, shows how it is possible to meet the challenge through energy codes and priority permitting.

Intern programme

Produced during the 2008 EDAW AECOM intern programme, the transformation of highway to park produced some powerful imagery. To reduce the dominance of cars and other road traffic in the heart of downtown Los Angeles, the concept was to cover over Highway 101, shown above, with a park, opposite bottom left and right. Opposite left, students taking part.

Form follows fusion

Gateway Parcel Design, Tuolumne River Regional Park, California, USA

Finding the balance between the apparently conflicting needs of humans and nature, plans for an area of riverside parkland in central Modesto, California, combined the expertise of designers and scientists. Working as an integrated team including biologists, hydrologists, engineers and architects, the goal was to create high quality and accessible public recreational space alongside areas with restored and protected habitat. Formerly a walnut orchard, the 35 hectare piece of land called the Gateway Parcel, was acquired to form a central part of the linear Tuolumne River Regional Park. Work on the Gateway design was focused on taking inspiration from the river, improving quality of life and acting as a catalyst for regeneration of adjacent commercial and industrial areas by providing an amenity that encourages new river-oriented development. Among the most innovative aspects of developing the design was the process which created a dynamic fusion of the expertise of designers and scientists. A fusion vocabulary was created which demonstrated that the design and restoration were not opposing forces, but rather gradations of intensity along a spectrum. For example, the concept of 'visibility' could be expressed as a gradient from more visible to less visible. When applied to planting this translates as low vegetation in areas where views can be enjoyed and dense vegetation in areas to provide wildlife protection. In a similar way, issues of accessibility were handled with great subtlety by making fewer and narrower pathways through environmentally sensitive areas closer to the river, while more and broader pathways served areas closer to the city where members of the public are more welcome. Plans for the park also include an amphitheatre for 3,000 people, a seasonal farmers' market, picnic sites, children's play areas, fishing piers, river outlooks, connections to the Tuolumne River regional trail system, an educational interpretive area and stormwater treatment swales.

Planting plan

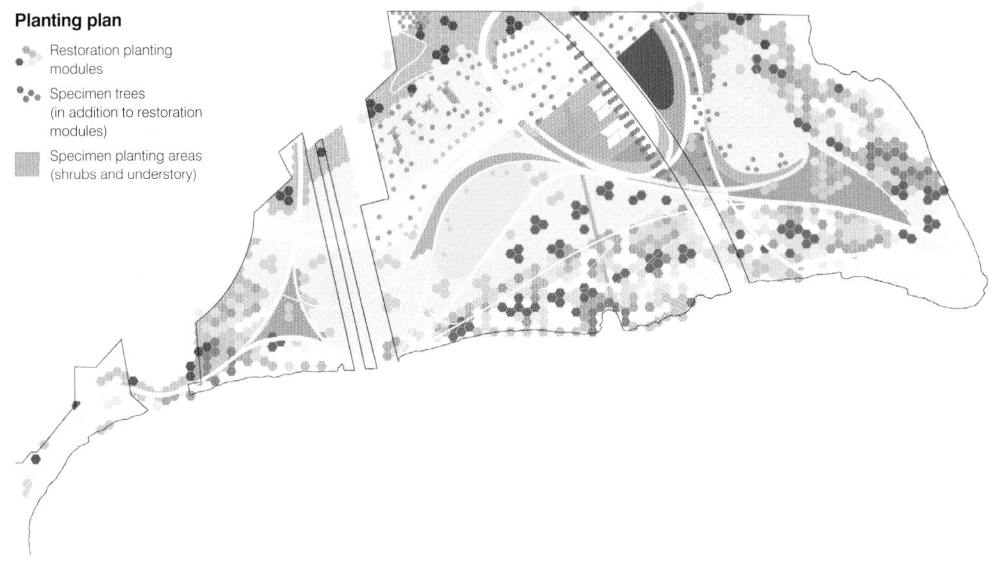

Grading plan

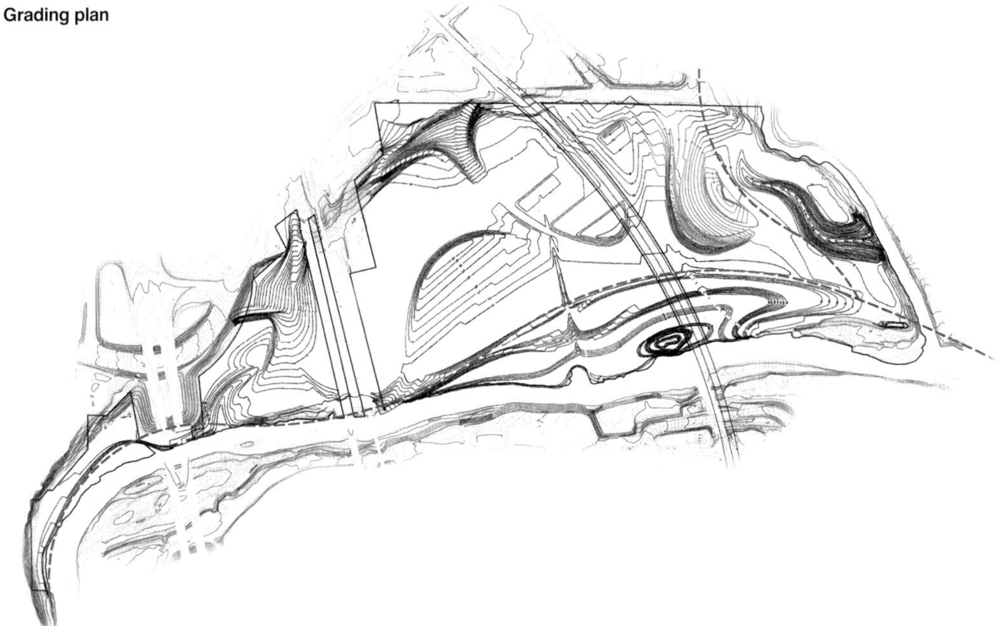

Circulation diagram

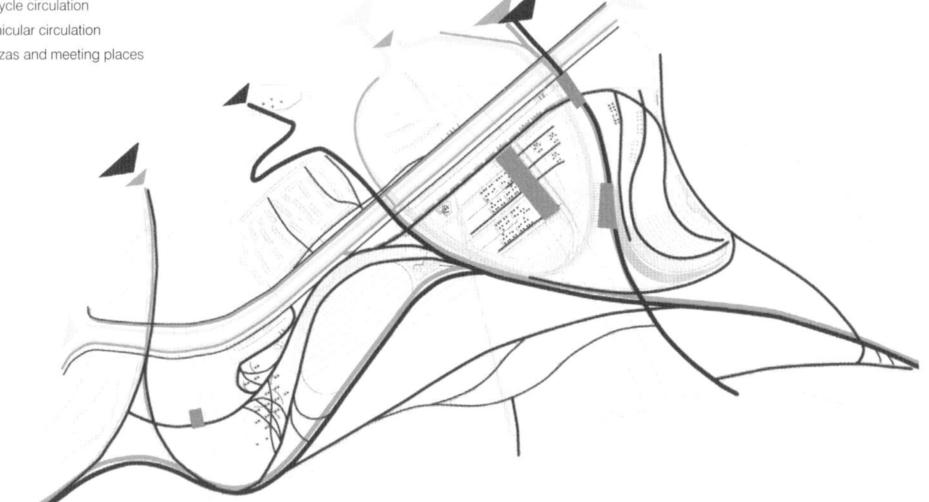

Protect and enjoy

Formerly a walnut orchard, the Gateway Parcel, has been identified as the location for a new public park that would also provide a catalyst for wider regeneration in the city of Modesto, California. Scientists and designers worked together to create a plan for the sloping riverside site that would balance the needs of people and nature.

The planting plan, grading plan, and circulation routes combine to accommodate the two seemingly incompatible goals by creating subtle transitions from intensely human occupied areas to wildlife-dominant zones. For example, planting is devised to maintain open vistas and views to the river in some places, while also providing areas of dense vegetation for wildlife protection.

The grading plan responds to the flowing landform, and circulation routes are devised to provide maximum public access in the least environmentally sensitive areas, guiding visitors away from the more sensitive areas.

Visualisations, opposite far left, show the upper terraces by the highway bridge in winter and in use as a farmers' market. Other images show the flowing circulation routes through the restored landscape.

Transforming the heart of Mexico City

Mexico City Sustainable Urban Regeneration, Mexico

Taking inspiration from the Plan Verde ambitions of Mexico City's mayor to create the world's Greenest Big City, one of the most innovative regeneration visions includes sinking a major road and creating a 1.5 kilometre long linear park over the top. Right at the heart of the city, the new green space would act as a catalyst for wider improvements in a truly self-sustaining urban regeneration scheme where more than a billion dollars of mixed-use real estate value could be created that subsequently generates the funding for three upgraded multi-modal transit stations, 23 hectares of new public domain and cultural facilities, plus 7,000 jobs. Proposed by a private development group, the concept plan is focused on one of the city's grand boulevards called the Avenida Chapultepec. Once the spine of the city's Aztecan aqueduct, the thoroughfare with up to eight lanes of traffic runs through several of the city's most important and affluent districts, but traffic and pollution have blighted the adjacent areas. New green space would be particularly welcome in the capital which has seen rapid recent population growth and urban sprawl. Greater Mexico City has a population of more than 22 million people, making it the largest metropolitan area in the Western hemisphere and the second most populated city in the world. In 2005, it ranked eighth in terms of GDP (PPP) among global urban agglomerations.

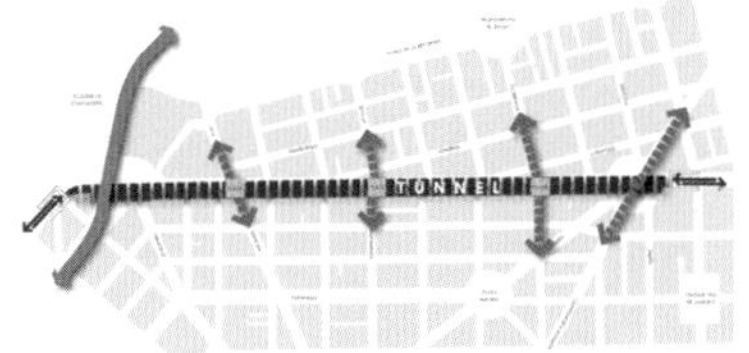

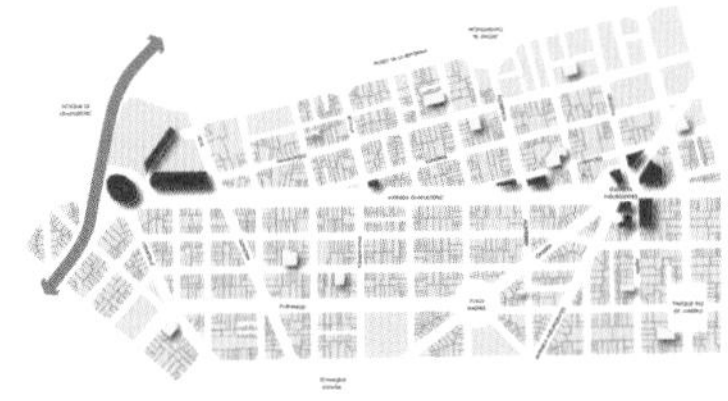

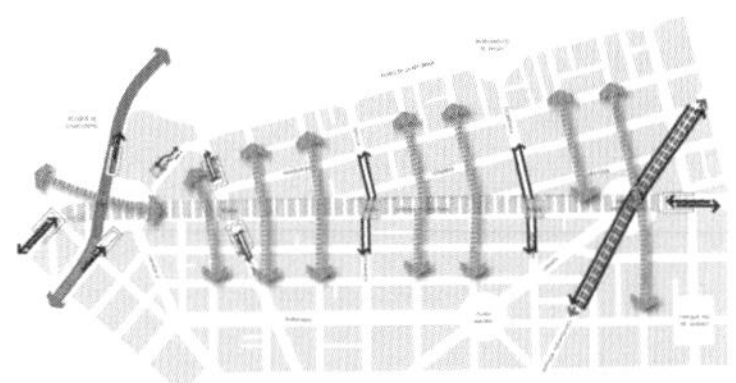

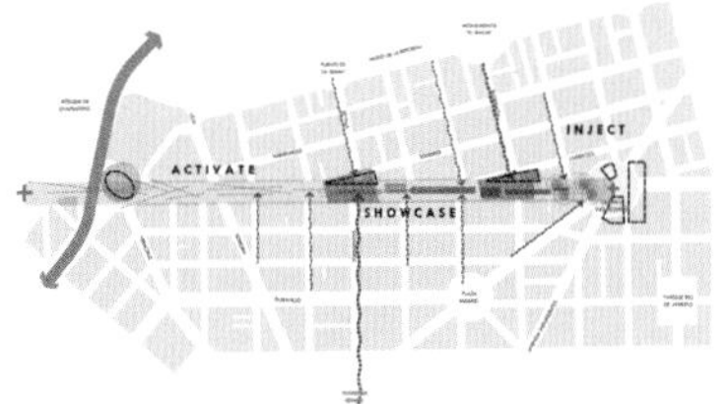

To the heart

A visualisation of the transformed Avenida Chapultepec, top left and bottom right, and as it is today, top right. Bottom left, from top, plans showing main circulation routes with new plazas at intersections, hot spots of development, ripple circulation and the introduction of water features.

The shape of things to come

Atlanta City of the Future 2108, Atlanta, USA

A model future

The vision of the future showing Atlanta as a city in the forest, top. The sustainable urbanism idea proposes the restoration of the city's hydrological systems, the return of above-ground streams and enhanced natural habitat, particularly on the city edges, bottom, which will be served by new transit systems.

When the US TV station The History Channel staged a City of the Future competition to visualise the Atlanta of 2108, the winning EDAW AECOM team opted for a design vision rooted in current issues. Looking at Atlanta's history and its modern needs, the team identified a central issue that would dominate Atlanta's future and the future of cities all over the world: water.

The competition provided seven days for teams to visualise their hundred-year plan, three hours to construct models, and 15 minutes to present the whole concept to judges. The proposed solution was the restoration of the city's natural hydrological systems. It was time to bring stormwater back to the surface, restore the natural creeks and wetlands, and allow nature to do its work. Collected and naturally processed in wetlands and streams, stormwater runoff would reduce the burden on drains and could instead be harvested for the city's water supply. With the lower ground returned to nature, development would concentrate densely along transit routes that followed the ridges. On the slopes, city and nature would intermingle. This combination of urban density with natural habitat would offer residents the best of both worlds and provide a unique and iconic pattern for the city. Sometimes known as the "city of trees", Atlanta in 2108 would become the "city in the forest", a model for ecological restoration and sustainable urbanism at the regional, national, and global levels.

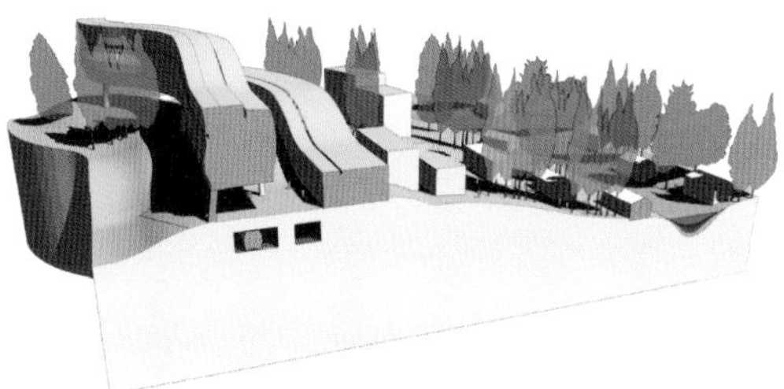

Plant a tree in NYC

PlaNYC Reforestation Initiative, New York, USA

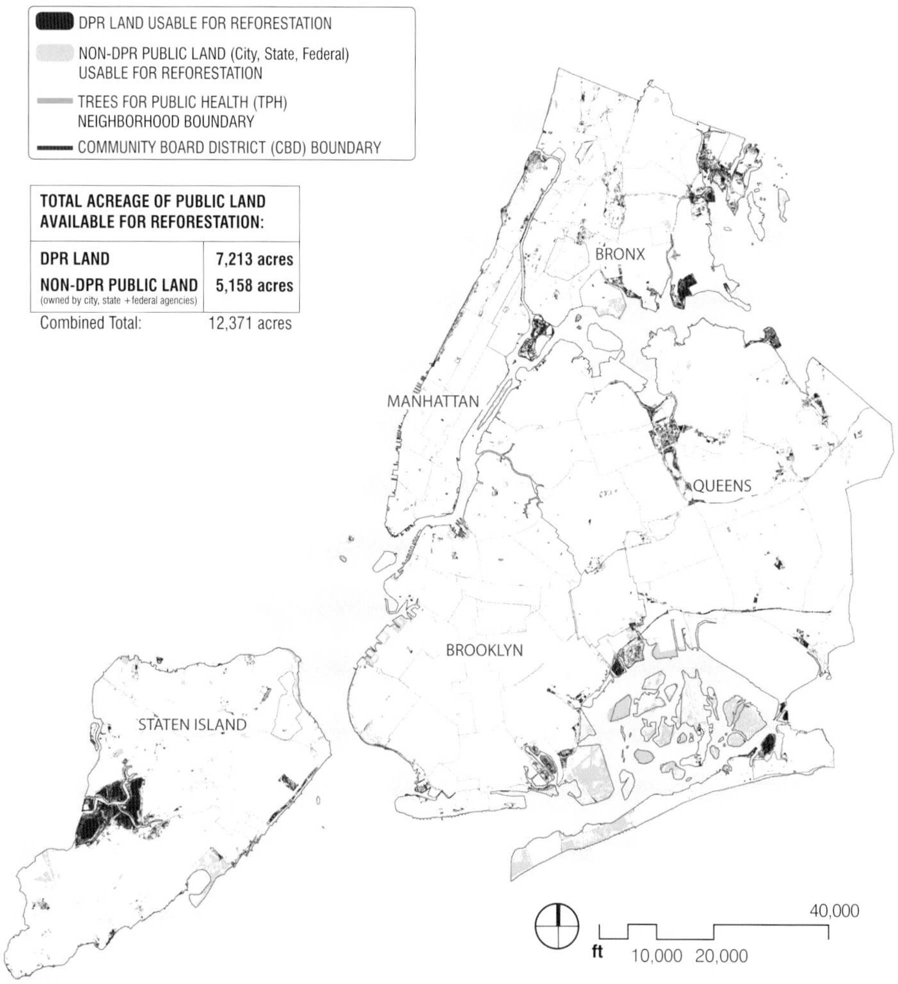

DPR LAND USABLE FOR REFORESTATION
NON-DPR PUBLIC LAND (City, State, Federal) USABLE FOR REFORESTATION
TREES FOR PUBLIC HEALTH (TPH) NEIGHBORHOOD BOUNDARY
COMMUNITY BOARD DISTRICT (CBD) BOUNDARY

TOTAL ACREAGE OF PUBLIC LAND AVAILABLE FOR REFORESTATION:	
DPR LAND	7,213 acres
NON-DPR PUBLIC LAND (owned by city, state + federal agencies)	5,158 acres
Combined Total:	12,371 acres

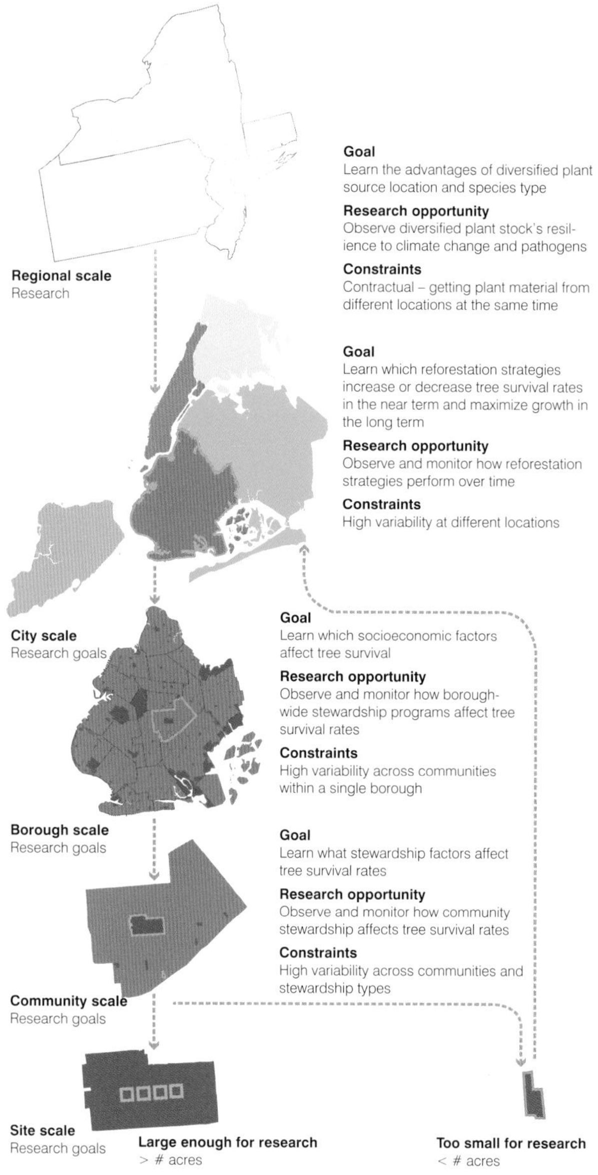

BRONX
MANHATTAN
QUEENS
BROOKLYN
STATEN ISLAND

ft 10,000 20,000 40,000

Regional scale
Research

Goal
Learn the advantages of diversified plant source location and species type
Research opportunity
Observe diversified plant stock's resilience to climate change and pathogens
Constraints
Contractual – getting plant material from different locations at the same time

City scale
Research goals

Goal
Learn which reforestation strategies increase or decrease tree survival rates in the near term and maximize growth in the long term
Research opportunity
Observe and monitor how reforestation strategies perform over time
Constraints
High variability at different locations

Borough scale
Research goals

Goal
Learn which socioeconomic factors affect tree survival
Research opportunity
Observe and monitor how borough-wide stewardship programs affect tree survival rates
Constraints
High variability across communities within a single borough

Community scale
Research goals

Goal
Learn what stewardship factors affect tree survival rates
Research opportunity
Observe and monitor how community stewardship affects tree survival rates
Constraints
High variability across communities and stewardship types

Site scale
Research goals

Large enough for research
> # acres

Too small for research
< # acres

On Earth Day 2007, New York's Mayor Bloomberg released PlaNYC 2030, a holistic set of 127 initiatives that address six key areas of sustainability for the city: land, air, water, energy, transportation and climate change. One of these initiatives, the PlaNYC Reforestation Initiative, has the long-term aim of foresting more than 800 hectares of public land across the five boroughs by 2017. This initiative is one of the three components of the MillionTrees NYC project which aims to increase New York City's canopy coverage from 24 per cent to 30 per cent by planting trees on streets, on privately owned land, and on public land. Through close collaboration with the client, the New York City Parks Department's Natural Resources Group, EDAW's role in the reforestation project has been pivotal. The production on this project has been remarkable both for its breadth and its depth. The first step was the production of GIS maps, site rankings, and databases to serve the client in locating and selecting appropriate sites for meeting the 800 hectare mandate. Next, a team was sent out to collect key data about all considered sites to provide a preliminary assessment of ground conditions, focusing on existing soil and existing invasive plants. This data was mapped in GIS and meticulously catalogued in a database. In conjunction with site selection and assessment, three diverse pilot sites were selected for fast-track implementation- the Hutchinson River Parkway, Kissena Corridor Park, and Willow Lake in Flushing. These sites broke ground in spring 2009. The final deliverable is a book with the working title of New York City Forest Restoration Guidelines. The book will be a comprehensive how-to manual, addressing a broad range of topics from urban forest typologies, and invasive plant control techniques, to the nuances of designing parks as forest. The book will serve practitioners and policymakers as the project evolves over the coming decade.

Greening the city

Bringing nature into the city, the PlaNYC reforestation initiative is to encourage tree planting throughout the New York area, top. Work has been completed to assess ground conditions, identify suitable sites and publish a comprehensive guide on implementing the planting.

Education and ecology drive economic development

Laguna Carén Masterplan, Santiago, Chile

With increasing urbanisation in South America, more than 40 cities have populations in excess of one million people. As part of this phenomenon, Chile's capital Santiago is experiencing rapid growth and to accommodate the expanding population an area west of the city has been identified as a new urbanisation zone. One of Santiago's largest municipalities, Pudahuel, was traditionally the city's agricultural and ecological reserve, defined by several major river courses, as well as a significant industrial zone anchored by the new international airport. Today, much of its remaining open space, the Valle lo Aguirre, will become home to 250,000 people within the coming decade. At the heart of this valley, a major area of land granted to the University of Chile is to become a recreational, educational, and technological hub. Learning from other cities where education and ecological assets have combined to inspire successful development, the masterplan is for a city in a park—a university campus and town centre set within a regional ecological reserve. The river and mountain ecologies of the site become the setting and defining characteristics of the new community. New public transportation and infrastructure investment ensures good connections with surrounding neighbourhoods, and, most importantly, provide a link to the airport and the urban centre. Pockets of vibrant urban density and water conservation strategies minimise the ecological impacts of development while enhancing the global competitiveness of Santiago with a better educated population. Pioneering the idea of student dorms in Chile, Laguna Carén will become home to 20,000 students and up to 25,000 new residents and it will be the focus of the next generation of economic investment creating valuable high-tech and green-collar jobs.

City in a park

To accommodate Santiago's rapid population growth, provide new educational opportunities and preserve and enhance the environment, plans have evolved for an urban extension that will become a residential, recreational, educational and technological hub. Set in the outstanding Valle lo Aguirre, above, the development, see masterplan right, is conceived as a city within a park.

From monumentality to sustainability

Brasilia II Sustainable Masterplan and Economic Analysis

More than half a century after Brazil's futuristic capital, Brasilia, was created by urban designer Lucio Costa and architect Oscar Niemeyer, proposals are in progress to create a satellite town called Brasilia II. Work has so far included a masterplan for the 2000 hectare site close to the capital. This inspiring plan preserves more than half the site as public open space and has entailed sustainable benchmarking for water, energy, green building, transportation and socio-cultural resources. A financial and economic analysis led to the final development strategy and phasing plans for more than 30,000 homes, a university and mixed-use development for a well-served community connected to the capital city by public and private transit routes.

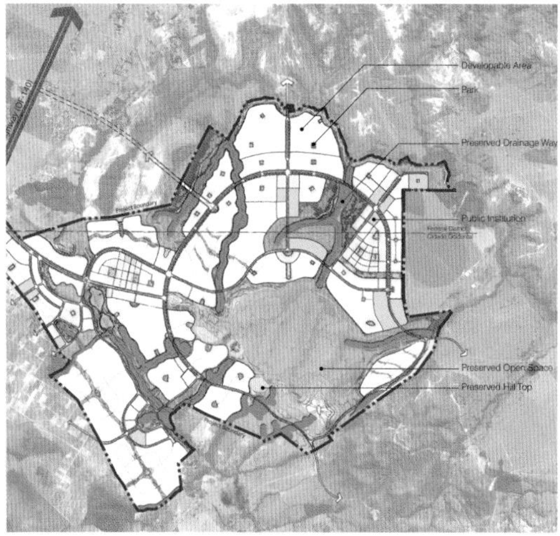

Green heart

Reflecting today's desire for a high quality of life achieved through full environmental, social and economic sustainability, the masterplan for Brasilia II is designed with generous public space and is also well served with community amenities including a public transport system.

Statistical summary

Total site	1996.5 Hectare 4931.3 Acre
Preserved drainage way	196.8 Hectare
Preserved hill top	15.0 Hectare
Preserved open space (20% of the site)	360 Hectare (required) 360 Hectare (provided)
Public area (40% of the site)	576 Hectare (required) 648 Hectare (provided)
Developable area	776 Hectare

* Public area includes public streets, district parks, regional community parks, lake parks, neighborhood parks, greenbelt, residual landscape within communities, retention facilities and public institution areas.

Measuring sustainability

Sustainable Systems Integrated Model

Drawing together the expertise of planners and environmental experts, the Sustainable Systems Integrated Model (SSIM)™ provides a holistic approach to measuring environmental, social and economic sustainability. Designed around the themes of energy, water, transportation, green building, ecology, carbon footprints and sociocultural factors, the land-planning tool measures the costs and benefits of different planning strategies. For example, in evaluating a number of alternative masterplans for new development, the SSIM makes it possible to measure components such as projected water consumption, energy use and greenhouse gas emissions and then identify the most sustainable plan option. The tool can also be used to achieve higher performance infrastructure and building systems and calculate their different costs and benefits. The overall result is a blueprint for new development ranging from the plan of streets and open spaces, along with the type and extent of public transport through the entire spectrum to the most detailed considerations of which light bulbs to use in streetlights and the performance of plumbing fixtures. For each component of a masterplan, the SSIM provides a rational basis for deciding how masterplan forms, primary infrastructure systems, building designs and ecological footprint should be configured to optimise sustainability within given cost and budget frameworks.

36%
Carbon footprint improvement including mobile emission

40%
Potable water reduction

134M
Gallons of gas conserved

8,401
Acres rescued from deforestation

50%
VMT reduction

4.1%
Direct building cost increase

4.6%
Direct building cost increase

Benchmark projects

This masterplanning project for the Tanggu District New Town in Tianjin, China, left, used the SSIM land-planning tool to assess different options on route to creating a benchmark eco city. Total project calculations were provided for energy and water consumption, vehicle kilometres travelled and total greenhouse gas emissions generated. The results showed that up to 50 per cent energy and water savings were possible depending on the acceptable cost impact. Graphs show, left, some sample SSIM results, and below, possible carbon reduction per $1000 invested.

Carbon Dioxide Equivalent (MMTCO2Eq)
10.0
8.0
6.0
4.0
2.0
0.0
0.7 Commercial Building Energy
1.2 Residential Building Energy
3.0 Industrial Building Energy
3.1 Retail Building Energy
5.9 Public Realm Energy
6.8 Employee-Housin Linkages

Carbon reduction per $1,000 invested
* Investment includes capital and annual costs over a 23 year period

Joined-up planning

South East Wales Networked Environment Region, Wales, UK

On the edge of the hilly Brecon Beacons National Park, the farmlands of Monmouthshire and the Vale of Glamorgan, former coalfields, the major coastal cities of Cardiff and Newport with the nearby wetlands of the Gwent Levels and the Severn Estuary, the South East Wales region is highly varied. In this post-industrial landscape fragmented by urban development, brownfield sites, infrastructure and modern intensive farming, concerns have been raised about helping wildlife adapt to climate change. A loss of the rich local biodiversity is likely to have a broader economic and social impact by adversely affecting the character of the place, reducing natural amenity and diminishing the quality of life. One solution is to protect existing wildlife sites and connect them by restoring habitat along strategically planned corridors. The concept is to make the landscape more permeable to wildlife enabling migration to more suitable areas as climate change takes effect. The fear is that continued isolation of protected wildlife sites will lead to the local extinction of species. This study for the Welsh Assembly Government and its partners used GIS analysis to identify potential ecological connectors in what will become a multi-functional Networked Environment Region. The project envisages a network of distinct but connected cities and towns supported by interconnected environmental infrastructure—such as river valleys, coastal wetlands, protected habitats, woodlands, upland heaths, peat bogs and semi-natural urban greenspace. Importantly, the proposed networks of green infrastructure will provide enhanced 'ecosystem services', which include food, timber, flood management, climate amelioration, wildlife habitat, carbon storage and pollination, which have a key role to play in underpinning social and economic development. Improving the environmental infrastructure will make the landscape more accessible to people, promote healthier lifestyles, increase tourism and improve the image of the region as an attractive place to live and work.

There is already considerable interest in using the networked environment region concept elsewhere as a policy framework to give clear direction and focus for investment in environmental improvement projects. This will include the creation of the Valleys Regional Park, reforestation, river and wetland restoration and urban green space provision, all projects that are due to take place, but which can be co-ordinated to produce maximum effect through this initiative.

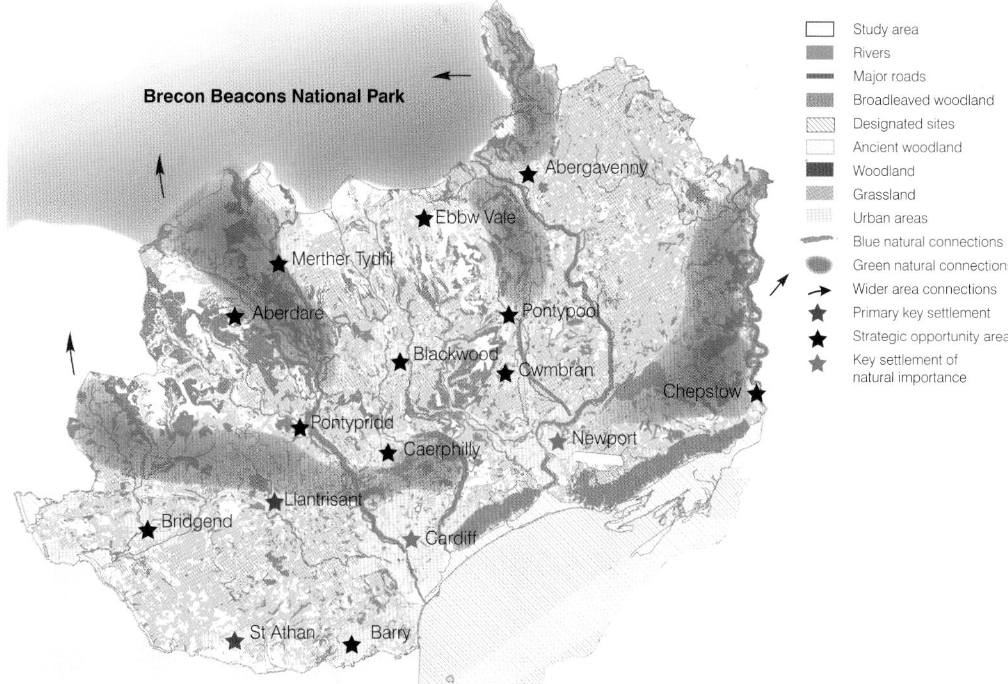

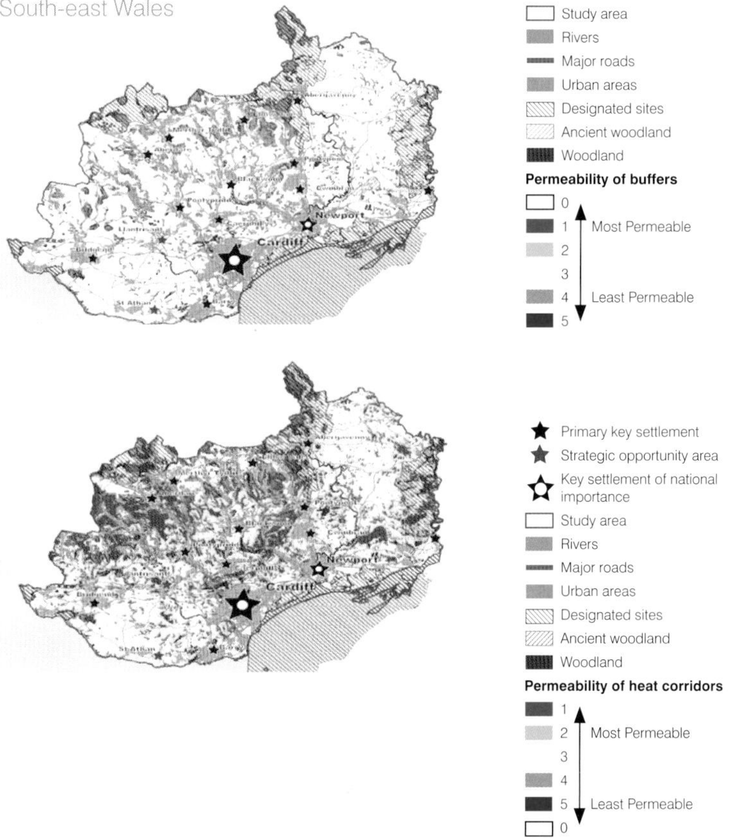

The strongest link

Making the link between a high-quality environment, a high quality of life and enhanced land values, this research project is focused on improving green infrastructure across an entire region. The model can be used in any area to direct investment in environmental improvements.

Landmark living wall

Westfield London Shopping Centre, London, UK

Among the landscape highlights at the high-profile retail centre Westfield London, is the 170 metre long living wall. At the western entrance to the 17 hectare scheme, the four metre high structure is a visually striking and ever-changing landmark creating the backdrop to an upbeat and inviting avenue lined with restaurants, cafes and bars. Standing between the centre and local homes, the north-facing living wall is planted predominantly with native woodland plants, primarily ferns and is incorporated into a massive contemporary-style water feature. In addition to being visually outstanding, the living wall contributes to the environment in numerous ways by helping to filter the air, creating a giant slice of new wildlife habitat in the middle of this retail complex and looking beautiful.

In addition to the wall, the distinctive landscape and public realm design creates a grand entrance, attractive and accessible pedestrian streets and vibrant interior and exterior public spaces. The streetscape incorporates a powerful graphic device of flowing lines in black and silver-grey granite paving which draws shoppers into the space from the new underground, overground rail and bus stations completed by the developer. The generous public realm includes seating, planters, street furniture, trees and ornamental planting. The scheme places great importance on integrating the new development into its urban context with landscape playing a key role in upgrading the local environment and providing screening and buffers between the development and existing houses and transport interchanges.

Green and seasonal

Described as a living wall, the vertical garden, above and right, at this west London shopping centre performs a range of functions. These include providing a visual and sound buffer between the shops and residential neighbours, creating a new slice of wildlife habitat, helping to filter the air and offering visitors a beautiful and seasonally changing garden. The wall forms part of the public-realm design scheme which also incorporates paving with a powerful graphic device of flowing lines in black and silver-grey granite, opposite, which draws shoppers into and through the development.

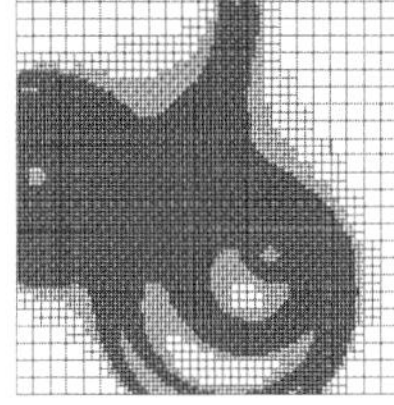

2.0
0.5
10

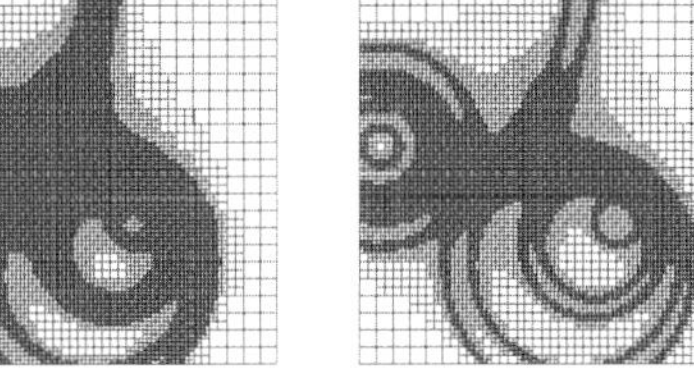

2.0
0.8
10

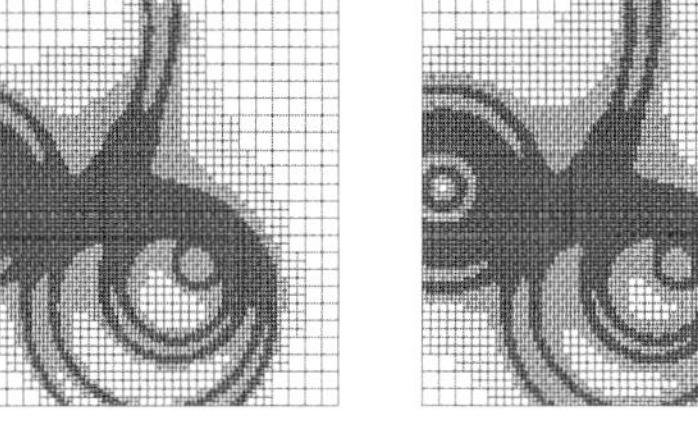

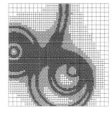

2.0
0.8
X

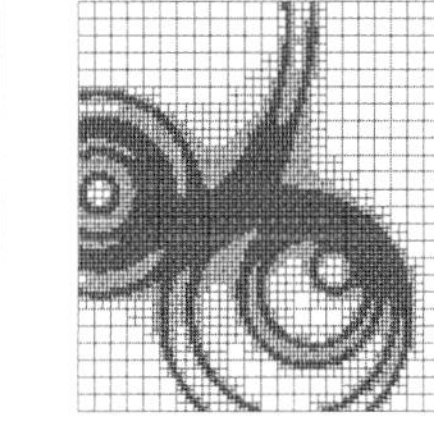

3.0
0.6
10

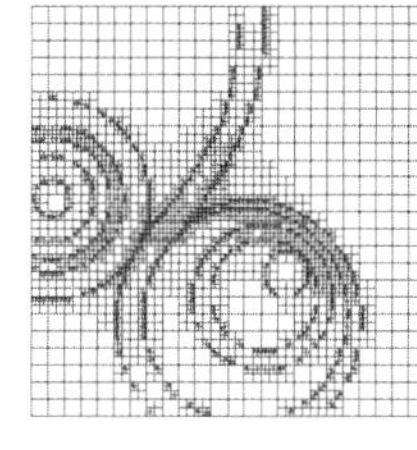

4.0
0.1
10

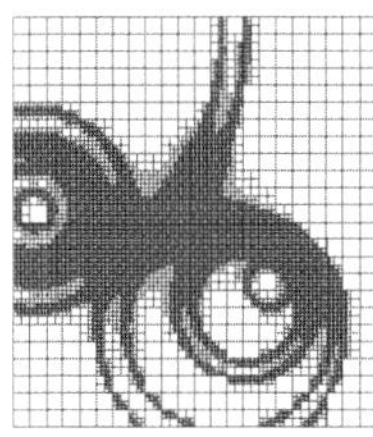

4.0
0.3
10

4.0
0.5
3

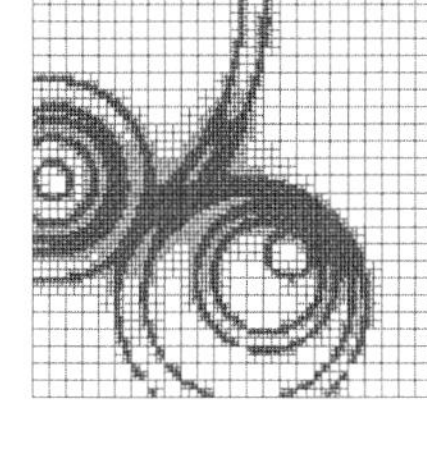

4.0
0.5
10

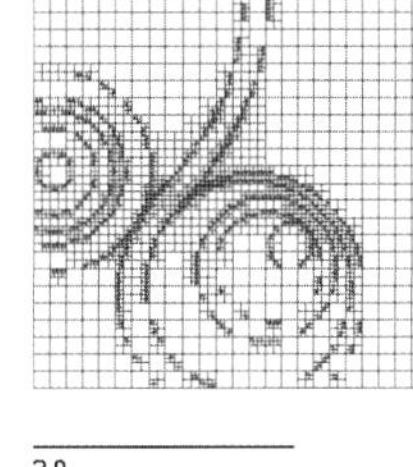

3.0
0.6
10

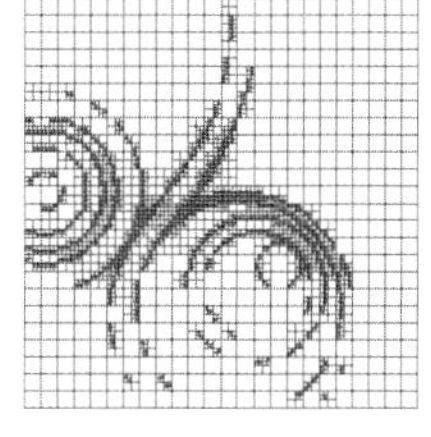

4.0
0.1
10

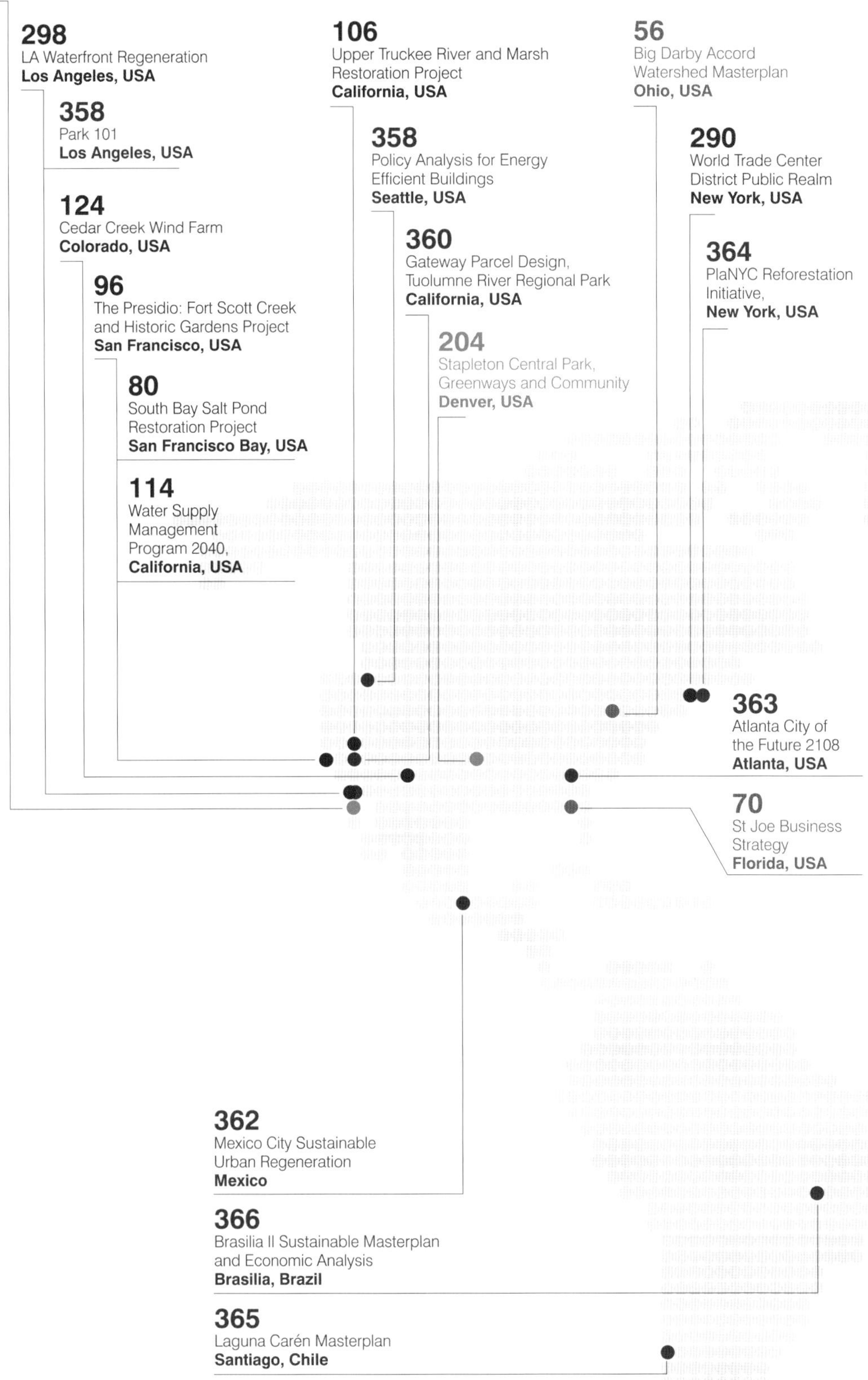

● **01** Megaprojects and Macroplanning

● **02** Environmental Systems

● **03** Regeneration

● **04** Communities

● **05** Public Realm

● **06** Culture and Leisure

● **07** The Future

320
Children's Gardens
Various Locations, USA

366
Sustainable Systems Integrated Model (SSIM)
USA

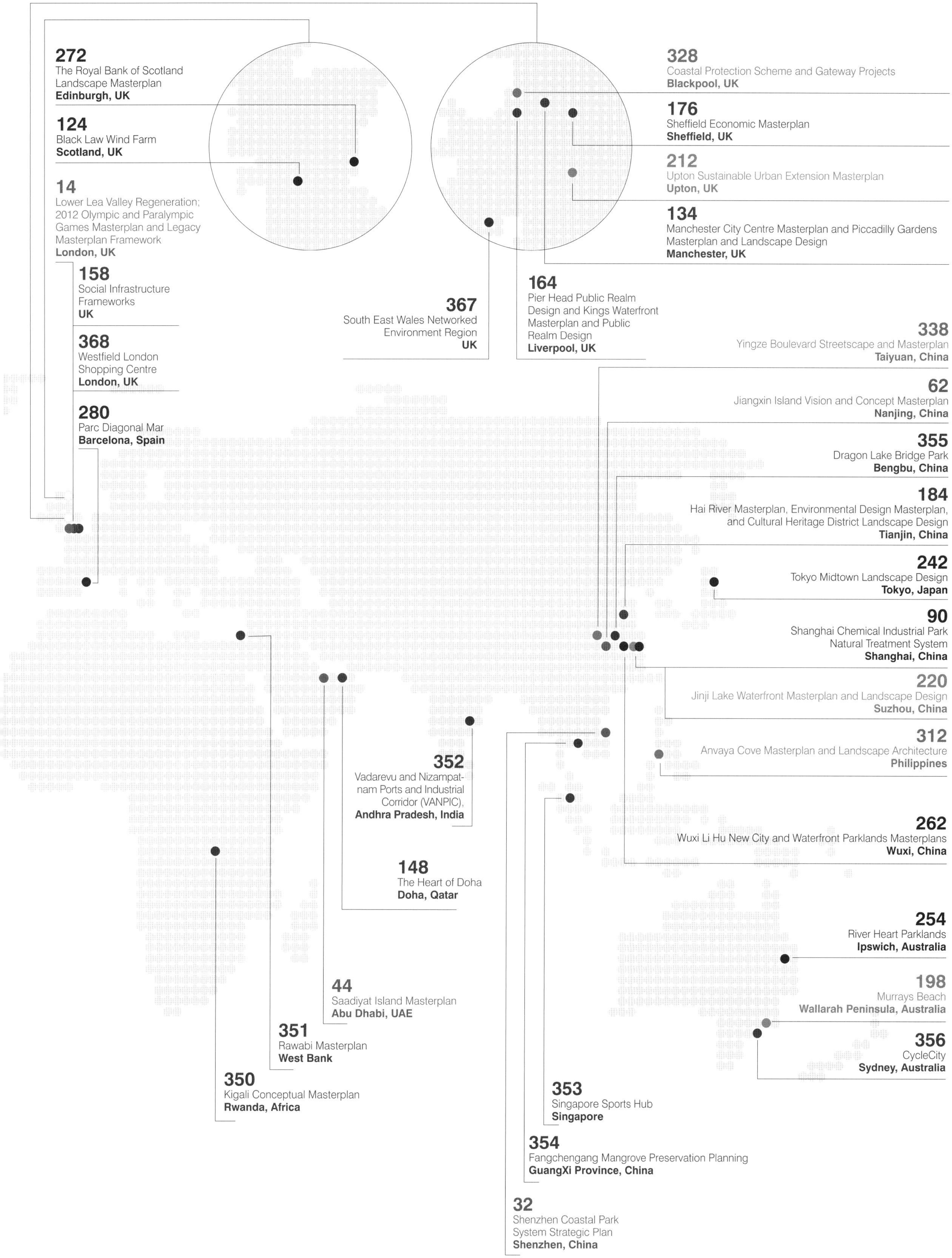

272
The Royal Bank of Scotland Landscape Masterplan
Edinburgh, UK

124
Black Law Wind Farm
Scotland, UK

14
Lower Lea Valley Regeneration; 2012 Olympic and Paralympic Games Masterplan and Legacy Masterplan Framework
London, UK

158
Social Infrastructure Frameworks
UK

368
Westfield London Shopping Centre
London, UK

280
Parc Diagonal Mar
Barcelona, Spain

367
South East Wales Networked Environment Region
UK

164
Pier Head Public Realm Design and Kings Waterfront Masterplan and Public Realm Design
Liverpool, UK

328
Coastal Protection Scheme and Gateway Projects
Blackpool, UK

176
Sheffield Economic Masterplan
Sheffield, UK

212
Upton Sustainable Urban Extension Masterplan
Upton, UK

134
Manchester City Centre Masterplan and Piccadilly Gardens Masterplan and Landscape Design
Manchester, UK

338
Yingze Boulevard Streetscape and Masterplan
Taiyuan, China

62
Jiangxin Island Vision and Concept Masterplan
Nanjing, China

355
Dragon Lake Bridge Park
Bengbu, China

184
Hai River Masterplan, Environmental Design Masterplan, and Cultural Heritage District Landscape Design
Tianjin, China

242
Tokyo Midtown Landscape Design
Tokyo, Japan

90
Shanghai Chemical Industrial Park Natural Treatment System
Shanghai, China

220
Jinji Lake Waterfront Masterplan and Landscape Design
Suzhou, China

312
Anvaya Cove Masterplan and Landscape Architecture
Philippines

262
Wuxi Li Hu New City and Waterfront Parklands Masterplans
Wuxi, China

352
Vadarevu and Nizampatnam Ports and Industrial Corridor (VANPIC),
Andhra Pradesh, India

148
The Heart of Doha
Doha, Qatar

254
River Heart Parklands
Ipswich, Australia

198
Murrays Beach
Wallarah Peninsula, Australia

356
CycleCity
Sydney, Australia

44
Saadiyat Island Masterplan
Abu Dhabi, UAE

351
Rawabi Masterplan
West Bank

350
Kigali Conceptual Masterplan
Rwanda, Africa

353
Singapore Sports Hub
Singapore

354
Fangchengang Mangrove Preservation Planning
GuangXi Province, China

32
Shenzhen Coastal Park System Strategic Plan
Shenzhen, China

00 The Bigger Picture

Cover image

Image credits: Image of salt ponds in South Bay, San Francisco, California, USA—see the South Bay Salt Pond Restoration Project

Alameda, Santa Clara San Mateo 2005 Digital Ortho Imagery Mosaic

National Agriculture Imagery Program (NAIP)

USDA-FSA Aerial Photography Field Office Salt Lake City, Utah

Key to EDAW AECOM role descriptions

Design—includes landscape architecture; architecture; design implementation

Masterplanning—includes GIS/physical context analysis; urban design; campus planning; community masterplanning

Strategic planning and economic development—includes GIS/social and economic analysis; regeneration planning; regional planning; socio-economic planning; policy planning

Environmental and ecological planning—includes GIS/environmental analysis; wetland ecology; natural resource analysis; water management; environmental restoration; energy planning

01 Megaprojects and Macroplanning

spread image EDAW AECOM

14

Lower Lea Valley Regeneration; 2012 Olympic and Paralympic Games Masterplan and Legacy Masterplan Framework, London, UK

Lower Lea Valley Regeneration, London, UK

Client: London Development Agency
EDAW AECOM's role: Design; masterplanning; strategic planning and economic development; environmental and ecological planning
Consultant team: EDAW AECOM Consortium—Allies and Morrison, Buro Happold, Capita Symonds, Foreign Office Architects, Mace

2012 Olympic and Paralympic Games Masterplan, London, UK

Client: London Development Authority for the 2004 masterplan and permission; Olympic Development Authority 2007 for the masterplan and permission
EDAW AECOM's role: Design; masterplanning; strategic planning and economic development; environmental and ecological planning
Consultant team: EDAW AECOM with Allies and Morrison, HOK Sport, Foreign Office Architects, Buro Happold, Capita Symonds

Legacy Masterplan Framework, London, UK

Client: London Development Agency
EDAW AECOM's role: Design; masterplanning; strategic planning and economic development; environmental and ecological planning
Consultant team: EDAW AECOM with Allies and Morrison, KCAP Architects, Buro Happold, Faber Maunsell, Beyond Green, VisionXS, JMP, Robert Camlin, Nick Ritblat
Image credits: EDAW AECOM; pg 15 EDAW AECOM, KCAP, Allies and Morrison; pg 17 LDA/DFL; pg 19 top EDAW AECOM, Allies and Morrison, Foreign Office Architects (FOA), HOK; pg 19 bottom LDA; pg 20/21 top EDAW AECOM with Allies and Morrison, FOA, HOK; pg 22/23 EDAW AECOM, Allies and Morrison, Buro Happold, FOA, HOK; pg 24 left and centre Allies and Morrison, right EDAW AECOM, Allies and Morrison, KCAP; pg 25 EDAW AECOM, Allies and Morrison, KCAP; pg 26–31 EDAW AECOM, Allies and Morrison, KCAP; pg 29, graphics—Smoothe.

32

Shenzhen Coastal Park System Strategic Plan, Shenzhen, China

Client: Municipal Planning Bureau, Binhai Branch
EDAW AECOM's role: Design; masterplanning; environmental and ecological planning
Consultant team: Sun Yat-sen University—biologist and horticulturist
Image credits: EDAW AECOM

44

Saadiyat Island Masterplan, Abu Dhabi, UAE

Client: Tourism Development & Investment Company (TDIC)
EDAW AECOM's role: Design; masterplanning; strategic planning and economic development; environmental and ecological planning
Consultant team: Frank Gehry—Guggenheim Museum; Zaha Hadid —performing arts centre; Jean Nouvel—Louvre Abu Dhabi; Tadao Ando—maritime museum; AECOM
Image credits: EDAW AECOM/TDIC

56

Big Darby Accord Watershed Masterplan, Ohio, USA

Client: City of Columbus, Ohio
EDAW AECOM's role: Strategic planning and economic development; environmental and ecological planning
Consultant team: MSI—planning, public facilities, public outreach; EMH&T—water quality regulations, water and sewer infrastructure analysis, water quality modelling, best management practices; The Ohio State University—water quality modelling; Squire, Sanders & Dempsey LLP—revenue generation mechanisms; Schottenstein Zox & Dunn—memorandum of agreement development; Trans Associates—transportation.
Image credits: EDAW AECOM, (additional images Avinash Srivastava)

62

Jiangxin Island Vision and Concept Masterplan, Nanjing, China

Client: Nanjing Jianye District Construction Bureau
EDAW AECOM's role: Design; masterplanning; strategic planning and economic development; environmental and ecological planning
Consultant team: Nanjing Academy of Urban Planning & Design—collecting site data and translating conceptual masterplan into regularity control plan according to local planning system.
Image credits: EDAW AECOM (additional images Yiwen Zhu, Janet Zhu, Jason Zhu, Kalla Gu)

70

St Joe Business Strategy, Florida, USA

Client: The St Joe Company
EDAW AECOM's role: Strategic planning and economic development
Image credits: EDAW AECOM; pg 74 The St Joe Company

02 Environmental Systems

spread image EDAW AECOM

80

South Bay Salt Pond Restoration Project, San Francisco Bay, USA

Client: California Coastal Conservancy, US Fish and Wildlife Service, California Department of Fish and Game
EDAW AECOM's role: Masterplanning; environmental and ecological planning
Consultant team: Philip Williams & Associates—team leader, hydrology and modelling, restoration design; Brown and Caldwell—water quality; HT Harvey & Associates—biology
Image credits: EDAW AECOM; pg 81 Pacific Gas & Electric Company, US Geological Survey

90

Shanghai Chemical Industrial Park Natural Treatment System, Shanghai, China

Client: Shanghai Chemical Industry Park Administration Committee
EDAW AECOM's role: Design; environmental and ecological planning
Consultant team: Tongji University, Qi Zhou, PhD; University of California, Berkeley: Alexander J Horne, PhD
Image credits: EDAW AECOM

96

The Presidio: Fort Scott Creek and Historic Gardens Project, San Francisco, USA

Client: The Presidio Trust
EDAW AECOM's role: Design: environmental and ecological planning
Image credits: EDAW AECOM (pg 97 Alex Felson)

106

Upper Truckee River and Marsh Restoration Project, California, USA

Client: California Tahoe Conservancy
EDAW AECOM's role: Environmental and ecological planning
Consultant team: ENTRIX—engineering design, hydrology and hydraulics; Western Botanical—botanical studies—Tahoe yellow cress; Susan Lindstrom, PhD—cultural resources; KD Anderson—traffic
Image credits: EDAW AECOM (additional images Mark Bibbo, Ellen Dean, Lorrie Jo Williams, Steve Patterson, Chris Fitzer); page 109 California Tahoe Conservancy

114

Water Supply Management Program 2040, California, USA

Client: East Bay Municipal Utility District (EBMUD)
EDAW AECOM's role: Strategic planning and economic development; environmental and ecological planning
Consultant team: RMC Water and Environment—engineering feasibilty; M Cubed—economic analysis; Maddaus Water Management—conservation programme; Karen Johnson—demand projections; TOVA—hazards and environmental justice; GTC—geology, soils, and seismicity; CBRE Consulting—demand study; TRG and Associates—public outreach; Weber Analytical—demand study normalisation
Image credits: EDAW AECOM; pg 121,122–123 East Bay Municipal Utility District

124

Cedar Creek Wind Farm, Colorado, USA, and Black Law Wind Farm, Scotland, UK

Cedar Creek

Client: Greenlight Energy and BP Alternative Energy
EDAW AECOM's role: Environmental and ecological planning
Consultant team: Babcock & Brown
Image credits: EDAW AECOM; Greenlight Energy/Cedar Creek Wind Energy

Black Law

Client: Scottish Power
EDAW AECOM's role: Environmental and ecological planning
Image credits: EDAW AECOM/ScottishPower

03 Regeneration

spread image EDAW AECOM /Wilkinson Eyre

134

Manchester City Centre Masterplan and Piccadilly Gardens Masterplan and Landscape Design, Manchester, UK

Manchester City Centre

Client: Manchester Millennium
EDAW AECOM's role: Design; masterplanning; strategic planning and economic development
Consultant team: Ian Simpson Architects; Benoy Architects; Nick Johnson; Martin Stockley; Faber Maunsell; BDP
Image credits: EDAW AECOM; pg 136 Manchester City Council

Piccadilly Gardens

Client: Manchester City Council
EDAW AECOM's role: Design
Consultant team: Tadao Ando—architecture; Arup—engineering; Chapman Robinson Architects—architecture; Peter Fink—lighting design
Image credits: EDAW AECOM

148

The Heart of Doha, Doha, Qatar

Client: Dohaland
EDAW AECOM's role: Design; masterplanning
Consultant team: Arup—project management and engineering; ERA—economics and market analysis; DTZ—property and real estate; Davis Langdon—quality surveying; Allies and Morrison—architecture
Image credits: EDAW AECOM; (pg 150 Rosanna Law); pg 149, 150 Qatar Museum Authority/The Centre for GIS, State of Qatar; pg 152 Mossessian & Partners; pg 154; 155 Allies and Morrison

158

Social Infrastructure Frameworks, UK

The London Thames Gateway Social Infrastructure Framework

Client: NHS London Healthy Urban Development Unit (HUDU)
EDAW AECOM's role: Strategic planning and economic development. development
Consultant team: Bevan Brittan LLP—delivery and implementation advice; YTP Strategic Regeneration and Partnership Consultants—delivery and implementation advice
Image credits: EDAW AECOM

The London Borough of Barking and Dagenham Social Infrastructure Framework (Pilot)

Client: London Borough of Barking and Dagenham
EDAW AECOM's role: Strategic planning and economic development
Consultant team: Bevan Brittan LLP—delivery and implementation advice; YTP Strategic Regeneration and Partnership Consultants—delivery and implementation advice
Image credits: EDAW AECOM

164

Pier Head Public Realm Design and Kings Waterfront Masterplan and Public Realm Design, Liverpool, UK

Pier Head

Client: Liverpool Vision; Liverpool City Council; British Waterways—canal link
EDAW AECOM's role: Design; masterplanning
Consultant team: 20/20 Liverpool—civil engineering; Arup—structural engineering canal; Faithful and Gould—quantity surveyor; Graham Festenstein—lighting; 3XN—architect of Museum of Liverpool
Image credits: EDAW AECOM, Liverpool Vision, Broadway Malyan; pg 165 Lynn Meacock; pg 168, 170/171 Lee Carus; pg 169 top left Alan Cookson

Kings Waterfront

Client: Liverpool Vision
EDAW AECOM's role: Design; masterplanning
Consultant team: Wilkinson Eyre Architects—architecture
Image credits: EDAW AECOM

176

Sheffield Economic Masterplan, Sheffield, UK

Economic masterplan

Client: Creative Sheffield
EDAW AECOM's role: Strategic planning and economic development
Consultant team: Ekos Consulting—economic intelligence; GVA Grimley—property and market intelligence; Greg Clarke—facilitator
Image credits: EDAW AECOM

Sheaf Square

Client: Sheffield City Council
EDAW AECOM's role: Design
Consultant team: Faber Maunsell; Sheffield City Council; Art 2 Architecture; Brett Payne, Chris Knight, Keith Tyssen and Keiko Mukade—artists
Image credits: EDAW AECOM

184

Hai River Masterplan, Environmental Design Masterplan, and Cultural Heritage District Landscape Design, Tianjin, China

Client: Tianjin Planning Bureau; Haihe Economic Development Office
EDAW AECOM's role: Design; masterplanning
Consultant team: for strategic masterplan—Callison, US; MVA, Hong Kong; Light Cibles; Calori & Vanden-Eynden—design consultant. For the environmental design masterplan—Light Cibles; Calori & Vanden-Eynden—design consultant. For the landscape design—TMWSDI, Tianjin
Image credits: EDAW AECOM

04 Community

spread image EDAW AECOM

198

Murrays Beach, Wallarah Peninsula, Australia

Client: Lensworth Wallarah Peninsula (until 2005); Stockland Wallarah Peninsula
EDAW AECOM's role: Design; masterplanning
Consultant team: for the peninsula masterplanning—Architectus—built-form management plan; Conacher Travers—bushfire management plan; Sinclair Knight Merz—construction management strategy; Manidis Roberts—ecological site management plan; Sinclair Knight Merz—physical infrastructure management plan; SGS Economics and Planning—social equity management plan. For the Murrays Beach development—Sinclair Knight Merz—infrastructure and water management; Manidis Roberts—environmental reporting; Conacher Travers—bushfire management and tree surveying
Image credits: EDAW AECOM

204

Stapleton Central Park, Greenways and Community, Denver, USA

Client: Forest City Development and Park Creek Metropolitan District
EDAW AECOM's role: Masterplanning; strategic planning and economic development; environmental and ecological planning
Image credits: EDAW AECOM

212

Upton Sustainable Urban Extension Masterplan, Upton, UK

Client: English Partnerships/Northampton Borough Council/ The Prince's Foundation
EDAW AECOM's role: Design; masterplanning; strategic planning and economic development; environmental and ecological planning
Consultant team: Alan Baxter Associates—transport engineer; Pell Frischmann—implementation engineer; Quartet—implementation landscape architect
Image credits: EDAW AECOM

220

Jinji Lake Waterfront Masterplan and Landscape Design, Suzhou, China

Client: Suzhou Industrial Park Administrative Committee
EDAW AECOM's role: Design; masterplanning
Image credits: EDAW AECOM

232

Ladera Ranch New Community Masterplan, California, USA

Client: Rancho Mission Viejo Company
EDAW AECOM's role: Design; masterplanning
Consultant team: Land Concern—master landscape architect; William Hazmalhalch Associates—master architect; Huitt Zollars—civil engineering
Image credits: EDAW AECOM; Tom Lamb

05 Public Realm

spread image EDAW AECOM

242

Tokyo Midtown Landscape Design, Tokyo, Japan

Client: Lensworth Wallarah Peninsula (until 2005); Stockland Wallarah Peninsula
EDAW AECOM's role: Design; masterplanning
Consultant team: for the pennisula masterplanning—Architectus—built-form management plan; Conacher Travers—bushfire management plan; Sinclair Knight Merz—construction management strategy; Manidis Roberts—ecological site management plan; Sinclair Knight Merz—physical infrastructure management plan; SGS Economics and Planning—social equity management plan. For the Murrays Beach development—Sinclair Knight Merz—infrastructure and water management; Manidis Roberts—environmental reporting; Conacher Travers—bushfire management and tree surveying
Image credits: EDAW AECOM

254

River Heart Parklands, Ipswich, Australia

Client: Ipswich City Council
EDAW AECOM's role: Design; masterplanning
Consultant team: SZCZ—architecture; Bligh Tanner—structural engineering; Webb Australia—lighting design; Irrigation Design Australia—irrigation design; Turner and Townsend—quantity surveying; Gary Wenk—hydraulic consultant; Synerg—energy consultant; ARUP—traffic engineering; Buchanan Heritage Services—heritage consultant; Douglas Partners—geotechnical engineering; Golder Associates—slope and flood modelling engineer
Image credits: EDAW AECOM; Christopher F Jones; pg 258/259 Ipswich City Council

262

Wuxi Li Hu New City and Waterfront Parklands Masterplans, Wuxi, China

Client: Wuxi Lake District Planning and Construction Leading Team Office
EDAW AECOM's role: Design; masterplanning
Consultant team: Wuxi Landscape Architecture Design Institute—construction design; Wuxi Architecture Design and Research Institute Liability Co—construction design; Szczepan Urbanowicz—architecture; LLA Consultancy—traffic consultant; CB Richard Ellis—economic consultant
Image credits: EDAW AECOM (additional image Cinndy Zhou)

272

The Royal Bank of Scotland Landscape Masterplan, Edinburgh, UK

Client: The Royal Bank of Scotland
EDAW AECOM's role: Design
Consultant team: Michael Laird Architects; RHWL; Mace; WSP Engineering; Lovejoys
Image credits: EDAW AECOM; pg 273 Hawkeye Photography

280

Parc Diagonal Mar, Barcelona, Spain

Client: Hines Madrid
EDAW AECOM's role: Design
Consultant team: Enric Miralles and Benedetta Tagliabue of EMBT; Europroject Consultores Asociados—engineer; Benjumea—construction
Image credits: EDAW AECOM

290

World Trade Center District Public Realm, New York, USA

Client: The Port Authority of New York and New Jersey
EDAW AECOM's role: Design; masterplanning
Consultant team: Fisher Marantz Stone—lighting; Two Twelve Arakawa—wayfinding and signage
Image credits: EDAW AECOM

298

LA Waterfront Regeneration, Los Angeles, USA

Client: Port of Los Angeles
EDAW AECOM's role: Design; masterplanning
Consultant team: Moffatt & Nichol—project engineer; Selbert Perkins Design—environmental graphics; Lighting Design Alliance—lighting; WET Design—water feature design; Tom Eliot Fisch—architect; Fine Arts Services—fine art consultant; John Greenlee—ornamental grass expert; Doug Hollis, Roberto Delgado, Adrian de la Pena, Harold Greene, Frank Charles Dante Minuto, Stuart Bender, Veralee Bassler, Ned Kahn, Carl Cheng, Slanguage, and Trace Fukuhara—artists; DCA—civil engineering; EEK—architecture; and KOA—traffic engineering
Image credits: EDAW AECOM (additional images Yan Mei, Taso Papadakis)

06 Culture and Leisure

spread image EDAW AECOM

312

Anvaya Cove Masterplan and Landscape Architecture, Philippines

Client: Ayala Land
EDAW AECOM's role: Design; masterplanning
Consultant team: GHD—inframasterplanning; LVLP—architecture; APDG—interior design
Image credits: EDAW AECOM

320

Children's Gardens, Various Locations, USA

Client: Children's Garden at Red Butte Garden and Arboretum—Red Butte Garden and Arboretum; Gateway Science School—Kennedy Associates; Cheyenne Mountain Zoo—Cheyenne Mountain Zoo; The Morton Arboretum Children's Garden Masterplan—The Morton Arboretum; The Gardens at Spring Creek Children's Garden—City of Fort Collins; Children's Garden at Marie Selby Botanical Gardens—Marie Selby Botanical Gardens; Olson Family Terrace Garden—St Louis Children's Hospital
EDAW AECOM's role: Design
Image credits: EDAW AECOM; pg 323 models by Emmanuel Didier, Techmedia, photographed by Jim Cambon

328

Coastal Protection Scheme and Gateway Projects, Blackpool, UK

Client: Blackpool Borough Council
EDAW AECOM's role: Design; masterplanning; strategic planning and economic development; environmental and ecological planning
Consultant team: Masterplan—The Jerde Partnership. Coastal Protection Scheme—Halcrow and Blackpool Borough Council—engineering; DPA Lighting Consultants—lighting design; Birse—main contractor. Southern Gateway—Arup and Blackpool Borough Council—engineering; DPA Lighting Consultants; Birse. George Bancroft Park—Blackpool Borough Council—engineering; DPA Lighting Consultants; Gordon Young and Why Not Associates—artists; Volker Stevin—main contractor
Image credits: EDAW AECOM; pg 330 Blackpool Borough Council; pg 330, bottom, EDAW AECOM and The Jerde Partnership; pg 336 bottom, 337 Jerry Hardman-Jones

338

Yingze Boulevard Streetscape and Masterplan, Taiyuan, China

Client: Taiyuan Landscape Bureau
EDAW AECOM's role: Design
Consultant team: OLP Lighting Solution—lighting
Image credits: EDAW AECOM; pg 341 Taiyuan Landscape Bureau

07 The future

spread image EDAW AECOM

350

Kigali Conceptual Masterplan, Rwanda, Africa

Client: Rwanda Ministry of Infrastructure
EDAW AECOM's role: Masterplanning
Consultant team: OZ Architecture, EDAW, Tetra Tech, ERA, Engineers without Borders
Image credits: EDAW AECOM; Antje Ilbert

351

Rawabi Masterplan, West Bank

Client: Bayti
EDAW AECOM's role: Design; masterplanning
Consultant team: AECOM Design—architecture; Faber Maunsell—transportation, water
Image credits: EDAW AECOM

352

Vadarevu and Nizampatnam Ports and Industrial Corridor (VANPIC), Andhra Pradesh, India

Client: VANPIC Projects Pvt
EDAW AECOM's role: Masterplanning; strategic planning and economic development; environmental and ecological planning
Image credits: EDAW AECOM (Kimberlee Myers)

353

Singapore Sports Hub, Singapore

Client: Dragages + HSBC
EDAW AECOM's role: Design; masterplanning
Consultant team: ArupSport; DPArchitects
Image credits: EDAW AECOM

354

Fangchengang Mangrove Preservation Planning, GuangXi Province, China

Client: Fangchengang Xindi Co
EDAW AECOM's role: Masterplanning: strategic planning, environmental and ecological planning
Image credits: EDAW AECOM

355

Dragon Lake Bridge Park, Bengbu, China

Client: Xincheng Comprehensive Development Zone, Benbu
EDAW AECOM's role: Design; masterplanning
Consultant team: Shanghai Institute of Architectural Design & Research/ SZCZ Architects
Image credits: EDAW AECOM

356

CycleCity, Sydney, Australia

Client: n/a, an inhouse research initiative
EDAW AECOM's role: Strategic planning and economic development
Consultant team: Maunsell
Image credits: EDAW AECOM

358

Policy Analysis for Energy Efficient Buildings, Seattle, USA

Client: City of Seattle
EDAW AECOM's role: Strategic planning and economic development; environmental and ecological planning
Image credits: EDAW AECOM

358

Park 101, Los Angeles, USA

EDAW AECOM Intern project
Image credits: EDAW AECOM

360

Gateway Parcel Design, Tuolumne River Regional Park, California, USA

Client: Tuolumne River Regional Park Commission
EDAW AECOM's role: Design; masterplanning; environmental and ecological planning
Consultant team: EDAW AECOM—lead design; McBain & Trush—riparian ecology; HDR Engineering—site/civil engineering
Image credits: EDAW AECOM

362

Mexico City Sustainable Urban Regeneration, Mexico

Client: confidential at time of going to press
EDAW AECOM's role: Design; masterplanning; environmental and ecological planning
Consultant team: AECOM PM/CM
Image credits: EDAW AECOM (Stephen Engblom)

363

Atlanta City of the Future 2108, Atlanta, USA

Client: City of the Future: A Design and Engineering Challenge by The History Channel. Entry title The City in the Forest
EDAW AECOM's role: Design; masterplanning; strategic planning and economic development; environmental and ecological planning
Consultant team: Praxis3, BNIM, Metcalf & Eddy
Image credits: EDAW AECOM

364

PlaNYC Reforestation Initiative, New York, USA

Client: City of New York Department of Parks and Recreation
EDAW AECOM's role: Design; strategic planning and economic development; environmental and ecological planning
Image credits: EDAW AECOM

365

Laguna Carén Masterplan, Santiago, Chile

Client: confidential at time of going to press
EDAW AECOM's role: Design; masterplanning; strategic planning and economic development; environmental and ecological planning
Consultant team: AECOM Design (legacy DMJM+HN), ERA
Image credits: EDAW AECOM (Lisa Fisher)

366

Brasilia II Sustainable Masterplan and Economic Analysis, Brasilia, Brazil

Client: Alphaville Urbanismo
EDAW AECOM's role: Masterplanning; strategic planning and economic development; environmental and ecological planning
Consultant team: AECOM International Development
Image credits: EDAW AECOM

366

Sustainable Systems Integrated Model (SSIM)

Sustainable development model
EDAW AECOM's role: Masterplanning; strategic planning and economic development; environmental and ecological planning
Image credits: EDAW AECOM

367

South East Wales Networked Environmental Region, Wales, UK

Client: Welsh Assembly Government
EDAW AECOM's role: Environmental and ecological planning
Consultant team: Forest Research
Image credits: EDAW AECOM

368

Westfield London Shopping Centre, London, UK

Client: Westfield Group
EDAW AECOM's role: Design
Consultant team: Fountain Workshop; Spiers and Major—lighting
Image credits: EDAW AECOM

Acknowledgements

Compiling this book has required true global collaboration involving AECOM Design + Planning offices around the world, our professional colleagues in other organisations and, of course, our clients. We would like to thank everyone who has helped draw together such an impressive publication. Key contributions have been made by the Pentagram team—Beatrice Blumenthal, Kate Shepherd, Kevin Purdy and Domenic Lippa, publisher Black Dog with Duncan McCorquodale and Sophie Hallam, our in-house photographers Dixi Carillo and David Lloyd with contributions from the Firmwide team including Fran Hegeler, Daniel Elsea, Jessica Anderson and Amanda Walter, graphics support from Alix Baer, Toby Humphreys, Rachel Lowry, Adam Rothwell, Stafford Trowse, Sarah Winge Sorensen, and additional support from Mary Banker, Sally Geldard, Rachael Pengilley, Yates McCullum and Heather Topel. We'd also like to thank our think piece contributors—David Higgins, Chief Executive of the Olympic Delivery Authority; Dr Kongjian Yu, Dean and Professor at the Graduate School of Landscape Architecture, Peking University, President of Turenscape; Sir Howard Bernstein, Chief Executive of Manchester City Council; Professor Nasser Rabbat, Aga Khan Professor of Islamic Architecture, MIT; John Beardsley, senior lecturer at Harvard's Department of Landscape Architecture and Adele Chatfield-Taylor, President of the American Academy in Rome.

Additional thanks must of course be extended to all Principals and staff who have contributed to the inspiring and often groundbreaking projects featured here. This book is a testament to their professionalism and creative talents which have helped shape our unique working culture and produced so many impressive and successful schemes.

And finally, a special thanks is reserved for the late Sandy D'Elia who provided the original idea for a monograph.

AECOM Design + Planning book team: Jason Prior, President, and Bill Hanway, Chief Operating Officer, editorial overview; Erik Behrens, project director; Fay Sweet, project manager and author.

AECOM Design + Planning is part of AECOM, a global provider of professional design, technical and management support services within a broad range of markets, including buildings, transportation, facilities, environmental and energy. With 43,000 employees around the world, AECOM is a leader in all of the key markets that it serves. AECOM provides a blend of global reach, local knowledge, innovation, and technical excellence in delivering solutions that enhance and sustain the world's built, natural and social environments. More information on AECOM and its services can be found at www.aecom.com.

Index

G

H

I

J

K

L

N

O

P

T

U

V

W

AECOM Design + Planning is part of AECOM, a global provider of professional design, technical and management support services within a broad range of markets, including buildings, transportation, facilities, environmental and energy. With 43,000 employees around the world, AECOM is a leader in all of the key markets that it serves. AECOM provides a blend of global reach, local knowledge, innovation, and technical excellence in delivering solutions that enhance and sustain the world's built, natural and social environments. More information on AECOM and its services can be found at www.aecom.com.

Black Dog Publishing Limited
10A Acton Street
London WC1X 9NG
United Kingdom

Tel: +44 (0) 20 7713 5097
Fax: +44 (0) 20 7713 8682
info@blackdogonline.com
www.blackdogonline.com

Design + Planning book team: Jason Prior, President, and Bill Hanway, Chief Operating Officer, editorial overview; Erik Behrens, project director; Fay Sweet, project manager and author.

Designed by Pentagram.

ISBN 978-1-906155-79-7
British Library Cataloguing-in-Publication Data.
A CIP record for this book is available from the British Library.

Black Dog Publishing Limited, London, UK, is an environmentally responsible company. The Bigger Picture is printed on Arctic the silk, an FSC certified paper.

Printed in the EU.

ISBN 978-1-906155-79-7
9 781906 155797 56000>

architecture art design
fashion history photography
theory and things

www.blackdogonline.com